Implementing the
Capability Maturity Model

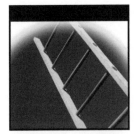

Implementing the
Capability Maturity Model

James R. Persse

Wiley Computer Publishing

John Wiley & Sons, Inc.

NEW YORK · CHICHESTER · WEINHEIM · BRISBANE · SINGAPORE · TORONTO

Publisher: Robert Ipsen
Editor: Robert M. Elliott
Assistant Editor: Emilie Herman
Managing Editor: John Atkins
Associate New Media Editor: Brian Snapp
Text Design & Composition: MacAllister Publishing Services, LLC

Library of Congress Cataloging-in-Publication Data:

ISBN: 0-471-41834-X

Printed in the United States of America.

10 9 8 7 6 5 4 3 2 1

Contents

Introduction

The software community has been struggling with a questionable quality image for a long time. The vaporous, amorphous essence of software creation is only partly understood within our business and is often completely misconstrued outside the business.

In the digital age, IT organizations are stretched thinner than they have ever been in the past. The prolific rise of automation within the business environment means more and more software development projects are being initiated. It's been a tough job keeping up with demand, and as a result, some of the work is being hurried through with the expectation that it can be fixed later. At the same time, the industry itself is awash in a wave of technological change. Twenty years ago if you walked into the MIS shops of a handful of large Fortune 500 companies, you could expect to see pretty much the same thing: Cobol, JCL, Mainframe systems, and batch processing. Today that commonality is gone. Now an amazing variety of tools and standards are in place in the industry: client-server computing, object-oriented development, distributed processing, Web development, applets, thin clients—the list goes on and on. IT organizations have to work just to keep up with current technology and sometimes, in haste or from incomplete directives, they adopt new technologies before they have mastered them.

The user also has a place in this failure. The age of personal computing has made the fields of software development and systems engineering *appear* to be simple and straightforward disciplines, with software creation as easy as clicking a mouse. This impression can drive users to expect too much out of development projects. They don't see the need to allow ample time for development or to provide the necessary funding, or to trim functional expectations in line with what can be reliably constructed.

Demand will continue to escalate, as will system criticality, while resources grow strained in response. For this reason, quality has become a bigger issue than ever before. The costs, liability, and reach of a failed or badly derailed software project have never been more significant. IT has become so integrated into the way America conducts not only business, but much of its daily life that poorly planned and marginally managed development efforts are increasingly difficult to tolerate.

Because of this, many companies today insist on dealing with only those IT shops that can demonstrate a level of quality management. The Software Engineering Institute's Capability Maturity Model (CMM) has become the most influential quality management system in the U.S. software industry. Alternative programs such as the ISO 9000 series, Deming's continuous quality improvement (CQI), Baldridge, and others have proven beneficial and effective within the IT community, but the CMM provides an edge that was quickly recognized and appreciated. CMM, from its inception, was designed specifically for the software engineering process, whereas the others are generic quality programs applicable to most *any* manufacturing/services industry. This distinction of focus constrains the scope of CMM , making it relatively compact and (by my experience anyway) easier and more cost-effective to implement. Over time, the program has been shown to reduce costs, decrease development time, and trim error rates in finished products. IT shops that operate under CMM guidelines and recommendations have a strong tendency to be much more efficient and responsive that IT shops that don't.

And when you realize that CMM also has wide international support and is a publicly sponsored program, free to anyone who wants to adopt it, you can understand why it's becoming so widespread within our industry. It's a good thing, too, because the IT community could use the help. Contrary to what many think, CMM is not a proprietary process to rigidly adopt, implement, and live with. Nor is it a rulebook that spells out the unbreakable laws of quality management. In fact, CMM (strange as it sounds) is not really concerned that much with quality or a particular way of doing business. It is rather a guidebook to process maturity. It is a set of broad boundaries, conceits, and assumptions that, when followed, allow you to establish a software management process within your organization that will result, by way of byproduct, in higher quality output.

Things work out that way because CMM contains at heart a continuous process-improvement philosophy. At its most basic, the CMM philosophy can be described as a spiral of planning, implementing, and evaluating, with the evaluation leading to improvements and the cycle then starting over. Follow this path and you will eventually end up with a proven, optimized way of doing business. In the mind of the SEI, that's process maturity.

Another way to look at process maturity is to evaluate the balance between predictability and risk on a software project. In a process-poor organization (one that does not plan well, or track its activities, or regularly evaluate its performance) predictability is typically low. You don't really know what the future holds until it arrives. You're busy looking at the here and now, not steps ahead. This means risk is high, risk for schedule slippage, or cost variations, or scope changes. High risk is directly related to project failure. Reduce the risk and the chance for project success rises proportionately.

You reduce risk by increasing predictability. You increase predictability through planning, careful implementation, and consistent evaluation. The guidelines for planning, implementing, and evaluating are contained in CMM. As you first start out, your drop in risk might be small; but as you refine over time, you'll find that the drop continues until you are operating in a highly predictable environment. This leads to smoother internal management, better planned versus actual balances, increased customer satisfaction, and increased overall quality.

This leads to another central and often misunderstood idea of CMM: CMM is not about good or bad process. It doesn't mandate total quality now. Rather it provides a framework by which you can grow a quality environment. Many who implement CMM, especially when shaping a Level 2 program, worry that they need to be the best, right on the money, right out of the gate. But that's not quite right. CMM would actually prefer for you to start off small and refine over time than to start off with a broad, all-encompassing solution that is only halfway implemented. To the CMM, the guy who runs the 100-meter dash in 14 seconds is just as much a winner as the guy who does it in 9.5. Think of CMM as the "just do it" company of the software industry.

CMM is built as a series of five maturity levels. As your organization gains in process maturity, you move up a level on the scale. All unassessed organizations start at Level 1, called Initial. These are IT shops that have no real process program in place and follow no rigid methodology for software development. The SEI estimates that roughly 73 percent of all major IT shops in the nation are operating at Level 1. The first step into CMM philosophy occurs at Level 2, where the structures and processes are put into place to effectively plan and manage software projects. At Level 3, these structures and processes become institutionalized across the organization. At Level 4, the structure and processes are refined for measured performance. And at Level 5, the whole approach of continuous process improvement is adopted for continuous care from the executive branch on down. (For a more complete overview of CMM, see Chapter 2.)

This book has been written as a practical guide for implementing CMM Level 2 and 3 requirements. I have tried to make it as readily applicable as possible, avoiding a lot of process theory, but at the same time trying to communicate the spirit of CMM. That's important, because the CMM book[1] is often taken too literally, as a set of commands rather than what it more closely resembles, a series of active boundaries and directions representing the current state of thinking in the process improvement arena. With CMM, the goal is more important than the way you achieve the goal. So if there are any major lessons in this book concerning implementing CMM compliant process programs in your organization, it would be:

- You have an enormous amount of flexibility in how you accomplish the CMM goals.

- The key to success with CMM is the consistent and considered implementation of your program.

In the end, with true commitment, demonstrable quality improvement should begin to become a tangible reality.

How This Book Is Organized

This book is divided into four parts:

- **Part 1: Overview of the CMM as a process improvement framework.** Here we'll look at the various parts of the Capability Maturity Model, with first a discussion of each level of the five-level tier, and then with a look at how each Key Process Area (KPA) is built of common elements. We'll also discuss the "spirit"

NEW VERSIONS OF THE CMM?

The CMM spec that is currently in the field (at the date of this writing) is version 1.1, and the contents of this book reflect that release of the CMM. At the same time, however, the Software Engineering Institute (SEI) has been working over the last few years to update the specification. Unreleased modifications, available for review at the SEI's Web site, mainly clarify the current content in the model, delineating some points for better detail and adjusting language for clearer understanding. Where appropriate, and where the intention has been quite clear, I have included some of the updates in my explanations. This should give you a full and current appreciation for what is intended in the model without straying from or introducing concepts not found in the official v1.1 offering.

The CMM can be a valuable, resourceful tool for all software practitioners. It is a process improvement model that has been show to generate tangible benefits. Cost savings, time savings, clarity of mission, and better end-product quality have all been measured from its proper use. I hope in adopting the CMM, and in using this book along those lines, you find that it does the same for your shop.

---

of the CMM, looking at how to implement the CMM in a way that supports your business missions, allows for flexibility, and relies on your professional judgment.

- **Part 2: A detailed series of recommendations for building a Level 2 compliant process improvement program.** In this section we'll look at the six KPAs of this, the *repeatable* level: Requirements Management, Software Project Planning, Software Project Tracking and Oversight, Software Configuration Management, Software Quality Assurance, and Subcontract Management. We'll examine setting up each one in your shop by focusing on four basic management areas: recommended structural components, processes, training, and policies. We'll also look at a series of typical processes, plans, and artifacts that you can use as starting points for your own program.

- **Part 3: A detailed series of recommendations for migrating your Level 2 program into a Level 3 compliant process improvement program.** In this third section we'll look at how to move from operating as a Level 2 organization to operating under Level 3 guidelines. Our discussion of the *Defined* level covers its six KPAs: Organization Profess Focus, Organization Process Definition, Training Program, Integrated Software Management, Software Product Engineering, Intergroup Coordination, and Peer Review. We'll examine setting up each one in your shop by building on what is in place for Level 2. As in Part 2, we'll also look at a series of typical processes, plans, and artifacts that you can use as starting points for your Level 3 program.

- **Part 4: Implementation and assessment processes.** In the last section we'll discuss some ideas surrounding the best ways to implement CMM in your organization. This will focus on how to prepare your people for the migration. Then we'll go over the assessment process, explaining how a typical process is usually run, and then identifying your participation in the process. Here we'll look at what you should have ready, the roles you'll be expected to perform, and how to ensure the best outcome.

Each part addresses the structures, processes, training, and policies for an organization to consider when implementing the CMM. To support this I provide examples of

- Practical CMM-compliant process outlines.

- Plan Templates for each of the Level 2 and 3 KPAs.

- Breakdowns of the resources, funding and tools helpful to each KPA.

- Outlines of the policies the CMM suggests you formulate within your organization.

- Lists of sample artifacts that could be used to support your use of processes and practices, and serve as compliance data during an assessment.

- A table and a statistical summary at the end of each KPA chapter. The table summarizes the activities discussed in the chapter. These usually tie directly to specific CMM key practices. Each KPA chapter ends with a rough statistical projection of what percent complete you'll be when you implement the recommendations in each chapter. This only as a friendly benchmark; it has not been scientifically calculated. I thought it would help you get a quick gauge of where you stand you move through the book and implement the CMM program in your shop.

The result is a basic, hands-on approach to setting the model into place, be yours a large, medium, or small IT operation.

Who Should Read This Book

I have written this book as a casual but hopefully full discussion of the CMM. Because of its tone and its scope, it's probably best suited to four general audiences:

- **People thinking about adopting CMM.** If you're interested in learning about CMM from a general perspective, this book can help you. Simply focus on Part 1 of the book. This part will give you an efficient overview of the CMM. It will also give you a feeling for what implementing the CMM will require of your organization. This material should give you a fairly solid foundation in the scope and spirit of the CMM and provide with some of the data you might need in order to make a decision as to whether the CMM could be right for your shop.

- **People planning to adopt CMM.** If you have been charged with implementing the CMM in your shop, this book can help in several ways. First it's a good companion to the CMM specification itself (Paulk, et al., 1994, Addison Wesley Longman, Inc.). In fact you'll probably find it handy as an interpreter of the spec, taking the precise recommendations and discussing how they are typically implemented in a practicing IT shop. The book will also help you by providing a series of practical implementation steps for each area under Level 2 and Level 3. IT can serve as your on-the-shelf program consultant.

- **Active CMM Managers.** If you're currently managing a CMM program, you will find that this book contains ideas and practical program examples that you might wish to adopt for your own program. If you're at Level 2 the book can help you understand and begin to move to Level 3. If you're at Level 3, you may find that the templates and process descriptions can be used to refine your program even further.

- **Those studying Software Process Management and Software Process Improvement.** Finally, any understanding of the Capability Maturity Model will create, as a byproduct, a better understanding of two rising disciplines in the IT world: software process management and software process improvement. We cover a lot of ground in these areas as we discuss implementing the CMM in real world environments.

From Here

The CMM is a practical, proven process quality framework, one that's been shown to work time and time again, across a wide variety of software development organizations. If you take the care and the time to implement it properly in your organization, you'll find that you reap a series of distinct, tangible benefits. You'll operate in an environment that's more predictable, where risk is reduced. You'll experience better planning, with more effective management views. You should see a rise in quality, a drop in errors, misdirection, and faulted assumptions. And, at the highest level, increased software quality, a better focused work force, and increased client satisfaction. I hope this book will help take you toward that goal.

Acknowledgments

For her help in the preparation of this book in its final form, I would like to thank Emilie Herman, my editor at John Wiley & Sons. Her recommendations and rearrangements greatly improved the flow of the material. I would also like to thank my friend Shannon Richardson for reviewing an early version of the material, and Michelle Wegan for her general drafting assistance. Finally I'd like to dedicate this book to my family, immediate and extended, from Thomas to Winifred, from the Pacific coast to the front porches of Tybee Island, Georgia. Finally, from the perspective of the craft of creating a book, I'd like to acknowledge Mrs. Elaine Stephens for teaching me the value of the written word.

PART

One

Introduction to the Capability Maturity Model

Overview of the Capability Maturity Model

The environments [we looked at] lacked an independent ability to perform. Development activities and the resulting products were unpredictable, and success or failure was totally dependent on the staff assigned.
Software Engineering Institute introductory literature

The PC revolution of the early 1980s only aggravated the quality problems within the IT community, so much so that the situation was now becoming widely known as a chronic crisis. This was beginning to attract a lot of attention, not only from corporate America but from the government as well. In the early 1980s the U.S. Congress began to look at the impact technology was having on the economy and on U.S. competitiveness on a global scale. Congress saw an impact that was both deep and broad. Technology, it saw clearly, was going to shape the future, and the best way to get ready for the future was to get the present in order. Congress fortunately also had a bead on the state of the IT industry in terms of its ability to perform in a standardized, consistent manner. In 1984, working with major U.S. corporations and research centers, Congress founded a non-profit, federally funded organization called the Software Engineering Institute (SEI) and housed it at Carnegie-Mellon University in Pittsburgh. The purpose of the SEI was to work to establish protocols and methodologies in the field of software development that would assist America in keeping a competitive edge in its technological endeavors. The SEI would accomplish this through a comprehensive program of research, training, and professional development.

According to the SEI's introductory literature:

The Software Engineering Institute was created as a research body to help improve the practice of software engineering. At its founding, the software engineering community lacked a shared view of the state of practice and agreement about what constitutes good practice. Development activity and resulting products were unpredictable, and success or failure was totally dependent on the staff assigned. While many technologies offered significant promise, most organizations were not in a position to adopt the new technology; and if they did, organizations could not evaluate its effect.[1]

To address this issue the SEI embarked on a strategy to bring engineering discipline —the same type of structured environment that architects and bridge builders and airplane designers work in—to the development and evolution of software. To do this the SEI needed to document this emerging discipline and then prepare to train industry professionals and organizations on how to improve their software development practices.

One of the early results was the SEI's Capability Maturity Model (CMM). The beginnings of the CMM were largely the work of Watts Humphrey, who in 1986 after 27 years with IBM began to investigate issues of quality in the development community at large. He soon became affiliated with the SEI, and in 1989 he published *Managing the Software Process* (Addison-Wesley). This was the first real version of CMM. From this publication point, the SEI began to refine the work with the help of Mark Paulk and a team of engineers and researchers from across the industry.

The focus of the SEI's CMM is to assist software development agencies in the maturing process. The word "mature" here means an environment in which predictability is high and risk (the unknown) is low. The CMM is structured as a five-scale tier. If an organization assesses at 5 on the tier it has reached full maturity. Full maturity implies that the organization has in place the practices, policies, and disciplines that allow the group to produce quality software in a predictable, reliable, repeatable manner. The SEI estimates that only about 1 to 2 percent of IS organizations worldwide operate at Level 5.

An organization that assesses at Level 1 naturally lacks these abilities, and so quality becomes somewhat of an unpredictable or unmanageable goal. Success here is not so much dependent on the organization as it is on the individual. The SEI estimates that the vast majority of IT shops around the world would assess at the first tier on the CMM. Though the SEI calls the first tier "Initial," it actually implies "organized chaos." Quality on the first tier is achieved through heroic individual efforts; it is neither a planned or an organized process.

The five levels are termed as follows:

5. Optimizing

4. Managed

3. Defined

2. Repeatable

1. Initial

Beginning with Level 2, the CMM calls for an organization to take on a successive series of process tools, methodologies, and policies geared to helping the organization stabilize and control its environment. The CMM first sets general goals at each level and then begins to define how the environment should operate at each level by defining a series of *Key Process Areas*.

The Key Process Areas are major functional areas that need to be properly shaped when working within the CMM. This is fulfilled by what's called *Key Practices*. Key Practices are specific activities that need to be carried out under each Key Process Area.

Following is a description of each of the five levels of the CMM, including a brief overview of what each level "looks like," an estimate of how many companies fit each particular level, and Key Process Areas for each level. Figure 1.1 illustrates improvement of software process at each of the five tiers of the CMM. At Level 1 there is a great deal of risk and low degree of predictability. But as you move up the ladder of maturity, predictability should increase while risk decreases.

Level 1: The Initial Level

Your group will qualify at the initial level for one of two reasons: Either you are totally process absent, or you have processes in place but just haven't been formally assessed yet. Every entity starts out as a Level 1 organization. The detriment to continuous operation at this level is that the environment is *unpredictable*.

At the Initial level, you'll find that the organization typically lacks a stable environment for developing and maintaining software. Any stable environment should include a set of sound management practices that are developed and used by the organization to control its activities. When these practices are missing the emphasis can easily shift from planning and tracking to reaction-driven commitment systems. The environment becomes very heat-sensitive: Attention is dumped on whatever issue happens to be the hottest at the moment.

Most Level 1 organizations by their nature pay short shrift to following whatever processes may be in place. During a crisis especially, teams will abandon planned procedures and revert to on-the-fly, ad hoc coding and testing. Success under these conditions depends entirely on the individuals on the team. Having an exceptional manager and a seasoned and effective software team becomes critical. But the problem with this

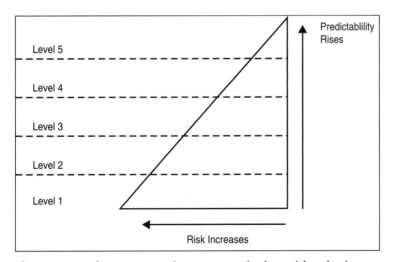

Figure 1.1 Software process improvement is about risk reduction.

reliance is that you end up tied to your people. They run the show. This may work occasionally—either because you have a bunch of heroes on your team or because you have a manager who is implementing sound practices despite their lack of definition in your organization. But when these people leave the project you are right back where you started, with their stabilizing influences gone. As CMM puts it, "Even a strong engineering process cannot overcome the instability created by the absence of sound management practices."[3]

A big problem with pure Level 1 shops (aside from the chaos) is that very little learning goes on in the environment. Because efforts from project to project are not measured or documented, they are not repeatable or share-able. New projects don't get the benefit of things done right on prior projects. Instead, the new project is managed by stress factors; pressure points get the most attention; it often takes heroic efforts to carry the project through. You may produce quality in such an environment, but you can rarely do it the same way twice.

Take heart, though. If you bought this book, chances are you are not a pure Level 1 shop. If you are serious enough about process improvement, project management, and accountability then you probably have many of the structures in place that are expected of a Level 2 or higher shop. But there are thousands of IT shops in the United States and across the globe that are truly Level 1. Many are small organizations, with fewer than 25 employees; some are quite large, with thousands of employees.[4]

The SEI estimates that in the industry as a whole—everyone included—between 75 and 85 percent would assess at Level 1. To bear this out, a little over 70 percent of all the shops that actually are assessed come out at Level 1.[5]

NOTE Level ratings are discrete. You are rated 1, 2, 3, 4, or 5. But in reality the ratings represent a spectrum of capability. You may be a 1 with many good attributes of level 2 and 3 shops.

Level 2: The Repeatable Level

Some people say Level 2 is the hardest step to achieve when adopting CMM. And I believe them. Here you leave the Initial world behind for good, taking on a whole new way of doing business. At Level 2 you implement processes and then you study them, repeating what works, discarding what does not. You become a "conscious" organization, able to learn and improve. At the Repeatable level, you begin to formalize the way you plan and manage individual projects. Level 2 is, indeed, a project-focused tier. At this level you create documented policies that establish the realm and boundaries for managing a software project. You also create processes and procedures complementary to the policies that channel project management along certain defined paths.

Also at Level 2, the way that you plan and manage new projects becomes heavily influenced by experience with similar projects. By identifying and documenting what worked on previous projects you can then enhance your processes to emphasize these strengths. New plans and processes should contain the elements of success from prior projects. Therefore, you should be able to *repeat* successful practices developed on earlier projects.

Formal control is another concept introduced at Level 2. Organizations at Level 2 operate with a set of basic management controls in place. These controls bind the reach of planning efforts. Project commitments are based mainly on results observed from previous projects and on the requirements of the current project. Little intuition or "swagging" is accommodated. These controls also shape the project management approach. The software managers for a project should track a set of defined variables, including software costs, schedules, and functionality. If any problem occurs in any of these areas it is addressed as it arises. Problems in meeting commitments are identified when they arise. At the same time, documentation and work product version control are set into place, with baselining to protect integrity. And quality assurance practices begin to monitor project compliance with established procedures.

The SEI estimates that 5 to 10 percent of the industry would probably assess at Level 2.

The key process areas for Level 2 focus on managing the software project by establishing a set of basic project management controls. Key process areas for Level 2 are as follows:

- Requirements management
- Software project planning
- Software project tracking and oversight
- Software quality assurance
- Software configuration management
- Subcontractor management

Level 3: The Defined Level

When you conduct your business practices consistently well at Level 2 you will eventually derive a set of tried and proven processes shown to enhance productivity and improve quality within your organization. At this point your organization is ready to institutionalize what it has created. You move from Level 2, which is really a project-centered level, to Level 3, which encompasses the whole organization. At this Defined level, the processes for planning, developing, and maintaining software across the organization are documented. This set of documentation includes software engineering processes as well as management and tracking processes. Together they make up a coherent whole—a set of organization-wide management tools.

Processes established at Level 3 are used to help software managers and technical staffers perform more productively, efficiently, and effectively. Whenever a new project begins, the defined set of tools is adopted and used. The project does, however, have the ability to tailor the organization's processes in order to extract a custom-shaped process that accounts for the unique characteristics of the project.

At Level 3, two new groups appear within the organization. The first is the training group. At this level an organization-wide training program is implemented to ensure that staff and managers have the resources ready by which they can acquire knowledge and skills to fulfill their duties.

The organization also creates a group that is responsible for the organization's software process activities. This group—the Software Engineering Process Group (SEPG) —manages the evolution of the defined processes for the organization as a whole.

The two chief qualities of software process activity in Level 3 organizations are standardization and consistency. Here, software engineering and management activities have become stable and repeatable. Institutional tracking keeps a regular eye on product costs, schedules, functionality, and overall quality. This approach is based on a common, organization-wide understanding of the activities, roles, and responsibilities in the defined software processes.

The SEI estimates that only about 3 to 7 percent of IT shops today are sufficiently mature to assess at Level 3.

The key process areas at Level 3 address both project and organizational issues, as the organization establishes an infrastructure that institutionalizes effective software engineering and management processes across all projects. Key process areas for Level 3 are as follows:

- Organizational process focus
- Organizational process definition
- Process training program
- Integrated software management
- Software product engineering
- Intergroup coordination
- Peer reviews

Level 4: The Managed Level

If Level 2 is mainly about process experimentation (this works, this doesn't) and Level 3 is about process definition, then Level 4 can be seen to be about process measurement: gauging the effectiveness of the defined processes with an eye toward continuous process improvement. At the Managed level the organization monitors the defined processes across all active projects, gathering metrics for performance improvement. This is done through a combination of quantitative process management and software quality management. What that means is that the organization sets *quantitative* (i.e., measurable) quality goals for both software products and processes. This stage is called managed because you are now managing virtually every aspect of product and process.

To support the focus on metrics for improvement at Level 4, the organization introduces an organization-wide software process database to collect and analyze data available from ongoing projects. Measurement becomes very important at this level because these measurements provide the quantitative foundation for establishing and evaluating each project's processes and product quality.

The maturity ability of Level 4 organizations has finally reached a stage that can be called predictable because the entire organization is using processes and tools that have been shaped through careful screening and scrutiny. They have been proven to work, and when implemented again they should produce the same results. This level of process capability allows an organization to predict trends in process and product quality and so manage a project with much more certainty.

The SEI estimates that only 2 to 3 percent of IT shops would assess at Level 4.

The key process areas at Level 4 focus on establishing a quantitative understanding of both the software process and the software work products being built. The two key process areas at this level are these:

- Quantitative process management

- Software quality management

Level 5: The Optimizing Level

Level 5 is the Optimizing level. Notice the form of the label "optimizing." "Repeatable," "Defined," and "Managed" all have an air of finality about them: You achieve, then you move on. But the Optimizing level, as its expression implies, is an ongoing, continuous state of operation. At the Optimizing level the entire organization is focused on continuous process improvement. By this stage the organization has arrived at the means to identify weaknesses, anticipate problems, and strengthen the process proactively. The prevention of defects becomes a major goal here. To address this, the project teams in Level 5 make a conscientious effort to analyze defects in order to determine their causes: what happened, how they slipped in. Using knowledge gained, they then adjust the different software processes to prevent similar types of defects from occurring.

At Level 5 the organization is in a state of continuous improvement because its members are consistently striving to improve the range of their process ability, thereby improving the process performance of their projects.

According to the SEI, no more than 2 percent of IT shops could meet Level 5 assessment requirements.

The key process areas at Level 5 cover the issues that both the organization and the projects should address to implement continuous and measurable software process improvement. Key process areas for Level 5 are these:

- Defect prevention

- Technology change management

- Process change management

The "Spirit" of CMM

Many people, when first exploring CMM implementation, take the model the wrong way. In their enthusiasm to put a productive model in place they read the CMM as a literal didactic, as a set of laws that should be followed exactly as stated. That's wrong, of course, but it is a common misconception. I have struggled through consulting sessions where the managers I worked with would pour over every nuance of language in the

CMM Key Practices, debating just what the words actually meant and what they called for, anxious to hit the mark exactly. They were taking a too-granular approach to the subject. They couldn't see the forest because all the trees were in the way.

It's important, even essential, to understand the true spirit of CMM. Let's start with the fact that the SEI's CMM is not a methodology for software development; it is not a production template, nor is it a set of process laws. If you read the CMM book you'll notice this is in the language. Abilities, activities, and other elements of the model are expressed in nonspecific terms; most are conceptual, and broad boundaries are established. CMM is an approach for process improvement, a set of guidelines that will help you forge and refine a development environment based on consistent repetition, measurement, and refinement. Even the concept of "quality" is not a central issue here. CMM assumes if you implement a program of repetition, measurements, and refinement then quality improvement will arise naturally as a byproduct of the environment.

Instead of a set of rules, think of CMM as a discipline, as a general approach to doing business. Operate within the guidelines, and you'll find lots of room to custom tailor and shape the program to the specific needs of your organization.

At the same time that CMM is not a do-it-this-way tome, it is also not a quick fix for IT shops having problems. CMM is a compass to direct you out of the storm. Many organizations (and this is understandable) want to magically appear at Level 2 or 3 or 4 without having to go through a cycle of documentation, tracking, measurement, refinement, and repetition. It's like the person who wants to be rich but doesn't want to spend the time or the energy to get rich. CMM is a program that requires a solid, long-term commitment on the part of your entire IT organization, from executive management down to line workers. The process of maturing does not happen overnight.

Finally it's important to understand that CMM allows a tremendous amount of flexibility in how you interpret its recommendations. CMM recognizes that all IT shops are different. They have different clients, different tools, different degrees of talent and specialty; they work on different kinds of projects, are of different sizes, and have different needs. So they should all approach maturity in their own ways. What works in one place might not work in another. What cements quickly in one place may not take so well in another place. Flexibility, professional interpretation, and thoughtful implementation are key ingredients to working well under CMM.

To illustrate these points, consider that it takes on average (in studies done by the SEI) 23 months of effort for an organization to move from Level 1 to Level 2. Once operating smoothly at Level 2, it takes an average of 25 months to move from Level 2 to Level 3.

Summary

The CMM is a framework for managing software process improvement activities. It is a means to an end, not an end in itself. When an organization adopts the CMM, it is making a conscious effort to become, in effect, self aware, to begin to analyze how it builds software for the purpose of improving that process. To facilitate this the CMM structures its framework of recommendations on a 5-tier scale, moving from Level 1, the Initial level where process is absent, up to Level 5, where an organization is continually optimizing its practices. Not all companies may need to achieve Level 5 in order to see distinct cost and quality benefits. Level 2, the Repeatable level, and Level 3, the Defined level, can bring to an organization the structures and disciplines that foster sustained process improvement. In this book we'll take a close look at Levels 2 and 3, beginning in the next chapter with an overview of Level 2.

Level 2:
The Repeatable Level

Overview of Level 2

At Level 2 your organization becomes "conscious"–able to learn from its successes and then take those successes and repeat them onto new projects.
Mindy Gilbert, West Conklin Computer Association

The CMM is a robust model for improving the software process in any IT organization. When properly implemented, it effectively reduces risk—the risk of ineffective planning, the risk of cost overruns, the risk of misinterpretation, and so on—and raises quality in a measurable way. The CMM has quickly become the industry's leading process improvement model, and the Software Engineering Institute has taken a lead role in producing research and refinements in the area of technology management.

For these reasons more and more companies are adopting the CMM as a way to help control their IT businesses. As mentioned in Chapter 1, about 70 percent of all software development organizations are probably Level 1 shops. That's why this book is focused on Levels 2 and 3, the tiers of the CMM where process and control mechanisms are fully introduced. People getting into CMM for the first time have to overcome the Level 2 hurdle, and this may be the biggest hurdle in the program because it's a turn away from an old way of looking at business to a new way. If you can make the successful transition from being a Level 1 Initial group to operating at Level 2, the rest of the steps up the maturity ladder should come in due order.

When you go into a Level 2 effort you are making, in effect, one big change in your group. You are going from being people-centered to being process-centered. That's not to say that the CMM does not care about people, but at Level 1 you are people-dependent. The success of your projects relies on the talent and the spunk of the individual. The project with high achievers assigned to it will perform significantly better than the project staffed with professionals of average capability. In an organized, well-run shop, the difference should not be so great. You should be able to manage productivity and quality through the use of management tools. This is what happens at Level 2. As important as your people are, what's needed is a set of generic processes and procedures that drives your projects in a consistent, definable manner. At Level 2 you turn from counting solely on your project's talent pool to management through process. You move from a degree of unpredictability ("How well will they do this time?") to a greater degree of prediction.

Though I consider Level 2 to be the biggest jump to take when working with the CMM, you may find it to be not such a big adjustment. The fact that you have purchased this book demonstrates your commitment to quality, management accountability, and process improvement. Pure Level 1 shops operate as if they don't have time to think about those issues. You are probably close to being a Level 2 shop already. You almost certainly have many of the Level 2 components in place to some extent. For you, going to Level 2 may very well be a process of refining and directing what you already have.

But before we look at just what Level 2 requires from a high-level perspective, let's briefly go over what kind of commitment it's going to take to make the CMM work, regardless of how close your structure is to Level 2 recommendations.

Finding the Right Motivation to Achieve Level 2

Adopting any quality program (even CMM), because that's what the executives say to do, happens a lot in the IT industry. It may even be prevalent. There's a good side and bad side to this. The bad side is that such a directive almost always leads to an effort that fizzles out slowly over time until it evaporates from the environment completely. This is what I call an improper motivation. By "improper" I mean a motivation that the CMM, in its application, cannot support. This can happen easily, especially when a group does not investigate the merits and requirements of the CMM up front but hungrily wants its rewards.

Improper motives include adopting the CMM as a "flavor of the month," an effort to be up on new trends or to be operating in a state-of-the-art manner. Another is to adopt the CMM as a quick fix or as a cure-all for your development problems. Another is lack of commitment. If a group gets into CMM just to "be there" they will in all likelihood not get there. In these cases there is no real motivation to change or improve the environment.

A proper motive is going to call for commitments along three lines. Take a quick look at these three and see if your group can take these on.

Broad Organization Support

For you to make a firm commitment to continuous process improvement, you need strong cross-company endorsements of the strategy from the executive, managerial, and line workers in the organization. The members of the group should understand what the CMM is all about and how it works, and they should agree on its utility within the organization. The group should want what CMM has to offer.

Commitment to a New Way

Moving to Level 2 of the CMM requires defining and adopting a new way of doing business. You are moving from a people-centered strategy to a process-centered one, one focused on continuous improvement. You will need to define a process, follow it for its course, analyze the results of the process, then improve the process and try again. This approach is not a luxury to follow when things are running smoothly and then abandon when things go wrong. It's a fixed path for process development, one that is not deviated from. If you don't have faith in your Level 2 processes or the stick-to-it-iveness to stand by them, CMM will not have a chance to help you realize its benefits.

Resource Support within the Organization

CMM requires a dedication of resources to support its implementation. You'll feel this especially at first when it appears that there's a lot of overhead involved. The key is that this overhead (such as the need for quality assurance analysts and configuration managers) is required in the long run to reduce costs and rework, and to improve delivery times and end quality. This requires people, resources, and funding. You must be comfortable developing your team along these lines. If you're not, you may find that you are implementing the CMM in a halfway manner. And CMM won't work well when done half way.

Taking That First Step: Entering Level 2

With Level 2 you are moving away from the Initial level, which resembles organized chaos, to the level called Repeatable. Initial organizations (this is a generalization, I know, but the concept is accurate) spend much of their time focused on the here and now. They are overly occupied with problem solving, crisis management, and reactive positioning. That begins to change significantly with Level 2.

The "Repeatable" label of Level 2 implies two things. The first is a process: You have to have something to repeat. And the second is learning: You study how the process worked on one project, then you lift out what worked well, discard what didn't, and then refine the process for the next project. That's continuous quality improvement in a nutshell.

But let's take a moment to clarify one point. Level 2 is a *project*-focused effort. It is not designed to bring your entire organization to process maturity. Here the focus is on repeating processes from *project* to *project*, studying the results, and improving for the next. The intent is to have you work out your basic processes on individual projects; once they have become refined enough to be proven generally successful, you can institutionalize them (at Level 3) across your organization.

Level 2 brings you into the process maturity realm through a project focus. Because of this you have to start Level 2 implementation using two broad disciplines: project planning and project management. Level 2 is heavily project management-oriented.

In fact, the tools and procedures you implement here all have direct bearing on how a project is planned and managed. The planning techniques help you anticipate (predict) how the project will roll out. And the management techniques help you stay on track with the plan (through status and measurement checks).

Key Process Areas of Level 2

CMM is a process improvement framework, so at Level 2 you're expected to introduce some processes on which to improve. As mentioned, these processes will help you manage projects in a way that ensures better control, reduces risk, and increases quality output.

The processes you'll introduce at Level 2 fall into what are called are called *Key Process Areas*. As the name implies, these are key processes that are implemented within certain areas of your development shop to better manage projects. There are six KPAs at Level 2:

- Requirements management
- Software project planning
- Software project tracking and oversight
- Software configuration management
- Software quality assurance
- Software subcontract management

Requirements Management

The requirements management process area should be built so that you can do two things effectively from project to project: track the requirements as they change, using some form of version control and change control, and make sure all software plans are adjusted when requirements change. The CMM phrases this as two general KPA goals:

Goal 1: System requirements allocated to software are controlled to establish a baseline for software engineering and management use.

Goal 2: Software plans, products, and activities are kept consistent with the system requirements allocated to software.[1]

Here you establish the resources and process needed to analyze the requirements for planning purposes and then keep project work efforts consistent with the approved requirements.

Software Project Planning

Software project planning is a key process area for Level 2. Planning—*realistic* planning—is a critical management activity. This KPA, properly designed, ensures that your project estimates, activities, and commitments are properly documented (in a software development plan) and then reviewed and approved by all parties concerned. CMM describes this in three separate KPA goals:

Goal 1: Software estimates are documented for use in planning and tracking the software project.

Goal 2: Software project activities and commitments are planned and documented.

Goal 3: Affected groups and individuals agree to their commitments related to the software project.[2]

Here you establish the resources and processes needed to shape the design and approval of a detailed software development plan. This plan will become the chief project management tool when the project gets underway.

Software Project Tracking and Oversight

Software project management is the core function at Level 2. Here we track project progress against the software development plan, make adjustments to the plan or project when goals deviate from actuality, and review all changes with affected parties before they are approved for implementation. CMM describes this in three KPA goals:

Goal 1: Actual results and performances are tracked against the software plans.

Goal 2: Corrective actions are taken and managed to closure when actual results and performance deviate significantly from the software plans.

Goal 3: Changes to software commitments are agreed to by the affected groups and individuals.[3]

Here you establish the resources and processes needed to manage the project on an ongoing basis. This includes regular status meetings and making approved adjustments as project variables change.

Configuration Management

This key process area brings version control and change control into a project. These configuration management activities should be planned for each project, a change control method should be set in place, project products need to be version controlled, and the release of new software baselines should be announced to all affected parties. CMM describes this in a series of four goals:

Goal 1: Software configuration management activities are planned.

Goal 2: Selected software work products are identified, controlled, and available.

Goal 3: Changes to identified software work products are controlled.

Goal 4: Affected groups and individuals are informed of the status and content of software baselines.[4]

Here you establish the resources and processes to implement change control for project changes/adjustments and to implement a version control system for project documentation, source code, and other output.

Software Quality Assurance

SQA activities ensure process compliance across the project. This Key Process Area should be designed so that SQA activities are planned for each project, SQA project evaluations are documented, affected groups are informed of the results, and noncompliance issues are resolved through upper management review.

Goal 1: Software quality assurance activities are planned.

Goal 2: Adherence of software products and activities to the applicable standards, procedures, and requirements is verified objectively.

Goal 3: Affected groups and individuals are informed of software quality assurance activities and results.

Goal 4: Senior management addresses noncompliance issues that cannot be resolved within the software project.[5]

Here you establish independent resources and processes to manage compliance with process standards within a project. This group becomes an independent arm within the group, not tied to any project team but rather reporting on compliance matters to senior management.

Software Subcontract Management

Shops that use the development services of outside agencies should track the agencies' own process and quality control activities. This Key Process Area should be designed so that you are not forfeiting necessary management oversight with each development piece you take outside the shop.

Goal 1: The prime contractor selects qualified subcontractors.

Goal 2: The prime contractor and the subcontractor agree to their commitments to each other.

Goal 3: The prime contractor and the subcontractor maintain ongoing communications.

Goal 4: The prime contractor tracks the subcontractor's actual results and performance against the documented commitments.[6]

Here you establish the management and communication chain within the project that will allow you to effectively control your outside vendors during the course of the project.

Looking at Your Organization

These six Key Process Areas represent focused centers of functionality that address specific requirements for operating at Level 2. Take a look now at the structure of your

IT shop. Do you have a project tracking and oversight position or group? Do you have a configuration management system or analyst? Do you have a configuration control board? We'll discuss this more in depth in Chapter 3, but right now, consider this: The CMM does not identify these 5 KPAs as distinct agencies or full-blown teams you should implement within your organization. In other words, you aren't expressly required to create a project planning organization in your shop if you don't currently have one. Perhaps that function is adequately handled within your project management team as whole. And if you don't have a full-time software quality assurance analyst, you might not need one. If you're a small shop, CMM would recognize as valid a business analyst who served part-time as SQA analyst for a certain project. Along these lines there are two important concepts to remember: "appropriate implementation" and "professional judgment."

The KPAs are key *process* areas. Your design for Level 2 within your organization need account only for the functionality required. The facilities and resources are left up to you. No IT shop is exactly like another. Customer focus, project size, technical specialty—these all differ as much as company size and culture. If you can make the KPA functionalities fit in the current structure of your teams ("appropriate implementation") and you can do so in a way that does not compromise the spirit and intent of CMM ("professional judgment") then you should have no problems during an appraisal or assessment.

To better understand just what functions are required of you in each of the six KPAs, you need to understand what is called for under each area.

Key Practices within Each Key Process Area

The six Key Process Areas of CMM are high umbrella domains for Level 2. The Key Process Areas focus your process improvement efforts in five functional areas within your organization. These are areas in which you need to institute management processes. CMM gives you great flexibility in addressing the structure and design of the KPAs within your group, but there are certain elements it expects to see in place and it defines these through what it calls key *practices*. These practices can be thought of as a set of behaviors that organizations adopt to help in the maturing process.

Each KPA is composed of five key practice areas (kpa, in lowercase). Under each area there may be multiple activities to conduct. The five key practice areas are as follows:

- Commitment to perform
- Ability to perform
- Activities performed
- Measurement and analysis
- Verifying implementation

For example, the requirements management function in your group will have to be designed in such a way that you demonstrate a commitment to its operation, that you can show a set of ready abilities that support the function, that you conduct a set of process activities, that you measure the performance of the activities, and that you verify that this overall design is being followed and works well.

Each of the six KPAs is built this way. Here's a brief, kick-start definition of each key practice area:

Commitment. Each key process area needs a formal commitment from management that supports its form and function within the organization. This commitment is typically evidenced by way of a written policy that defines the purpose, scope, and role of the area.

Ability. Each process area should have a certain set of abilities ready to carry out the function properly. These abilities are usually such things as having staff appointed specifically to certain roles and having the staff trained to carry out their duties.

Activity. Each process area should contain a series of activities that make up the heart of the processes for each area. These are usually the procedures and methods used to fulfill the commitments in each of the areas.

Measurement. For each key process area you need to conduct measurements of the processes in order to gather quantitative data to be used in continuous process improvement. These measurements can be status oriented or flow oriented, whatever gives you a better picture of the efficacy of the processes.

Verification. You need to review the functions of each KPA on a regular basis. This review includes regular SQA reviews to ensure process compliance, as well as reviews with management to ensure workability and gauge the need for revisions.

In the following section, we'll look at the key practices for each of the six Key Process Areas.

Requirements Management

The KPAs described by the CMM for this Key Process Area work together to protect the integrity of the software requirements across the life of the project.

Commitment to Perform

CMM, as you'll see in the other commitment sections, feels that no true process improvement program can begin without executive endorsement of that mission. One example of this endorsement is an executive mandate. For requirements management, CMM calls for a written policy that is disseminated to all relevant staff.

Commitment 1: The project follows a written organizational policy for managing the system requirements allocated to software.[7]

Ability to Perform

In order to meet CMM stipulations for requirements management, your group needs to have four abilities—four prerequisites standing by. The requirements you are gouing to be working with have to be documented; someone or some team has to be officially assigned to analyze these requirements, identifying which ones are software related. Funding has to be in place to support (that is, pay for) the team; finally, the people in your group who have to analyze the requirements need to be trained to use a set process when doing it.

Ability 1: For each project, responsibility is established for analyzing the system requirements and allocating them to hardware, software, and other system components.

Ability 2: The allocated requirements are documented.

Ability 3: Adequate resources and funding are provided for managing the allocated requirements.

Ability 4: Members of the software engineering group and other software-related groups are trained to perform their requirements management activities.[8]

Activities to Perform

To promote effective requirements management, CMM wants to see you conduct three general activities. You can even (and you might as well because it's easy and helpful to do so) integrate these into your requirements management process (see Chapter 4). You need to make sure the key players of your software engineering group review the requirements allocated to software. You need to make sure that the software requirements are used as a foundation for project planning and estimating. And you need to make sure any changes to the requirements are reflected in appropriate changes to the project plan.

Activity 1: The software engineering group reviews the allocated requirements before they are incorporated into the software project.

Activity 2: The software engineering group uses the allocated requirements as the basis for software plans, work products, and activities.

Activity 3: Changes to the allocated requirements are reviewed and incorporated into the software project.[9]

Measurement and Analysis

In order for you to evaluate how your requirements management process is working, you will need to measure certain portions of it. For example, you might track how many times a single requirement changed over the course of the project. Or you might compare the number of requirements at the start of the project to the number at the end.

Measurement 1: Measurements are made and used to determine the status of the activities for managing the allocated requirements.[10]

Verifying Implementation

You can't just put requirements management on auto-pilot and trust it to get where you want it to go. You, as management, have to periodically check the process for effectiveness (does it need to be changed in any way?). Your software project manager needs the same opportunity for review. And you need to make sure your SQA people are doing compliance checking at a more micro-level—at certain defined stages of every project in the works.

Verification 1: The activities for managing the allocated requirements are reviewed with senior management on a periodic basis.

Verification 2: The activities for managing the allocated requirements are reviewed with the project manager on both a periodic and event-driven basis.

Verification 3: The software quality assurance group reviews and/or audits the activities and work products for managing the allocated requirements and reports the results.[11]

Software Project Planning

The KPAs described by the CMM for this Key Process Area ensure full software planning through the use of planning categories, procedures, and guidelines.

Commitment to Perform

To demonstrate that your organization is committed to effective and realistic (that's an important word for this KPA) project planning you need to have two things in place: a formal executive-level policy citing executive endorsement of the mission and tactical structure of project planning, and a manager appointed to carry out planning activities for the project.

Commitment 1: A project software manager is designated to be responsible for negotiating commitments and developing the project's software development plan.

Commitment 2: The project follows a written organizational policy for planning a software project.[12]

Ability to Perform

CMM wants to see four abilities in place for project planning. You need, as a very initial starting point, a statement of work for the software project. The people who will be contributing details to the project plan are assigned. Funding is available to support the staff and facilities required for the planning effort. And those people who participate in planning activities are trained in the methodology of planning, negotiating, and estimating.

Ability 1: A documented and approved statement of work exists for the software project.

Ability 2: Responsibilities for developing the software development plan are assigned.

Ability 3: Adequate resources and funding are provided for planning the software project.

Ability 4: The software managers, software engineers, and other individuals involved in the software project planning are trained in the software estimating and planning procedures applicable to their areas of responsibility.[13]

Activities to Perform

Software project planning requires 15 activities. You might find it handy to integrate these (or to make sure they are present) in your project planning processes. Because CMM is really all about giving you more control and insight into your projects, planning becomes a very critical activity. That's why it's treated in such a detailed manner here. The common threads that run through most of these activities are shared knowledge and opportunity for input. The objective is get the whole organization involved in creating the project plan so that all have common stakes in the plan and a common understanding of the plan.

The activities describe an environment in which the whole group participates in project planning, the planning effort is initiated early in the project life cycle, and the software engineering group participates with other (perhaps nontechnical) groups in higher-level project planning. All commitments contained in the plan that affect outside groups are reviewed by senior management. The developmental methodology is selected early in the project life cycle. Estimate formulas are derived and used for determining project scope, size, duration, cost, and resources. And the resulting plan is built and published following the established plan creation guidelines. Finally, all planning data (estimates, assumptions, etc.) are archived for future reference, measurement, and review.

Activity 1: The software engineering group participates on the project proposal team.

Activity 2: Software project planning is initiated in the early stages of, and in parallel with, the overall project planning.

Activity 3: The software engineering group participates with other affected groups in the overall project planning throughout the project's life.

Activity 4: Software project commitments made to individuals and groups external to the organization are reviewed with senior management according to a documented procedure.

Activity 5: A software life cycle with predefined stages of manageable size is identified or defined.

Activity 6: The project's software development plan is developed according to a documented procedure.

Activity 7: The plan for the software project is documented.

Activity 8: Software work products that are needed to establish and maintain control of the software project are identified.

Activity 9: Estimates for the size of the software work products (or changes to the size of software work products) are derived according to a documented procedure.

Activity 10: Estimates for the software project's effort and costs are derived according to a documented procedure.

Activity 11: Estimates for the project's critical computer resources are derived according to a documented procedure.

Activity 12: The project's software schedule is derived according to a documented procedure.

Activity 13: The software risks associated with the cost, resource, schedule, and technical aspects of the project are identified, assessed, and documented.

Activity 14: Plans for the project's software engineering facilities and support tools are prepared.

Activity 15: Software planning data is recorded.[14]

Measurement and Analysis

In order for you to evaluate how your planning efforts are working you will need to measure certain portions of the activities. For example, you might track how your estimate for duration matched the real length of the project or compare the estimated size of the staff against the actual number used.

Measurement 1: Measurements are made and used to determine the status of the software planning activities.[15]

Verifying Implementation

You need to review your planning processes periodically to make sure they are current and reflect the condition of your projects. To facilitate this, executive management should periodically review the processes. Your software project managers should do the same thing from a more practical, line-oriented level. And you need to make sure your SQA people are doing compliance checking at a more micro-level—at certain defined stages of every project in the works.

Verification 1: The activities for software project planning are reviewed with senior management on a periodic basis.

Verification 2: The activities for software project planning are reviewed with the project manager on both a periodic and an event-driven basis.

Verification 3: The software quality assurance group reviews and/or audits the activities and work products for software project planning and reports the results.[16]

Software Project Tracking and Oversight

The kpas (I'll use small kpa to denote key *practice* area) described by the CMM for this Key Process Area work together as tools and methods to monitor project work products and activities over time. Let's look.

Commitment to Perform

To show your organization is just as committed to effective project management as it is to realistic project planning, you need to have two things in place: a formal, executive-level policy citing executive endorsement of the mission and tactical structure of project tracking and oversight. You also need to have a manager appointed to carry out tracking and oversight activities for the project.

Commitment 1: A project software manager is designated to be responsible for the project's software activities and results.

Commitment 2: The project follows a written organizational policy for managing the software project.[17]

Ability to Perform

CMM wants to see five abilities in place to manage the project. First and foremost, you need to have a software development plan (SDP) approved and in place. Then you need to have a project manager assigned and funding available to support that role. The people who will be involved in managing the project need to be trained in their duties; they should also have an orientation on the technical aspects of the project.

Ability 1: A software development plan for the software project is documented and approved.

Ability 2: The project software manager explicitly assigns responsibility for software work products and activities.

Ability 3: Adequate resources and funding are provided for tracking the software project.

Ability 4: The software managers are trained in managing the technical and personnel aspects of the software project.

Ability 5: First-line software managers receive orientation in the technical aspects of the software project.[18]

Activities to Perform

You've got to account for 12 activities to manage a project at Level 2. But if you get your project planning activities done and in place, these activities should be readily managed and should fall into place nicely. Just as in planning, you might find it handy to integrate these individual activities (or to check to make sure they are present) in your current project tracking processes.

Ongoing observation, management, and judgment are required on every project. To give you the tools to follow through with this you need to begin with an approved software development plan (SDP), and you need to use it as your chief project tracking tool. It's the Book of Law for your project. Any changes that come about during the project that deviate from the SDP should be assessed following set procedures. And any commitment changes that emerge from these changes will need first to be reviewed by senior management. During the project, the software project manager will need to track the project's scope, size, resources, effort levels, schedule, and risk factors regularly. This tracking should be done in conjunction with representatives of the software engineering group. Finally, all your tracking data should be documented for use later as measurement data.

Activity 1: A documented software development plan is used for tracking the software activities and communicating status.

Activity 2: The project's software development plan is revised according to a documented procedure.

Activity 3: Software project commitments and changes to commitments made to individuals and groups external to the organization are reviewed with senior management according to a documented procedure.

Activity 4: Approved changes to commitments that affect the software project are communicated to the members of the software engineering group and other software-related groups.

Activity 5: The size of the software work products (or size of the changes to the software work products) is tracked, and corrective actions are taken as necessary.

Activity 6: The project's software effort and costs are tracked, and corrective actions are taken as necessary.

Activity 7: The project's critical computer resources are tracked, and corrective actions are taken as necessary.

Activity 8: The project's software schedule is tracked, and corrective actions are taken as necessary.

Activity 9: Software engineering technical activities are tracked, and corrective actions are taken as necessary.

Activity 10: The software risks associated with the cost, resource, schedule, and technical aspects of the project are tracked.

Activity 11: Actual measurement data and planning data for the software project are recorded.

Activity 12: The software engineering group conducts periodic internal reviews to track technical progress, plans, performance, and issues against the software development plan.[19]

Measurement and Analysis

In order to evaluate how your project tracking efforts are paying off you will need to measure certain portions of your PM activities. For example, you might track how many change requests have come in over the life of the project. Or you might tally the number of schedule shifts that had to be introduced into the plan due to unforeseen circumstances.

Measurement 1: Measurements are made and used to determine the status of the software tracking and oversight activities.[20]

Verifying Implementation

Just as with project planning, you need to review project management activities and processes on a periodic basis. Executive management should periodically review the processes. Your project managers should do the same thing at a more practical, line-oriented level. And your SQA people should be doing micro-level compliance checking at certain defined stages.

Verification 1: The activities for software project tracking and oversight are reviewed with senior management on a periodic basis.

Verification 2: The activities for software project tracking and oversight are reviewed with the project manager on both a periodic and an event-driven basis.

Verification 3: The software quality assurance group reviews and/or audits the activities and work products for software project tracking and oversight and reports the results.[21]

Software Configuration Management

The kpas described by the CMM for this Key Process Area work together to protect the integrity of the software work products across the life of the project. Let's look.

Commitment to Perform

To demonstrate your organization's commitment to the purpose and role of configuration management you need to develop a formal, executive-level policy citing executive endorsement of its mission and tactical structure.

Commitment 1: The project follows a written organizational policy for implementing software configuration management.[22]

Ability to Perform

You'll need five abilities in place to carry out Level 2 configuration management activities. You'll need to establish and define the role of a Change Control Board. You'll need to create a configuration management job or group and you will need to fund it appropriately. Then you'll need to train your Configuration Managers in their mission and the tools available to them; you will also need to train the members of the engineering group who will have to work within Configuration Management (CM) boundaries.

Ability 1: A board having the authority for managing the project's software baselines (i.e., a Software Configuration Control Board, or SCCB) exists or is established.

Ability 2: A group that is responsible for coordinating and implementing Software Configuration Management (SCM) for the project (i.e., the SCM group) exists.

Ability 3: Adequate resources and funding are provided for performing the SCM activities.

Ability 4: Members of the SCM group are trained in the objectives, procedures, and methods for performing their SCM activities.

Ability 5: Members of the software engineering group and other software-related groups are trained to perform their SCM activities.[23]

Activities to Perform

Configuration management, because it contains both version control and change control duties, is made up of 10 specific activities. You should first make sure a software configuration plan exists for each project, and you have to use this SCM plan as the basis for project-related SCM activities. To manage project-related output you should set up some form of a version control library system, identify the work products that will be tracked, and create the SCM procedures for tracking documented baselines, version controlling, and status reporting to the team.

Activity 1: A SCM plan is prepared for each software project according to a documented procedure.

Activity 2: A documented and approved SCM plan is used as the basis for performing the SCM activities.

Activity 3: A configuration management library system is established as a repository for the software baselines.

Activity 4: The software work products to be placed under configuration management are identified.

Activity 5: Change requests and problem reports for all configuration items/units are initiated, recorded, reviewed, approved, and tracked according to a documented procedure.

Activity 6: Changes to baselines are controlled according to a documented procedure.

Activity 7: Products from the software baseline library are created, and their release is controlled according to a documented procedure.

Activity 8: The status of configuration items/units is recorded according to a documented procedure.

Activity 9: Standard reports documenting the SCM activities and the contents of the software baseline are developed and made available to affected groups and individuals.

Activity 10: Software baseline audits are conducted according to a documented procedure.[24]

Measurement and Analysis

To intelligently plan improvements to your configuration management processes, you will need to measure certain portions of your CM activities. For example, you might track how many new baseline versions of certain documents have been issued over the life of the project. Or you might tally the number of change requests that came in for a certain project.

> **Measurement 1:** Measurements are made and used to determine the status of the SCM activities.[25]

Verifying Implementation

For configuration management as well as change control you need to review project activities and processes on a periodic basis. Executive management should periodically review the processes. Your project managers should do the same thing from a more practical, line-oriented level. Your SCM managers should be doing their own internal quality checks now and then. And your SQA people should be doing micro-level compliance checking at certain defined stages.

> **Verification 1:** The SCM activities are reviewed with senior management on a periodic basis.
>
> **Verification 2:** The SCM activities are reviewed with the project manager on both a periodic and an event-driven basis.
>
> **Verification 3:** The SCM group periodically audits software baselines to verify that they conform to the documentation that defines them.
>
> **Verification 4:** The software quality assurance group reviews and/or audits the activities and work products for SCM and reports the results.[26]

Software Quality Assurance

The kpas described by the CMM for this Key Process Area are designed to monitor compliance by the software project team with documented processes and procedures.

Commitment to Perform

To demonstrate your organization's commitment to the purpose and role of quality compliance you need to develop a formal, executive-level policy citing executive endorsement of its mission and tactical structure.

> **Commitment 1:** The project follows a written organizational policy for implementing software quality assurance (SQA).[27]

Ability to Perform

You'll need four abilities in place to carry out Level 2 software quality control activities. You'll need to create an SQA job or group, and you'll need to fund it appropriately. Then you'll need to train your SQA people in their mission and in the tools available to them; you will also need to train the members of the engineering group who will have to work with SQA analysts on projects.

Ability 1: A group that is responsible for coordinating and implementing SQA for the project (i.e., the SQA group) exists.

Ability 2: Adequate resources and funding are provided for performing the SQA activities.

Ability 3: Members of the SQA group are trained to perform their SQA activities.

Ability 4: The members of the software project receive orientation on the role, responsibilities, authority, and value of the SQA group.[28]

Activities to Perform

The SQA group is "project independent." It is not directly accountable to the project manager (although it does present reports to the project team.) It is accountable to executive management. SQA's role is to help project teams stay in compliance with the processes and procedures designed to manage the project. To do this, eight activities are specified in CMM. SQA should develop an SQA plan for the project, then use that plan as the main SQA management tool during the project. Though an "independent" arm of the project team, SQA is included in all team plan reviews and activity reviews. During the course of the project the SQA team will audit project activities and issue periodic compliance reports. If there are significant process deviations, SQA will work with project management to realign them.

Activity 1: An SQA plan is prepared for the software project according to a documented procedure.

Activity 2: The SQA group's activities are performed in accordance with the SQA plan.

Activity 3: The SQA group participates in the preparation and review of the project's software development plan, standards, and procedures.

Activity 4: The SQA group reviews the software engineering activities to verify compliance.

Activity 5: The SQA group audits designated software work products to verify compliance.

Activity 6: The SQA group periodically reports the results of its activities to the software engineering group.

Activity 7: Deviations identified in the software activities and software work products are documented and handled according to a documented procedure.

Activity 8: The SQA group conducts periodic reviews of its activities and findings with the customer's SQA personnel, as appropriate.[29]

Measurement and Analysis

SQA needs to measure itself in much the same way it measures performance in other groups. This way SQA can determine the areas it needs to refine or improve. For example, SQA might track the number of compliance issues that arise in each project. Or SQA might calculate a compliance percentage for projects and compare one to another.

Measurement 1: Measurements are made and used to determine the cost and schedule status of the SQA activities.[30]

Verifying Implementation

With SQA you need to review project activities and quality control processes on a periodic basis. Executive management should periodically review the processes. Your project managers should do the same thing from a more practical, line-oriented level. And your SQA people should be doing their own quality checks (with the assistance of outside consultants, if available) as to how their work is succeeding.

Verification 1: The SQA activities are reviewed with senior management on a periodic basis.

Verification 2: The SQA activities are reviewed with the project manager on both a periodic and an event-driven basis.

Verification 3: Experts independent of the SQA group periodically review the activities and software work products of the project's SQA group.[31]

Software Subcontract Management

The kpas described by the CMM for this Key Process Area are designed to monitor compliance of the subcontract by the prime contractor and the vendor.

Commitment to Perform

To demonstrate your organization's commitment to effective and proactive contract and vendor management, you should develop a formal, executive-level policy citing executive endorsement of its mission and tactical structure.

Commitment 1: The project follows a written organizational policy for managing the software subcontract.

Commitment 2: A subcontract manager is designated to be responsible for establishing and managing the software subcontract.[32]

Ability to Perform

You'll look to three abilities for this KPA. You'll want to make sure the right levels of resources and funding are in place; you'll want to make sure your contract managers are trained; and you'll want to ensure that the software managers and other members of the project team are oriented to the role and processes of subcontract management.

Ability 1: Adequate resources and funding are provided for selecting the subcontractor and managing the subcontract.

Ability 2: Software managers and other individuals who are involved in establishing the software subcontract are trained to perform these activities.

Ability 3: Software managers and other individuals who are involved in managing the software subcontract receive orientation in the technical aspects of the subcontract.[33]

Activities to Perform

The activities of the subcontract management group serve to cement the working relationship between the prime contractor (your shop) and the selected vendors. If there are significant work plan or process changes, the prime contractor and the subcontractor will work closely to align the changes against a set of common commitments.

Activity 1: The work to be subcontracted is defined and planned according to a documented procedure.

Activity 2: The software subcontractor is selected based on an evaluation of the subcontract bidder's ability to perform work, according to a documented procedure.

Activity 3: The contractual agreement between the prime contractor and the subcontractor is used as the basis for managing the subcontract.

Activity 4: A documented subcontractor's software development plan is reviewed and approved by the prime contractor.

Activity 5: A documented and approved subcontractor's software development plan is used for tracking the software activities and communicating the status.

Activity 6: Changes to the software subcontractor's statement of work, subcontract terms and conditions, and other commitments are resolved according to a documented procedure.

Activity 7: The prime contractor's management conducts periodic status/coordination reviews with the software subcontractor's management.

Activity 8: Periodic technical reviews and interchanges are held with the subcontractor.

Activity 9: Formal reviews to address the subcontractor's software engineering accomplishments and results are conducted at selected milestones according to a documented procedure.

Activity 10: The prime contractor's software quality assurance group monitors the subcontractor's SQA activities according to a documented procedure.

Activity 11: The prime contractor's SCM group monitors the subcontractor's SCM activities according to a documented procedure.

Activity 12: The prime contractor conducts acceptance as part of subcontractor product delivery according to a documented procedure.

Activity 13: The software subcontractor's performance is evaluated on a periodic basis, and the evaluation results are shared with the subcontractor.[34]

Measurement and Analysis

Subcontractor management should periodically measure its performance. This way project management and executive management can evaluate areas that may require refinement or improvement in the future.

> **Measurement 1:** Measurements are made and used to determine the status of activities for managing the software subcontract.[35]

Verifying Implementation

Management should review subcontract management activities and quality control processes on a periodic basis. Executive management should periodically review the processes. Your project managers should do the same thing on a more practical, line-oriented level. And your SQA people should be doing their own quality checks (with the assistance of the outside vendor).

> **Verification 1:** The subcontract management activities are reviewed with senior management on a periodic basis.

> **Verification 2:** The subcontract management activities are reviewed with the project manager on both a periodic and an event-driven basis.

> **Verification 3:** The SQA group periodically reviews and audits the activities of the subcontract management.[36]

Summary

Looking at the various key practices under each Key Process Area, you may have noticed a pattern emerging. The pattern is this: Each KPA requires four facets to be in place for compliance:

- Structure
- Process
- Training
- Policy

If you design your Level 2 program one KPA at a time using the SPTP approach—that is, thinking about each one in terms of its policies, its structure, its processes, and its training requirements—you should be able to build a Level 2-compliant program economically and efficiently within your organization.

In the next chapter we'll look at the how to create the right structure for each KPA to support a Level 2-compliant program.

Creating Level 2 Structures

*The structure of an organization gives momentum to its activities.
The right structure—designed for adequacy and efficiency—can move a
group well on the way toward predictability in output.
Dan Payne, Senior Analyst, Lockheed-Martin Corp.*

In order to move toward Level 2 compliance within your software development group, you want to make sure (among other things) that you have the right team structure in place to support the methodologies of the CMM at Level 2.

By the "right structure" we mean that you have the right people, tools, and space needed to get the job done in a way that supports process quality activities. Naturally, the actual form of the structure will vary from organization to organization, and probably even from project to project. Large organizations working on large projects would probably have a Level 2-compliant structure that looks quite different from that of a small company working on smaller projects.

When looking at your current structure consider each of these factors: the assignments of your people (how they are organized into teams on the projects), the tools and resources available to them, the funding and corporate support given to the teams, the size of your projects, and your general corporate culture.

At heart here is the responsibility to match the structure to your mission. This being the case, there is some flexibility in the law of this matter. But the spirit carries in it a set of common considerations you should adequately address when assessing if your structure is truly Level 2 compliant.

In this chapter we'll look at ways to accommodate some of the recommendations found in the CMM through the implementation of a series of structural elements for your projects. These usually include role assignments, providing adequate funding for activities, and acquiring any tools required for performing the activities. We'll explore this breakdown for each of the Key Process Areas of Level 2. But let's first begin with how the CMM itself promotes structure.

What Kind of Structure Is Required?

All software development shops have some things in common, no matter what their size. For example, there are people on board who write code, people who perform testing, people who design, and people who write technical documentation. Of course, in today's world there are countless little hacker shops out there: small, informal organizations that adopt a take-it-as-it-comes attitude toward development. There everyone does a little of everything. These are perpetual Level 1 shops. They run on raw talent and heroic efforts, often in crisis mode. Their structures are very informal, and their market niches (usually small projects under $50,000) don't demand much of a change.

On the other hand, your IT shop is probably a step or two (at least) above the hacker level; it's probably a much more formal organization, dealing with multiple high-end projects. Crisis mode is probably considered a negative thing where you work. The CMM program was not really intended for hacker shops. It was meant for organizations like yours, with a formal MIS foundation in place. The traditional steps of requirements engineering, analysis, design, coding, testing, documentation, implementation, and support are structural components that serve as the bedrock of any process-oriented program. The Software Engineering Institute (SEI) assumes that any organization adopting its CMM program is in some way already in sync with these traditional steps. The CMM, especially at Level 2, uses these steps as a base on which to build an *enhanced* structure for project management.

At Level 2, the CMM expects you to have a structure in place that supports five general activities (activities that may or may not be new to your group). These are requirements management, project planning, project tracking, configuration management, and software quality assurance. (I'm holding off discussing subcontractor management until I treat it on its own in Chapter 7.)

The CMM defines what it expects of this enhanced structure chiefly through a series of qualities it terms "Abilities." (Some activities affect structure as well, as we shall see later.) Each of the five Key Process Areas at Level 2 should possess certain ability attributes that demonstrate each area's preparedness and readiness to carry out a quality program from the start and from within the traditional MIS environment. Without the right structure in place, any quality program is doomed.

Does this mean that you will be obligated to expand your organizational structure, to have five new and separate groups in place, one dedicated to each of the five KPAs?

No. In fact, the CMM is generously open not only about how you assign these responsibilities, but also about how you define a responsible group. According to *The Capability Maturity Model: Guidelines for Improving the Software Process* (Paulk et al., 1994),

> A group is a collection of departments, managers, and individuals who have responsibility for a set of tasks or activities. A group could vary from a single individual assigned part-time, to several part-time individuals assigned from different departments, to several individuals dedicated full-time. Considerations when implementing a group include assigned tasks or activities, the size of the project, the organizational structure, and the organizational culture.1

In terms of the enhanced structure required for Level 2 compliance, you have a lot of latitude in how you define and assign the resources necessary to account for the specific abilities. These assignments can be part-time; they can be contracted out. The only hard rule is that they should be assigned in a manner appropriate to the scope of the project. And at Level 2 they should always be project specific.

What Minimum Resources Are Required?

Just as there are Key Process Areas and Key Practices in the Capability Maturity Model, so are there also—in my view—key players. Key players are those people on your team who take on very job-specific roles when you are working in a Level 2 program. While there are six key roles that need to be supported, they can be supported by as few as four key players. Chances are, you already have a few of these roles accounted for in your organization today. The CMM expects two things in this area: First, the different roles are explicitly assigned for each project, and second, adequate funding and resources are available to carry out the roles.

Here are the areas in which you will need to evaluate your structural situation for Level 2:

- Requirements management
- Software project planning

Figure 3.1 The CMM supports the idea of committed process improvement with recommendations that call for the organization's supporting each project with adequate funding, people, and tools.

- Project tracking and oversight
- Configuration management
- Software quality assurance

We will now examine each of these topics in greater depth.

Requirements Management

The CMM is not very concerned with requirements *definition*. That job is usually done by members of the systems engineering group. The CMM is a process quality program for software engineering groups, groups that design, build, and implement software systems. Because of this, the requirements definition process is external to the scope of the CMM. It is a prerequisite for the program. The CMM assumes that the requirements are defined and in place prior to the beginning of any project. And while this is not always true in the realm of the business world, a line of demarcation is important. The CMM is chiefly concerned with the *management* of the requirements. The CMM understands that requirements can change over the life of a project, so it emphasizes two main management techniques. The first is that the requirements are analyzed up front to aid in general understanding and planning. The second is that all changes to the requirements are closely tracked, with plans being adjusted accordingly.

In terms of the right structure needed for effective requirements management, the CMM calls for the following:

- For each project, responsibility is assigned to team member(s) to analyze and allocate the requirements to hardware, software, and other components.
- Adequate resources and funding are available for managing the allocated requirements.

A person on the software engineering team will take the system requirements (presumably from the systems engineering people) and perform a technical analysis to allocate them to software, hardware, and other architectural areas. This assignment provides data used for planning the project and for understanding the requirements within the software engineering group. This type of role is usually handled by an analyst or a designer or some other similar specialist. It need not be full time, but it does need to be an "officially designated" role. Sometimes this role will be assigned to a "business expert" on the team, someone who understands the business domain under which the system falls. Other times it may fall to a technical analyst.

How you account for the position depends on your project and your resources. Just remember to appoint the position and to assign it the two tasks of understanding the requirements and providing allocation data for project planning efforts. And finally make sure you fund and support the position within your organization or group.

Software Project Planning

When you are moving your organization to Level 2 you are taking it into a process-oriented mindset. The goal of the CMM is to implement a series of management techniques that will make your approach to systems building predictable, successful, and manageable. Project planning is one of the first milestones to demonstrate this. Planning is a key technique throughout the CMM program, and it takes on a special relevance at Level 2. Because the CMM looks for up-front project planning, it calls on your organization to have the ability to create a realistic project plan using recognized resources.

For Level 2 you should appoint someone, usually the project manager who will run the software project portion of the project, to create a project plan. The CMM puts it this way:

- A project software manager is designated to be responsible for negotiating commitments and developing the software development plan.
- Adequate resources and funding are provided for planning the software project.

This is usually a project manager, but in any event the role calls for someone to take the analyzed requirements and negotiate with all the teams in the software engineering group the cost, schedule, scope, deliverables, and commitments for the project. The project plan that comes out of this effort is the main tool used to manage the software portion of the overall project. The appointment of someone to create the project plan is an important aspect of Level 2 activity.

Project Tracking and Oversight

If the CMM at Level 2 is focused on anything, it is focused on project management. The process of planning, evaluating, and adjusting is key to smooth operations. At the same time, it is required to ensure the eventual realization of specific objectives. Naturally, the CMM looks for a strong project management structure within a Level 2-compliant group. Project management involves up-front project planning (see the previous section) and extensive project tracking and oversight activities. The appointment of a project manager for each project is a major attribute of CMM Level 2.

- A project software manager is designated to be responsible for the project's software activities and results.
- Adequate resources and funding are provided for tracking the software project.

Management of the software development plan usually falls to the software project manager, just as the planner is usually also the project manager. Once the plan is approved the project is ready to go. The software development plan is then used by a project manager to help measure and track project progress over time. This is perhaps the central role of the Level 2 philosophy: tracking actual activity against planned activity and making adjustments (to both) as needed.

The project manager you assign does not have to be dedicated full time to the project, if such dedication is not required. But the PM should be given the proper amount of time, funding, and resources to manage the project effectively.

Configuration Management

As already mentioned, Level 2 is very focused on management techniques and activities. Configuration management is an extension of this, and CM can be viewed as a project management tool external to the project management role. Configuration management is the process by which a project's output (source code, documentation, etc.) is carefully monitored and cataloged in order to keep the data current and to retain an audit trail from prior versions. Additionally, the configuration management role is designed to provide a form of change control (typically in the guise of a change control committee) through which all changes to project commitments, scope, and resources should pass.

The chief responsibility of configuration management is to make sure all changes are carefully scrutinized and assessed before they are incorporated into existing plans.

At Level 2, the configuration management structure requires three things. First is a committee appointed (usually over all projects) to review, assess, and approve any changes requested for a project. Next is a position in which the project's output is carefully tracked and version controlled. Finally is the requirements for some kind of library system to assist in the tracking and version controlling of the project's output.

To support this the CMM calls for the following:

- A board having the authority to manage the project's software baselines (a Software Configuration Control Board) exists or is established.

- A group that is responsible for coordinating and implementing SCM activities for the project exists.

- Adequate resources and funding are provided for carrying out configuration management activities.

- A configuration management library system is established as a repository for the software baselines.

The Configuration Control Board is a committee convened to review and approve any changes to the scope, schedule, cost, or other plans for the project. Often it is referred to as the Change Control Board (CCB) because its chief task is to control the request for changes that come in while a project is underway. The Configuration Control Board can be as large or as small as your project calls for, but it should be composed of people who are familiar with the project and who are able to ascertain the relevance and criticality of change requests that come in. The CCB can meet on a frequent or periodic basis, again depending on the activity for each particular project. For Level 2, each project should be under the guidance of a CCB; all changes to the project should be passed first through the CCB.

A software project requires the production of a lot of software code as well as a lot of supporting documentation. All of this information needs to be version controlled so that up-to-date copies of current configurations are always available to the software engineering group (SEG) team, executive management, and the customer. This is a fairly specialized functional area and is usually handled by a configuration analyst using a specific set of tools (see the next section). Configuration management can be an easily manageable job on smaller projects, and it can become a complex, resource-intensive job on large projects. Depending on the scope of your project, the configuration management tasks can be handled by a range of talent, from an administrative assistant to a technical writer, on up to an experienced technical analyst.

Next to the software development plan, the chief tool used to manage any Level 2 software project is some form of a configuration management system. This system need not be elaborate as long as it suits the needs of your project. The system could be as simple as a hard-copy library of plans, documentation, and source code, organized to keep current copies clean and older versions clearly marked. Complex projects may require more complex systems. There are many functionally extensive configuration management software systems available on the market today. If you have a system in place in your organization already you may find that it suits the Level 2 needs just fine. If not, make adjustments to help the match fit.

Software Quality Assurance

The software quality assurance (SQA) role is another key one in the CMM. SQA is the person or group who oversees the activities of a project to make sure each project follows established processes and methodologies as closely as possible. The concept of "compliance" falls under the SQA umbrella. SQA, in essence, scores compliance from project to project, but its role is actually much more supportive. SQA should be proactive in helping a project and its members follow the process path in a direct, straightforward manner.

To define a structure that will allow such assistance, the CMM calls for the following:

- A group that is responsible for coordinating and implementing SQA activities for the project exists.
- Adequate resources and funding are provided for performing the SQA activities.

The SQA role within CMM is introduced at Level 2. For each project you should appoint an "independent" resource to monitor the project's activities in relation to what's called for in your development processes. The SQA's responsibility is to make sure that the established processes are being followed in every phase of the project. The role is called "independent" in the CMM because this role does not report to the project manager, but rather to executive management. It is independent of the project reporting hierarchy.

What Is Meant by Adequate Resources and Funding?

You will notice that the CMM calls for "adequate funding and resources" to be made available for each of the four structural areas discussed previously. This simply means that your organization should support these roles through financial and operational support. These roles should become an integrated part of your IT team structure. It might be tempting to keep these roles in an "unofficial" state, pulling them into use when you have to, but such an approach is at odds with the consistent quality approach of the CMM.

As mentioned in the Introduction, adoption of the Capability Maturity Model will require you to take on some additional overhead. And while this overhead has been proven to pay for itself over time, it does require an up-front commitment.

For your organization and for your Level 2 program, check to make sure that these roles have official recognition on your organizational chart and that there is some indication of budgeting and capital expenses available for each area.

In the end, your judgment will ensure proper resource allocation for this part of the CMM. As stated in the specification:

Organizations should (ultimately) determine the organizational structure that will {best} support the activities that require focus.

This means that you will have to use professional judgment when implementing the enhanced structure called for by the CMM. As an example, for Level 2 compliance you would probably count a structure as being lacking if you found that the software project manager on a project team was also serving in the role of quality assurance analyst and configuration manager, too. That's splitting the focus too much for any one job to be done properly, and a CMM assessment would probably see it that way as well.

On the other hand, for a relatively small project it would be perfectly acceptable to have a structure in which the project manager did both the project planning and the project tracking, and in which the requirements analyst, the SQA analyst, and the CM analysts all worked only part time on the assignment.

NOTE Training is a topic that touches every KPA in Level 2 of the CMM program (though it is not the same as the formal training called for at Level 2). The CMM requires that you have an infrastructure in place to support two broad types of training activity. The first is process training for employees. This is formal training in the process methodologies used for software development in your organization. The other is project orientation. This is a training mechanism by which various members of the software engineering groups are given business-specific orientations as to the scope and nature of the project in order to better carry out their own roles. Therefore, your organization should also support a training structure that is not addressed in this chapter. Level 2 training is addressed on it own in Chapter 5 of this book.

Supporting the Implementation of Level 2 Structures

The structure you build into your organization to support Level 2 requirements can be supported through a series of artifacts that will readily demonstrate that the structure is indeed in place. An artifact is any piece of tangible evidence (such as a document, a report, a form) that rises out of the activity on a project. Some people term artifacts "process documents." You will need a structure that contains not just the traditional developmental groups (coding, testing, etc.), but also requirements analysis, project planning and management, configuration management, and software quality assurance. Each of these four areas needs official recognition within your organization. This can be achieved in many ways, including the following:

Presence on the project's organizational chart. Each project's org chart should include boxes for project management, configuration management, and software quality assurance (if they are not present already). Depending on how you assign your resources, you may also want to include a box for requirements analysis and project planning, though these roles could fall under a number of other already existing boxes.

Presence on operational/personnel charts. If your organization uses charts showing what employees are on what teams, be sure to include your assignment identifications for requirements analysis, project planning, project tracking, configuration management analysis, members of the configuration management board, and members of the SQA group.

Job descriptions. The roles of requirements analysis, project planning, project tracking, configuration management analysis, and CCB membership all require specific job descriptions. Create these job descriptions to finalize the scope and responsibilities of each role using Level 2 requirements as a foundation. These descriptions will also be useful as training and orientation material for new hires.

Funding and budget allocation. On each project and for each new area within the Level 2 structure, assign an official budget code and funding code (if practical and if they do not exist already) so that each area is treated as an official organizational function.

Staff assignment form. Finally, document your resource allocation activity through the use of staff assignment forms. For each project, use the form to official assign staff members to the roles of requirements analysis, project planning, project management, configuration management, and software quality assurance. Keep these forms as they make excellent artifacts for proof of compliance during CMM assessments.

Table 3.1 demonstrates some of the artifacts you many need for each KPA.

Table 3.1   Evidence of Program Compliance

KEY PROCESS AREA	ARTIFACTS
Requirements Management	Staff assignment form, general organizational chart, job description, budget allocation/capital account
Project Planning	Staff assignment form, general organizational chart, job description, budget allocation/capital account
Project Tracking and Oversight	Staff assignment form, general organizational chart, job description, budget allocation/capital account
Configuration Management	Staff assignment form, general organizational chart, job description, budget allocation/capital account
Software Quality Assurance	Staff assignment form, general organizational chart, job description, budget allocation/capital account

Naturally these artifacts are not mandated by the CMM, but they are fairly common examples of what organizations tend to put into place when they create the corresponding project structures. You may have your own type of artifacts in mind. As long as they are able to help you and your team demonstrate how you are working they will no doubt be fine.

Summary

By way of a rough calculation you could consider that implementing the recommendations in this chapter takes you to (about) 20 percent of Level 2 compliance. Consider that number as a handy yardstick to help track the progress of your effort. Setting the right structure in place for your Level 2 projects is important in several ways. It's the first step to assigning people to specific process improvement roles. It requires a potential commitment of funding and tools from the executive level of the organization. And it provides an infrastructure adding on other components of the model. We'll take a look at one of these components—Level 2 processes—in the next chapter.

Table 3.2   Key Practices Discussed in This Chapter

KEY PROCESS AREA	CHAPTER TASK	KEY PRACTICE OBLIGATION
Requirements Management	Assign analysis and allocation responsibility, provide funding and resources	Ability 1, Ability 2
Project Planning	Assign project planning responsibility, provide funding and resources	Commitment 1, Ability 3
Project Tracking and Oversight	Assign project tracking responsibility, provide funding and resources	Commitment 1, Ability 3
Configuration Management	Establish a Configuration Control Board, establish a configuration management library system, assign configuration management responsibility, provide funding and resources	Ability 1, Activity 3, Ability 2, Ability 3
Software Quality Assurance	Assign SQA responsibility, provide funding and resources	Ability 1, Ability 2

Creating Level 2 Processes

The heart of systems improvement lies in the activities that are conducted by way of published processes and procedures. These are key to staying on the improvement track and to knowing where you stand from project to project. It's the practice of the methods that count and the practice is in the process.
Seane Devenshire, Process Consultant

Process can be defined any number of ways, but one of the simplest is "a path built to reach a defined outcome." A process is a series of steps that, when combined, result in an outcome, often a product. You bake a cake using a process. If you've got a good process you can gain a reputation as a talented baker. If the cakes turn out bad most of the time—they fall or burn—there's probably something wrong with your process. Somewhere in there something doesn't work for cake baking. If you want to improve as a chef you will need to find out what that thing is, fix it, and then have a go at it again. The same is true for software engineering at Level 2 of CMM. As mentioned in Chapter 1, Level 2 is termed the Repeatable level. Here an organization should become conscious where previously it had been pretty much unconscious. What I mean by this is that at Level 2 the organization will begin to pay attention to something new: itself. Level 1— Initial—organizations are typically focused just on the end product, on getting it out any way possible. Level 1 organizations don't analyze their work habits to make them better. They can't in many instances because their habits are ad hoc, undefined. Level 1 organizations don't use consistent processes, and without process, learning and improvement become significantly more difficult.

In the CMM, process is introduced at Level 2. The organization becomes not only process focused but process centered, and this is reflected in software project planning and management. In fact, a strong commitment to honor and follow process is just about the only thing on which CMM absolutely and invariably insists. Think of a typical midrange IT project, and you'll see how process can affect most aspects of it. Without some form of process the project cannot be realistically planned, it cannot be effectively tracked, and it can't be properly evaluated for goodness-of-fit. And that's at the macro level. Go granular, and the complexities increase. To help an organization grow in maturity, CMM calls for a process commitment beginning with Level 2, and it is looking for a series of processes in its Key Process Areas. The processes will help manage requirements, create a project software development plan (SDP), track and manage the project, provide for effective change control, provide for consistent configuration management, and provide for the oversight of software quality assurance.[1] In this chapter we'll discuss each of these areas and the activities required for each process on this tier of the CMM.

Look at Your Existing Processes

Nearly 50 percent of assessed organizations tracked at the SEI have fewer than 100 employees. About 25 percent have from 100 to 200, and about 25 percent have more than 200.[2] An "organization" does not necessarily mean the entire IT arm of a company. Different organizations within the same company may assess independently of each other. The point is that organizations of all shapes and sizes are moving to adopt the CMM, and to do this they must all begin by defining and then refining their processes.

What's your organization like? If you are truly a pure Level 1 shop, then you have no processes in place at all. Zero. And if that's the case, you will find it a big task to research, create, publish, implement, and train people on the series of processes you might use at Level 2. On the other hand, your organization is probably not a pure Level 1 shop. You probably already have a number of processes in place, and many aspects of them might perfectly fit CMM guidelines. But whether you are wholly Level 1 or somewhere on the way to Level 2, remember these two series of *Dos* and *Don'ts*.

Process Don'ts

Here are two tips that that will help you know what your process boundaries might end up leaning toward:

> **Your processes don't have to be extensive.** Many people think their beginning processes have to be all-encompassing management systems, wide reaching and perfectly integrated into the environment. That's not true. You can implement small processes at the start—processes that address basic needs—and then expand and grow them through use and analysis. In fact, as far as the CMM is concerned, that's a great way to do things.

> **Your processes don't have to be perfect.** This is another common misconception. The CMM is all about improvement over time. It does not expect that everything you implement will be complete and effective. It assumes it won't. CMM really begins at the Repeatable level because it is at this level that you begin to repeat your success and discard your failures. Don't agonize over every little detail of your processes. Don't sweat the small stuff. Define, implement, analyze, and improve, then start the cycle again, and you'll be on your way.

Process Dos

These two ideas will help you position your efforts to effectively support and manage your processes.

Your processes have to be documented. Documentation is a CMM cornerstone. You have to document your processes for all projects. For the sake of consistency, tracking, and training, the processes must be written in clear, concise, unambiguous terms.

Your processes have to be followed. Adherence is another CMM cornerstone. Once you have documented your project processes your people have to follow them, and any deviations have to be carefully reviewed and tracked. The key to improvement is to follow the path and then measure how well that path worked for you. If you don't consistently follow the path, your measurements become significantly less meaningful.

What Processes Are Useful at Level 2?

For Level 2 you should think through a series of processes, some more extensive than others. Here is a brief list:

Requirements management. A process to bring documented requirements into the software engineering group and then manage them over the course of the project.

Project planning. Processes to create the project's software development plan (SDP) and also to have it reviewed and approved.

Estimating. A series of processes that guide how members of the SEG estimate project planning variables, including component size, work efforts and costs, required resources, and schedule.

Project tracking. A process used to govern the tracking and oversight responsibilities of software project management. This, with planning above, are perhaps the core process areas of Level 2. All project activities aimed at managing the project are coordinated through this central process. Requirements management, configuration management, and even SQA tasks merge into the tracking process and should be accounted for in the tracking process.

Configuration management. A process for the management of project work products, using some form of library management system to formally version control the products. These products might include output such as source code, project plans, and change requests, among other things.

Change control. A process to help govern how the Configuration Control Board manages, assesses, and approves requested project changes.

Software quality assurance, A process for the SQA analyst to use when monitoring and auditing project activities from a compliance standpoint.

Executive review. A process or procedure used by management to review the processes and policies in each of the CMM Level 2 KPAs periodically.

CMM avoids describing how each process should work in detail. It has to take this position because all IT shops are different. One master process won't work every place. Instead, CMM identifies a series of activities (and I include measurements here also) that need to take place to support each of the five Key Process Areas. In the next sections we'll briefly outline what you can consider including in your processes to make sure you are operating in a manner consistent with Level 2 recommendations.

NOTE Though I have organized this process discussion around the individual Key Process Areas, you don't have to define individual processes as I have done here. You can elect to create one large "Project Management" process that encompasses all the activities you should undertake; you might decide to define two or three major processes. Select the approach that best suits the way your project teams conduct business.

Requirements Management Process

A sound requirements management process is about three things: receiving documented software requirements, reviewing them for acceptance, and then managing any changes to them that may come along during the project.

The process is not about investigating, identifying, or describing the requirements. Software engineering comes after systems engineering has established that baseline. So, when the software project starts, the requirements definition should already be complete or, at least, well underway. This Key Process Area—look to the word "management"—is about the bridge between systems engineering and software engineering.

CMM defines a need for a requirements management process because it sees the requirements as a chief tool of agreement among parties: customer, management, and technical team. If all are in common agreement on what the requirements are, the process of creating the subsequent functionality should go that much smoother. For that reason it is important to implement a process that encourages some form of finalization (via documentation) with upfront review and continuous monitoring over time. Following are steps you might want to include in your requirements management process:

1. **Assign requirements review responsibility.** In this step, usually as a prelude to software project planning, members of the project team are assigned to allocate the requirements to software, hardware, and so on. The purpose of this step, from a software engineering perspective, is to isolate those requirements that have to do with software so that the software engineering group (the SEG) can focus on these.

2. **Receive documented software requirements.** In this step, the documented software requirements are taken into the software engineering group for analysis by the previous group. This step ensures that the requirements are documented—that they are written down for the purposes of tracking and version control before they begin to be considered in terms of project scope and commitments.

3. **Review software requirements.** Here members of the SEG review the software requirements to become familiar with them and to become satisfied that there are no missing, contradictory, or ambiguous requirements to be dealt with. Here the SEG can request clarification of the requirements and then review them again when the clarifications come in. The purpose of this step is to ensure that the team understands what the requirements are so that its members can plan and work in a way that is consistent with the requirements.

4. **Baseline software requirements.** The SEG accepts and baselines the approved requirements (after any needed clarifications or modifications), so they can be used for planning purposes. The key here is that planning starts with the acceptance of the approved requirements. Because the requirements will ultimately determine the size, effort, schedule, and cost of the project, it is important to use them as the foundation for all estimating activity. This task ties in with the estimating tasks in the project planning process.

5. **Submit requirements to version control.** With the baseline in place, the requirements are now formally version controlled. Any changes to the requirements that occur from this point on are change-controlled before they are incorporated into the software project. This step ties in with the role of configuration management.

6. **Record process measurements.** At defined stages during the project, measurements are made by appointed members of the SEG to determine the status of requirements management activities. These measurements might include such statistics as the average number of changes per requirement, the source of the change requests, and so on. These measurements are used later as one of the sources for process improvement initiatives.

7. **Provide an SQA window into the process.** At defined stages during the project, members of the SQA team review and audit the requirements management activities. This ties in with milestones identified in the project plan, as well as with the specific SQA process itself. The purpose of this step is to ensure that the activities used to manage the requirements fall in line with established procedures.

8. **Review process activity with management.** Usually at the end of the project, the project manager will review the requirements management activities to determine what worked well and what areas (if any) had problems. This step is used for future process improvement and process verification.

This basic eight-step process is both CMM compliant and practical for creating a sense of commonality between project team members, management, and the customer. If it, or one like it, is conscientiously followed, you should find that a large number of questions and problems concerning scope, intention, and direction are effectively quelled. As you begin to use this process and measure its effectiveness against your culture and project needs, you may find ways to improve or refine such that it becomes even more useful to you over time.

Project Planning

If you're looking for a common methodology within the CMM—a Level 2 rhythm of work—it's this: Plan your activity and then carry out that plan. For Level 2, one of the most important plans you'll create is to manage the software project as a whole. The process of creating a project's software development plan typically involves seven activities: creating (or receiving) a statement of work (SOW), using a template that guides the contents of the software project plan, utilizing procedures to estimate the size, cost, resources, and schedule for the project, and following a general process that aligns these activities with the overall planning effort.

We'll look at each these in brief detail, but first a general word on what the CMM looks for from project planning activities. CMM gives you wide latitude in this area, but it does so with the view that your planning numbers—costs, resources, schedule duration—are both reasonable and realistic. The resulting plan that emerges from this process will be your chief tool to manage the software project over the course of the effort. If you start out with an unrealistic plan, one filled with unreasonable expectations, the project will probably not go well. Try to ensure that you and your team members appreciate this essential point. Plan objectively and realistically, and the project will stand a strong chance for smooth rollout.

For software project planning you might consider having the following in place:

- A statement of work
- A template for the software development plan
- Estimating procedures for work product size, effort and cost, critical computing resources, and schedule/durations
- A process to follow when developing the software development plan

Let's review each item.

Statement of Work

You'd find it hard to start any serious project planning until you have a statement of work (SOW). This is a brief, written document that describes at a very high level the purpose, scope, and approach of the project. The SOW helps you align your planning efforts in the proper direction for the project. The SOW will usually contain descriptions of the technical goals and objectives for the project, any cost or schedule constraints that must be met, any resource constraints that exist, and any other pertinent assumptions that both the client and vendor need to recognize from the outset. In effect, the SOW is used as a common high-level agreement between the client and the vendor; it's a contract to begin planning along defined lines.

Who writes the SOW? Ideally, the client and vendor management should draft the SOW together, but often you might find that one party or the other creates it and the other party reviews and approves it. Usually the author will not be a member of your group, but it is not unheard of that the software project team helps create the SOW.

If you are called on to be a part of this writing effort, remember these three characteristics of a statement of work:

- The statement of work should be a short document. It is not a design document nor is it a full-fledged legal contract. Keep it high level and to the point. Its job is to help establish the scope of the work effort, to begin to define what the end product should be.

- Ensure that both the client and executive management thoroughly review and approve the statement of work before any other project activity commences in earnest.

- Once the statement of work is approved you should version control the document and include it as part of your software project plan.

Consider the SOW to be, along with the requirements, the beginning point of your software project planning efforts. Like the requirements, it is an important tool to align the expectations of the customer, management, and technical team along common lines.

Template for the Software Development Plan

All of the project planning activities undertaken by your group should be conducted in a consistent manner. Plans from one project effort to the next should look similar even if some of the detail content is different. Such an approach makes both management and measurement a lot easier. You can help ensure this through the use of a template for the project's software plan. The template is simply a high-level outline that shows the author what needs to be included in the plan.

What follows is a template that includes the items the CMM looks for in a well-designed plan. You can use this as a starting point for your own template. Yours might contain other items that are unique or special to your work environment or culture.

I. **Statement of Work.** Include the SOW in your software development plan.

II. **Introduction/Overview.** Include a brief introduction or overview describing the software's purpose, scope, goals, and objectives. This introduction should present the team with a high-level orientation to the work at hand. It can also be used in a manner similar to the SOW, as a bellwether demonstrating a common understanding of the project between client and vendor.

III. **Life Cycle Adopted.** Include a description of the software development life cycle to be used. You might select the spiral method, the waterfall method, rapid application prototyping, or any of the other established methods. You may even use your own proprietary method. Documenting the development life cycle up front positions the team to work in a defined direction.

IV. **Standards and Procedures.** Identify the standards and procedures you will use to manage the project over the course of its duration. This can be a boiler-plate-type insert, as you should use the same ones from one project cycle to the next , with some tailoring based on the unique characteristics of each. As you read through this chapter you'll get an idea for the kinds of standards and procedures you'll need to define for a project. Include these as you see fit.

V. **A List of the Work Products to Be Developed.** List and describe the project deliverables. These are the work products that will constitute the acceptance package for the client. Usually included in this set are software source code, compilers, technical documentation, and end-user documentation. It's also a good idea to define other internal work products that will emerge from project efforts. This will give your management efforts tangible benchmarks. Consider defining such products as system design, code segments, test plans, and so on. It is important that this list be complete to the degree you wish to manage. And remember, if an item is included here, it will need to be developed, tracked, and delivered.

VI. **Scope Projections.** In this section you should detail the projected scope of the project in terms of size, effort, and required resources. Include a statement as to the estimated size of the software product. This can be done using lines of code, number of function points, or any sizing method you use within your group. You should also include a projected level of effort. This effort can be in any form of units: the number of resource hours (Rhours) required, the number of man-months, or any other units that denote the commitment over time. Finally, you should include an estimate of the required use of critical computer resources. Scope projections can also apply to the other work products you identify for the software project. You'll find that your planning becomes more accurate over time if you produce size, effort, and resource estimates for each work product you plan to produce over the course of the project.

Note that the preceding information is data that you will need to solicit from your team leads early in the planning process. You will need to give them the estimating guidelines to use to come up with their own numbers for effort, size, and resource commitments (see the next sections on estimating procedures). You will then use the numbers turned in to you to shape the bulk of the software development plan, especially the sections describing the work products, the estimates, and the schedule.

VII. **The Schedule.** The software development schedule is the centerpiece of the project plan. The schedule should break down the project into a series of distinct, definable milestones and benchmarks, each representing a progression point for the project. This is typically called a work breakdown structure. The schedule should be of sufficient detail that team members understand when and what they need to focus on during the various stages of development. At the same time, the schedule should avoid excessively rigid detail that might encumber the process of managing and executing the project.

Here it is advisable to combine the plans of software configuration management and software quality assurance. These two teams will develop their own plans for the project, so their milestones and benchmarks need to be integrated into the project schedule as a whole. The schedule should, in the end, present a consolidated picture of the activities of the entire team across the life of the project.

VIII. **Measurements to Be Made.** Include the measurements that will be made over the course of the project life cycle, and identify at what point they will occur. This will include such project management measurements as deviations from expected timelines, average milestone duration, projected costs versus actual, or any measurements you specifically define. These measurements are important because they will provide you with raw data for analyzing performance and identifying areas for improvement. It is a good idea to include the SQA and SCM measurements in this section as well.

IX. **Facilities and Support Tools Available.** In this section describe the facilities and the support tools to which you will need access during the course of the project.

X. **Risks and Assumptions.** In this final section you describe two things: the risks that might affect the plan and any assumptions that were used to create the plan. These items can have a potentially large impact on the schedule, costs, effort, and size of the project. The number and scope of the risks and assumptions give a feeling for the solidity of the plan, and they help anticipate the possibility of plan adjustments down the road. For this reason, the risks and assumptions should be followed by a brief description of the contingencies that may be called into play should deviations occur.

XI. **Appendixes.** For the sake of reference and future measurement you should consider including an appendix at the end of the SDP that includes all the raw planning data used to create the plan. This includes the data given to you by the team members in the estimating phase of the planning process.

You might also consider appending the full software configuration management plan and the software quality assurance plan if you haven't already fully integrated them into the SDP. The next section gives you an overview of how to develop the estimating procedures that can be used to derive some of the critical content of the software development plan.

Estimating Procedures

In order to produce the software development plan for the project you will need to gather information from members of the software engineering group (SEG). You will need their input to gauge the scope, cost, and schedule for the project accurately. In order to provide this information, the SEG will need to study the statement of work and the system requirements. They will also need a set of four procedures that they can use to produce the needed estimates. For the SDP, they will have to provide estimates on the size of their work components, estimates on the cost/effort required to produce the components, estimates on the timeline for the effort (the schedule), and estimates of any critical computing resources required by the team.

People produce estimates in many ways, which means that estimates can sometimes have solid validity and can sometimes prove to be meaningless. CMM understands this and therefore supports the use of common procedures by all members of the SEG to estimate consistently, using past experience and appropriate projections.

For your Level 2 program you'll need to define the four estimating procedures for your team. These procedures will have to be documented in brief form (a paragraph or two, or a set form, will suffice in most cases), then distributed to the selected SEG members for their use.

In building the SDP you will identify the work products (the deliverables) that will be produced over the course of the project. These products can range from the software source code and end-user documentation to test plans, system designs, training materials, installation schedules, and technical documentation. The range of work products will depend on your project and on the agreements reached between you, your management, and the client.

For each work product you will need to identify an SEG team member responsible for its creation and then, for each product, solicit estimates on size, effort, timeline, and critical resources.

Estimating Component Size

Estimating the size of the work product gives you a starting point for considering the work involved in producing it. Size can be stated along any number of lines. For software it can be in terms of function points or lines of codes or procedures. For documentation it can be number of pages or number of chapters. For your procedure, ensure that you document the way you will describe size for each work product identified in the software development plan. In the procedure you should also state the following: The estimator will decompose the work products to the level necessary for estimating; the estimator will use historical data as a consideration point when it is available; the estimator will document all sizing assumptions used to produce the estimate; the estimator will review the sizing estimates with project management, software management, and any contributing parties prior to the estimate's official inclusion in the SDP.

Estimating Component Effort/Cost

Once the component size has been estimated, you can approach an estimation of the level of effort required for producing the product. And then from effort you can derive cost. Effort can be described in many ways. It can be counted as resource hours, man months, and so on. It's usually expressed, though, in units of time multiplied by the number of people required. To derive cost, a dollar value per time unit is usually provided for each resource position level, and that is calculated into the effort totals. For your procedure, ensure that you document the way you will describe effort and how cost will be derived from total effort. In the procedure you should also state that the estimator will calculate cost/effort based on work product size; the estimator will use historical data as a consideration point when it is available; the estimator will document all cost/effort assumptions used to produce the estimate; and finally, the estimator will review the cost/effort estimates with project management, software management, and any contributing parties prior to the estimate's official inclusion in the SDP.

Estimating Critical Computer Resources

With work product sizes estimated you can estimate what critical computing resources are going to be required to support each one. Often in development shops, projects must queue up for use of some dedicated resources, such as production mainframe time or use of training facilities. It is important to identify these critical resources in the SDP and document what level of their use the project will require. For this procedure, ensure that you document the way you will describe reserving these resources for project use. You should also state that the estimator will estimate the need for critical resources based on the sizing and effort estimates and on the projected data processing loads of the project. Finally, the estimator will need to review the assignment of critical resources with project management, software management, and any contributing parties prior to the estimate's official inclusion in the SDP.

Estimating Work Timelines and Schedules

Once you have calculated the estimates for size, effort, and resources needed for the project's work products you have a firm basis for producing a project schedule. Here you want to follow a consistent procedure as well. The schedule is an important part of the overall software development plan. It will be used to gauge progress and to track milestones across the life cycle. You therefore want to prepare it properly. Many schedule management software tools are available to help with this. Products like MS Project, Workbench, and LBMS are common in development shops today and help you automatically create schedules based on a common work breakdown structure. Whatever tool you use, or whether you even use a tool, make sure that your schedule estimation policy contains the following standards:

The schedule will identify all milestones and benchmarks needed to track progress of work product creation. The schedule will be consistent with the sizes and efforts defined for the various work products. The schedule will be based in part on an analysis of similar projects from the past, if any are available. All milestone and benchmark durations are reasonable and reflect common industry standards. All scheduling and timeline assumptions will be documented. And, finally, the schedule will be reviewed with project management, software management, and any contributing parties prior to its official inclusion in the SDP.

Software Plan Development Process

You can use the statement of work, the software development plan template, and the estimating procedures to create the software development plan within the following process:

1. **Statement of work created.** Early in project startup, the statement of work is distributed to the software engineering group. The SOW is the starting point for all planning efforts. It is the first look at the mission, objectives, and approach for the project. You can not begin to plan adequately until your team has been introduced to the SOW.

2. **Assign project planning responsibility.** At this time, software management assigns a project planner to create the software development plan. Usually this is the software project manager, but the job can be assigned to any appropriate person on the team. The idea here is to explicitly assign the responsibility for developing the SDP to an individual who will take ownership of the job.

3. **Review the SOW.** The planner reviews the SOW, the system requirements, and available analyses to identify needed work products. Identifying work

products is a major task in creating the SDP. The work products will define the scope and effort required for bringing the project to fruition. The work products will also shape your team's estimates for size, cost/effort, and other factors. Work products can be anything from source code to user documentation to test plans and database schema.

4. **Designate estimating resources.** The planner assigns work product estimating tasks to designated members of the software engineering group. Because different teams in the group will need to build certain portions of some of the work products, each will need to provide estimates to the planner to construct its portions. The project planner must assign this responsibility to specific members within the team to ensure that the estimates are produced.

5. **Plan with the SEG.** The planner and the members of the software engineering group participate in overall project planning activities. In order to ensure that the efforts and expectations of the software engineering group are consistent with those of the project team as a whole, the SEG should participate in general project planning activities.

6. **Derive estimates.** Estimates are derived according to documented procedures. When you assign estimating tasks to the members of the SEG for the identified work products, you will want your team to make their estimates in roughly the same way, using a common set of estimating procedures. This approach ensures consistency and predictability.

7. **Review and approve estimates.** Once reviewed and approved, the estimates are given back to the planner. The project planner should not include any estimates in the SDP until the teams have reviewed and approved the estimates. There must be cross-team commitment to the estimates before they become a formal, contractual element of the SDP.

8. **Draft software development plan.** The planner finalizes the software development plan using an established format and process. Once the estimates and other planning data have been created for the SDP, the project planner will bring this information together in a standard format for formal review and acceptance. The use of a common SDP template ensures that plans for various projects are developed in a consistent and measurable manner.

9. **Define and review commitments.** Prior to release, senior management reviews software commitments in the plan that affect external groups. This step helps to ensure that all commitments made in the SDP, especially those that affect the expectations of the client, are first reviewed by senior management to make sure that the company can securely face up to the commitments being made.

10. **Review the SDP.** The SDP is reviewed by all affected internal groups prior to release. This step is related to step 9. Here it is important to give the members of the SEG and any other affected groups the opportunity to review and clarify the plan prior to its official adoption. Both steps 9 and 10 are designed to get cross-level commitments from all levels in the organization prior to making any promises to the client.

11. **Baseline SDP.** Upon approval, the SDP is placed under version control for consistent and continuous management. This final step makes sure that the SDP is version controlled so that any future changes are assessed for impact before they are incorporated into the official plan.

This process is important because it coordinates the software planning efforts across the SEG. The software development plan will become the chief tool by which the project is tracked and measured, so it should be constructed in a well-organized and informed manner. Here is a look at each step in the process.

Software Project Tracking and Oversight

The process of software project tracking and oversight represents the consolidation of most CMM Level 2 activities. Here requirements management, project planning, software configuration management, and software quality assurance all come into coordinated play. The preparation and planning that went into each of these areas to make them Level 2 ready are put into active practice in this Key Process Area.

The central mission of this KPA is the careful and regular tracking of the progress of the project once software development starts. This is typically done by comparing the current status of the project against what was estimated in the software development plan. But there is more to it than that. You also need to manage the peripheral activities of the project. This includes facilitating the oversight work of the software quality assurance team and the version control and auditing responsibilities of the software configuration management team. All three of these areas work best when consolidated into a smooth and organized effort.

To make sure that you have the right work structure in place for software project tracking and oversight you can use four things:

Tracking process. A formal process that outlines the sequential steps you will take to regularly gauge the progress accomplished and the issues facing the project.

SDP revision procedure. A brief procedure that outlines how the SDP will be revised when such action becomes necessary.

Commitment review procedure. A brief procedure that outlines how new commitments that arise from project changes will be reviewed and approved before being incorporated into the SDP.

Status review procedure. A brief procedure that outlines how the software project manager will structure regular tracking and oversight efforts to get feedback on the progress and issues of the project.

Following is a brief description of each of these four items.

SDP Revision Procedure

This procedure is a written statement that describes how changes in the software project are assessed and approved so that they may be officially included in the software development plan. Such a procedure usually includes acknowledgment of the version control activities for the SDP and outlines the major steps to recognize adjustments, the commitments that go along with the adjustments (see the procedure that immediately follows), and the process for getting the changes approved.

Naturally this procedure should be tied closely with your configuration management, version control, and Software Change Control Board practices. Keep the procedure aligned with these , and ensure that your software project managers (and any other team members you select) have easy access to it.

Commitment Review Procedure

This procedure is a written statement that describes how new software commitments arising from project changes are approved by senior management before they are officially included in the SDP. This procedure typically includes the following points: assessing the changes in terms of the commitments, assigning new schedule, cost, and resource values to the new commitments, and then presenting that data to senior management for review, clarification, and approval. This procedure is closely tied to the previous procedure, and the two may be integrated into one if you find that path more convenient.

Status Review Procedure

The purpose of this procedure is to define how the software project manager will regularly track the progress of the project, along with the activities, issues, and risks that face the project over time.

This procedure should describe the frequency and the mode of status checks. It should call for status reviews that look at the size, effort, costs, resources, schedule, activities, risks, and assumptions that affect the project.

The procedure should also state that the status reviews will be used to document current issues, assess the effects of these issues on plan activities and commitments, document and review any corrective actions that need to be taken, and then revise the SDP accordingly.

Software Tracking and Oversight Process

The software project tracking and oversight process lies at the heart of all Level 2 activities. The project revolves around this process. At its foundation you will find two things: the software development plan and the procedures (see the preceding text) required for managing all project activities against the plan.

You can create as complex or as streamlined a Software Project Tracking and Oversight process as your organization calls for, but it should probably include (in some form) the following:

1. **The software development plan is published.** A complete and approved SDP exists for the project. Before work on the project officially begins you should have a complete software development plan that has been reviewed,

approved, and baselined. Also, by way of extension, you should have the same for the software configuration management plan and the software quality assurance plan.

2. **Assign software project tracking responsibility.** The software project manager assigns responsibility across the software engineering group to track the work products in the plan and report on cost, effort, time, and resources. This is key to the status review activities. The software project manager needs to designate representatives across the various development groups (design, coding, testing, etc.). These representatives then track the project attributes that apply to their piece of the overall effort and report back to the software project manager at the scheduled status review meetings. To facilitate this the SDP must be distributed to all designated trackers.

3. **Conduct project team orientation.** Project team leads and first-line managers receive an orientation to the business and technical attributes of the project. This step educates the team about the overall mission and direction of the project and prepares them to begin work on the project aligned in the same direction. This orientation should include a review of the business purpose of the system and the technical approach and development methodology being used, as well as a review of the key elements of the software development plan.

4. **Technical work begins.** With the plan in place and the team properly oriented to the direction of the project, actual work can now begin.

5. **Hold regular status review meetings.** Regular status review meetings are held. This part of the process establishes the frequency of status meetings across the life of the project. The software development plan should contain in its schedule the times when project status meetings are held. Some projects may require meetings once a week; others may require them only when defined work products are due. You will have to make the call as to how often your project team meets formally. Remember that the software project manager can conduct informal or ad hoc meetings with members of the software engineering group as needs dictate. Whatever your approach to status meetings, consider including the following at each formal one: a report from your leads on the size of work products, the amount of effort/cost being devoted to the work products at this point in the project, the computer resources, the amount of time this phase has taken in the schedule, and a general review of technical activities, risks, and assumptions that may have arisen.

Compare the reported actuals to the estimates contained in the SDP and determine if any variances that crop up are OK or need corrective action. Document the reported status, then discuss any changes that need to be made. With team agreement, submit the changes to the Software Change Control Board. On SCCB approval, you can then incorporate the changes into the SDP and reissue a revised version to the members of your team, management, and the client, as required. At the same time you are receiving status reports from designated members of the SEG you should also allow for any scheduled SQA and SCM activities. For SQA this includes verifying activities for commitment changes, activities for plan revisions, activities for tracking project status (its costs, effort levels, etc.), and reviews of the plan estimates as compared to actuals reports. For SCM this includes auditing and reporting on the use of the configuration management library system.

6. **Track project milestones.** The software development plan will identify key project milestones in which defined work product deliverables are due. These work products can include a range of items, from software design documents, to source code, to acceptance test plans. These milestones need to be anticipated. When they come due, each product needs to be reviewed for conformity (is it built as it was planned to be built?). Then measurements should be taken to compare the actual size, effort, resources, and timeline of the work product with the estimated numbers contained in the SDP. You are free to choose those measurements that have the most meaning for your team for the specific project.

7. **Final project review.** At the end of the project (and perhaps during the project), the software project manager should meet with senior management, general project management, and SQA in order to ascertain the condition of the project to, in effect, answer the question, did the project go pretty much as we had planned?

8. In this stage of the tracking process you should meet with senior management and general project management to review such items as commitment impacts, staffing, costs, resources required, risks addressed, and unanticipated issues. The meeting minutes from this assessment should be documented and distributed to the SEG as necessary.

The software project manager should also meet with SQA to gauge the level of process compliance that was in evidence on the project. This assessment should point out areas of strong compliance and areas of weak compliance. This can be used later as a basis for process improvement plans.

Software Configuration Management

Software configuration management has three major roles within CMM at Level 2: establishing a change control process to handle requests for fixes or enhancements, tracking and auditing all prior versions of the software, and effecting the release of new software baselines in an organized, coordinated manner.

All three of these roles are in place to protect the integrity of the software and to help protect the alignment between requirements and product. During the course of a project, a software system may quickly evolve. Prior versions may be radically different from later ones. Without proactive and somewhat rigorous version control, baselines can blur and new releases can become corrupt. With proper SCM processes in place, the integrity of each version and each new release can be better ensured.

Software configuration management can be initiated broadly or narrowly at Level 2. In its broadest sense, configuration management can be used to control almost every work product that comes out of a project: software source code, requirements documentation, work schedules, project estimates, project plans, and more. At its narrowest, you can use SCM simply to control the core products released to the client: the requirements, the resulting software code, any needed compilers, and the technical documentation needed to reconstitute the software.

There are merits to both approaches. The broad approach gives you a high degree of control in a volatile environment and an audit trail for almost all facets of the project. The narrow approach gives you basic controls and does so in a simplified, direct manner. Whichever approach you elect to take in your Level 2 program it is important to understand what processes you need in place to carry out this function.

NOTE *Version control* **is that less rigorous form of change management that you can in use in place of configuration management for many project products. Many organizations choose to version control such products as the software development plan, the SQA, designs, and test plans rather than formally placing them into the configuration management system.**

You should consider accounting for about six processes to implement SCM properly in your Level 2 environment:

- A procedure to develop the SCM plan
- A template to create the SCM plan
- An SCM process
- A change control process
- A procedure to create software baselines
- A software baseline audit process

Let's look at what's needed for each.

Procedure to Develop the SCM Plan

A Software Configuration Plan should be created for every project. This plan, which dovetails with the overall software development plan, describes what SCM activities will take place over the course of the project. From project cycle to project cycle, the SCM plan should be developed in a consistent way. To support this you will need a general procedure that details for your SCM team the manner in which the SCM plan is created. You will need to write this procedure for your Level 2 program. To help with this, consider positioning your process to include the following:

- SCM planning for the project is begun early in the project cycle and in parallel with other planning efforts.
- The SCM plan is built according to a defined and approved template.
- The SCM plan, before it is incorporated into the overall project plan, is reviewed by all affected parties.
- Once approved, the SCM plan is version controlled (and may even, if desired, be configuration managed).
- The approved SCM plan is the chief management tool used by the SCM team to manage SCM activities on a project.

Incorporating would produce a series of process steps that might look something like this:

1. Assign a configuration manager early in the project life cycle.

2. Confirm that adequate configuration management resources (library space, etc.) are available for project use.

3. The configuration manager works with the software project manager and the project team in the planning phase to identify the work products that will be formally configuration managed.

4. Based on the planning activities the configuration manager then uses the project's configuration management plan template to create a draft of the configuration management plan.

5. Upon completion, and perhaps in parallel with other reviews, the configuration management plan is reviewed by the project team prior to approval.

6. After any necessary revisions are made to the plan, the plan is baselined for the project and then placed under version control (or, if desired, under configuration management).

7. The plan is then followed over the course of the project.

8. Any changes to the plan are handled under the project's change management processes.

This procedure, as the preceding points demonstrate, can be quite short and to the point. Consider including it with your SCM policies or training materials as a way to make sure that it is communicated to the members of your SCM group. (For more on these steps, see the "Software Configuration Management Process" section that follows in this chapter.)

Template to Create the SCM Plan

Just as the SCM plan should be developed in a consistent manner, so should it be produced in a consistent manner. The content should be structured similarly across project cycles , using a broad, common outline and customizing at a lower level based on the needs of cycle. To support this, you might consider creating a content template for the SCM plan.

You can create this template as a simple outline, as a detailed table of contents listing, or as a robust procedural guide. Whichever path you take, consider the following content items:

1. **A statement of the purpose and scope of SCM on the project.** This can be a brief statement that aligns the software configuration management mission and objectives with those of the software project overall. This is necessary because the SCM plan will eventually become a chief reference to the software development plan.

2. **A description of the work products that will be managed by the SCM group.** At the least, these should be the software source code, any software

tools related to the main system, and the requirements document on which the system is based. You are also free to include such items as work plans, schedules, and estimates, as you see fit. Identifying these products will emerge from your work with the software project planner in the project planning stage.

3. **A description of the SCM activities to be performed on the project.** This can include such items as the scheduled dates for Change Control Board meetings, SCM audits, major software baseline release, the release of various SCM reports, SQA review of SCM activity, and project management review of SCM activity.

4. **A description of the SCM activities to be performed by the members of the software engineering group project team.** This ties directly in with the activities detailed previously. It's a description of what activities the group will perform in order to support SCM activities. These can include such actions as following the change control process (see the text that follows), preparing for SCM audits, and setting dates for reviews by SQA and project management.

5. **A description of the library system to be used, along with its various control levels.** This is a description of the management library you'll be using, which should serve as a quick reminder of the level of control you'll be placing on the configuration units. This will help inform the team members of the level of control they will need in order to check in and check out material. This should also include a description of the configuration units—and the breakdown layers for version control tracking.

6. **A description of the SCM reports to be issued over the life of the project.** These can include such reports as the following:

   - Change Control Board meeting minutes
   - Change request summary and status
   - Defect report summary and status
   - Baseline/version status reports
   - Audit reports

7. **A description of configuration management measurements**. Finally you might consider identifying the measurements you'll be collecting over the course of the project. These tie to a series of reports or remain independent of them. The important thing to remember about measurements is to define those that really mean something to your project and the team. As they will be one of your chief improvement sources, you'll want them to be useful.

Software Configuration Management Process

Software configuration management protects the integrity of the software product. It forges a direct link to the accepted requirements and so works to establish a common plateau of expectation between the customer, project management, and the project's technical team. Further, configuration management protects the quality of its products, providing a mechanism to keep each release of a managed product clean and free from previously identified defects or obsolete functionalities. Configuration management systems always include some kind of controlled library, and access to the library is managed along a set of rules. You check in and check out material in a manner that facilitates the smooth integration of new feature sets across a set of parties. The library system can be as simple as a controlled hardcopy closet or as robust as one of the recognized electronic SCM tools available in the IT marketplace. In the eyes of the CMM both are valid. And both involve a series of practices and procedures. A full SCM program typically includes most of the processes and procedures described in this section. You need to have a high-level process, though, that shows the direction of SCM over the course of a typical project. This concise process should include these items as a start:

Assign SCM planning responsibility. Near the start of a development project responsibility is assigned within SCM to create the SCM plan for the project. Each project should have an SCM analyst assigned to manage and oversee the configuration management activities for that project. This appointment must be made in an official way and should be documented and then communicated to the software project manager and software project team.

The SCM plan is created. Once the SCM analyst is appointed to the project, this person should set about developing the SCM plan for the project. The SCM analyst should work closely with both the software project manager and the SQA analyst to ensure that the SCM plans are in harmony with those of project management and SQA.

The SCM plan is reviewed. Once the SCM plan has been created, it needs to be reviewed by the project team to ensure that it is consistent with overall plans and is clear and understandable to the team. During this review questions and comments can be addressed and clarifications made. The plan should then be revised as necessary.

The Plan is approved. Once the SCM plan has been approved, it must be managed against change by being placed under version control. You may choose to place the document under the full realm of configuration management if you choose.

Library space is allocated for the project. When the project begins, the SCM analyst must ensure that the SCM library is configured to house the expected project documents and work products. Ample space in the system must be allocated to the project.

As the project begins, SCM activities are carried out and recorded. The purpose of any plan of course is to follow it once it has been created. Here the appointed CM analyst will use the SCM Plan as the chief tool to manage configuration activities. This is an activity that really works closely with software project management. SCM activities in the plan should be coordinated across the whole team through integration into the higher activities of the software development plan.

SCM audits are conducted as scheduled and SCM reports are issued as scheduled. The SCM Plan will identify with work products that will be managed in the CM library and also identify at what points the library will be audited to inspect it for proper use and product integrity. It is important to keep to the plan in terms of the audits, unless some project variation requires an adjustment to the audit schedule. The logical conclusion of each audit is to produce a report for the project team that encapsulates the finding of the audit. This report will help correct any deviances that currently exist in the library and also help avoid the occurrence of similar problems in the future.

SCM measurements are made as scheduled. These measurements can include such items as the number of CRs processed during a set time, the number of software baselines released, and the amount of SCM funds expensed on the project to date.

SCM activities reviewed with SQA scheduled. Part of the role of software configuration management is to serve as auditor on the project. But this role needs to be audited too, from time to time, and the body that does this is SQA. At selected points during the project life cycle, SQA should check on the activities of SCM to ensure that they are being carried out according to plan and that each is executed following established process paths.

SCM activities reviewed with Project Manager as scheduled. This step may be integrated with regular project status meetings or set up as an independent review. Either way the idea is to periodically keep project management informed as to the progress of software configuration management for the project. There are two objectives at work here. The first is to simply ensure that SCM services are being provided to the project team in an efficient and effective manner. The second is to provide an opportunity to review SCM activity from a process level, to provide project management feedback that it can use to begin to refine or augment the process to meet changing or un-addressed needs. The measurements cited above can tie into this discussion and can serve as a basis for examining specific attributes of the processes.

Change Control Procedure

Integral to the success of SCM is the role of the Software Configuration Control Board. This is a board you establish to review and assess any proposed changes to the software (or to any project output you want to change-manage). The board can be any size you see as appropriate, and it should meet at preset times during the project life cycle. The SCCB should conduct its role using an established procedure, a procedure you need to create. Just as in the procedure for creating the SCM plan, this procedure can be concise and to the point. You may want the procedure you write to include some or all of the following ideas:

- Any change request or defect report must be presented to the SCCB using approved CR and DR forms/documentation.

- All *change requests* (CRs) and *defect reports* (DRs) will be reviewed and assessed by the SCCB.

- The board may elect to reject a request, assign it to a certain release, or delay it for further evaluation.

- No CRs or DRs are incorporated into the project plan until approved by the SCCB.

- All approved CRs and DRs are tracked as revisions to the project.

This procedure can be quite short and to the point if you'd like it to be. Consider including it with your SCM policies or SCCB training materials as a way to ensure that it is communicated to the members of your SCM group.

Software Baseline Creation Procedure

Creating reliable software baselines is required throughout the cycle of a project; therefore it's important they be up to date and reflect the current integrity of the project.

The process of creating baselines should be governed using an established procedure. Again, this is a procedure you need to create. Like the previous ones, this procedure can be concise and to the point. Make sure that the procedure you write includes the following statements:

- Only new functionality approved by the SCCB, through the change control process, can be integrated into any new baseline release.

- Regression testing is done on all new baselines prior to release to ensure functionality and integrity.

- Baselines can be created and released only by using the project's library management system.

This procedure will help guide both your SCM group and the members of the SEG concerning software releases. Consider including it with your SCM policies or with general SCM training and orientation materials.

Software Baseline Audit Procedure

Because creating reliable software baselines is such an important activity during a project, it is important to periodically audit the baseline library and baseline procedures to see if the process is upholding the integrity of the software. Audits need to be managed using an established procedure. Consider including the following statements:

- The baseline audit schedule will be included in the SCM plan and (by extension) in the project plan.

- Members of the SCM group and the SEG will receive adequate notification of an audit in order to prepare properly for it.

- The audit will assess and document the integrity of the released software baseline versions.

- The audit will assess and document the integrity of the contents of the project's library management system.

- The audit will assess and document the integrity of the library system's structure and operational capabilities.

- The audit will measure the degree to which the software baseline process adheres to SCM processes and standards and project standards and processes.

- An audit report will be issued from this assessment and delivered to the project manager.

- Action items identified in the audit will be tracked.

Software Quality Assurance

The SQA role provides process oversight for each project. The SQA group is an "independent" group within the project team. This means that SQA does not report directly to project management (even though SQA does provide reports to project management and must work closely with them). SQA reports to executive management; they are management's view into process compliance across the various projects within an organization. SQA monitors the various stages and activities of each project to ensure that the projects are being conducted according to published plans and established procedures. When SQA encounters any deviations, they investigate with the project manager and work out a plan to set the variation back on track.

Consider accounting for these processes to implement SQA in your Level 2 environment:

- A procedure used to develop the SQA plan

- A template used to create the SQA plan

- An SQA process used to implement the plan

- An SQA audit procedure

- An SQA noncompliance escalation procedure

Let's look at what might be included in each.

Procedure to Develop the SQA Plan

A software quality assurance plan must be created for every project. This plan will dovetail with the overall software project plan. The SQA plan describes what SQA activities will take place over the course of the project. It's important to develop the SQA plan in a consistent way from project to project. Therefore, you should manage the creation of your SQA plans through the guidance of a general procedure that details for your SCM team the manner in which the SCM plan is created. You will need to write this procedure for your Level 2 program. Your procedure might contain (at least) the following considerations:

- SQA planning for the project is begun early in the project cycle and in parallel with other planning efforts.

- The SQA plan is built according to a defined and approved template.

- The SQA plan, before it is incorporated into the overall project plan, is reviewed by all affected parties.

- Once approved, the SQA plan is version controlled (and may even, if desired, be configuration managed).

- The approved SQA plan is the chief management tool used by the SQA team to manage SQA activities on a project.

An unwritten part of this procedure should contain the endorsement that a good SQA plan comes from working closely with software project management to establish expectations, specific roles, and activities and to establish milestones and reporting benchmarks. SQA should be shaped and positioned as a complementary effort to that of project management, as an overall project support tool.

Template to Create the SQA Plan

SQA must be conducted in a consistent way across all projects. This is necessary to ensure that compliance is supported in a smooth way within the organization. For this reason, the SQA plan must be produced in a consistent manner. The content of the plan should be structured similarly from project to project, using a broad common outline and customizing at a lower level, based on the needs of the project. To support this, it is helpful to have a content template ready each time an SQA plan needs to be produced.

You can create this template as a simple outline, as a detailed table of contents listing, or as a robust procedural guide. Whichever path you take, be sure to include the following content items in your template:

A statement of the purpose and scope of SQA on the project. This should be a brief statement that aligns the software configuration management mission and objectives with those of the software project overall. This is necessary because the SQA plan will eventually become a part of the software development plan.

A description of the SQA resources allocated to the project. This should include an assignment of the SQA staff appointed to work on the project as well as a description of the SQA tools, equipment, and facilities set aside for use on the project.

A description of SQA's role in developing the overall software development plan (SDP). This should include the responsibility of SQA to adequately review the SDP to make sure that it works within established processes and procedures. SQA should have the authority to request plan changes when the plan is out of sync with current operational standards.

A description of the SQA activities to be performed on the project. This can include such items as scheduled dates or milestones for SQA audits and scheduled release of SQA reports.

A description of the audit procedure. This should describe how SQA will perform its audits during the project, citing the forms to be used and the reports to be issued. All units should be conducted in a consistent manner; this positions SQA as a neutral party within the project team.

A description of the noncompliance correction procedure. This is a description of the steps SQA will take to correct deviations from planned activity or processes when they are encountered. This procedure should include several things including a description or definition of what constitutes noncompliance, the establishment of a severity/criticality level to assign to each noncompliance situation, and a resolution path. This contains a description of how the situation is first corrected within the project team, with the project manager forging the correction. Only if SQA and PM cannot agree on a correction course should SQA escalate the situation to project management and then executive management.

A description of the SQA measurements to be made on the project, and the dates/milestones for their collection. These reports can include such items as the number of process deviations to date, deviations by severity, and the average resolution time frame.

A description of the milestones/dates for project management review of SQA activity. You can see how closely the SQA plan must fit in with the overall software development plan. For this reason, SQA and software PM must work closely together in the planning stages.

SQA Process

The SQA role is central to effective Level 2 activities. As mentioned earlier, the SQA role as defined by CMM is an independent role. That is, it does not report to project management but rather reports to executive management. SQA's chief purpose is to help ensure that all project activities, across the various projects ongoing in your shop, are conducted in a manner that is consistent with approved processes and procedures. SQA serves here in an oversight role. At the same time, however, SQA must work very closely with the software project manager and the software engineering group. This means that SQA, while being independent, is not detached from the project team. The process that SQA uses to manage its activities must blend in harmoniously with the general project management plan.

A typical SQA process will contain the following steps:

1. **SQA responsibility assigned.** Responsibility is assigned within SQA to create the SQA plan for a project. In this step, an SQA analyst is appointed to create an SQA plan specifically tailored to the project at hand. This analyst will have to work closely with the software project planner to coordinate the efforts of SQA with project activity overall.

2. **SQA in project planning.** SQA participates in project plan development. This step is needed because SQA is an integral part of process compliance across the organization. For SQA to be able to help oversee the various phases in a project, the SQA analyst must work closely and in tandem with the project planner to map out SQA mileposts and check points consistent with those of software development.

3. **SQA plan created.** The SQA plan is created by the SQA analyst according to the needs of the project.

4. **SQA plan reviewed.** The SQA plan is reviewed. Before the SQA plan can be officially adopted as part of the overall project plan, it must reviewed and

approved by software project management and the software project team. During this step, questions and comments are addressed, and the plan is then revised as necessary.

5. **SQA plan approved.** The SQA plan is approved. Once the SQA plan has been reviewed by the team, and once all clarifications and adjustments have been made, the plan can be officially approved for inclusion in overall project planning.

6. **SQA plan is version controlled.** The SQA plan is put under version control. As the project begins, there may come times when the contents of the SQA plan must be adjusted to balance with other project activity. This must be accomplished through the proper change control process, and any revisions must be entered through a written change control procedure.

7. **SQA activity begins.** As the project begins, SQA activities are carried out and recorded. This is the heart of the SQA process. The plan must identify when SQA activities will take place, and then the action must be carried out. These activities include SQA audits and reviews to ensure that the project as a whole is in compliance with accepted processes and practices.

8. **SQA reviews held.** SQA reviews are conducted as scheduled. This is the highlight of step 7. The SQA plan will identify specific times when formal SQA reviews are carried out on the project's activities. The results of these reviews will be recorded.

9. **SQA audits held.** SQA work product audits are conducted as scheduled. This is an extension of steps 7 and 8. The SQA plan will identify specific benchmarks during the project when formal SQA audits are made. These audits will seek to match planned activity against actual activity and to ensure that all activity being conducted follows accepted processes and practices.

10. **SQA reports issued.** SQA reports to the SEG are issued as scheduled. The end result of an SQA review and/or audit is to issue a compliance report to the software project manager. The frequency and due dates for the reports should be itemized in the SQA as well as the audience to which the reports will be distributed.

11. **SQA measurements taken.** SQA measurements are made as scheduled. These measurements can include such items as the number of process deviations encountered over a period of time and the resolution outcome of each deviation.

12. **SQA activities are reviewed.** SQA activities are reviewed with project management as scheduled. The SQA will finally contain a list of meeting times when the SQA analyst will meet with the software project manager to discuss compliance issues and assign action items that come from the issues.

SQA Audit Procedure

When you shape your software quality assurance program you'll want to define how your SQA analysts will conduct audits. This is important for two reasons. First you want to conduct audits in a consistent manner. Doing them the same way during a project and then across future project releases will enable to take meaningful measurements for the purpose of improvement. Second, and perhaps more importantly, you should want your project team members to know up front exactly how an audit will be handled so they are prepared to participate fully and they know what to expect. You can shape your procedure in a way that best suits your organization but you might want to consider the following points for possible inclusion.

To begin with, make sure that an SQA plan exists for the project before any audits are conducted. The work products and team activities that you audit should be identified in the SQA Plan.

The project team should be briefed on the contents of the SQA plan. This up front work will help ensure that everyone knows ahead of time what role SQA will take on the project. Then at a preset time prior to each scheduled audit, notice of the audit should be sent to the Software Project Manager and the owner of the work product or activity to allow time for preparation. The audit is then conducted at the specified time. Typically the SQA analyst will review work products for proper contents, completeness, and format, and review project activities for proper procedure, documentation, and artifact creation. For both, the auditor can solicit improvement feedback/comments from audit members as a way of getting line information on how the processes and practices are working in the production environment. If any noncompliance issues are encountered the SQA analyst will deal with them following a documented procedure (see the next section). As a final step, the SQA auditor and the members of the audited team should probably acknowledge (through some sign-off mechanism) the audit's completion. The SQA analyst can then notify software project management that the specific audit has been completed.

Shortly after the audit is completed, the SQA analyst should present to the team an audit report. The audit report documents the action of the audit, items that were found to be in compliance, items that were found to be out of compliance, and recommended actions to correct the noncompliant items.

This procedure, or one like it, will help align SQA actions to the needs of the team and do so in a coordinated and supportive manner. Here's a summary of these steps:

Entry Criteria

1. An SQA plan exists.
2. The work products and team activities to be audited are identified in the SQA plan.
3. The project team has been briefed on the contents of the SQA plan.

Audit Process

1. At a preset time prior to each audit, notice of the audit is sent to the Software Project Manager and the owner of the work product or activity.
2. At the identified time, the audit is conducted.
   - Work products are reviewed for proper contents, completeness, and format.
   - Activities are reviewed for proper procedure and artifact creation.

- For both, the auditor solicits improvement feedback/comments from audit members.

- For noncompliance, see below.

3. The SQA auditor and audit members acknowledge (sign-off) the audit.

4. The SQA auditor notifies the software project manager that the specific audit is complete.

Exit Criteria

Shortly after the audit is completed, the auditor presents to the team an audit report. The audit report documents the action of the audit, items that were found to be in compliance, items that were found to be out of compliance, and recommended actions to correct the noncompliant items.

SQA Procedure to Manage Non-Compliance

When SQA encounters a situation in which process or practice has not been followed, for whatever reason, the situation needs to be handled in a consistent manner. This helps to ensure balanced realignment and team cooperation. Having a documented procedure for handling noncompliant events and making sure the team knows what this procedure is take you a step in that constructive direction.

Basically noncompliance can fall into one of three categories. There's a process/practice deviance but a good reason for it. There's a process/practice deviance and both the SQA auditor and audit team agree it needs to be corrected. Or there's a disagreement between the SQA auditor and the audit team that a process/practice deviance has occurred.

In the first case you might shape a procedure like this: The SQA auditor finds a product or activity to be out of compliance. The audited team agrees but is able to offer an acceptable reason for the deviation. The SQA auditor accepts the reason and documents the noncompliance and the reason. No corrective action is necessary, but the event is noted in the audit report.

In the second case you might shape a procedure like this: The SQA auditor finds a product or activity to be out of compliance. The audited team agrees and acknowledges the noncompliance. The SQA auditor and the audited team agree to a current or future corrective action. The SQA auditor documents the noncompliance, the reason, and the agreed upon action. The event, reason, and corrective action are then included in the audit report.

In the third case you might shape a procedure like this: The SQA auditor finds a product or activity to be out of compliance. The audit team disagrees that the product/activity is out of compliance. The SQA auditor documents the situation. The situation is brought to the software project manager and audit team lead for a discussion/decision. Afterwards if disagreement still exists, the situation is brought to the Project Manager for decision. The Project Manager should have the authority to decide either way: no deviation, acceptable deviation, or unacceptable deviation. The ultimate resolution is then documented and the SQA auditor and the software project management take action to follow through on the agreed-upon corrective course.

Here's a summary of these steps:

Entry Criteria

- An SQA Audit occurs.
- Non-compliant situation #1 (acceptable noncompliance).
    1. The SQA auditor finds a product or activity to be out of compliance.
    2. The audited team agrees but is able to offer an acceptable reason for the deviation.
    3. The SQA auditor accepts the reason and documents the noncompliance and the reason.
    4. No corrective action is necessary, but noted in the audit report.
- Non-compliant situation #2 (unacceptable noncompliance).
    1. The SQA auditor finds a product or activity to be out of compliance.
    2. The audited team agrees and acknowledges the noncompliance.
    3. The SQA auditor and the audited team agree as to a current or future corrective action.
    4. The SQA auditor documents the noncompliance, the reason, and the agreed upon action.
    5. The corrective action is then included in the audit report.
- Non-compliant situation #3 (disagreement on noncompliance)
    1. The SQA auditor finds a product or activity to be out of compliance.
    2. The audit team disagrees that the product/activity is out of compliance.
    3. The SQA auditor documents the situation.
    4. The situation is brought to the software project manager and team lead for a decision.
- If disagreement still exists, the situation is brought to the Project Manager for decision.
- The Project Manager has the authority to decide either way: no deviation, acceptable deviation, or unacceptable deviation.

Exit Criteria

The SQA auditor and the software project management take an action to follow through on the agreed-upon corrective course.

Executive Review

The final process that needs to be accounted for at Level 2 is that of executive review. CMM requires that executive management conducts periodic reviews of the projects over-all, as well as SCM activities, SQA activities, and requirements management activities. The term "periodic" can mean once a quarter, once a year, or at whatever frequency is deemed by your executives to be the most effective.

The key at these reviews is to examine the current processes in place and to gauge their level of effectiveness and then identify any actions that might arise to improve them. To fulfill this need, executive management should adopt this simple four-step process:

- Executive management will review the requirements management processes and policies on a periodic basis.

- Executive management will review the project planning and project tracking processes and policies with project management on a periodic basis.

- Executive management will review the software configuration management processes and policies with SCM and project management on a periodic basis.

- Executive management will review the software quality assurance processes and policies with SQA on a periodic basis.

This executive review process can work as a standalone procedure or it may be integrated into your other processes. Either way the idea is to periodically meet with executive management to keep them informed as to the efficacies of the processes you are using on the project. As with the regular meetings with project management, there are two objectives at work here. The first is to simply ensure that the project team has been able to implement the established processes and practices, and that they are serving something of a useful purpose. The second is to provide an opportunity to review all process activities from a management level for the purpose of software process improvement.

Supporting Processes

Establishing a Level 2 CMM program requires in part a series of processes used to manage and coordinate activities across several key management areas. The artifacts that emerge from your use of processes will usually be the documented processes themselves as well as the forms and other materials that emerge from their regular and practical use.

The following is a sample list—albeit a pretty detailed one—of the kinds of processes you may have created for your Level 2 program:.

- Requirements management process
- Software development plan template
- Work product sizing estimating procedure
- Work product effort/cost estimating procedure
- Critical computing resources estimating procedure
- Scheduling/duration estimating procedure
- Software plan development process

- Software development plan revision procedure
- Commitment review procedure
- Project status review procedure
- Software tracking and oversight process
- SCM plan development procedure
- SCM plan template
- SCM process
- Change control process
- Software baseline procedure
- Software baseline audit procedure
- SQA plan development procedure
- SQA plan template
- SQA process
- Executive management review process

Evidence of the processes being fully used could include items such as the following:

- Staff assignment forms relevant to each KPA
- Requirements analysis report
- Requirements document
- Requirements measurements
- Project's statement of work
- The software development plan
- Estimate review forms
- SDP review and approval form
- Training/orientation notice
- Training/orientation meeting minutes
- Status meeting minutes
- Project tracking measurements
- Final project review minutes
- Change request form
- Library audit report
- SCM plan
- SCM plan review form
- Baseline audit report
- SCM measurements
- SQA plan review form

- SQA plan
- SQA audit report
- SQA measurements
- Meeting minutes review with project management
- Meeting minutes review with SQA
- Meeting minutes review with SCM
- Meeting minutes review with requirements management

These items are summarized in Table 4.1. However, note this: The processes and artifacts you develop for your organization do not have to match this list. Use this list simply as a guide or reference. What you develop for your organization may be similar or it may distinctly different. The strategy that should guide you is to develop processes and practices and forms and templates and so on that meet the needs of your business environment. Useful applicability that can be further refined over time is the key to suc-

Table 4.1   Evidence of Program Compliance

KEY PROCESS AREA	ARTIFACTS
Requirements Management	Staff assignment form, RM analysis report, requirements document, requirements measurements
Project Planning	Staff assignment form, statement of work, SDP creation process, SDP template, software development plan, estimate review forms, SDP review and approval form
Project Tracking and Oversight	SDP review procedure, commitment review procedure, status review procedure, project tracking process, PM staff assignment form, orientation notice, orientation meeting minutes, status meeting minutes, project tracking measurements, final project review minutes
Configuration Management	Staff assignment form, SCM plan development procedure, SCM plan template, Change request form, Library audit report, SCM process, SCM plan, SCM plan review form, Software baseline procedure, baseline audit procedure, Baseline audit report, SCM measurements
Software Quality Assurance	Staff assignment form, SQA plan development procedure, SQA plan template, SQA plan review form, SQA plan, SQA process, SQA audit report, SQA measurements
Executive Review Process	Meeting minutes review with project management, meeting minutes review with SQA, meeting minutes review with SCM, meeting minutes review with requirements management

cessful software process improvement. Develop within the model to address your internal development needs and you'll almost certainly meet the intention of the model.

Summary

Level 2 processes focus mainly on management activities concerning software development. Software project planning and software project tracking and oversight were supplemented by activities under software quality assurance, software configuration management, and requirements management. There are two common elements to each of the areas we've discussed in this chapter. First is the need to create a plan of action for each of the KPAs. Then there is the need for a process to follow to review and approve each plan. After that these elements are usually integrated into the overall software development plan (SDP). Implementing the recommendations in this chapter takes you to about 45 percent Level 2 compliance. Together with the recommendations contained in Chapter 3, you should be at about 65 percent compliance.

In the next chapter, we'll taker a closer look at the training needs that typically surround Level 2.

Table 4.2 Key Practices Fulfilled in This Chapter

KEY PROCESS AREA	CHAPTER TASK	KEY PRACTICE OBLIGATION
Requirements Management	Create requirements management process	Ability 1, ability 2, activity 1, activity 2, activity 3, measurement 1, verification 3, verification 2
Project Planning	Create statement of work, create software development plan template, create work product sizing estimating procedure, create work product effort/cost estimating procedure, create critical computing resources estimating procedure, create scheduling/duration estimating procedure, create software plan development process	Ability 1, activity 6, activity 9, activity 10, activity 11, activity 12, activities 5, 6, 7, 8, measurement 1

Creating a Level 2 Training Program

The issue of training is important because it prepares the team to conduct its activities according to the established procedures and processes, and it provides the background to judge the effectiveness of these methods.
Mackie May, Quality Assurance Consultant

Training is an important area to the CMM program as a whole. In fact, it becomes its own Key Process Area (Training Program) at Level 3, but it is introduced at Level 2. The difference in training at Levels 2 and 3 is that Level 3 calls for a formal "required" training program based on set roles and responsibilities within the group. At Level 3 the organization becomes, in part, an educational institution, with its employees assigned to an ongoing and defined curriculum.

At Level 2, the CMM assumes that the organization is not yet established enough within the process methodology world to have firmly fixed roles and responsibilities. The training at Level 2 is therefore more informal and flexible. The main goal of training here is to prepare staff members to operate within each project in a way that conforms to the quality processes and procedures in place.

Unfortunately, too many Level 2 programs treat training as an afterthought or attempt to account for it under "on-the-job training." That approach doesn't work well. Training is an important ability that prepares members of the group to begin a project in a consistent way and to work through it in a smooth, predictable way. Even though the training should be explicitly designed and developed, you do not need to make a major structural commitment to it at Level 2. As the CMM specification states,

> Different organizational situations are likely to drive different specific training needs.[1]

In this chapter we will look at what kinds of training the CMM calls for, who needs to be trained, and how to begin to create the kinds of training materials you need to support Level 2 training requirements.

THE IMPORTANCE OF TRAINING YOUR STAFF AT LEVEL 2

At CMM Level 3, training becomes its own Key Process Area, so at that stage it should be adopted formally. At Level 2, however, it is often given short shrift. Because it's not a formal regimen at this level, project managers can be inclined to treat it with a less than efficient informality. Yet training at Level 2 is, at the very least, a key discipline (if not a Key Process Area) and a strong general indicator of a group's ability to meet CMM requirements overall. Let's look at why I view training as an important activity for organizations trying to get their programs recognized at Level 2 on the CMM scale.

The first reason comes back to the word "commonality." Training helps ensure a consistency of understanding across the project team. The structural training sessions and the orientations serve to move everybody on your project team onto the same path, pointed in the same direction. The members know what is expected of them in their assignments, and they have an appreciation for the scope and the purpose of the project.

This leads to the next reason: enhanced cross-team recognition. The training sessions and orientations give each team member an understanding of (and appreciation for) the various groups and their roles at work on the project. This exposure helps members follow through with process steps because they understand the purpose and reach of the steps, and it enhances intergroup communications by establishing functional and operational boundaries within the project.

But the single most important reason is that training prepares you to operate smoothly in a new environment. Consciously moving your organization to CMM Level 2 means you are making a commitment to a new way of doing business. Your IT shop is going to begin operating on the foundations of organization, planning, and documentation. These may be foreign concepts to a number of people on your staff. Introducing them to this new environment through a well-planned and well-delivered series of training sessions is an excellent way to move them productively into this new business model. You can use this opportunity not only to train them in their structural job roles but also to introduce them to the scope, mission, and objectives of this Level 2 effort.

What Kinds of Training Does the CMM Call For?

The CMM calls for two types of training. For the sake of delineation I'll call these Structural Training and Application Domain Orientation.

Structural Training is the "deeper" of the two. This type of training is usually implemented in a somewhat formal teacher-student environment (though it does not have to be). Structural Training is used to prepare a person to do a specific job and (as related to us) to do it within Level 2 boundaries.

There are four areas in which a person can be trained in this area. The first is called *direct process training*. This is training to help the employees understand how to execute their specific job responsibilities. It's training in the processes that they will have to follow on a day-to-day basis.

The second is *indirect process training*. This is training to help the employees learn how to interface with other groups when communicating and managing project data. These are the processes that serve other groups. Training a requirements analyst in the rules of estimating is an example of indirect process training. The estimating process is really owned by the project planning group, but it should be used by staff members outside that group.

The third is *tool training*. Many roles within the software engineering group require the use of specialized tools. Groups such as project management and configuration management will probably adopt tools to specifically manage some Level 2 activities. The staff members in these areas need to be trained in the use of these technical tools.

The fourth is *role training*. At Level 2, the CMM looks to project teams to support a series of specific roles. To do this, members of the teams need to have an appreciation for the roles different groups undertake on a project. This type of training does need to be in depth. It should be structured, though, to give the individual a broad appreciation for the scope and value of the roles within the organization.

Each of these areas—direct process training, indirect process training, tool training, and role training—represents training that need be given only once to an employee. It can be done when the person is first hired or when first assigned to a project. This type of one-time training does not have to be repeated. As times evolve and your processes change, you may need to put people through a refresher course to keep them up to date.

Application Domain Orientation is the other main kind of training. The word "orientation" here is used to indicate a lesser depth of knowledge being transferred than would be expected via training. An orientation is an overview or introduction to a topic. Orientations can be formal or informal, long or short. Two kinds are called for at Level 2. The first is *business/operations orientation*. When a new project is begun, members of the software engineering group should be given an orientation to the business background of the project. This is an overview of the business solution that the system will support. This kind of overview gives the members an appreciation for what the software will do in the real world. The second is a *technical architecture orientation*. This orientation is complementary to the first. When a new project is begun, members of the software engineering group should be given a technical orientation to the architectural requirements of the project. This is an overview of the environment in which the system will be built. This kind of overview gives the members a heads-up on the technical direction the project will take.

While Structural Training is usually given only once for a project (or as things change), the Application Domain Orientations are given with each new project or as new members join a project. Because with each project, the business mission and the technical requirements may be very different, these orientations are ongoing and should become, in effect, a distinct part of the overall project management process. Table 5.1 summarizes the types of training one can consider for Level 2.

Who Should Be Trained?

Not everyone in your project group needs to be trained in all things. But there is a core set of people that you should plan to include in the specialized training that prepares them to do their jobs. The requirements analysts, the project planners and managers,

Table 5.1   Types of Training Supported at Level 2

STRUCTURAL TRAINING	APPLICATION DOMAIN ORIENTATION
Direct process training	Business/operations orientation
Indirect process training	Technical orientation
Tool training	
Role training	

the software quality assurance analysts, the configuration managers, and the members of the Configuration Control Board (CCB) will have to be specifically trained to carry out their roles.

There is a final group that has to be trained, and it is referred to in the CMM book as "members of the software engineering group and other impacted groups." Just who these people are is largely up to you, but the basic idea is easy to grasp. Across your various project teams—analysis, design, coding, testing, implementation—there will be certain members who will represent a team or who will be involved in the project in such a way that they need to interface and work with other teams. These people, who may have these set positions or who may change from project to project, will need a certain regimen of training in order to prepare them to perform in compliance with your processes and with Level 2 requirements.

We will cover what areas in which the members of the software engineering group need to be trained. Selecting the specific members is up to you, using your professional judgment as it relates to the scope, nature, and needs of your projects.

At Level 2 training prepares your project members to work effectively in your process improvement environment. When you think about your project training needs you can plan along five general areas of need: direct process training, indirect process training, tool training, role training, and high-level orientations.

Requirements Management Training Requirements

To address the Level 2 training requirements for requirements management you need only review the single training requirement for this area:

> Members of the software engineering group and other software related groups are trained to perform their requirements management activities.[2]

This means you should ensure that the members of the SEG who are responsible for analyzing and allocating the requirements are trained in how your project will approach this task. This might involve direct process training: a seminar on how the requirements analysis process works, what it covers, and how it is documented. It might also involve some tool training, especially if you use a specific requirements management tool to help analyze the individual requirements.

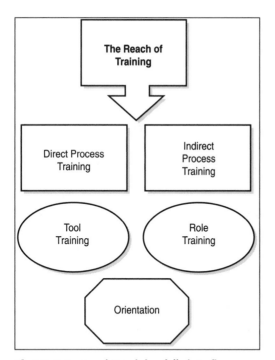

Figure 5.1   Level 2 training falls into five common categories.

This type of training can be given once to an individual, then refresher courses can be offered as the process changes over time or as project needs evolve.

Who: Requirements analysts

What: Requirements analysis and allocation process

When: As hired or on assignment

Scope: The methodology, rules, and tools used to allocate requirements to hardware, software, and other project elements

Type: Direct process training, tool training

The CMM also recognizes (simultaneously) the need to orient the project team to the business domain of the application. That is, to present to members of the team an orientation about the business solution that the project they are working on will address. This type of orientation gives the members of your project team a foundation on which to understand the nature of the system they are building. This helps them relate to and account for the real-world business needs of the system and to construct the system with the job of the end user in mind.

Who: Software engineering group

What: Orientation to the business background of the project

When: At project initiation

Scope: An orientation to the business solution that the project will address, expressed in terms of real-world application

Type: Orientation

Project Planning Training Requirements

To address the Level 2 training requirements for the project planning function, you need to understand that the single statement from the CMM that follows implies a fairly robust sequence of training programs. The main reason is that planning a project involves input from just about every area of your software shop. A lot of your people will need to know such things as what input is required from what area and the rules for estimating time, capital costs, and resource costs. Together with this, the software project manager will need to know what is expected in a project plan, what process is used for constructing one, and how to work any software tools that are used to automate software planning tasks.

Here's what the spec says:

> The software managers, software engineers, and other individuals involved in software project planning are trained in the software estimating and planning procedures applicable to their areas of responsibility.[3]

Sounds simple, but there's a lot in that statement. You won't find it overpowering from an implementation standpoint, but you need to understand the scope involved. Let's start first with the software managers. In order for them to do their jobs, your project software managers will need training in three areas.

The first is direct process training in how your group manages a software development project. The project managers have to be instructed in the processes you support, and they need to have a thorough understanding of the steps involved in project management as well as the different teams represented on each project. This should be considered the main training that the project manager receives. It could come as soon as a person is hired into the role or at least before the person is assigned to a real project.

The second is another session of direct process training, this one in the rules and regulations surrounding the estimating process. As the project manager will be negotiating and documenting commitments to form the software development plan, the project manager will need to have a sound knowledge of how estimates are derived and interpreted.

The third course of training for project planning is a session of tool training, training in the system that your project management team uses to produce a software development plan. If your system is something as simple as using MS-Word against a basic project plan outline, then your training could be fairly simple. If, like many IT shops, you have adopted some form of project management tool, perhaps complex and detailed in operation, you will have to make sure your new project manager has a strong understanding of how the tool(s) work.

Who: Project managers

What: Project planning methods and processes

When: As hired or on assignment

Scope: The methodology and rules used to plan a software project and create a software development plan

Type: Direct process training

Who: Project managers

What: Project planning rule for estimating

When: As hired or on assignment

Scope: The contacts and rules applied to the process of estimating costs, schedules, and resources for a project

Type: Direct process training

Who: Project managers

What: Project planning tools and utilities

When: As hired or upon assignment

Scope: Training on the system tools and applications used to develop the software development plan

Type: Tool training

The training regimen cited here takes care of job-specific training for your software project managers. Those three courses will not only prepare the SPMs for active, effective assignment to a project, but they will fulfill the major points for training covered under the project planning KPA. The rest of the requirements are fulfilled by training members of the software engineering group in the project's rules and regulations for project component estimating.

As mentioned earlier in this chapter, the phrase "members of the software engineering group" is deliberately vague. For the sake of effective project planning, the various teams within the development group will probably contribute input and direction in the specific technical details of the project. For these teams to provide this, some members should be trained in the rules and regulations of how to estimate schedules, resources, and materials and how to cost efforts.

Who: Software engineering group

What: Project planning rule for estimating

When: As hired or upon assignment

Scope: The contacts and rules applied to the process of estimating costs, schedules, and resources for a project

Type: Indirect process training

Project Tracking and Oversight Training Requirements

One of the tricks to effective performance at Level 2 is a properly implemented software project tracking program. Project tracking, of course, involves a host of activities. These include schedule management, cost management, resource management, change control management, and negotiating any necessary adjustments to the software development plan.

In order to carry out such a multifaceted role, the software project managers should be trained in the mechanisms of their jobs as related to each project. In addition, members of the SEG (especially first-line software managers) need orientation on the scope and technical nature of the project in order to get in sync with the software project manager's mission. To support this the CMM defines training recommendations as follows:

- The software managers are trained in managing the technical and personnel aspects of the software project.[4]

- First-line software managers receive orientation in the technical aspects of the software project.[5]

The software project manager will typically conduct business using two methods. The first is that the SPM will track the project using the steps and activities contained in the project tracking process (see Chapter 4). The second is that the software project manager will (usually) follow this process with the assistance of some sort of automation tool. It could be something as basic as a calendar application or something more intensive, like MS-Project, or even a custom-designed piece of tracking and management software.

This duality—process and tools—requires a two-pronged approach to training. The SPM will need to be trained in both your project tracking processes and the tracking tools you use to supplement the process.

Who:	Project managers
What:	Project tracking processes
When:	As hired or upon assignment
Scope:	Training on the steps and activities defined in the software tracking process
Type:	Direct process training

Who:	Project managers
What:	Project tracking tools
When:	As hired or upon assignment
Scope:	Training on the system tools and applications used to track the software project
Type:	Tool training

NOTE The CMM suggests that your software project managers might also benefit from some formal, external training in the general discipline of project management. After all, project management is more than just a set of processes and software tools. It involves people skills, writing skills, and communication skills. It is also a field with its own set of operational theories and methodologies.

Recognizing this, the CMM mentions (but does require) that your software managers might benefit from some discipline-generic training. You will find that many institutional organizations (like the Project Management Institute) and many academic organizations offer training and certificate courses in the field of project management.

The process of project tracking usually begins with some form of project initiation. This is typically conceived as a kick-off meeting or as a startup workshop. One of the areas that could be covered at the start of any project, no matter how it's done, is to orient the team to the technical aspects of the project. This orientation should cover such things as the hardware environment, the software architecture, the tools being used, third-party vendor support, and so on. The goal of this effort is to get the technical team aimed along a common technical line. I have mentioned the term "commonality" a few times already. It applies here as well. The smooth operation of a project can be better ensured when everyone involved has a common understanding of the scope and the approach the project will take.

Who: Software engineering group

What: Orientation to the technical aspects of the project

When: At project initiation

Scope: A presentation of the architecture, tools, and technical approach the project will take

Type: Orientation

Software Configuration Management Training Requirements

Next to the direct activities of project management, the role of configuration management is central to successful software project control. There is a lot of output on any project: source code, technical documentation, project plan documentation, and more. All this needs to be continually managed to ensure that current copies of this output reflect the current project stasis and provides an audit trail for this documentation, a traceable history of project changes and adjustments.

To support this, the CMM defines training here this way:

- Members of the SCM group are trained in the objectives, procedures, and methods for performing their SCM activities.[6]

■ Members of the software engineering group and other software-related groups are trained to perform their SCM activities.[7]

To effectively establish a configuration management program within your group, you will need to train three specific resources in the workings of CM. The first is the configuration managers who will be active in version control activities during the project. Each CM will need a session of direct process training and a session of tool training.

The direct process training covers the daily activities required for carrying out the CM program from a project standpoint. The configuration manager will need to know just what your processes are and what the boundaries are when it comes to following them. The configuration manager will also need to know how to effectively interact with members of the SEG who may be participating in the configuration management process (checking project material in and out).

The tool training gives the configuration manager a working knowledge of any CM tools your project/functional groups use for version control purposes. The scope and depth of this training, of course, depend on the tool(s) you have selected. Some (like PolyVersion Control) can be quite complex and sophisticated; others can be relatively simple and straightforward.

Who:	Configuration managers
What:	Configuration management methods and processes
When:	As hired or upon assignment
Scope:	The methodology and rules used to conduct version control activities across a project
Type:	Direct process training

Who:	Configuration managers
What:	CM tools and utilities
When:	As hired or upon assignment
Scope:	Training on the system tools and applications used for version control during the project
Type:	Tool training

The role of configuration management within the CMM does not stop at version control. It includes, by extension, change control. To fulfill all the requirements of this KPA at Level 2 you should develop a change control process and establish a change control committee, a Configuration Control Board. You will need to create adequate change control procedures and then educate the board members as to their duties and responsibilities in this area.

Who:	Members of the Configuration Control Board
What:	CCB rules and procedures
When:	As appointed or prior to project start
Scope:	Training as to the rules and processes that should be followed by members of the CCB when performing their duties
Type:	Direct process training

With the configuration managers and the members of the Configuration Control Board trained, one group is left. To carry out configuration management activities in an efficient manner you should now train members of the software engineering group to interface effectively with the CM process across the life of a project. This means training them in the processes they will need to carry out when seeking changes to the scope, resources, cost, or schedule of the project.

It is important to note that, also included in this training, there should be a presentation on the general role and *value* of configuration management within the organization. Some people may view CM activities as too time-intensive or as calling for too much overhead. It is helpful to express the important role CM plays at the start of the project. The appreciation gained will help members of the SEG follow the specified process more closely and in a manner in which they can comprehend its contributions.

Who: Members of the SEG

What: Processes required to participate in CM activities

When: As hired or upon assignment

Scope: The steps and rules applied to the process of configuration management; as well as training on the general role and value of CM within the organization.

Type: Indirect process training

Software Quality Assurance Training Requirements

Software quality assurance is the umbrella function under which CMM Level 2 compliance is monitored. To make sure that the SQA team is ready to encourage, educate, and enforce process compliance you need to make sure that your SQA resources are trained in their duties and activities and that the members of the SEG are trained in how they should participate in process compliance. To support this the CMM promotes SQA training in this way:

- Members of the SQA group are trained to perform their SQA activities.[8]
- The members of the software project team receive orientation on the role, responsibilities, authority, and value of the SQA group.[9]

To launch the SQA role within your group you will need to train two specific resources in the workings of SQA. First are the SQA managers who will be active in process compliance activities during the project. Each SQA resource will need a session of direct process training and a session of tool training.

The direct process training covers the daily activities required to carry out the SQA program from a project standpoint. The SQA analyst will need to know just what your processes are and what the boundaries are when it comes to following them. The analyst will also need to know how to interact effectively with members of the SEG who will be participating in process compliance.

The tool training gives the SQA analyst a working knowledge of any SQA tools your groups use for process compliance purposes. The scope and depth of this training, of course, depends on the tool(s) you have selected.

Who: SQA managers

What: SQA methods and processes

When: As hired or upon assignment

Scope: The methodology and rules used to conduct SQA activities across a project.

Type: Direct process training

Who: SQA managers

What: SQA tools and utilities

When: As hired or upon assignment

Scope: Training on the system tools and applications used for SQA during the project.

Type: Tool training

NOTE As with project management, the CMM again suggests that your SQA analysts might benefit from some formal, external training in the general discipline of software quality assurance. Because the job calls for strong interpersonal communication skills, effective management and negotiation skills, and some degree of arbitration skills, some specialized training in these areas may be of great use to your SQA analysts.

To conduct the activities of SQA in an efficient manner you should now train members of the software engineering group to interface effectively with SQA expectations. This means training them in the SQA processes they will need to be aware of for the projects they are working on.

It is important to note that, like configuration management, there should be included in this training some form of presentation as to the general role and *value* of software quality assurance. The appreciation gained will help members of the SEG follow the specified process more closely and in a manner in which they comprehend its uses and importance.

Who: Members of the SEG

What: Processes required to participate in SQA activities

When: As hired or upon assignment

Scope: The steps and rules applied to the process of configuration management; as well as training on the general role and value of SQA within the organization.

Type: Indirect process training

How Formal Should the Training Program Be?

This is the most frequently asked question about training at Level 2. People want to know what kind of program they have to put into place. There is no firm answer here. If your plans get the job done, then, chances are, the approach aligns with the CMM (and an assessment will probably find them acceptable). Remember, training becomes an important KPA in its own right at Level 3 (see Chapter 13). From that standpoint you might wish to begin instituting a formal training program so that you are closer to the Level 3 KPA when the time comes. On the other hand, when you are building a Level 2 program, having come up from Level 1, you may find that you have to implement and watch over enough new stuff; adding a training program that is close to Level 3 may be taking on too much too soon.

In fact, the CMM takes a broad view of the training structure:

> Although classroom training is a common mechanism that many organizations use to build the skills of their employees, the CMM also accommodates other vehicles such as facilitated video, computer aided instruction, or formal mentoring.[10]

As indicated previously, many training avenues are open to you. The key is to make sure that the avenue you choose is well designed and thorough. This can mean different things for different types of training. In this chapter we defined two types of CMM training: Structural Training and Application Domain Orientation. Structural Training covers the processes and tools you will need to carry out a specific job role. Application Domain Orientation is a topical introduction to or an overview of a certain subject.

Structural Training Forms

Structural Training is the more classical of the two. This training (we've identified 11 courses in this chapter) is typically given once to a staff member, with refresher courses offered periodically over time. You can handle this type of training in many ways, but the four most common are formal classroom sessions, private one-to-one or small group tutoring, on-the-job mentoring, and media-based (VHS, CBT, etc.) instruction.

Whichever form you adopt, you should make sure that you are covering the necessary topics, that the student has opportunity for questions and feedback, and that you in some way assess the student's retention of the matter at the end. As simple and flexible as the CMM tries to make it, many IT shops (in my experience) try to skirt around the training issue. They feel that it takes too much time to prepare training material (it *does* take time), that it costs too much money, or that it takes time away from actual project work. So they try to "cheat" a bit in this area.

Two forms of training are actually violations of the intent of the CMM. They are what's known as "throw-em-in-the-fire" training and "gentle osmosis."

"Throw-em-in-the-fire" training is euphemistically referred to as "on-the-job training" —although it's usually all job and no training. Here you learn by the mistakes you make. The problem with this approach is that you start off not knowing which mistakes could be easily avoided. You usually run into them all, and that can't help but impact in some ways the schedule, cost, scope, and integrity of your product. Take the time to train properly, and people will start off in the right direction, well prepared for the road ahead.

Gentle osmosis is another form of training-denial. A more accurate term might be pseudo-mentoring. This occurs when managers fudge on training requirements by aligning a new staff member with a senior one, mimicking the mentoring strategy but not owning up to the serious mentoring responsibilities. What's left is a form of training that is nothing more than a question queue. What makes it worse is that the new guy on the team may not even know enough yet to ask the right questions. These training arrangements quickly dissolve into the "throw-em-in" approach.

Resist the temptation to follow either of these "easy" paths. Except in the most special of circumstances they almost always turn out to be more trouble than they are worth. Meet your structural training requirements with a series of small-scale but well-designed training sessions, and you'll find that your team is well on its way toward Level 2 compliance.

Application Domain Orientation Forms

This form is much less formal than Structural Training and can usually be accomplished in short sessions or during informal project meetings. Because the purpose of an orientation is to give you a general flavor for a topic, a feeling for the scope and depth of a subject, it need not be intricately planned or prepared. On top of that, the orientation subject matter changes from project to project, so there is no way to hard-script an orientation.

At Level 2 you present orientations to the project team covering the business realm of the application and the technical aspects of the project itself. Both of these can typically (again, it depends on your project and the experience of your team) be conducted in short informal sessions, using a presenter-audience format or a simpler question/answer round table discussion format.

The goal of the orientation is to leave the team with a broad understanding of two high-level positions. The first is the business solution the project is attempting to address. That is, what is this system used for in the real world? How does it interface with and benefit the business environment?

The next is an understanding of the project's technical architecture. Because you are running a technical team here your people are going to need an introduction to the technical architecture in which they are going to have to build. This aligns everyone with the same technical objective, a set of complementary technical tools, and a common direction of effort.

Accomplish these two things, and your orientation sessions will be successful.

Supporting the Training Responsibilities

In Chapter 1, we saw that a CMM assessment will look for certain artifacts of your program as proof that your program is Level 2 compliant. "Proof" is really the wrong word to use. The CMM does not expect you to prove anything to it. Its sole goal is to get you and your group working in the realm of process preparation, practice, and improvement. An assessment will then look not for proof but rather for indicators that you are following a process methodology. These indicators—the artifacts of the process (like the wake of a boat)—are seen as natural byproducts of a thought-out process. In the area of Level 2 training there are a number of materials that you may create during the course of planning and training delivery that produce artifacts perfectly suited to what an assessor may be hoping to see.

Here is a brief overview of some of those materials you might have shaped for the projects in your shop:

General training program scope sheet. Your Level 2 program requires about 11 sessions of training aimed at various members of your SEG. Naturally you will have to devise the course content for each of these sessions. The scope sheet can be as a simple as a "Courses Currently Available" check sheet. It's used as a summary sheet that gives you a quick look at the extent of your current training program.

Instructor's course guidebook. For each course you will have to select suitable course content, then bring this content together into some form of a "tutor" guide. The size and formal presentation of this material will naturally vary from shop to shop. One place might simply use a general outline, given that the presenter/tutor is well versed in the material at hand. Another place might create very formal course presentation material, including the specific and detailed information to impart, a formal agenda, even A/V support materials. Either approach is valid. The benefit each possesses is that the training has been thought out in advance and documented for consistent presentation. Just shape your training materials to the needs of your group, and you should satisfy Level 2 expectations.

Participant material. To reinforce the participant's exposure to the course, it's a good idea to provide each with some handout course material. This material can be directly derived from the course outline or developed on its own. Either way, its purpose is twofold. During the course it gives the student a guide to follow in understanding the presentation. And after the course it can serve as an on-the-job reference for the graduate.

Training invitation memo. For any course to be a good use of time, you have to identify the participants who need to attend, then you need to formally invite them well in advance of the training date. In such an invitation include the title and objective of the course, the place, date, and time, and other information the attendees might find helpful. Issue and keep the training invitations you distribute.

Training certificate. When new members complete a course it's a good idea to present them with some form of completion certificate. The individuals can keep these as their own artifacts for demonstrating training compliance.

Training audit form. Tied to the previous items, management should keep a running list of everyone who has been trained in their programs. This list should include the staff member name, course title, and date trained. This can serve as a useful audit trail, showing, in effect, a history of your training efforts.

Table 5.2 gives you some examples of the kinds of artifacts you may wish to design to help support your training activities for Level 2. You don't need all of these and you may come up with some others that aren't mentioned. You might also notice that the artifacts are pretty much the same for each KPA. The idea is to be able to show that you are making sure your project members are being adequately prepared to take on their assignments.

Summary

Implementing the recommendations in this chapter would take you to (about) 25 percent of Level 2 compliance, and if you add on the recommendations in Chapter 3 and 4 you would be at about 90 percent. Almost there. Training is an often overlooked area, but it is of central importance. It's the cornerstone that allows your people to begin their Level 2 practices. In this chapter, we have looked at five different areas where training might occur, and we have seen how each applies to the Level 2 KPAs. How you shape your training is largely up to you and the needs of your group. At Level 2, training is not seen as a formalized practice, yet that does not diminish its importance. People lie at the heart of CMM implementation success, so properly trained people should help take your organization to that goal faster. As you and your people become more experienced, your training needs should stabilize.

We'll take a look at a final area for Level 2 consideration in the next chapter, "Creating Level 2 Policies."

Table 5.2 Evidence of Program Compliance

KEY PROCESS AREA	ARTIFACTS
Requirements Management	Training scope sheet, training invitation, training course material, student hand-out material, completion certificate
Project Planning	Training scope sheet, training invitation, training course material, student hand-out material, completion certificate
Project Tracking and Oversight	Training scope sheet, training invitation, training course material, student hand-out material, completion certificate
Configuration Management	Training scope sheet, training invitation, training course material, student hand-out material, completion certificate
Software Quality Assurance	Training scope sheet, training invitation, training course material, student hand-out material, completion certificate

Table 5.3 Key Practices Fulfilled by Implementing the Training Lessons in This Chapter

KEY PROCESS AREA	CHAPTER TASK	KEY PRACTICE OBLIGATION
Requirements Management	Train requirements analysts in process for analyzing and allocating, Orient members of the SEG to the business domain of the project	Ability 4
Project Planning	Train project managers in the software development plan production process, Train project managers in the use of SDP tools, Train project managers in the rules and regulations for project estimating, Train members of the SEG in the rules and regulations for project estimating	Ability 4
Project Tracking and Oversight	Train project managers in the use of project tracking processes, Train project managers in the use of project tracking tools, Orient the members of the SEG in the technical scope of the project	Ability 4
Configuration Management	Train configuration managers in the use of CM processes, Train configuration managers in the use of CM tools, Train members of the CCB in their duties and responsibilities, Orient the members of the SEG to the role and value of CM	Ability 4
Software Quality Assurance	Train software quality assurance analysts in the use of SQA processes, Orient the members of the SEG to the role and value of SQA	Ability 3, Ability 4

Creating Level 2 Policies

*Policies show a high level commitment to process and improvement.
It is important that the executive position be clearly and concisely
stated so that a common understanding and common boundaries
are widespread within the group.*
Mindy Gilbert, West Conklin Computer Association

A policy is a written opinion as to a method of conduct or a position of attitude. We encounter policies every day in the working world. "No shirt, no shoes, no service" is a common policy at many restaurants. "You break it, you buy it" is a policy often seen hanging in glassware and pottery shops. And, of course, in the field of information technology, we encounter any number of policies on a daily basis. Does your organization have a policy that prohibits downloading shareware from the Internet onto company PCs? Or a policy that requires you to perform a virus check on any diskette you bring in from home? Policies are all around us, some simple and generally inconsequential, some complex and critical to working in a smooth, organized environment. Whether simple or complex, all policies we encounter (or create) share four qualities in common.

First, as mentioned previously, they have to be written. They need to be documented statements. A policy becomes real only when it is published. Until then it is a nebulous cloud of ideas.

Next, policies are created to be understood as representing a formal commitment to a process. In the shirt-and-shoes policy, the understood process is this: *The restaurant wishes to serve only fully dressed clientele; if an ill-clad patron enters, service will be politely denied.* If that process is not followed, if random exceptions are made or personal favors are used to bypass the rule, the policy ceases to have any power. A sincere and unwavering commitment is essential to give a policy weight.

Third, once policies are documented they should be made available to those they affect. Policies are used to influence behavior. If the targeted audience is not receiving the message, there's no point to having a policy at all. Policies therefore should be treated as public documents—and by public I mean made available to the group you define. In the glassware shop, the break-it policy would be appropriately displayed next to a stand of crystal. If it was instead posted on the door to the manager's office we could argue that the policy wasn't in force because it had not been disseminated properly.[1] Properly distributing the policy is as important as creating and documenting it.

Fourth, and this is worth special attention, a policy should be created as a brief, concise summary of conduct, attitude, or position. A well-shaped policy is not a long tome or a dissertation. It is not a description of the program or attitude being endorsed; it's a high-level depiction.

These four qualities—written, committed, distributed, and short—are essential to any policy; within the CMM program they prove beneficial to the process of achieving Level 2.

The creation and use of policies occupy an important and critical place in the CMM program. Not only are they introduced at Level 2—the first step up from being essentially ad hoc—but they shape the foundation of any CMM program, from Level 2 up to Level 5.

To move toward Level 2 you will need to create and maintain five policies, one for each of the five Key Process Areas defined for Level 2 (Requirements Management, Project Planning, Project Tracking and Oversight, Software Configuration Management, and Software Quality Assurance.) Each project will need to operate under these policies, but each project can use its own versions. In this chapter we'll look at how to design and create the policies you need to operate a Level 2-compliant process quality program.

What Policies Are Recommended?

All Key Process Areas at Level 2 require a specific governing policy be in place for each project. In this chapter we'll discuss the following five:

Requirements Management. A policy directing the conditions and use of requirements within a project.

Project Planning. A policy governing how project planning materials are developed and approved and how formal commitments are made concerning the project.

Project Tracking. A policy directing the manner in which project resources and commitments are kept consistent with project progress.

Configuration Management. A policy describing the use and availability of configuration management resources and tools for each project.

Software Quality Assurance. A policy governing the oversight and reporting duties particular to the SQA mission.

Who Creates These Policies?

You'll notice that these five areas typically represent (in most IT shops) four or five different teams or groups of workers in the organization. Often separate managers oversee

WHY DOES THE CMM LIKE TO SEE FORMAL POLICIES IN PLACE?

The Capability Maturity Model establishes Level 2 as an integrated five-link chain. Requirements Management flows into Project Planning; Project Planning flows into Project Tracking and Oversight; Project Tracking flows into Configuration Management; and they are all integrated with Software Quality Assurance. (The KPA Subcontractor Management is not addressed until Chapter 7.) The CMM expects that certain conditions and actions exist in each of these areas. The use of policies can support this expectation in many ways. Four of the major ways are briefly described here.

Because a policy is an official announcement declaring a formal adoption of and commitment to a program or a position within the corporate environment, policies are the equivalent of laws. When you are building a process quality program, like the CMM, it helps to have the force of written policies to back you up.

The use of policies also shows executive positioning. Because policies are created from the highest offices in a company/division/group, they reflect executive management's on-the-record stand regarding broad strategic missions within the organization. More importantly, successfully creating an effective Level 2 process-quality program requires the whole organization, from executive management on down.

Policies also serve as a functional step toward a condition the CMM strives for that I term "commonality." The CMM recognizes that one of the keys to successful project management is effective interteam and cross-team communications. The result of such effective communications is that everyone comes away with a "common" understanding of the mission and issues surrounding it. Policies can help establish such commonalities. By their nature they are concise statements, brief and to the point, establishing high-level positioning; they are available to all.

Finally, policies can serve as the foundation for continuous quality improvement (CQI). Level 2 is all about CQI: trying, reviewing, improving, trying again. And this process holds true for the policies, too. Once you create a policy you should follow its success/problems within the organization from project to project, adjusting it from time to time, as change calls for, and refining it over time. Beginning CQI with executive policies is a good way to cement CQI within your Level 2 program.

each of the groups. Who then is responsible for writing and issuing each of the policies?

Basically, anyone can write the policies for you. The CMM has no rules on who creates them. It could be a consultant you hire, or an experienced employee who happens to be a strong writer; or the CEO. Chances are pretty strong that if you are reading this book it may be *you* who has to write the policies or, at least, guide them through creation. However you select an author, you should remember three things:

First, these policies are law in the workplace. They have to be well expressed, accessible, and (above all) correct.

Second, they should truly reflect your positioning and plans for action. Make sure your executive team knows what should be accounted for in each policy. Then communicate that to the author.

Third, whoever writes the policy is just ghost-writing. Whatever policy is released, it should be approved and signed by executive management. All policies should be seen to come from this level of management. Such a level is required for the policy to carry the weight of company-wide endorsement.

Knowing that, how do you choose an author?

There's again no answer to that because there are many dependent factors. For example, who the author is depends on how big you are as an organization; it depends on the nature of your chain of command. IBM would handle the creation of policies much differently than, say, my little company, LightTouch Systems. People in the telecommunications industry would probably handle the tasks differently than those in the health care industry.

So, I get back to my earlier point: If you're reading this book, it's probably up to you or someone you work with or directly report to create and manage the policies for your CMM Level 2 program.

I hope that whoever it is (what individual, what team) will find the next section beneficial. In it we'll go through a quick seven-step process to get your policies created and in place as you begin your Level 2 program.

The Seven Habits of Highly Effective Policy Managers

Follow these seven habits, and you'll have few problems getting your required policies into place.

Identify the Owners

There are five policies that need to be created: one for Requirements Management, one for Project Planning, one for Project Tracking and Oversight, one for Software Configuration Management, and one for Software Quality Assurance. In your organization, who owns these functional areas? Is it project specific? Group specific? Who is responsible for creating policies that affect the operation and direction of these areas? You may have a single executive who oversees these areas, or different executives may manage each one. It all depends on your business. But it's a good bet that you know who it is who should own the policies for these areas.

As part of the CMM implementation for Level 2, you will probably already be working with the owners. In any event, identify the owner for each required policy and contact him or her. Brief the owner on the need for a policy in the specific area and what it should contain. (This chapter will tell you in detail what each policy should include as a minimum.)

Think It Through

Think carefully through what each policy ought to contain. The policy should accurately reflect two things: the issues CMM expects for Level 2 compliance and the operational characteristics unique to your program.

NOTE It is important to remember that the policy should be an accurate reflection of how your program operates. Because of this you should probably have your structures, processes, and training plans worked out (see Chapters 3, 4, and 5) before writing the policies.

The policy author needs to know from a broad perspective how a specific team operates. You can get this information from line managers and workers as well as from executive-level management. Gather this data together as a series of outline points and then run it by the policy owner for a quick review.

Write the Policy

With the content of the policy in fairly solid shape, the author should commit the information to final form: a policy statement. As mentioned earlier, the policy statement need not be an extensive, florid document. In fact, the best-shaped policies are the opposite: brief, concise, clearly expressed. What you are creating is a formal commitment to a process, not the process itself. Paragraphs can suffice. One or two pages is certainly plenty. If you find that you are churning out a 12-page policy statement, go back and reexamine the contents against your outline notes.

To make sure the policy is as compact as possible, put the points into succinct form, keep them high level, and express them in language that is clear and accessible for all to read.

When you have a draft in place, you are ready to publish it for review.

Review the Policy

Each draft policy should be reviewed by two main audiences. First are the line managers, the people on the front line of the work who will be responsible for implementing and following the policies. Without their approval and endorsement of each policy, your CMM program will be off to a rough start. Request feedback from line management on each draft.

Next, review the drafts and any changes with executive management. These people are the true owners of the policies so it is critical that they understand, endorse, and provide for all stipulations expressed in the policies.

Based on feedback from line management and executive management, make changes to the policies as required. You are now ready to submit them for signature.

Approve the Policy

With final forms of the policies in place, you can either review them again or submit them to executive management for approval. The approval process requires two basic steps. First, executive management should unequivocally support the policy content; to demonstrate this, executive management should sign each one. This "imprinting" marks the policy as officially adopted.

This step is critical to the spirit of the CMM. It shows dedicated ownership and formal commitment to a plan of doing business, two things that the CMM promotes by its nature.

Publish the Policy

With the policies approved and signed, they are ready for publication. The key in this step is thorough distribution. Each policy should be easily accessible by those workers who need to work within the boundaries of the policies. This is so important to the CMM that it should be closely monitored.

You can properly disseminate the policies to affected employees a number of ways.

Printed copies can be placed into new hire orientation materials. You can post a copy on a company intranet site. You can send copies to employees via e-mail. You can even post a copy on a bulletin board in the employees' work area.

Whatever options you select, make sure the policies are freely and openly accessible to the people they affect. It is of major importance that the line workers—those people who are following your Level 2 CMM program—understand their roles from the policy-level perspective.

Maintain the Policy

Policies should not be static, rigid documents. Things change in the business world, and things change rapidly in the IT world, often from project to project. And because the CMM Level 2 program expects you to be constantly measuring your jobs in order to improve them, the same holds true for your policies. You should review the policies on a regular, periodic basis. You should keep them up to date with changes in the workplace or new executive directions. And you should also inspect them to make sure that any changes do not deviate from or conflict with the CMM expectations of your program.

This approach is a set of seven quick steps to creating your Level 2 policies. Though somewhat simplified and condensed, the process is basically complete; if you follow it, even as a broad outline, you and your team will be in good shape for this part of the Level 2 program.

In the next section we'll look at what specific points you should include in each of your five policies to make sure they are Level 2 compliant.

Creating Level 2-Compliant Policies

In this section, we'll look at what the CMM recommends for each policy. Remember, like many of the facets of the CMM program, these points are not doctrine. They are not rules or commands; they are suggestions. But, as suggestions, they have been carefully thought out to reflect the inherent needs of the program. You do not have to include each item in your policies if you have a good reason not to and if the absence does not result later in a deviation from CMM philosophies.

You should also read this section with the understanding that these policy points are minimums. That is, they simply account for what the CMM suggests be addressed. You may very well need to include other policy points that specifically address any unique characteristics of your IT management programs.

Requirements Management Policy

The CMM calls for a Requirements Management policy that highlights three points:

- The requirements are documented.
- Requirements are approved by the software managers and affected groups before commitments are made.
- Software plans and activities are kept consistent with changes to the requirements.

These three points are very basic. The CMM wants to see the requirements written because that is the best way to define, analyze, measure, and track them. Because the requirements form the foundation for the beginning of any software development, it is important that the project begins with the requirements in solid, tangible form.

Reviewing the requirements is also an important feature. The requirements will naturally affect all those working on the project. It is important that all affected parties (managers, team leads, etc.) have a chance to review the requirements and comment on them before internal and external commitments and plans are made.

Finally, the CMM stresses the need to keep the project defined along a base line of clean requirements. Over the course of a project, requirements are bound to change to one degree or another. When requirements do change, project management should adjust commitments, schedules, and resources accordingly.

You can see even from these brief policy requirements that the CMM is pursuing the concept of "commonality," of providing the avenue and obligation for everyone on the project team to share a common, documented understanding of the project and to manage its evolution in a predictable, tangible way.

Project Planning Policy

The CMM calls for a Project Planning policy that covers five areas concerning project preparation:

- Requirements are used as the basis for planning.
- The project's commitments are negotiated among the project manager, the software managers, and other impacted managers.
- Affected groups get to review the software size estimates, effort and cost estimates, schedules, and other commitments.
- Senior management reviews all commitments made to external organizations.
- The software development plan is managed and version controlled.[2]

If you read these points you'll see that they all share a common objective: The CMM at this stage wants everyone involved in the project—client, managers, team members—to have a chance to shape the project plans (again, the concept of commonality). Project planning should never be conducted without regard for the team, the executive management, or the client. The project plan will set the work level and expectation level for all concerned, so it needs to be done with as much input as necessary and with formality. To support this, the CMM calls for the requirements to be used as the basis for the client-vendor-worker relationship. All affected parties should approve any issues or commitments that arise from this foundation and provide the feedback necessary to shape a realistic, achievable plan. Finally, the software development plan that arises from this process should be closely managed and controlled.

Software Project Tracking and Oversight Policy

The CMM calls for a Project Tracking and Oversight policy that covers five areas concerning project monitoring:

- A software development plan (SDP) is maintained as the central tool for tracking the project.
- The software project manager is kept informed (by all subgroup and team managers) of the project's status and issues.
- Adjustments to the SDP or to the project team are made by the software project manager when the SDP is not being achieved.
- Changes to the SDP are reviewed by all affected groups before the changes are implemented.
- Senior management reviews all changes to the SDP that affect commitments to external groups.[3]

As we touched on in Chapter 1 of this book, Project Tracking and Oversight lies at the heart of the CMM Level 2 program. Project monitoring ensures two things: That a defined plan is being used to manage progress on the project and that communications concerning the project are spread to all relevant project members. The points here enforce this twofold benefit.

Basically, the policy mandates the use of a software development plan by which project progress is tracked. The team is responsible for updating the project manager on any issues or conditions that might affect achieving the objectives of the plan. If such conditions or issues arise, the project manager may elect to adjust or change the plan or the components of the project team to keep the overall project on track. Any changes that are made should first be reviewed by all impacted groups. Finally, if the changes or adjustments affect any of the external commitments for the project, senior management should review and approve such modifications.

Configuration Management

The CMM calls for a Software Configuration Management policy that covers five areas concerning how the project's deliverables and documentation are kept current and up-to-date:

- Responsibility for SCM is specifically assigned for the project.
- SCM processes are implemented throughout the project life cycle.

- SCM is implemented for all projects within the organization.

- The projects are each given adequate access and resources within the SCM environment.

- Software base lines and general SCM processes/results are audited by management on a regular basis.[4]

Like Software Quality Assurance (see the next section), Software Configuration Management is a CMM component that resides *outside* the immediate project team. It is viewed as a tool or resource that the project team uses to manage evolving versions of its deliverables and documentation. The policy therefore enforces the availability and use of SCM in and across projects.

The policy covers several important points. It calls for SCM responsibility to be specifically assigned for each project. This means that formal and official notice is given to the SCM team that a new project should now be included under SCM activities. The project team, at the same time, is given responsibility for following SCM processes for the life of the project. To support this, the policy states that each project will be given adequate "space" within the SCM environment and access to the SCM tools appropriate to the needs of the project. Finally, the policy concludes with a call for regular reviews by software management members of the SCM activities and repository.

Software Quality Assurance Policy

The CMM calls for a Software Quality Assurance policy that covers three areas concerning process quality management:

- Software Quality Assurance practices are in place on all projects.

- The SQA team retains an independent channel for reporting to executive management.

- Senior management periodically reviews SQA activities and results.[5]

Software Quality Assurance plays an intricate role in CMM. Because of this it is important that the policy establishes the unique position SQA maintains within the model. First, the policy states that SQA practices will be implemented for all projects. This helps ensure compliance to organizational (and CMM) standards. The policy also identifies the direct reporting avenue for SQA. SQA reports directly to executive management; SQA is not an interteam, interproject role. It is an extra-management tool.

The SQA role sits beyond the team—it is the role of objective observer. The policy also includes a statement that executive management will periodically review the activities and mission of the SQA role with an aim toward continuous quality improvement.

Supporting Policies

The CMM uses the creation and dissemination of policies as a measure of the commitment to process quality improvement your organization is willing to make. When you are assessed for being Level 2 compliant one of the things that the CMM assessors will want to see is verification that you do have the required policies and that you have implemented them properly within your organization. Such "proof" can be readily demonstrated with what are called "process artifacts." These are the papers, reports, and processes that serve as evidence that you are implementing what has been recommended.

Providing such evidence for the creation and use of specific policies is easy. You will need to provide artifacts for three broad areas: the existence of current policies, the means of broad distribution, and efforts at refinement and improvement.

Produce the policies themselves to demonstrate that they exist. You might also want to keep early draft copies or content notes as evidence of the definition process (although this is not absolutely necessary). You will also want to show how you distributed the policies, so have some sort of evidence for your distribution avenue (a Web page, an e-mail, a bulletin board, whatever method you used as long as it shows thoroughness). Finally, if you have had a chance to reassess any of your policies or change them to support CQI, keep any updates notes of meetings you may have taken when the evaluation was underway. The notes serve as proof of evaluation and measurement. Examples of the kinds of artifacts you can use to show your policy work is included in the Table 6.1.

Summary

Implementing the recommendations in this chapter takes you to (about) 10 percent of Level 2 compliance. Implementing the recommendations in Chapters 3, 4, 5, and 6 takes you to (about) 99 percent compliance. And that's pretty much the whole program.

In this chapter we've looked at some ways to plan for and create policies in each CMM Level 2 KPA. Policies are important because they are documented evidence of your entire organization's commitment to a program of process improvement. And

Table 6.1 Evidence of Program Compliance

KEY PROCESS AREA	ARTIFACTS
Requirements Management	The policy, any policy drafts or notes, distribution avenue, assessment or change notes or memos
Project Planning	The policy, any policy drafts or notes, distribution avenue, assessment or change notes or memos
Project Tracking and Oversight	The policy, any policy drafts or notes, distribution avenue, assessment or change notes or memos
Configuration Management	The policy, any policy drafts or notes, distribution avenue, assessment or change notes or memos
Software Quality Assurance	The policy, any policy drafts or notes, distribution avenue, assessment or change notes or memos

because they should come from the executive level of the organization they should carry the weight of authority. Three characteristics are important for any policy: It should an accurate statement of your expectations; it should come from the "top"; and it should be disseminated to the people who need to know what it promotes.

So far, we've looked at the structures, processes, training, and policies that should be considered when implementing a Level 2 program. But we've carried our discussions omitting one Key Process Area, Subcontract Management. This omission has been intentional. This KPA applies only to a limited number of software development shops —shops that farm out substantial parts of their work to other shops.

We'll take a look at Subcontract Management in the next chapter.

Table 6.2 Key Practices Fulfilled by Implementing the Lessons in This Chapter

KEY PROCESS AREA	CHAPTER TASK	KEY PRACTICE OBLIGATION
Requirements Management	Write a Requirements Management policy	Commitment 1
Project Planning	Write a Project Planning policy	Commitment 2
Project Tracking and Oversight	Write a Project Tracking and Oversight policy	Commitment 2
Configuration Management	Write a Configuration Management policy	Commitment 1
Software Quality Assurance	Write a Software Quality Assurance policy	Commitment 1

Subcontract Management

Managing quality is not simply an interteam discipline. The process
extends past the walls of your business and touches on those
you work with, those who supply you with product,
and those who end up with your product in their hands.
West Wicker, Quality Test Associates, Inc.

We've kept subcontract management out of our discussion so far in this book. You may find the reason valid, maybe not. But, in my work with CMM, especially with companies that are consciously working toward Level 2 certification, subcontract management is usually attended to as a side issue. Not because it's unimportant, but simply because the project teams are usually more focused on what they should be doing. In fact, many of these companies outsourced only on a sporadic basis. I am guessing that that same situation probably applies to most of the people buying this book. Therefore, I've kept this discussion separate from the others. If you and your project teams don't do a lot of subcontract management, you can skip this chapter, maybe saving it for later when you might need it. For those people to whom it does apply, you'll find that the processes and practices dovetail nicely with the other kinds of KPA activities your projects have adopted so far through this book.

In this chapter we'll look at subcontract management from the view adopted for the other KPAs: structure, process, training, and policy. We'll focus first on the purpose and goals of this KPA, and then look at the kind of structure you might want to put into place to support subcontract management activities. We'll then look at some processes you could adopt to shape and guide those activities. Next we'll look at the kinds of training you may have to offer to get your people ready to work within those processes. And finally we'll look at what you might set into place in terms of a subcontract management policy.

Subcontract Management as an Extension of Project Reach

Using outside vendors to expand the capabilities of your project team will extend the reach of your management activities. That's why subcontract management is a practical extension of project tracking and oversight. You have to track a new set of work activities and oversee a new set of commitments. Given the choice, most companies probably wouldn't outsource. Sometimes, though, you just have to.

For example, another company might have a piece of code that addresses some functionality you need to account for. They might even have modules of an entire system ready to go. Usually these are called COTS solutions, for custom/off-the-shelf systems. This area ranges from generic code that might require extensive modification to plug-and-play software used as is, like word processors, pop-up calculators, and more. You might decide that it is faster and more economical to purchase this software from a third party than to develop it yourself from scratch. In this case, you'll have to draw up a contract that spells out such factors as condition of the code to be purchased, modification rights, ownership rights, functionality in the code, support available, and delivery time frames. You'll have to manage the vendor as you would if you were buying a prepackaged system, like a house or a car.

Another reason to outsource is to have access to special expertise. Many IT shops specialize in certain technical and/or business disciplines: One shop might concentrate on Java-based solutions; one shop might mainly serve the point-of-purchase industry. In fact, specialization is probably the rule in the IT industry. From time to time your shop might need access to some expertise it does not possess. Maybe there's a specific technical solution you need to implement; maybe there are certain rules you need to automate. You may have to buy these skills on the outside. In this case, you can bring the vendor in-house to join your team, in which case you'll keep direct control. Or (perhaps more likely) you'll farm out those certain pieces of work to the vendor and they'll turn finished product back to you. In this case, you'll have to develop a contractual relationship that controls the type of solution, the amount of time involved, the work product to deliver, the acceptance criteria, and so forth. It's the same as buying consulting time: You should define it thoroughly up front so you'll know just what you'll be getting.

A third reason for outsourcing is simple economics. It could be cheaper for your shop to hire out the work than do it inside. Maybe you've got a sudden surge in work levels, or perhaps schedules have unexpectedly shrunk. You could find yourself with a temporary bulge in activity. Meeting the demand by hiring in permanent positions may be overkill for the situation, a commitment of long-term resources to meet a short-term problem. Hiring it out could be the more fiscally responsible alternative. But just like managing outside expert resources, you'll have to treat this management extension in the same way—define it up front so that you know just what you are getting.

The important thing to understand about moving some of your development efforts outside is that, for all the benefits you get, you also lose a degree of control. Loss of control results in decreased predictability, and decreased predictability equals risk. The more control you give up, the greater the risk. You can mitigate the risk somewhat by selecting the absolute best outside help you can get, but a better way is to increase control through a conscientious subcontract management program. The mission of subcontract management is to protect the integrity of the project when control is dissipated. It might be tempting, especially if you have first-rate help, to leave things to the experts and trust that it will be fine come plug-in time, but that's turning a blind eye to the management issue. The best path to smooth outsourcing is to define the outsource effort proactively and then manage to that definition.

You'll notice in the CMM that there is talk about the customer, the prime contractor, and the subcontractor (or vendor). Here you may think of yourself as the customer. After all, the subcontractor is servicing your needs. But the CMM takes the view that you are the prime contractor and you are providing services to a certain customer of yours. In order to provide the best services, you are seeking the help of a subcontractor to perform certain work on behalf of you for the customer. In this chapter we'll discuss how the prime/subcontractor relationship might be shaped to make the experience successful on each of your projects.

Goals of Subcontract Management

If you are going to the trouble of building a quality program in your shop you are probably not inclined to hire idiots. You need people with a certain level of quality. It's the same thing with your outside subcontractors. If they are no good at what they do, no degree of quality management will make the result significantly better. That's why the CMM has defined a Subcontract Management Key Process Area for Level 2. It's a way to make sure your process and quality awareness reach beyond the walls of your shop. To make this a practical reality for your software development projects, the CMM has established four general goals for this area. They neatly summarize the keys to effective subcontract management.

- To begin with, you need to choose only qualified subcontractors. If you don't start out with basic competence you won't find it magically materializing later.

- Once you have chosen a vendor for a project, both you (software project management) and the vendor will first agree to the commitments (work, cost, time, products, management steps) that define what the assignment is before any work begins.

- Once the project gets underway, you and the vendor will maintain ongoing communications.

- You will track vendor progress against the documented, agreed-to commitments for the assignment.

In the next sections we will look at some tangible ways to address each of these goals tactically. First you might notice that this KPA is somewhat different from the others. It's structured pretty much the same, but its intention makes it unique. The other KPAs focus more on work-related activity—that is, direct steps in a certain situation to help ensure an outcome. Here, with subcontract management, the activity is a little more passive. The focus is more on management and measurement, on tracking what has been set into motion. It can also end up being in a very real way a branch of contract management, which you might find tied to the legal side of your business.

A Level 2 Structure to Support Project Management

Two things are required to provide adequate support for subcontract management on your projects. One, you will need to appoint a subcontract manager for each project that is farming out work to an external vendor. Two, you will need to make sure that project management allocates an appropriate amount of funding and resources for subcontract management to perform the designated duties.

The role of subcontractor manager is very much like that of software project manager. For certain projects it might be appropriate for the software project manager to work in this capacity, too, especially if the external work is not very extensive. On the other hand, it might be better to appoint someone other than the software project manager to handle subcontract management. You might decide to appoint one person full time or part time, or to divide the work among several people. In some organizations, the role of subcontract management might automatically fall to someone with specialized legal knowledge or contract interpretation training. The key is to make the appointment suit the work. The guidelines you use to appoint a subcontractor manager will depend on the scope of your project, the resources available, and the culture of your IT shop. However you handle this, the subcontractor manager will be the external vendor's chief point of contact for the software project.

The Role of the Subcontract Manager

When you reach the point where you must appoint a subcontractor manager for one of your software development projects, take care to appoint someone with the skills and the orientation required to carry out the job. The most obvious responsibility this person will have is that of tracking vendor progress and activity against what has been defined in the agreement between you and the vendor. But there's more to the job than just this version of software project tracking and oversight. In fact, the duties are so varied that it really might take more than one person to address them all. Take a look at the following tasks and judge how to best see them through for your project.

Create the Subcontract Management Plan

This may be the single most important job the subcontractor manager takes on. Three things are involved in this effort. First, the work to be done by the vendor must be carefully identified and defined. Second, the timelines, work products, and checkpoints that will arise from the vendor's efforts must be just as clearly identified and defined. Finally, legal issues such as costs, payment schedules, delivery expectations, and other such issues have to be defined. Together all of these things will culminate into the contract that forms the basis of the agreement between you and the vendor. Can one person put all this together? You'll have to make that call within your own shop. But take care in this step. All further management activity will stem from what you build and agree to here.

Address Issues and Conflicts

Once the contract is in place and work on the project has begun, subcontract management will be charged with keeping a steady eye on the vendor's progress. Using the contract and the vendor's software development plan, the manager will follow the vendor's activities and work through any issues or conflicts that arise during the course of the work.

Take Measurements

During the course of vendor tracking, the subcontractor manager should also be taking regular measurements of vendor activity. The exact nature of these measurements will depend on what kind of data is valuable to you. You might want measures of actual delivery dates versus planned dates, or of projected costs versus actual costs, or of full-time resource measures during each phase of the effort. Whatever measures you define, make sure your manager is able to collect them on a regular basis.

Report to Software Project Management

As part of regular management duties, the subcontractor manager should make regular reports to the software project manager as to vendor progress and any pending issues or risks. This can be handled any number of ways: through regular status meetings, through defined milestone audits, or through the delivery of scheduled reports. The main objective here is to keep a channel of communication open between project management and vendor management. Such activity does not have to exclude the vendor. It might be good idea to bring vendor representatives in for certain status meetings. However you configure this relationship, make sure that both parties are able to exchange information in such a way that if any problems do begin to materialize they can be caught and addressed early.

Manage Team Interfaces

A final duty of the subcontractor manager is to facilitate interactions between the vendor and members of the primary software project team. Part of the subcontract management plan should include scheduled audit points, stages in the project where your project managers, software quality assurance people, and software configuration management people have the opportunity to review the work of the vendor in respect to their areas of specialty. For example, the SQA people may need to visit the vendor from time to time to perform scheduled SQA audits on certain planned work products or activities. The subcontractor manager, as the chief point of contact, is the ideal person to coordinate and facilitate this interaction.

Provide Resources and Funding for the Role

The previous section defines the general duties of the subcontractor manager. Of course, the exact duties will depend on the needs of your shop and your projects. For every project that will make use of this role, you should ensure that adequate funding and resources are made available from the project budget and schedule to accommodate the required duties. You might find that these resources and funding and spread across several job titles or involve the acquisition of special tools. However the job shapes up in your IT shop, help it be effective by giving it the business support it needs to operate.

In the next section we'll look at what processes and practices you might think about putting into place for use by your subcontractor manager. The items we'll be presenting should be treated as a series of generic recommendations. As you think each through and assess its role you can decide what role, if any, each might play in your own process mix.

Subcontract Management Processes and Procedures

The person (or people) you appoint to manage subcontractor activities on your project should do so according to a set of defined processes. These processes will help regulate how the tracking and oversight works; they will lend a degree of predictability to the task. If you take an ad hoc approach you are really operating at Level 1. What you are striving to do in this area is really two things at once. First, you are implementing a set of processes to guide your management activity specific to this project. You are also working to develop a set of subcontract management processes that will one day be so refined that your whole organization can adopt them and use them for all projects. This requires repetition from project to project, refining the steps along the way. That's why an ad hoc approach won't work well. Being reactive by nature and undocumented, an ad hoc approach is not very repeatable. The best approach is to put what you're going to do down on paper and do it within a certain context.

To help you with this, we'll briefly discuss nine processes or procedures (a procedure is a shorter, maybe even nonsequential, process) that will address the areas of subcontract management we talked about. The processes are as follows:

- Vendor selection process
- Contract development process
- Work plan template
- Work plan development process
- Vendor SDP review and approval procedure
- Work plan change procedure
- SCM review procedure
- SQA review procedure
- Acceptance verification procedure

Vendor Selection Procedure

Your organization should create a process used to choose vendors that will do work for you. In the absence of such a process you don't have much to go on. You can rely on the good-old-boy network and hire cronies and friends to come by and take on the work for you. Or, for the sake of convenience, you can go with the people down the hall, or you can go with your cousin's recommendation, that group of kids who work really cheap. None of these avenues is likely to pay off in the long run. Two business factors should jump to the forefront at any time you must work with an outside vendor: competence and value. The chief goal of building a subcontract management function is to avoid incompetence, to avoid hiring a group to perform a job that they are not (for whatever reason) ready to perform. In this area it is important to screen for quality up front, to make sure that you are dealing only with shops of a certain caliber, ones that show a commitment to quality similar to that of your shop. When you have confined your choices to competent shops you are then in a position to judge value. "Value" is a nebulous term and may well mean different things in different shops. Value to you, though, will in some way combine the attributes of cost, schedule, effort, and work product deliverables. Each vendor will be somewhat different in this regard, and you will have to look at the specific needs of your project to determine the blend that will make your project team most comfortable.

You can think of a vendor selection procedure as being a basic seven-step process:

1. **Proposal preparation.** In order to choose a vendor, you'll have to know what that vendor proposes to do for you, and that will happen only if you tell the vendor what the job is. For each selection process, you must begin with a proposal to the vendor that spells out just what the work is. This is a critical part of the whole process. Everything that follows will be based on this work description. You should take the time to make sure you completely define what you need done. Many people can be involved in this effort: project management, executive management, the various software group managers, the requirements analysts, and others. Get the proper input, document the result, and then get the group's approval before the proposal is released.

2. **Solicitation.** Step 2 can come before or after Step 3; they are related. The idea of this step is to get the proposal out into the community of vendors. You may have a list of qualified vendors to which you distribute the proposal, or you may send it out blind and then screen the respondents later. Either way, make sure the vendor knows the timeline for response and any rules or formats required of the response. Give the vendors a window of response time that reflects the scope of work you are asking them to consider.

3. **Entrance criteria.** To ensure that you are entertaining the partnership of only qualified development shops, you should establish an entrance criteria for proposal consideration. These can be any criteria you think will work for you. Many times the criteria aim to screen for such things as companies with a certain degree of financial strength, companies of a certain size, specific industry experience, number of years in business, or any business or industry certifications. Select criteria that will help you screen according to your needs. Just be sure to hold all respondents to the same set of criteria.

4. **Inspection criteria.** The entrance criteria will help you screen out proposals that don't meet your initial standards. The inspection criteria will help you narrow the field even further. Once you have received proposals from qualified

vendors, you should then inspect each in an organized way. This usually begins with a review of the proposal and then some form of scoring that will serve as a first-round value rating. After this you may wish to go deeper with your evaluation, inspecting the vendor against other criteria. This might include an on-site inspection of facilities and tools, inspecting resumes of proposed team members, perhaps a series of product demos, and follow-ups about client references.

5. **Award criteria.** The selection process proper ends with the award, which should itself be made against an objective set of criteria. Your selection team should devise a scoring mechanism that can weight such factors as cost, schedule, proposal completeness, ability, and that intangible called "goodness of fit" in order to decide the best value among the respondents.

6. **Contract negotiation.** Once the award is made, you and your organization can enter into formal contract negotiations to devise the contract that will guide the relationship from this point forward.

7. **Record keeping.** Keep all proposal and evaluation records for later reference. They can be helpful in improving and refining your vendor selection process.

Contract Development Process

Another process you will need for subcontract management is one that guides how your organization will create a contract to establish the legal agreements between parties. A discussion of contract writing and negotiations is out of the scope of this book and probably requires some experienced legal counsel. Nonexistent contracts leave a wide path open for later misunderstandings or disputes. Poorly written contracts are sometimes just as bad and often worse. The best protection that both you and the vendor have for a consistent understanding and smooth working relationship is a professionally drafted contract that acknowledges the expectations of both parties. You may have people internal to your shop who are experienced at this line of work, or you may have to go outside to get this expertise. Either way, it's a good investment of your time and attention.

However you proceed with contract development, make sure to include references to the initial proposal, the response delivered by the vendor, the work plan you derive for the project, and the vendor's software development plan. All of these should become part of the contract by way of attachment. This material is important here because the contract will be ultimately viewed as the guiding source for all decisions made regarding the work.

Work Plan Template

Just as your project team will use its software development plan to track the progress it makes, so too should the outsourced portion of your project. In fact, a work plan is doubly important when it comes to managing external sources. It's not only your progress roadmap; it becomes a mechanism to link two disparate groups, to sync and harmonize work efforts. Make the effort to develop a good work plan, and you will find that it benefits both you and your outside partner. A plan that is poorly thought out, ambiguous, or incomplete may leave open the possibility for confusion and misdirection later. What goes into your work plan is pretty much up to you. Because it resembles nothing more than a software development plan you might treat it as a mini version of that. Just as in a formal SDP, you'll want to set a work schedule, define deliverables, identify review dates, and more. The following table of contents can be used as starting point for your plan.

Table of Contents

    I. Statement of Work
   II. Reference Documents
       1. Work Description
       2. Contract
       3. Vendor's SDP
  III. Work Products
       1. Description
       2. Delivery Mechanism: Phase, Size, Format
  IV. Work Breakdown Structure
       1. Timeline
       2. Deliverables
       3. Status Reviews
       4. Formal Milestone Reviews
       5. CM Review/Audits
       6. SQA Review/Audits
       7. PM/Exec Reviews
   V. Measurements
  VI. Relevant Process Documents

The following sections will cover how the document is reviewed and approved.

I. Statement of Work

This is a brief narrative summary describing the vendor's assignment. Usually no more than a page or two, the statement of work may also contain the high-level deliverables and milestone dates expected over the course of the project. In that form it can be used as an executive overview.

II. Reference Documents

The vendor work plan, if it to be kept to a manageable size, can't contain every detail of the agreement between you and the vendor. Its job is to define the work and provide a mechanism for tracking it. These details, though, can sometimes be influenced by other documents dealing with the relationship. For this reason it's often a good idea to term these other documents a referential part of the plan. You'll probably want to include your initial work description here, along with the vendor's proposal response, the contract both parties signed, and a copy of the vendor's software development plan.

This last item has special importance. To a large extent, your vendor work plan should appear very similar to the vendor's work plan. You want a copy of the vendor's plan to ensure a few things: first, that the vendor is even planning to begin; second, that its plan matches your schedule; and third, that its plan builds the products you bargained for. As much as possible you will find it beneficial to work with vendor planning in developing these two plans. If the plans start out close and on track, they'll probably end up that way for you.

III. Work Products

In this section you'll identify the individual deliverables that the vendor has been contracted to produce. This may include a wide scope of items, depending on the nature of the vendor assignment. The list may be as basic as source code, user documentation, and technical documentation. Or it might be so extensive that it includes items like design document, network test plan, test plan results, baseline library, and more.

You'll have thought this through during the proposal stage of the project, so chances are that you can incorporate that description here. What you typically associate with each work product is a description of each and the details of the method of delivery. This will include such items as date due, format due in, estimated size, and delivery location. Once completed, this section will be a useful quick reference for what exactly it is that you are having built.

IV. Work Breakdown Structure

This is the heart of the vendor plan. It identifies activities over time and sets the boundaries for the vendor's work. The work breakdown structure can be very detailed or very high level. At the minimum, it should follow the delivery of the work products you described in the previous section. A good starting point for developing a work breakdown structure is to plot the following items along a timeline that ends with acceptance testing:

Deliverables. Dates on which the major work products are due, with an owner associated with each product. Include any dependent steps that might be gatekeepers for each product.

Status reviews. Dates on which general status meetings with take place with the vendor and members of the project team. The vendor will probably be conducting its own status meetings, but this section describes those meetings between the prime and the vendor.

Formal milestone reviews. Dates in which formal progress reviews will be made. These are usually milestone dates that coincide with the delivery of a major work product. These meetings are used not so much to discuss work details but to discuss broader issues, such as schedule compliance, quality assurance, resource availability, and downstream risks. Usually both project management and vendor management are included at these meetings.

SCM review/audits and SQA review/audits. Dates on which you have scheduled software configuration management audits and software quality assurance Audits. Both your SCM group and your SQA group will play an important role in vendor management. Because the vendor team is a very real extension of the project team, this team will need to operate in the same vein as the rest of the project. This includes checks by software quality assurance and CM library audits by the software configuration manager. These activities do not have to appear together, but each one needs to be scheduled, and the teams being reviewed should be notified in advance regarding what will be reviewed and what needs to be ready. It's the same Level 2 processes you'll be using for your internal team, now applied outside.

PM/executive reviews. Finally, if you plan to have formal executive review dates (perhaps at kick-off and then at project end), note these activities on the timeline.

V. Measurements

The last management portion of the vendor plan is a defined series of measurements that the subcontract manager is going to record over the life of the project. These measurements will be used later in process improvement analyses. You might want to measure such things as number of planned vendor resources versus actual, planned cost versus actual cost, number of delays and types of delays, number of vendor-requested changes, and disposition of changes.

VI. Relevant Process Documents

Finally, it's a good idea to include in the appendix of the vendor plan a copy of your change control procedure, your SQA/SCM review procedure, and your final acceptance criteria. Both the vendor and the project team will have to know these processes and follow their guidelines. A description of each follows later in this chapter.

Work Plan Development Process

Once your have a project plan in place (your own SDP) and you know what work the vendor will be doing (you have defined that already), then you can put together a vendor plan for the project. This is an extension of the work definitions you developed for the proposal and will eventually merge with the rest of the project's SDP. (For an example of the contents of a work plan, see the previous section.) As you may have to work with project management, SQA, SCM, and the vendor team in developing this plan, you might consider this seven-step process:

1. **Investigate plan detail.** This is the stage in which the real work of the vendor plan gets done. Here you define the elements that will eventually make up the work breakdown structure. To acquire the information needed for this your subcontract manager (or whoever is the author of the vendor management plan) will need to begin as early in the overall project planning as possible. The author will have to work with your project planners so that one plan will fit into the other. The author will also have to work with the software quality assurance and software configuration management teams to define when quality checks and audits should occur. The author will also have to work with the vendor team to help coordinate activity and timelines across the work plans of each.

2. **Create plan draft.** Once the investigation is complete, the subcontract manager can use the data gathered to create a first draft of the plan.

3. **Distribute draft for review.** Once the draft is ready, it can be distributed for review. The plan should go out to any group that is affected by its detail. And it's usually a good idea to allow a couple of weeks for thorough review of the material, especially if the plan is comprehensive. With the distributed plan you should include a meeting notification for the upcoming review of the material.

4. **Formal review.** The formal review should be an opportunity for affected parties to come together and review the vendor plan as a group. The meeting should be used to clear up ambiguities in the plan, correct errors, or make notes of any issues that may need to be worked. Notes should be taken at the meeting and then used as the basis for revision.

5. **Revise plan.** Based on the notes taken during the review meeting, the author makes the corrections necessary to the document and then redistributes it to the review team, usually with a copy of the meeting notes. The team is given a span of time (adequate to its length) to take a final look at the contents. An approval date is set with this review time. That's the date on which no further comments to the document will be accepted.

6. **Approve plan.** After all changes have been incorporated into the plan, the document can be submitted for signature. It is usually the project manager or the software project manager who will approve the plan, but it's a good idea to get the vendor to approve it, too.

7. **Publish and distribute plan.** Once the plan has reached its final form—approved and signed off—it can be officially distributed to the organization and vendor as needed. The plan at this point becomes the major tool for tracking vendor activity and progress. Any changes to the plan will have to be made through formal change control channels. The plan itself should be placed under version control to keep its change history organized and clearly delineated.

NOTE This type document review/approval process is expanded in the CMM at Level 3. There it becomes its own KPA, Peer Review. We will look at the processes of Peer Review, which break the preceding process down into a few more detailed steps, in Chapter 12.

SDP Review and Approval Procedure

One of the major documents the vendor should provide to you as part of the prime/subcontractor arrangement is a detailed software development plan that will clearly spell out what the vendor teams will do over what period of time to comply with the assignment you have given them. This vendor SDP should map closely with your vendor management plan; the plans should complement each other to a large degree and ideally should be developed together. Requesting an SDP from the vendor should become a part of the contract. Reviewing and approving the vendor's SDP should become one of the first activities the prime does to manage the subcontract. Because the process is almost exactly the same (given your vendor's own way of doing business) as for the vendor work plan, we will let those sections apply here as well.

The main objectives in this process are to confirm that an adequate plan is in place from your vendor and that all members of the project team, internal and external, have had a chance to review their assignments ands get comfortable with all the commitments contained in the plans. You might even consider (as I recommended previously) making the vendor's software development plan, by way of attachment, part of your official vendor management plan.

Work Plan Change Procedure

At Level 2 your projects will be following a change control procedure of your design to address the need for any changes that come up during the course of the project. We have seen this functionality set up by means of a Configuration Control Board (see Chapter 3). The board is responsible in the long run for clean software base lines, but in the short term the board is also often responsible for change management in general. In your own shop you may call this board the Change Control Committee or the Scope Management Committee. It may consist of several members or just a couple. However you set up the body, one of its duties is to manage change. The need for change management will exist in your outsourcing efforts, too. In fact, you'll probably find it convenient to run your subcontract changes through the established change management system you use for the project at large.

Of course, change management with the subcontractor may involve a few additional steps. Changes will ripple through several new areas, such as contract authorities, vendor's executive management, and the vendor management and vendor SDP plans. For these reasons it's important to keep close tabs on subcontract changes. We discussed the basics of a change request/control procedure in Chapter 4, and you may elect to adopt that process here. Here's a quick review of it, with some steps added to recognize the special channels of subcontract management.

1. **Document change request.** Any change requests that surface during the course of the subcontract effort should be well documented. Some shops will use a specific form for all change requests; others will forgo a form but insist on the presence of some basic information. Whichever path you take, consider the following kinds of data when your or your subcontract team wants to initiate a change to the project. Start off with a description of the change, a brief narrative that summarizes precisely what the change is and why it is needed. You may wish to give this description a summary title, too. Next, think about including such support data as date submitted, date change is needed by, and requestor ID. You might also want to indicate which development areas are likely to be affected by the change, an estimated size of the change (S, M, L), and a criticality factor (Cool, Warm, Hot). All these data elements can be analyzed later and collected as change control performance measures for this KPA. This data also provides a good documented foundation for tracking changes over time, in the interests of software project management, configuration management, and vendor performance.

2. **Submit CR to the change control authority.** Once the CR is documented, you may wish it to move through a few channels of inspection before it goes to the change authority. For example, you may want any vendor-oriented change requests to pass first through the vendor's management for initial approval. If a change is not needed, if it is an embellishment, or if it is substantially out of the scope of the contract, the vendor may not wish to push it through the prime's channels. Only after vendor management has approved the request may it go on. The next step may be to have all vendor approved CRs pass by the subcontract manager. This person may have the proper perspective to judge if the change is viable and if it is OK to move it ahead or better to table it for later consideration. After that you might want the subcontract manager to pass all approved CRs by the software project manager. Only then, after the vendor, subcontract manager, and software project manager have reviewed them, do the CRs go to the Change Control Committee. Tailor this approval path to the needs of your projects, but try to establish a route everyone can follow for all potential change requests.

3. **Assess the CR's impact.** When the CR is officially submitted, someone (or some group) affiliated with change management will assess the effect of the change. The change will be analyzed in terms of time to create, cost to create, resources required, and effect on final project deadlines. This analysis should be just as finely documented as the initial request, and the two should be paired as a single decision point.

4. **Approve/disapprove/table.** The timetable of your change control process will shape how changes are submitted and moved through the various approval stages. Some change boards meet weekly, others monthly. Time-sensitive requests may have to be submitted in deference to the review schedule. At some point in the process, based on the nature of the request and its impact assessment, the CR will be approved, tabled for later consideration, or denied. Approved changes will move through the next steps:

5. **Adjust schedule/costs/effort as needed.** When a change is approved for the subcontract, software project management must work with vendor project management to fit the change into the plans for the development. Timelines, budgets, resource allocations, and deliverables may all have to be revised. These revisions should occur in at least three places: the SDP used by software project management, the subcontractor manager's vendor management plan, and the vendor's SDP. The subcontractor manager should review all points of revision across these plans to make sure they all match before the revised plans are distributed.

6. **Amend contract as needed.** There is a possibility, depending on the type of contract you are using or on the scope and nature of the approved changes, that some content in the contract must be revised in order to keep it current with the project. If this is the case, consult the contract authorities in your shop concerning this, and make sure executive management, project management, and vendor management have an opportunity to review and approve the changes that are being made. Fortunately, most of the time contracts are written in such a way as to avoid the need for frequent modifications, and when they need to be done they can be handled by way of reference.

7. **Release updated plan.** Once the change has been approved and all adjustments have been made to planning material, the revised planning documents can be distributed to the affected parties. This is an important step. It's one thing to carefully document and analyze changes; that's important, too. It's just as important, though, to communicate the changes to the work groups that must create or live by the changes. Get the revised plans and specs into the hands of the right people. You may even consider giving the groups an overview of the changes in a presentation or a brief training session that gives the groups a chance to ask for clarification or further explanation.

8. **Implement change.** At this point, with the change documented, analyzed, approved, incorporated, and communicated, you can now proceed in the new direction mandated by the change.

SCM and SQA Review Procedure

An integral part of subcontract management comes in the form of configuration management audits and software quality assurance reviews. Both of these activities are woven into the flow of your overall project life cycle. Your SQA people monitor work products and activities at certain defined points. And your configuration managers regularly inspect the software base line library and releases. Both regularly check for process compliance and overall product integrity. When you elect to use outside help for substantial parts of your project effort, you will need to extend the roles of SCM and SQA to perform their review work on the outside team now as well.

This can become a delicate area between the vendor and the prime (you). Having one party come in to inspect another might be seen, in an ill-informed light, as evidence of mistrust or micro-management, and it may lead to a degree of resentment on both sides. The vendor might resent the prime for not "leaving it alone to do its job." The prime might resent the vendor for "operations that have to forced open, like pulling teeth." Both these attitudes can and should be avoided up front. For one, you're probably better off anyway picking a vendor that appreciates the value of configuration management and active SQA reviews and that is implementing both on their part of the project by way of course. Also, your up-front discussions with the vendor should include your expectations for SCM and SQA involvement. Added to this, your efforts in building the vendor management plan and the vendor's own SDP should allow plenty of opportunity to discuss and schedule the checkpoints needed by these teams. Preparing your vendor for this process will help ensure that the work goes smoothly and that the two teams work well together to produce useful audit and review results.

The process of handling the SQA and SCM inspections is relatively straightforward. It's based on planning and mutual consent, with ample prep time and use of established criteria for determining acceptable performance. The criteria should be established in the planning phase of the project. It is at this time that you may need to train any members of the vendor team in the formats and processes they will be expected to use. The vendor's people should have plenty of time to get up to speed on any practices they will be expected to follow. Only after that can they be expected to conform to any quality standards you have in place. The process of conducting the SQA and

SCM reviews can be thought of as a basic eight-step process. Here's a brief look at each step:

1. **Identify each inspection point in the project.** During the project planning phase, the subcontract manager should work with the vendor's project manager and with the prime's SCM and SQA resources to identify what points in the project life cycle will be open to SQA and SCM inspection. As you know, for each project your people will develop some form of SQA plan and SCM plan. These plans can be used as the basis for planning the activities with the subcontractor. The objective in this planning effort is to let all parties know the inspection milestones before work begins.

2. **Schedule the inspections/work products/participants.** This step is an extension of the previous one and also figures into planning. Once the inspection points are identified, you can assign to these points the work products and the team activities that will be reviewed. If possible at this time, assign participants in the reviews from both teams, vendor and prime. Steps 1 and 2 here ensure that all inspections are defined up front and are part of the general knowledge concerning, in part, how project progress and quality will be measured.

3. **Notify participants of pending inspection.** After the plan is in place and work is underway, the inspection times will eventually roll around. Some time prior to the inspection (usually 2 weeks or so, but any time that you judge adequate is fine), the subcontract manager or the SQA/SCM analyst (whoever is appointed to be the coordinator) should send a formal announcement to the participating members noting the upcoming review date, what products will be reviewed, and what activities will be reviewed. The notice might also include the list of participants and any meeting facility data (conference room, floor, and so on). This advance notice should give the team time to organize the products to be inspected. The notice should end with a confirmation request.

4. **Confirm meeting, arrange facilities.** Once the participants have confirmed attendance (the quorum you require should be defined by your software project management) the coordinator is free to set up the room reservations and make any other arrangements the meeting might require.

5. **Conduct inspection.** On the agreed date the inspection will occur. If the steps have been followed to date the right materials and people ought to be present for a productive review. The review should be an open forum of exchange and feedback. A person serving as a note-taker should be present to officially record all issues and action items that might come out of the review.

6. **Prepare inspection report.** Sometime shortly after the meeting (again, 2 weeks is typical but choose a span of time that works for your team) the inspector will prepare an inspection report, which will summarize the points of the inspection and compare them to the published standards. It should also contain a list of recommendations for going forward. The tone of the report should be constructive in nature; the idea of the inspections is not to identify faults but to help the project efforts stay on track with what was planned.

7. **Distribute inspection report.** The inspection report should not be constructed as a private analysis, suitable only for executive eyes. It's more like a public progress report, which should be distributed to all affected parties. The idea of the report (from its contents) is to help teams stay on track with what was planned for the project. This report then should be openly distributed to software project management and maybe even executive management. It should also go to vendor project management as well as the specific vendor team that was inspected.

8. **Meet to discuss/resolve as necessary.** Based on the recommendations contained in the inspection report, the teams may agree to meet and discuss future actions to address any issues or compliance problems that may have been identified during the inspection.

This inspection/review procedure can be used for both the software quality assurance activities and the software configuration management activities. You may also find this procedure helpful for planning any type of formal meeting called for in the software development plan. The process of identifying the meeting, announcing it well in advance, carrying it out, and the reporting on it will work for a wide range of project activities you may undertake.

Acceptance Verification Procedure

One of the key details of your relationship with an outside vendor is to define what criteria must be met in the end for final acceptance of the vendor's work products. The nature of this definition will, of course, depend on the type of work you are requiring the vendor to perform for you. Your acceptance criteria will be different for a set of user documentation than for a software module that integrates into a larger system. By different I mean that the things you'll be looking for in each case, things that confirm to you that the job has been acceptably completed, will differ. Having acceptance criteria on hand is a critical tool in the process of subcontract management. It benefits both parties. The key to making it a productive tool lies in the up-front disclosure of the process.

Creating acceptance criteria is not something you want to put together once the vendor's work efforts are well under way. In fact, it should emerge as a natural extension of the proposal process. Once you have defined what work the vendor will be required to perform you can then develop acceptance criteria for that work. Determining acceptance criteria is such a significant gate-keeping function that it should be reviewed with the vendor as soon as is practical. Some organizations may do this as part of the selection process, having the vendors sign off on the criteria as part of the proposal. Other organizations may have the review as part of the planning process with the chosen vendor. However you decide to handle it, make sure the vendor knows in advance what the criteria are so that work may be directed to meet them. Above all, make sure the criteria description is in harmony with the other published work documents you have shared wit the vendor, such as the vendor management plan and the vendor' s own SDP.

Whether your vendor is performing a documentation task for your team, delivering software code, or providing ready-to-plug-in software, there are some things that all acceptance criteria can have in common. We'll look at these now.

Entry Criteria

The process of acceptance verification (or acceptance evaluation or acceptance testing) should not begin until you have determined that things are ready on that front. For this to be case, you should define a minimum set of readiness standards that needs to be in place before the process can move forward. For example, if it is time, as scheduled, for the verification to begin, but you and the vendor team are still wrestling with pending change requests, the acceptance process might be delayed. Based on the work assigned to the vendor, you will need to come up with a list of items that need to be ready in order for you to consider moving forward with acceptance verification. This list will follow closely with the type of work the vendor has been assigned. The main goal of using an entry criteria checklist is to provide an objective means of confirming that a level of quality and completeness exists to make acceptance a practical consideration.

Deliverables List

This item is related to the entry criteria. This is a listing of all products that should be delivered in order for acceptance verification to begin. The list may include such items as software source code, compiler, technical documentation, user documentation, and database tables. This deliverables list will align the expectations of your organization with those of the vendor. You might even consider applying an individual acceptance criterion to each of the items on the deliverables list.

Test Plan

This can be a test plan in the traditional sense of a test plan—that is, a series of software test cases run to measure the consistency of the delivered code against the published requirements. Many times such a test plan will become the major tool for acceptance verification in an organization. But a test plan can also be as simple as a series of inspection steps to make sure a deliverable is up to snuff. With many outsourced projects you will probably need a combination of both: some software test cases and some general inspection steps. Your test plan (or test plans) should be a series of inspection points mapped to your acceptance threshold (the line that separates acceptable and unacceptable). The vendor should know these points well in advance of the actual test run. In fact, if the vendor knows them at the start of the project, it will wisely track progress against these points.

Acceptance Date

As part of overall planning, you should establish a date on which the acceptance verification of each identified deliverable will be conducted. For larger deliverables you might establish a date range. It's common here to actually identify a series of three dates: date of delivery (by the vendor to the prime), date range to carry out the verification test, and date to present an accept/no accept decision (with reasons) to the vendor.

Acceptance Threshold

Just as the vendor deliverables should enter the verification process in a certain condition, they can leave the process only in a certain condition. This is the ultimate acceptance judgment, and it is called a threshold because it allows for a degree of variance from what might be called "perfect," with the understanding that the variances are minor. Naturally, the terms critical errors, major errors, and minor errors can be highly subjective. The acceptance threshold you establish is a way to objectify the weight of these possible outcomes. The idea is to first define what the minimally acceptable performance standard is and then define what measured product variances will result in straying from that standard. One way is to define a series of error levels, detailing critical, major, and minor errors and then deriving a number for each over which acceptance cannot be recommended.

Undoubtedly in the acceptance test process, you and the vendor will come across items that need to be corrected or adjusted. Your job here is to quantify a point at which those corrections/adjustments seriously compromise the integrity of the product being inspected.

Repair Window

As a nod to the possibility that an acceptance verification may uncover issues that push the acceptance threshold past the point of go-ahead, you may consider providing the vendor with a repair window in order to address the issues. Naturally, this window may have to be established after you have performed the inspection as it may depend on the type of problems identified. This step can be seen as a provisional step and is usually invoked when it is clear to all parties that the issues at hand can be readily addressed.

Sign Off

The final step in acceptance verification will come in two forms: If the products are accepted there should be a sign-off indicating this by vendor management, subcontract management, and software project management (and perhaps by your organization's legal contract management people). This will demonstrate final, executive acceptance of the products and the formal completion of work. If the products are unacceptable, you are then in a position to grant an extension or to explore the "failure to perform" clause of the prime/vendor contract. Of course, if you have chosen your vendor carefully and defined and managed the work in a manner consistent with that we have discussed so far in this chapter, failure to perform should be a very rare occurrence, one you are not likely to face.

Level 2 Training for Subcontract Management

The role of subcontractor manager may be spread out over several members on your project team or handled by one person who specializes in this function. As we have seen from the previous sections, the role of subcontractor manager calls for varied set of responsibilities. The person may be involved in vendor selection, in creating a vendor management plan, in documenting acceptance criteria, in managing changes to the scope of the vendor's work, to conducting quality reviews and status reviews. How you spread this responsibility out among the members of your project team will depend on the composition of your team and the type of work you have farmed out to the vendor. Because these responsibilities can prove to be focused on critical project areas, whomever you appoint to handle them should be adequately prepared to perform their duties. This involves appointing people who have the right background or the right level of practical, in-house experience. In order to ensure this, you may have to train your people in the area of subcontract management, specifically in what the project calls for in relation to subcontract management. So far we have talked about the following activity areas: vendor selection process, work plan development, work plan change procedure, SCM review and SQA review procedure, and acceptance verification. Following is a list of potential training topics you may wish to shape in order to prepare your people to function in the realm of subcontract management for your project.

Who: Subcontractor management team

Course: Vendor selection process

When: As hired, or upon assignment

Scope: Training for the manager on how to manage the process of vendor screening and selection when outsource help is required on a project

Type: Direct process training

Waiver: Adequate experience; prior training

Who: Subcontractor management team

Course: Vendor management plan—process and template

When: As hired, or upon assignment

Scope: Training for the manager on how to work with various project team entities to create the vendor management plan, how to facilitate its review and approval, and how to manage vendor activities based on the plan

Type: Direct process training

Waiver: Adequate experience; prior training

Who: Subcontractor management team
             Vendor groups as applicable

Course: Change control process

When: As hired, or upon assignment

Scope: Training for the subcontract manager and members of the vendor project team that instructs them in how to work the project's change control process for introducing change requests

Type: Direct process training

Waiver: Adequate experience; prior training

Who: Subcontractor management team
           Vendor groups as applicable

Course: SQA/SCM review process

When: As hired, or upon assignment

Scope: Training for the subcontract manager and members of the vendor project team that instructs them in how to work with the SQA and SCM teams at various points in the project to prepare for and conduct quality inspections of work products and team activity

Type: Indirect process training

Waiver: Adequate experience; prior training

Who: Subcontractor management team
           Vendor groups as applicable
           Software project management
           Vendor management as applicable

Course: Acceptance testing process

When: As hired, or upon assignment

Scope: Training for all who require it on the formal steps involved in the acceptance testing process

Type: Indirect process training

Waiver: Adequate experience; prior training

A Level 2 Policy for Subcontract Management

So far in this chapter we have discussed the CMM's subcontract management KPA in terms of structure, management processes, and some potential training requirements. As you implement all or a portion of these ideas you see your Level 2 subcontract management program shape into an effective control mechanism for the projects in your shop that outsource portions of their work. But a final element is needed to cement the program's effectiveness for your projects, and that is a policy that sets in place the official mission of the program and its broad duties for your projects.

We discussed policies in Chapter 6 of this book, and that discussion still holds true here. Each of your projects should be guided by a series of policy statements that control your direction of work in various activity areas. You should have policy statements to guide requirements management, project planning, project tracking, software quality assurance, and software configuration management. These policy statements are short summaries covering the mission and objectives of each of these areas.

The policies are important for several reasons. One, they encapsulate acceptable bounds of behavior. Two, they establish high-level goals. And three, and perhaps most important, they show executive endorsement for a project's activities in certain areas. Take a look at Chapter 6 for points on how to create a policy.

You'll need to create a policy for your project that governs the high-level approach to subcontract management. You might want to consider the following base elements to include in your project's subcontract management policy:

- The project will use a defined process to select vendors for outsource assignments.

- The documented commitments associated with the assignment will serve as the basis for tracking vendor progress.

- Both prime contractor and the subcontractor will agree to any change in the commitments before they are adopted.

These three areas cover at a high level what we discussed so far in this chapter. In short, they reinforce the idea that vendor selection will be an objective process (as much as possible) and will be guided by a documented process that implicitly serves to identify qualified vendors. After a vendor is chosen, the details of the work assignment will be documented as a series of commitments (contract and work plan), and then those commitments become the basis for measuring vendor progress on the project. Finally, any changes to the commitments that arise during the course of the project will need to be documented and reviewed by both parties in order to come to a consensus on how to act on each.

You'll notice that these points cover again the general goals of this KPA. Because the use of outside vendors for their expertise and/or economic benefits is becoming more and more common in the software development industry, you will find it beneficial to have a well-thought-out subcontract management program in place. It is also very important to continually measure the performance of this program across multiple projects—each potentially using its own processes—so that you can refine the program and improve on it through experimentation over time.

Supporting Subcontract Management Activity

When you put a conscientious subcontract management program in place for a software development project, you'll find that a series of artifacts will naturally arise out of the activities and processes you undertake. This is especially true if you follow the recommendations we have outlined in this chapter. You can use these artifacts as a means for tracing the history of your program's evolution and as a basis for process improvement. You can also use these artifacts as evidence during a formal CMM assessment that you have worked to operate within recommended CMM guidelines.

Following are some artifacts, falling into four separate areas, that you might consider formalizing for your subcontract management efforts.

Appointment of a Subcontract Manager

To show that you have appointed project team members to handle subcontract management and that you have properly funded the person's job role, you might produce the following: an organizational chart showing the position for the project, a budget showing capital allocations for the job role, a resume for the manager, a staff assignment form for the job role, and a team composition chart.

Training

To show that you have properly trained the manager (or managers) in the role and duties of subcontract management, you might show a series of available courses and for each, any of the following materials: training scope sheet, training invitation, training course material, student hand-out material, and completion certificate.

Process and Management Documents

To help show that you are following a defined set of vendor management processes for the project you might show some of the following: vendor selection process, work proposal, vendor responses, proposal scoring, award notification, vendor contract, vendor SDP, and a copy of the vendor management plan for the project.

Management Materials

Finally, these management materials will help demonstrate consistent progress during the course of the work: status meeting minutes, formal review notes, other communiqués, and measurements taken over the life of the project.

Table 7.1 presents a breakdown of the kinds of artifacts you might wish to develop in order to meet CMM Level 2 Subcontract Management recommendations. These items

Table 7.1 Evidence of Subcontract Management Compliance

KEY PROCESS AREA	ARTIFACTS
Structure	Organizational chart with SubMan role, appointment/assignment forms, capital budget, job descriptions
Processes	Vendor selection process, contract development process, work plan development process, work plan template, vendor SDP review and approval procedure, work plan change procedure, SCM review procedure, SQA review procedure, acceptance verification procedure
Training	For each Course: Training scope sheet, yraining invitation, yraining course material, student hand-out material, completion certificate
Policy	Policy statement, early drafts of statement

address each area of focus: structure, process, training, and policy. As with the other KPAs, this is just a list of suggestions. Your organization may require different items, but these are ones commonly employed.

Summary

We devoted this chapter to a discussion of subcontract management, keeping it separate from the other KPAs, for a couple of reasons. First, many organizations won't have a need to implement this KPA. They do all work in house. Secondly, the reach of subcontract management is different from the other KPAs. The others are internal, impacting your team directly. Subcontract management is more of an outreach program, ensuring that your selected vendors are providing you efforts and products in a planned and manageable fashion.

However, you will have noticed that the regimen of structure, process, training, and policy still applies. The goal with subcontract management is ultimately to blend outside efforts harmoniously with inside efforts.

In a way, our discussion of subcontract management wraps up Part 2 of this book on implementing the CMM. We have now covered the six KPAs of Level 2 and looked at a series of practical examples on how to bring about the model's recommendations in your own shop. Naturally such knowledge is important; but just as important is your commitment to working within the repeatable level, your dedication to looking at what you do, and your ability to improve upon it. That takes patience and time, and a team ready to take that path to quality.

Success in this area should eventually take one into the real of Level 3, the defined level. We'll look at Level 3 in Part 3 of this book.

Table 7.2   Key Practices Fulfilled by Implementing the Concepts in This Chapter

MANAGEMENT AREA	ACTION	KEY PRACTICE
Structure	Create the SubMan role, Fund the role for each project	Ability 1
Process	Vendor selection process, contract development process, work plan development process, work plan template, vendor SDP review and approval procedure, work plan change procedure, SCM review procedure, SQA review procedure, acceptance verification procedure	Activity 1, activity 2, activity 3, activity 4, activity 5, activity 6, measurement 1, verification 1, verification 2, verification 3
Training	Train SubMan in the various processes and practices in the program	Ability 4
Policy	Create SubMan policy	Commitment 1

PART

Three

Level 3:
The Defined Level

CHAPTER 8

Overview of Level 3

Two of the main motivations for moving to Level 3 are the
economies of scale and unification of efforts. A single tool set
becomes available to whole organization, and that tool set
can be centrally maintained.
Cynthia Schnabel, Quality Analyst

In previous chapters we discussed how to implement a Capability Maturity Mode (CMM) Level 2 process improvement environment in your organization. We looked at the six Key Process Areas that are introduced at Level 2, and we looked at the key practices that are typically used to support each of these areas. To help plan a practical implementation strategy we then looked at the structure, process, training, and policies you should consider when shaping a program designed for your group. We also discussed the different kinds of artifacts you might consider creating and using to help you manage the Level 2 environment and, also, to use as evidence that might support a formal assessment should you seek that recognition from the Software Engineering Institute.

In Part 3, we'll look at the concepts and structures that go into a Level 3 program. But before we start to think about Level 3, it's important to briefly revisit the purpose of Level 2. Understanding the one leads to a better understanding of the other.

First, remember that working toward being a Level 2 shop is probably the first step in what is probably a new realm for your organization: software process improvement. Many people mistakenly think that the CMM is a software process improvement (SPI) program in and of itself, but that's not the best way to look at it. You should think of SPI as a larger domain than just CMM. Think of CMM as a framework onto which you can build an effective SPI program. CMM is all about thoughtful, planned process improvement. In order for CMM to be effective in your shop, you have to be committed to it; but first you have to be committed to SPI.

Another thing to remember is that the commitment to SPI doesn't mean that you have to be perfect or complete. CMM is a model based on levels of maturity—in this case process maturity. It assumes that organizations at Level 1 are process immature because they lack the environment in which the organization is self-aware, and that it monitors its activities, measures the results, then tries to improve next time. Pure Level 1 organizations wear blinders in many ways. (I know this firsthand because I ran a Level 1 organization for years.) All these type shops can usually see is the product. They will pull out any stops to get the product out. They often rely on the heroic efforts operating in controlled chaos to pull the job off. They might turn out a good product, close to the schedule and budget, but the odds are against this. And if they get and do it once, there's nothing in place to guarantee they can do it again.

Level 2 shops have moved beyond this frying-pan/fire environment. A Level 2 shop is not just product conscious. You can see the big picture, and your group becomes process-conscious, as well. You understand that part of effective management and a significant part of quality management involves looking at how you create the product, what steps you take, what activities work well, and which ones work poorly. This new realm of organizational consciousness is not a part-time activity, nor is it an objective with a definitive end in sight. It is a new way of doing business. You need to make a long-term commitment to this new awareness, and at Level 2, CMM provides distinct areas that will promote and foster the creation of process-focused activities within your environment.

But don't put too much of a burden on your Level 2 efforts right out of the gate. The idea behind Level 2 structures and activities is not to solve your process/quality problems once and for all. It's to introduce a mechanism that will help you start that process, but it's an effort you grow into. For that reason, remember this: Level 2 is a project-focused SPI program.

Many people read the CMM book and come away thinking that Level 2 is just an organizational solution, and I have seen many organizations implement it as such. That's the wrong approach; it rubs against the true spirit of CMM. At Level 2, CMM assumes that the organization is not mature enough to adopt an organizational solution regarding its software development and management processes—that's too much to do all at once. The true intention at Level 2 is very different, and much smaller in scope. At Level 2, CMM wants you to implement processes only on the different projects you are working on. The processes used for one project can be different—even radically different—from the processes used on another project. The only real requirement is that the processes are documented, followed, and then measured. You should feel free to experiment from project to project. In fact Level 2, called the Repeatable Level, is an opportunity for experimentation. In the hard sciences, experimentation and repetition are the hallmarks of discovery. You try out an idea, see how it works, improve it, then try it again.

It's hard for many to grasp, but at Level 2 success is not all-important—learning is. Level 2 should help your organization to reach a gradual understanding of what processes work best for it in the management and control of software development efforts. The six Key Process Areas of Level 2 give you a framework for the essence of repeatability. For each project you plan, execute according to plan, and measure. Then analyze the measurements, and improve by discarding the useless and the ineffective, keeping and refining the good, and then repeating on the next project.

Most organizations that adopt CMM as their model for software process improvement are not what you would call "pure" Level 1 shops. If you know what CMM is and you can appreciate its value, chances are you are not wholly process absent. In the majority of the organizations I have worked with to shape a Level 2 program I found that most of the Level 2 characteristics were in place to one degree or another. That's good in that these shops start off on the CMM journey already pretty much on the right track. But there's something of a negative side to this also: The shops that find themselves close to their goal, often by accident, want to hop to it and get to the end of the trail as quickly as possible. In more than a few organizations—major Fortune 500 companies at that—I have found that executive bonus plans have been tied to receiving Level 2 certification or Level 3 certification within x amount of time. That's like (with slight exaggeration) telling a freshman college class that they all have exactly four years to finish their degrees, and if anyone varies from that path they all flunk.

The important idea here is that process improvement, within CMM or without, is not a race. Speed is irrelevant, and in many places a push to the end goal might actually hinder progress. It takes time to move from the Initial Level to smooth operation at the Repeatable Level. How long? That depends of course on your own environment. But taking a year, 14 months, even two years to reach Level 2 maturity is not uncommon. You could even argue that the longer it takes you to get there (the more you experiment, the more you refine) the better off you'll be when you arrive.

Time is involved (and is important here) because it takes time to learn, to discover what works best for your projects and, ultimately, your organization as a whole. To apply CMM in a conscientious fashion at Level 2 requires that you experiment across many projects, and to give each one close and continuous scrutiny. This way, over time, you will slowly derive a foundation of core processes proven effective on you projects. You will have reached full Level 2 maturity at this stage and can then begin moving up the SPI ladder and implementing a Level 3 program.

Another reason to spend time developing Level 2 competencies is that you will have to develop not just new habits and new ways of doing business, but you will have to implement a solid infrastructure to support Level 2 activities. You will have to design, fund, and shape this new infrastructure until it becomes a natural part of the fabric of your development culture. At first, you may think of this as pure overhead, but in time you will see its value and it will begin to pay dividends in terms of better planning, increased predictability, and improved quality.

For example (and this is very common even in advanced Level 1 shops), you will probably have to create and fund a new software quality assurance position/team within your shop. This will involve developing the SQA role, appointing staff, documenting processes, training staff, setting up work resources, and so forth. That in itself, apart from the effort it takes to refine the role, takes time. Same thing for configuration management, and requirements management, project planning, project tracking, and subcontract management. It takes time to set each of these areas up, get their responsibilities and activities in place, and then set them out on their missions. Setting this infrastructure in place and then combining it with a conscientious program of measurements and refinement is your starting point down the road to quality improvement.

As mentioned back in the Introduction, the high-level goal of software process improvement is to reduce risk and increase predictability. This will lead to strong quality control. Risk of course leads to poor quality; where risk is high, you are less in control. When risk is low you are more in control; you can better predict what will happen down the road.

All your problems don't magically go away when you implement a Level 2 program. As you implement greater quality controls, risk will shrink and predictability will expand. In terms of CMM, operating at Level 1 will entail higher risk and lower predictability; operating at Levels 4 and 5 will mean levels of low risk and high predictability. If you are implementing a Level 2 program, you will still have to deal with a level of risk; not everything at this stage is solidly predictable. The idea is to begin the journey of process improvement. While achieving Level 2 is a notable accomplishment for any software development shop, it's not really what you would think of as a typical ending point. Level 2 is project-oriented, but out of the Level 2 effort you should move toward identifying and the adopting a set of effective core processes that you can use to standardize your whole organization. This is what Level 3 is all about.

Parallel Implementation at Level 2

When you implement a Level 2 program, you are setting in place the foundation on which you can build a manageable software process improvement methodology. The six KPAs defined in CMM for Level 2 each serve a specific role in project management. What you should notice about each is that you can, to a large degree, construct each KPA independently of the others. For example, though Requirements Management and Configuration Management both help the project stay on track and guard project integrity, the two KPAs do not in essence rely on one another to function. You can build them separately as you shape your Level 2 program. This is true for the other KPAs at Level 2 as well (except for SQA, which needs the others in place first before it can take full shape). You are pretty much free to develop each KPA independently of the other, in parallel if you wish.

This parallel/complementary quality helps you establish Level 2 with efficiency. You set the pillars in place to support process improvement on your projects. But things change when you are ready to move to Level 3.

CMM labels Level 3 the "defined" level. It is at this point within the model that your organization has reached a level of process maturity where you can establish organization-wide software development processes. By this stage your organization, heretofore operating at Level 2, will have had considerable experience trying out software processes and management practices, refining them, and gradually shaping them into a set of methodologies proven over time to be effective. At Level 3 you are able to define what your organizational processes are (what they have become), and you can implement a structure to manage them from an organizational level.

At Level 3 you don't jettison anything you developed for Level 2; you build on it. The six original KPAs that you shaped into structured management areas remain intact throughout your Level 3 development. The main activities you'll engage in at Level 3 are centered on efforts to create an organization support structure that puts in place controls to help you institutionalize, manage, and further refine the processes you have created.

Note this difference between the work you do at Level 2 and at Level 3. The KPAs at Level 2 can be created, for all practicality, in parallel (with the possible exception of SQA). The KPAs at Level 3, however, are more sequential; one relies directly on the presence of the other. At this level some things have to be in place first before others can occur.

Key Process Areas at Level 3

There are seven Key Process Areas at Level 3. Roughly grouped into the order in which each should occur, they are as follows:

- Organization Process Focus
- Organization Process Definition
- Training Program
- Integrated Software Management
- Software Product Engineering
- Intergroup Coordination
- Peer Reviews

Let's take a high-level look at each.

Organization Process Focus

As a practical matter, this is the first KPA you should implement at Level 3. The other KPAs that follow rely in large part on the operations within this area. The label "Organization Process Focus" means pretty much what it says. When you begin to operate as a Level 3 organization you have reached a stage where you can institutionalize (make standard) your software development processes and management activities. You begin to align all project activities along the same lines. In order to do this you need to create a structure to support the management of your processes from the organizational level.

It is at this level that you will establish within your shop the group/entity generally responsible for this management: the Software Engineering Process Group (that's just the CMM name; you can call it anything you want). The SEPG will work to make sure that the standard software processes are available to the entire organization and that they are maintained, evaluated, and refined in a coordinated manner.

CMM cites three general goals for this KPA:

Goal 1: The activities for organizational software process improvement are institutionalized to support a defined process.

Goal 2: Strengths and weaknesses of the organization's software processes are identified.

Goal 3: Software process definition and improvement are coordinated across the organization.[1]

Organization Process Definition

This KPA is closely tied to the previous one. The SEPG created for Organization Process Focus is set into place to care for (to manage, evaluate, refine) the software processes and management activities on which you have standardized. This KPA is in place to make sure that the standards are formally documented, that they are made available, through whatever mechanism, to those team members who need access to them, and that methodologies are in place that guide how the defined process is maintained.

CMM cites three general goals for this KPA:

Goal 1: The activities for organizational software process definition are institutionalized to support a defined process.

Goal 2: A set of standard software processes for the organization is established and maintained.

Goal 3: Assets related to the organization's set of standard software processes are available to software projects.[2]

Training Program

When you establish an organization-wide software development process, you will not be able to carry it out unless your staff is properly trained in its workings. Training becomes very important at Level 3 (it also plays a significant role at Level 2). The idea here is to establish a company-wide training program that will educate your workers on the details of your software process development methodology and will do so in a consistent manner with existing employees as well as new ones. You will need to train your people in two general areas: how to use the defined software processes and how to perform the specific technical and managerial activities they have been assigned.

CMM cites three general goals for this KPA:

Goal 1: The activities for organizational software training are institutionalized to support a defined process.

Goal 2: Training that supports the organization's software process assets is provided.

Goal 3: Training to perform the software management and technical roles is coordinated across the organization.[3]

Integrated Software Management

The entire organization will use the defined software processes (DSP) to plan and manage software projects. This KPA deals with software development planning. It's really an extension of the Level 2 KPA, Software Project Planning. The idea here is simple: All new projects will use the defined software processes, but not all projects are alike. Size, scope, and mission may vary extensively from project to project. The organization needs to establish guidelines for tailoring the DSP to the specific needs of each project. In addition, the organization must also provide guidelines for the way software project status and issues are communicated to other arms of the project team and guidelines by which risks to the software project can be managed.

CMM cites four general goals for this KPA:

Goal 1: The activities for managing the software project are institutionalized to support the project's defined software process.

Goal 2: The project's defined software process is tailored from the organization's set of standard software processes.

Goal 3: Management of the software project is coordinated with the rest of the project and organization.

Goal 4: Software project risks are managed.[4]

Software Product Engineering

This KPA flows naturally out of Integrated Software Management, just as Project Tracking and Oversight flows naturally out of Project Planning at Level 2. And we can view Software Product Engineering as a more robust form of Project Tracking and Oversight. The focus of this KPA is to generate and maintain the software management procedures necessary to control the development, verification, and delivery of the project's software products. Included in this KPA are specific steps that shape how the defined software processes are actually implemented for the project.

CMM cites four general goals for this KPA:

Goal 1: The activities for software product engineering are institutionalized to support the project's defined software process.

Goal 2: Software work products of the project are developed and maintained that are kept consistent with each other.

Goal 3: Software work products are verified and validated against their requirements.

Goal 4: Software products and applicable support are delivered to the customer and/or end users.[5]

Intergroup Coordination

This KPA is related to and complementary to the Peer Review KPA that follows. Both are in place to enhance communication across various groups and to facilitate the coordination of activities across the groups. You can think of Intergroup Coordination as management coordination and Peer Review as technical coordination. For this KPA you'll establish procedures to guide formal work coordination across all project functions, including all disciplines, groups, or teams involved in the overall project.

CMM cites three general goals for this KPA:

Goal 1: The activities for project interface coordination are institutionalized to support the project's defined software process.

Goal 2: Commitments among project functions are established and maintained.

Goal 3: Activities among project functions are coordinated.[6]

Peer Reviews

The last KPA for Level 3 is Peer Reviews. Here the organization begins to work proactively on defect prevention. (This activity is further expanded at Level 4.) Peer review is a common practice in almost all engineering organizations. Level 3 organizations establish peer review procedures and policies so that work products, prior to being approved, are reviewed for technical integrity with a view to spot and remove defects up front. To do this, people knowledgeable of the material to be reviewed (peers) must have an opportunity for review, a mechanism for feedback, and a process for incorporating needed changes.

CMM cites three general goals for this KPA:

Goal 1: The activities for peer reviews are institutionalized to support the project's defined software process.

Goal 2: Software work products are reviewed by the producer's peers.

Goal 3: Defects in software work products are removed early in the software life cycle.[7]

Key Practice Areas at Level 3

Like Chapter 1, this chapter is designed to give you a high-level view of the Capability Maturity Model for Level 3. We'll cite each of the commitments, abilities, activities, measurements, and verifications that typically accompany a Level 3 operation. In Chapter 1, I gave an introduction to the CMM's use of commitments, abilities, activities, measurement, and verification (CAAMV) as a way to structure each Key Process Area. If you're jumping around in this book and you missed that explanation, you'll want to revisit it before getting too far into Level 3 definitions. Just as we did in Chapter 1, in this chapter we'll look at all of the commitments, abilities, activities, measurements, and verifications cited in the Maturity Model for Level 3. In later chapters we'll get into what's needed to actually put these attributes into operation, but for now it'll suffice to look at each to establish the scope and direction of the Level 3 effort.

The first thing you should notice as you read through the attributes for each of the KPAs is that, even more so than at Level 2, these KPAs are structured in a common manner.

To begin with, look at the commonality across the commitments for each KPA. Basically, they are the same for each KPA, with perhaps minor differences. In essence they are all alike; they all seek to accomplish roughly the same things. To begin with, they each call for the existence of a policy to show executive support for the goals of the KPA. Then, they might call for some form of further executive sponsorship or support of the KPA.

The abilities defined for each KPA at Level 3 are just as consistent. Four abilities are cited for each KPA, and they are alike across KPAs. Basically, the attributes call for you to establish and maintain a plan or process to support the KPA, provide adequate resources and funding for the KPA, assign responsibility and authority to manage the functions of the KPA, and train people as needed to support the KPA.

You'll see the same consistency with measurements and verifications across the KPAs. Only the activities defined for each KPA differ across KPAs.

Let's take a look now at the CAAMV structure of Level 3.

Organization Process Focus

To help establish and define an organization-wide focus on software process management and improvement, the following set of qualities has been defined for Level 3.

Commitment to Perform

To show that your organization is committed to an organization-wide focus on software process management and improvement, you should create a written policy that documents this commitment. The policy should be signed by executive management and made easily and readily available to members of the organization. You should also, through some official capacity, establish a sponsorship avenue for process-related activities. For tips on writing these policies for your organizations, take a look at Chapter 6.

> **Commitment 1:** Senior management establishes and maintains the written organizational policy for organizational software process improvement.

> **Commitment 2:** Senior management sponsors organizational software process improvement activities.[8]

Ability to Perform

Four abilities are defined for Organization Process Focus. First, you should create and maintain the plan used to establish the focus on process in your organization. Next, you should have a process or procedure used to establish and appoint process program responsibility. Adequate funding and resources should be made available to support the process maintenance role, and the people who will serve in this role should be trained as needed.

> **Ability 1:** Establish and maintain the organization's software process improvement plan.

> **Ability 2:** Allocate adequate resources and funding for organizational software process improvement.

> **Ability 3:** Assign responsibility and authority for organizational software process improvement.

> **Ability 4:** Train the people performing or supporting organizational software process improvement as required and needed.[9]

Activities Performed

Six activities are designed for Organization Process Focus. The purpose of these activities is to create an environment in which the organization can establish and maintain a software process improvement methodology. The activities help the organization create its processes, assess them periodically, coordinate changes, and disseminate changes to the workers at large.

Activity 1: Perform the activities for organizational software process improvement according to a defined process.

Activity 2: Appraise the organization's software processes to identify strengths and weaknesses periodically and as needed.

Activity 3: Establish and maintain action plans to address the findings of the software process appraisals.

Activity 4: Coordinate implementation of software process action plans across the organization.

Activity 5: Coordinate the deployment of the organization's software process assets.

Activity 6: Coordinate organizational learning on the software process.[10]

Measurement and Analysis

To measure the effectiveness of the Organization Process Focus activities, you should take an active series of measurements that cover these activities. These measurements, which should be meaningful and helpful to you, can be used in future process improvement evaluations. For example, you might record such data as the number and types of projects that have used the standardized process set, the number and versions of processes contained in the standardized process library, the number and kinds of meetings held to manage the process definitions, and the time and cost involved in process management activities.

Measurement 1: Define, collect, and analyze measures to provide insight into the performance of the activities for organizational software process improvement.[11]

Verifying Implementation

This use and the role of verification are very straightforward. From time to time, to ensure validity and effectiveness, executive management, project management, and sometimes SQA should meet with representatives of the Organization Process Focus function and review its mission, processes, and activities. The goal here is for thorough reviews on a periodic basis, reviews that can then be used as a basis for process improvement.

Verification 1: Objectively review designated activities of organizational software process improvement for adherence to specified requirements, plans, processes, standards, and procedures.

Verification 2: Objectively review designated software work products of organizational software process improvement for adherence to specified standards and requirements.

Verification 3: Review the activities for organizational software process improvement with senior management periodically and as needed.[12]

Organization Process Definition

For Organization Process Definition, the following are set in place so that your organization is able to create, manage, and maintain a set of standardized software processes that are used by the entire organization for managing software development projects.

Commitment to Perform

To show that your organization is committed to implementing and managing a defined software process set, you should create a written policy that documents this commitment. You should also establish an avenue for executive support of the activities for definition and maintenance. The policy should be signed by executive management and made easily and readily available to members of the organization. For tips on writing these policies for your organizations, take a look at Chapter 6.

Commitment 1: Senior management establishes and maintains the written organizational policy for organizational software process definition.

Commitment 2: Senior management sponsors the activities for organizational software process definition.[13]

Ability to Perform

This KPA, Organization Process Definition, is supported by four abilities. First, you should create and maintain the plan used to create, manage, and maintain the standardized software development processes. Next, you should have a process or procedure to establish and appoint process definition management responsibility. Adequate funding and resources should be made available to support the process maintenance role, and the people who will serve in this role should be trained as needed.

Ability 1: Establish and maintain the plan for organizational software process definition.

Ability 2: Obtain adequate resources and funding for organizational software process definition.

Ability 3: Assign responsibility and authority for organizational software process definition.

Ability 4: Train the people performing or supporting organizational software process definition as required and needed.[14]

Activities Performed

Six activities are designed for Organization Process Definition. These activities are closely tied to those for Organization Process Focus. The activities here provide a framework around which the organization can makes it processes available to the various projects within the shop. These activities support the maintenance of the processes, the definition of acceptable development life cycles, the creation of guides to tailor processes for projects, and the maintenance of a process library to which workers have access.

Activity 1: Perform the activities for organizational software process definition according to a defined process.

Activity 2: Establish and maintain the organization's set of standard software processes.

Activity 3: Establish and maintain descriptions of the software life cycle models approved for use by the projects.

Activity 4: Establish and maintain the tailoring guidelines for the organization's set of standard software processes.

Activity 5: Establish and maintain the organization's software measurement database.

Activity 6: Establish and maintain the organization's library of software process-related documentation.[15]

Measurement and Analysis

To measure the effectiveness of the Organization Process Definition activities, you should take an active series of measurements that cover these activities. These measurements, which should be meaningful and helpful to you, can be used in future process improvement evaluations. For example, you might record such data as the number and types of projects that have used the standardized process set, the number and versions of processes contained in the standardized process library, the number and kinds of meetings held to manage the process definitions, and the time and cost involved in process management activities.

Measurement 1: Define, collect, and analyze measures to provide insight into the performance of the activities for organizational software process definition.[16]

Verifying Implementation

This use and the role of verification are very straightforward. From time to time, to ensure validity and effectiveness, executive management, project management, and sometimes SQA should meet with representatives of the Organization Process Definition function and review its mission, processes, and activities. The goal here is thorough reviews on a periodic basis, reviews that can then be used as a basis for process improvement.

Verification 1: Objectively review designated activities of organizational software process definition for adherence to specified requirements, plans, processes, standards, and procedures.

Verification 2: Objectively review designated software work products of organizational software process definition for adherence to specified standards and requirements.

Verification 3: Review the activities for organizational software process definition with senior management periodically and as needed.[17]

Training Program

For the Training Program KPA, the following are set in place so that your organization is able to create, manage, and maintain an interdisciplinary training program that prepares workers both to perform their technical duties and to operate within the process bounds of the organization.

Commitment to Perform

To show that your organization is committed to the implementation of an organization-wide training program, you should create a written policy that documents this commitment. The policy should be signed by executive management and made easily and readily available to members of the organization. For tips on writing these policies for your organizations, take a look at Chapter 6.

Commitment 1: Senior management establishes and maintains the written organizational policy for software training.

Commitment 2: Senior management sponsors organizational software training.[18]

Ability to Perform

The Level 3 Training Program has been defined around a set of four abilities. First, you should create and maintain an overall Training Program plan for use by the organization as a whole. Next, you should have a process or procedure to be used to establish and appoint Training Program management responsibility. Adequate funding and resources should be made available to support the training role, and the people who will serve as trainers should be trained in their educational roles.

Ability 1: Establish and maintain the plan for organizational software training.

Ability 2: Allocate adequate resources and funding for organizational software training.

Ability 3: Assign responsibility and authority for organizational software training.

Ability 4: Train the people performing or supporting organizational software training as required and needed.[19]

Activities Performed

Six activities are designed for the Training Program. These activities help establish and maintain an effective corporate training program for your IT group. They call for you to create a formal training program plan, identify specific training needs in your organization, prepare appropriate curriculums and training support materials, develop skilled trainers, and keep appropriate training records.

Activity 1: Perform organizational software training according to a defined process.

Activity 2: Identify the software training needs of the organization.

Activity 3: Determine the organizational training support needed to address the specific training needs of software projects and support groups.

Activity 4: Establish and maintain software-training materials that address the needs of the organization.

Activity 5: Train people in the software skills needed to perform their roles.

Activity 6: Establish and maintain training records for the organization.[20]

Measurement and Analysis

In order for you to evaluate the use and effectiveness of your training program activities, you should take an active series of measurements over time for the program. These measurements, which should be meaningful and helpful to you, can be used in future process improvement evaluations. For example, for a given span of time, you might record such data as the number of training courses offered, the types, the number of participants in each class, the popularity of certain classes, the cost and effort associated with certain classes, and student ratings of courses and instructors.

Measurement 1: Define, collect, and analyze measures to provide insight into the performance of the activities for organizational software training.[21]

Verifying Implementation

This use and the role of verification are very straightforward. From time to time, to ensure validity and effectiveness, executive management, project management, and sometimes SQA should meet with representatives of the Training Program function and review its mission, processes, and activities. The goal here is for thorough reviews on a periodic basis, reviews that can then be used as a basis for process improvement.

Verification 1: Objectively review designated activities for organizational software training for adherence to specified requirements, plans, processes, standards, and procedures.

Verification 2: Objectively review designated work products of organizational software training for adherence to specified requirements and standards.

Verification 3: Review the activities for organizational software training with senior management periodically and as needed.[22]

Integrated Software Management

For Integrated Software Management, the following are set in place so that software project planning efforts have access to a set of standardized software processes that may be custom tailored to the needs of the software project. This KPA is an extension of the Level 2 KPA, Software Project Planning.

Commitment to Perform

To show that your organization, from the executive level on down, is committed to the implementation of Integrated Software Management practices, you should create a written policy that documents this commitment. The policy should be signed by management and made easily and readily available to members of the organization. For tips on writing these policies for your organizations, take a look at Chapter 6.

> **Commitment 1:** Senior management establishes and maintains the written organizational policy for managing the software project.[23]

Ability to Perform

Integrated Software Management has been defined around a set of four abilities. First, you should create and maintain a plan for use by the organization as a whole to tailor the standard software process set to the needs of the individual project. Next, you should have a process or procedure to be used to establish and appoint ISM management responsibility. Adequate funding and resources should be made available to support the ISM role, and the people who will serve as software managers should be trained in ISM-specific duties.

> **Ability 1:** Establish and maintain the plan for managing the software project.
>
> **Ability 2:** Allocate adequate resources and funding for managing the software project.
>
> **Ability 3:** Assign responsibility and authority for managing the software project.
>
> **Ability 4:** Train the people performing or supporting software project management as required and needed.[24]

Activities Performed

Eight activities are designed for Integrated Software Management. These activities are set in place to create an environment in which projects can be managed in a similar fashion, with the tools in place to custom tailor activity for the project and manage risks that might arise during the course of the project.

> **Activity 1:** Perform the activities for managing the software project according to the project's defined software process.
>
> **Activity 2:** Establish and maintain the project's defined software process.
>
> **Activity 3:** Ensure that the project's defined software process is appropriately reflected in the software development plan.
>
> **Activity 4:** Provide training needed to perform the project's defined software process.
>
> **Activity 5:** Coordinate management of the software project with the management of the rest of the project and organization.
>
> **Activity 6:** Establish and maintain mitigation strategies for the software project risks.

      Activity 7: Mitigate the software project risks.

      Activity 8: Contribute to the organization's software process assets.[25]

Measurement and Analysis

For Integrated Software Management, you should collect measurements to evaluate the use and effectiveness of that group's activities. These measurements, which should be meaningful and helpful to you, can be used in future process improvement evaluations. For example, for a given project you might record such data as the number of process changes made to tailor a specific effort, the amount of management time devoted to mitigating risk, and the total amount of process management time spent on the project.

      Measurement 1: Define, collect, and analyze measures to provide insight into the performance of the activities for managing the software project.[26]

Verifying Implementation

This use and role of verification is very straightforward. From time to time, to ensure validity and effectiveness, executive management, project management, and sometimes SQA should meet with representatives of the Integrated Software Management function and review its mission, processes, and activities. The goal here is for thorough reviews on a periodic basis, reviews that can then be used as a basis for process improvement.

      Verification 1: Objectively review designated activities of managing the software project for adherence to specified requirements, plans, processes, standards, and procedures.

      Verification 2: Objectively review designated software work products of managing the software project for adherence to specified standards and requirements.

      Verification 3: Review the activities for managing the software project with senior management periodically and as needed.

      Verification 4: Review the activities for managing the software project with the project manager periodically and as needed.[27]

Software Product Engineering

For Software Product Engineering, the following are set in place so that development efforts across the organization will adhere to an established regimen for managing software development. This KPA is an extension of the Level 2 KPA, Software Project Tracking and Oversight.

Commitment to Perform

To show that your organization, from the executive level on down, is committed to the process of Software Product Engineering you should create a written policy that documents this commitment. The policy should be signed by management and made easily and readily available to members of the organization. For tips on writing these policies for your organizations, take a look at Chapter 6.

> **Commitment 1:** Senior management establishes and maintains the written organizational policy for performing software product engineering.[28]

Ability to Perform

To conduct the Software Product Engineering activities effectively your organization should account for four abilities have been defined to support this KPA at Level 3. First, you should create and maintain a plan or process for use by the organization as a whole to manage software engineering projects. This plan or process will have arisen out of your Level 2 Software Project Tracking and Oversight process. Next, you should have a process or procedure in place to appoint SPE responsibilities. Adequate funding and resources should be made available to support software engineering functions, and the people who will serve as part of the software engineering team should be trained as appropriate in technical and process matters.

> **Ability 1:** Establish and maintain the plan for performing software product engineering.
>
> **Ability 2:** Allocate adequate resources and funding for performing software product engineering.
>
> **Ability 3:** Assign responsibility and authority for performing software product engineering.
>
> **Ability 4:** Train the people performing or supporting software product engineering as required and needed.[29]

Activities Performed

There are 11 activities designed for Software Product Engineering. These activities are closely related to those of Integrated Software Management, and they are focused on consistent project management across the organization. These activities guide the management of a project through a series of common and defined stages (defined in the ISM KPA). These include conducting requirements reviews, maintaining work products related to requirements, designs, and source code, conducting thorough product testing, and delivering and supporting the product as appropriate to the project.

> **Activity 1:** Perform the activities for software product engineering according to the project's defined software process.
>
> **Activity 2:** Establish and maintain an understanding of the customer requirements for the software project as appropriate.
>
> **Activity 3:** Develop and maintain the software requirements.
>
> **Activity 4:** Develop and maintain the software design.
>
> **Activity 5:** Develop and maintain the software code.
>
> **Activity 6:** Perform integration testing of the software.

Activity 7: Perform system testing of the software.

Activity 8: Perform acceptance testing of the software.

Activity 9: Develop and maintain the documentation that will be used to install, operate, and maintain the software.

Activity 10: Package and deliver the software to the customer as appropriate.

Activity 11: Support the operation and use of the software as appropriate.[30]

Measurement and Analysis

To better evaluate the use and effectiveness of your software product engineering activities, you should take an active series of measurements over the life of a software project. These measurements, which should be meaningful and helpful to you, can be used in future process improvement evaluations. For example, for a given project you might record such data as the number of change requests that came in during a set period of time, the number of modules or lines of code the project produced, the time and cost required to manage the effort, and the number and types of unexpected issues that arose during the life of the project.

Measurement 1: Define, collect, and analyze measures to provide insight into the performance of the activities for software product engineering.[31]

Verifying Implementation

This use and the role of verification are very straightforward. From time to time, to ensure validity and effectiveness, executive management, project management, and sometimes SQA should meet with representatives of the Software Product Engineering function and review its mission, processes, and activities. The goal here is thorough reviews on a periodic basis, reviews that can then be used as a basis for process improvement.

Verification 1: Objectively review designated activities of software product engineering for adherence to specified requirements, plans, processes, standards, and procedures.

Verification 2: Objectively review designated work products of software product engineering for adherence to specified requirements and standards.

Verification 3: Review activities for software product engineering with senior management periodically and as needed.

Verification 4: Review the activities for software product engineering with the project manager periodically and as needed.[32]

Intergroup Coordination

For Intergroup Coordination, the following are set in place so that, for each project, each functional group therein has access to the proper channels so that intergroup communication and activity coordination can easily take place.

Commitment to Perform

To show that your organization, from the executive level on down, is committed to the processes for Intergroup Coordination you should create a written policy that documents this commitment. The policy should be signed by management and made easily and readily available to members of the organization. For tips on writing these policies for your organizations, take a look at Chapter 6.

> **Commitment 1:** Senior management establishes and maintains the written organizational policy for project interface coordination.[33]

Ability to Perform

Four abilities have been defined to support Intergroup Coordination. First, you should create and maintain a plan or process for use by the organization as a whole to manage intergroup coordination. Next, you should have a process or procedure to be used to establish and appoint IC points of contact and status participation. Adequate funding and resources should be made available to support IC functions, and the people who will serve as group points of contact should be trained in IC-specific duties.

> **Ability 1:** Establish and maintain the plan for project interface coordination.

> **Ability 2:** Allocate adequate resources and funding for project interface coordination.

> **Ability 3:** Assign responsibility and authority for project interface coordination.

> **Ability 4:** Train the people performing or supporting project interface coordination as required and needed.[34]

Activities Performed

Six activities are designed for Intergroup Coordination. They all have to deal with the way the various members of a development project can communicate and coordinate their activities in an efficient and effective manner. The activities are designed to facilitate group interchanges with a view to raise pertinent issues and provide an avenue for their resolution.

> **Activity 1:** Perform the activities for project interface coordination according to the project's defined software process.

> **Activity 2:** Participate with other project functions to establish and maintain an understanding of the customer requirements.

> **Activity 3:** Participate with other project functions to coordinate technical activities.

> **Activity 4:** Participate with other project functions to identify, negotiate, and track critical project coordination dependencies and commitments.

> **Activity 5:** Ensure that work products produced to satisfy project coordination commitments meet the needs of the receiving functions.

> **Activity 6:** Resolve project coordination issues with the project functions.[35]

Measurement and Analysis

In order for you to evaluate the use and effectiveness of your intergroup coordination activities, you should take an active series of measurements over the life of a software project. These measurements, which should be meaningful and helpful to you, can be used in future process improvement evaluations. For example, for a given project you might record such data as the number of coordination meetings conducted for a project, the types and number of issues introduced and resolved, and the time and cost involved in the coordination activities.

> **Measurement 1:** Define, collect, and analyze measures to provide insight into the performance of the activities for project interface coordination.[36]

Verifying Implementation

This use and role of verification is very straightforward. From time to time, to ensure validity and effectiveness, executive management, project management, and sometimes SQA should meet with representatives of the Intergroup Coordination function and review its mission, processes, and activities. The goal here is thorough reviews on a periodic basis, reviews that can then be used as a basis for process improvement.

> **Verification 1:** Objectively review designated activities of project interface coordination for adherence to specified requirements, plans, processes, standards, and procedures.

> **Verification 2:** Objectively review designated work products of project interface coordination for adherence to specified requirements and standards.

> **Verification 3:** Review the activities for project interface coordination with senior management periodically and as needed.

> **Verification 4:** Review the activities for project interface coordination with the project manager periodically and as needed.[37]

Peer Reviews

For Peer Reviews, the following are set in place so that each project has a mechanism it can use to identify and remove defects early in the development process.

Commitment to Perform

To show that your organization, from the executive level on down, is committed to the process and purpose of Peer Reviews, you should create a written policy that documents this commitment. The policy should be signed by management and made easily and readily available to members of the organization. For tips on writing these policies for your organizations, take a look at Chapter 6.

> **Commitment 1:** Senior management establishes and maintains the written organizational policy for performing peer reviews.[38]

Ability to Perform

CMM wants to see four abilities in place to make the Peer Reviews activities relevant and effective. First and foremost, you should create and maintain the plan (or process) for conducting peer reviews. Next, you should have a process or procedure to establish and appoint peer review participation. Adequate funding and resources should be made available to support the function of peer reviews, and the people who will participate in peer reviews should be trained in peer review-specific duties.

Ability 1: Establish and maintain the plan for performing peer reviews.

Ability 2: Allocate adequate resources and funding for performing peer reviews.

Ability 3: Assign responsibility and authority for performing peer reviews.

Ability 4: Train the people performing or supporting peer reviews as required and needed.[39]

Activities Performed

Five activities are designed for Peer Review. The purpose of these activities is to provide an avenue by which the software development team can review work to find defects as early in the process as practical and then remove the defects. Peer Review activities address this by calling for a process by which the reviews are prepared for, conducted, and then used to document problems and their accepted resolutions.

Activity 1: Perform the activities for peer reviews according to the project's defined software process.

Activity 2: Prepare for the peer reviews of the software work products.

Activity 3: Conduct peer reviews of the software work products.

Activity 4: Address the action items identified in the peer reviews of the software work products.

Activity 5: Record data on the preparation, conduct, and results of the peer reviews of the software work products.[40]

Measurement and Analysis

In order for you to evaluate the use and effectiveness of your peer review process, you should take an active series of peer review measurements over the life of a software project. These measurements, which should be meaningful and helpful to you, can be used in software process evaluations. For example, for a given project you might record such data as the number and types of peer reviews held for the project, the number and types of defects uncovered during the different peer reviews, and how much time and cost were involved in peer review activities.

Measurement 1: Define, collect, and analyze measures to provide insight into the performance of the activities for peer reviews.[41]

Verifying Implementation

This use and the role of verification are very straightforward. From time to time, to ensure validity and effectiveness, executive management, project management, and sometimes SQA should meet with representatives of the Peer Review function and review its mission, processes, and activities. The goal here is thorough reviews on a periodic basis, reviews that can then be used as a basis for process improvement.

Verification 1: Objectively review designated activities of peer reviews for adherence to specified requirements, plans, processes, standards, and procedures.

Verification 2: Objectively review designated work products of peer reviews for adherence to specified requirements and standards.

Verification 3: Review the activities for peer reviews with senior management periodically and as needed.

Verification 4: Review the activities for peer reviews with the project manager periodically and as needed.[42]

Summary

At the end of Chapter 1, we discussed a way to implement the commitments, abilities, activities, measurements, and verifications the CMM calls for at Level 2. The approach was pretty uncomplicated: Most of the KPAs (with the sole exception of SQA) could be created, for the sake of practicality, pretty much independently of each other. We then moved our effort under the SPTP umbrella: Structure, Process, Training, Policy. For each KPA, we extracted those CAAMV attributes that supported structure or process or training or policy, and from that we shaped how we would shape a Level 2 environment and fulfill the Level 2 goals.

We're going to take a slightly different approach for Level 3. The seven KPAs for the Defined level are not as cleanly separate as the ones for Level 2. If you look at them you will see that the first three fall under a heading we might call "structural," while the final four fall under a heading we might term "procedural." Naturally, you can't have the procedure without first having the structure, so in the next section we'll look at how to create and implement a valid environment for Organization Process Focus, Organization Process Definition, and Training Program. Compared to the other KPAs at Level 3 these are more static in nature. They are defined, used, then refined over time. They represent the foundation you need in place to support Level 3 activities.

Most of those activities—at least in the sense of software development—take place within the four remaining KPAs: Integrated Software Management, Software Product Engineering, Intergroup Coordination, and Peer Reviews. These are the active KPAs, those efforts that use what Organization Process Focus, Organization Process Definition, and Training Program have put into place. These are ongoing, dynamic areas of effort, and from them come the data and results needed to refine and improve the core organizational structure.

We'll look at ways to implement these dynamic KPAs, but first a look at the foundation.

CHAPTER 9

Focusing on Organizational Process Improvement

At Level 3 the entire organization becomes focused on process improvement. It's an important step up the maturity scale. At this point your teams have developed a set of proven processes and practices that have been shown to work over time and across a wide variety of projects. The challenge now is to gather these into a single program and then to implement it across the organization, with the idea of measurement and improvement still in mind.
Alan Waklin, Micronetix Corporation

An IT shop operating at Level 2 makes continuous and conscientious efforts at process improvement. But while this commitment is typically organization-wide, at Level 2 the efforts are uncoordinated. They need to be uncoordinated. The focus at Level 2 is on discovering what processes work best for the array of projects your shop undertakes. Therefore, you conduct initial process improvement activities—SPI activities—at the project level. Using a common set of boundaries (the six KPAs of Level 2), each project is free to operate according to its own methodology. Out of this trial-and-error environment you will eventually discover a set of practices and processes that has proved to work well over time. At this point you can bring the processes and practices together into a standardized process set (SPS), and from that point on, each project will use the SPS to shape how the project is managed and worked. Whereas at Level 2 all projects were free to work in their own way, at Level 3 they are obliged to work the organization way. You can now begin to coordinate your SPI activities. Your shop has learned enough —become mature enough—that you can now institutionalize what you had previously been developing.

That's why Level 3 is called the Defined level. You have been able to define a process set that works not just for one project, but for your whole organization and the many projects it undertakes. At this point, a shift in quality management occurs. The ultimate responsibility for process (and product) quality rises to the executive level of the organization. At Level 2, the buck stopped (for all practicality) with the software project manager. At Level 3, the organization takes on that responsibility and provides a long-term commitment to it. The organization becomes, in a way, a kind of beefed-up quality assurance operation.

There are many advantages to reaching this point of institutionalization for your processes. Project management becomes more consistent, planning and forecasting become more accurate, and facility/resource coordination is streamlined. But Level 3 also introduces some new responsibilities that management should consider carefully in light of its focus on process improvement. We'll discuss all these in time, but it's best to begin with the first and biggest: your *strategy* for software process improvement.

This strategy is reflected in the CMM's three goals for the Organization Process Focus KPA:

Goal 1: Software process development and improvement activities are coordinated across the organization.

Goal 2: The strengths and weaknesses of the software processes are identified relative to a process standard.

Goal 3: Organization process development and improvement activities are planned.[1]

As we begin to look at the workings of CMM Level 3, it's important to make a distinction that is often misunderstood concerning CMM. That is this: The Capability Maturity Model is a framework that supports process improvement, but it is not itself a process improvement plan or strategy. You can use the Maturity Model to organize, manage, and evaluate your process improvement activities, but you must still create your own software process improvement plan, a plan that will work within the framework of CMM. If you have already implemented the recommendations for Level 2 in your shop, then you probably already have something of a software process improvement plan (SPI plan) in place, perhaps not on paper or as robust as it needs to be for Level 3, but a starting point anyway. Such an informal plan can work fine at Level 2, from project to project. At Level 3, though, you need an organization-wide plan for process improvement, an executive level plan used to guide the whole organization toward common goals.

We'll look at what might go into a basic SPI plan later in this chapter (and you might decide that this template works for your shop just fine as it is), but the details for developing a full-blown SPI plan are unfortunately beyond the scope of this book. Fortunately, there are many good sources for developing software process improvement strategies. Numerous books have been written on the topic, and the Software Engineering Institute itself has focused a lot of its efforts in this direction. The SEI supports several complementary SPI tools, such as IDEAL, INSPIRE, and CBA-IPI. You can get information on these by checking the SEI Web site, www.sei.cmu.edu. Of course, any SPI plan will first and foremost have to reflect the mission, structure, and practice of your own IT shop, so any path toward SPI you choose will probably have to be distinctly custom tailored to your unique needs.

A Different Approach to Describing KPAs for Level 3

In the first part of this book we discussed implementing the six KPAs of Level 2 using an approach labeled SPTP—Structure, Process, Training, Policy. As we saw, we can interpret all of the CMM's key practices at Level 2 as falling into one of these four categories. The SPTP approach is useful because it allows us to view CMM recommendations in light of what can be thought of as basic organizational building blocks. The SPTP approach is also handy for organizations wishing to operate under Level 2 guidelines in that the Level 2 KPAs are pretty much independent entities, areas that don't really cross each other except under project management conditions. They can be built somewhat independently of each other. They have their own structures, their own processes, their own training needs, and their own operating policies.

We are going to use the SPTP approach to describe Level 3 also, but with one difference. The SPTP approach will be used to describe the four "dynamic" KPAs of Level 2. These are Integrated Software Management, Software Product Engineering, Integroup Coordination, and Peer Reviews. I call these KPAs dynamic because they are the broad tools used to manage projects against corporate standards, and so they are used on all projects within your organization. Their make-ups (processes and practices) are continually monitored, assessed, and measured. They are scrutinized to provide feedback to improve the more static standards managed by the KPAs Organization Process Focus, Organization Process Definition, and Training Program.

Therefore, we will discuss how to shape the ISM, SPE, IC, and PR KPAs under one umbrella of SPTP. But we will look at OPF, OPD, and TP individually, still using the same SPTP approach. The reason is that these KPAs are somewhat dependent on each other, one shaped by the other. A discussion of each KPA separately from the others will make for a better structural foundation for those planning to implement a CMM Level 3 program.

Managing Software Process Improvement

Managing software process improvement organization-wide involves five high-level steps. These steps support the Organization Process Focus KPA of the CMM. Basically, what you need for this KPA is an internal structure that will help you, as an organization, perform the following activities:

- Periodically evaluate your defined processes for strengths and weakness

- Based on the results of the evaluation, establish concrete plans for improving the weak areas

- Coordinate the improvement efforts across the organization, assigning responsibility for refinement as appropriate

- Once the changes have been made, make the new/updated processes available to the organization as a whole

- Finally, make sure to reeducate your users so that they may properly use the updated processes and accurately follow new practices

If these steps look like the heart of a software process improvement plan, you are right. Use-Evaluation-Change-Notification: That is the kernel of all process improvement, whether it's building software systems or playing softball. It's the first step to a true process focus, to keeping a consistent, conscientious eye on the workings of your processes.

Unless you are an especially small IT shop, you will probably find that you need the services of an internal oversight committee to manage your software process improvement program across the organization. In the CMM this is called the Software Engineering Process Group (SEPG), but there's nothing magical or mandatory about that name. It's just a tag for a process steering committee. (If you are a tiny shop, your steering committee may be just one person.) In some organizations I have worked with, the group is called the Process Management Team; in others, it is the Process Oversight Committee. Different names, yes, but they share a basic common mission. For the sake of convenience, we'll stick to the SEPG tag.

The SEPG is sponsored by management as part of the long-term executive commitment to process improvement. The SEPG is a team of people appointed within the organization to manage the mission of SPI and coordinate the actions for SPI. CMM Level 3 activities are anchored by the Software Engineering Process Group. This is the entity that focuses the organization on process improvement. As we move into the details for fulfilling the recommendations of the Organization Process Focus KPA at Level 3, keep in mind that all of our discussions will be centered on three basic items:

- The operation of the SEPG

- The use and management of the organizational software process improvement plan (see Figure 9.1)

- The use and management of the standardized set of software processes (discussed in true detail in the KPA Organization Process Definition)

The Right Structure for a Focus on Process

The first logical step an organization takes when it begins to implement a CMM Level 3 program is to turn the organization to face process improvement issues as a unified

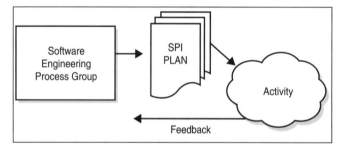

Figure 9.1 An organization uses two new structural elements to coordinate process improvement in a unified manner: the Software Engineering Process Group and the organizational software process improvement plan. The two should work together. The SEPG sponsors the SPI Plan and presents it to the organization for use. The organization uses and measures its performance, providing feedback for continuing refinement.

entity. You can't begin a Level 3 program (with any hope of success) until you first focus the organization on the tasks of process improvement. That's why the CMM lists Organization Process Focus as the first KPA of Level 2. To set this focus, and to support it as it begins to pinpoint specific SPI activities, you will need to make sure that you have the right structure in place within your organization to make sustaining the focus possible.

The CMM does not explicitly state what structure you need in place to be compliant with CMM guidelines, but the basic call for structure can be seen in the following three key practices:

Commitment 1: Senior management sponsors organizational software process improvement activities.

Ability 2: The organization allocates adequate resources and funding for organizational software process improvement.

Ability 3: The organization assigns responsibility and authority for organizational software process improvement.[2]

The structure that is implied in the above key practices begins at the highest levels of the organization. Since process is now being disseminated across the organization in a unified and coordinated manner, it is important to begin the effort with a solid measure of executive sponsorship.

Executive Sponsorship

The first practice (Commitment 1) represents a dedicated effort on the part of executive management to make process improvement a core mission of software development. Executive management should consciously and visibly sponsor SPI efforts. Management can take various routes in order to demonstrate such sponsorship. Most obviously, it can create a special organizational body to focus on process improvement plans and activities for the organization. It can make sure this body is adequately funded and staffed. But management can also integrate the mission of SPI into the higher missions of the company, perhaps by making SPI progress part of management bonus plans or part of identified goal accomplishment. As far as structure, it's good for IT management to wear the "banner" of SPI as part of its approach to management in general.

More specifically, executive management should assign "responsibility and authority" for software process improvement plans and activities (Ability 3). This ability usually translates into the establishment of a Software Engineering Process Group (SEPG), a body that takes on the duties of managing SPI in a planned and coordinated way across the organization.

Creating and Funding the SEPG

The central pillar in the organizational structure of a CMM Level 3 operation is the Software Engineering Process Group. This group, the SEPG, is the link between management and project work, between philosophy and implementation in the realm of process improvement. When you move from operating as a Level 2 shop to operating as a Level 3 shop, one of your first steps should be to create and fund the SEPG.

Your view of the SEPG should reflect the structure, culture, and needs of your organization. There are no hard and fast rules as to how it should be sized, how often it ought to meet, or what (specifically, that is) it ought to do on a regular basis. Set the SEPG up in a way that best serves your organization. Here are some ideas to consider as you begin to think about the shape and function of your shop's SEPG.

The Role of the SEPG

Your SEPG, as the link that coordinates process improvement across the organization, should be designed to carry out four basic functions:

- Create and manage the SPI plan
- Coordinate process improvement feedback
- Manage the smooth integration of SPI revisions
- Monitor CMM compliance

This first item is the critical one: *create and manage the software process improvement plan* for the organization. We'll discuss later in this chapter what might go into an SPI plan, but understand here that the SEPG is usually the body responsible for creating the plan and maintaining it for the organization. The creation part requires a considerable amount of up-front work. The plan need not be extensive, but it should be carefully thought out so that it not only matches management objectives for process improvement, but also puts forth a monitoring and review process that fits comfortably within the way your shop conducts business. The ongoing part of this is the management of the plan, its smooth execution within your organization. Most of the duties of the SEPG revolve around carrying out the SPI plan.

The next item is a logical extension of the first. The SEPG is the body best able to *coordinate process improvement feedback* within the organization. The SPI plan will contain a strategy for periodically analyzing the effectiveness of the processes and practices used to guide software development. Out of this analysis should arise ideas and suggestions for possible process improvement. This kind of feedback can come from just about any place in the organization, but it should flow (up or down) to the SEPG. In less well-managed shops, process improvement feedback can come flying from all directions, which is OK, but it might never land in the same place, ending up scattered across many people's to-do lists and agendas. Uncoordinated process improvement rarely leads to actual process improvement. The SEPG should be responsible for coordinating the feedback so that it can be properly assessed and evaluated as to its value to your process program.

What should result from coordinated feedback is action for tangible improvement. The SEPG should work to *manage the smooth integration of SPI revisions into the SPI plan and into development activities*. This is important because at Level 3 the entire organization is working in a common manner, one guided not only by the SPI plan, but also by use of the Standard Software Process Set (SSPS). And while there is a legitimate focus on process improvement here, improvement recommendations and changes cannot be introduced willy-nilly into the environment. Constant ad hoc change will serve only to unseat any quality controls already in place. The SEPG should work to make sure that all process improvement initiatives are introduced into the environment in a logical manner. To accomplish this, the SEPG should, after it has adopted specific process improvement changes, schedule when the changes should be incorporated, facilitate the introduction of the changes into existing SSPS documents, publish the new documents, announce to the organization the scope and nature of the changes, establish a dateline for adoption, and then provide the necessary route to educating workers on the new changes.

These three items deal with the management of software process improvement efforts in your IT shop. The fourth general responsibility of the SEPG might be considered secondary, or even unnecessary by some shops. I describe it here because you may find it relevant for your shop, especially if your mandate for adopting the Capability Maturity Model seeks official and formal compliance with Level 2 and Level 3 recommendations. This fourth responsibility for the SEPG is to monitor CMM compliance within the organization. This activity may emerge as a natural byproduct of the SPI plan, especially if it has been written to conform to CMM. Or it may become a separate yet related task of the SEPG. The emphasis you place on this responsibility will depend on your own shop's emphasis on CMM guidelines.

The Makeup of the SEPG

When I work with companies implementing CMM, one of the most common areas for discussion centers on the makeup and logistical function of the SEPG. The kinds of questions that are routinely tossed around include, "How large should the SEPG be?", "Who should serve on the SEPG?", and "How often should the group meet?". You can fret too much about building the SEPG, and you can take it too lightly. Try to strike a balance somewhere in the middle with the understanding that your first take on it need not be your last. You can change the SEPG as you need to change it. No laws govern its makeup. The only key consideration you should focus on is the idea that the SEPG should reflect how your IT shop conducts business. It should be built to support that operative paradigm.

That being the case, the size of the SEPG should be contingent on the size of your IT shop and the size of your SPI initiative overall. Knowing the typical responsibilities of the group as detailed previously, you should appoint enough people to carry out those duties as you ultimately define them. But refrain from making the SEPG a process-congress for your company. If you feel the obligation to appoint representatives from all corners of your shop to serve in the group, you may create such a bulky body that it can't make progress in any direction in an expedient or efficient manner. The best recommendation I can give is to make the SEPG as small *as possible*. Given its responsibilities, two people might be too small. On the other hand, if the group is 25 folks (in an IT shop of, say, 300) that might be a bit too much. A look at the type of people to appoint might help you get a better handle on what size is appropriate for your shop.

From a practical standpoint, try to appoint people to the SEPG who have the time to serve on the board (in 95 percent of cases, membership on the SEPG should probably not be a full-time assignment) and who have an interest in serving on the board. No matter how talented they are, if they lack these two qualities they will not bring much value to the SEPG. That done, you should make appointments that give the SEPG the background knowledge it needs to manage processes in your shop. Select people that can contribute to a composite knowledge base in the following areas: general process management, process improvement, and knowledge about how your organization develops software products. These three qualities are important because they reflect what the SEPG will have to concern itself with. The SEPG will have to create a software process improvement plan, manage it within the organization, and make sure it suits the needs of the culture and mission of your IT shop. Appoint the people who can make contributions in these specific areas.

There are other practical matters you'll have to consider when forming the SEPG. For example, how often should the SEPG meet? What process management tools will the team need? What training will be required to support the team? What amount of funding is adequate to support the SEPG? Once again, in these areas your professional judgment will produce the most practical answers. If you understand that the SEPG is not a body that affects the *detail* of process management, but rather a body that oversees the big picture, then you should be able to focus its energies in a way that does not impede process operations in your IT shop, but instead gently and methodically guides them in a direction that gradually leads to more efficient and effective operations.

Establishing Support Contacts for the SEPG

Together with appointing members to serve part-time on the SEPG committee, you should also consider appointing a second tier of people to act as liaisons between the project/worker level of the organization and the SEPG. This ties back to the need for coordinating process improvement feedback and activities. The SEPG should not be contrived or operated as (for lack of a better word) an intrusive group. That is, the SEPG should be a support body within your IT shop, one that collects data from the field and then uses that data to refine processes and practices. To foster this mission, it helps to have people at the line level—those working on specific projects or serving in specific functional areas—appointed to provide feedback to the SEPG, as noted in the SPI plan, or to help projects or areas work with the SEPG when problems or issues arise. This liaison role provides two benefits to the organization. First, it helps spread sponsorship of software process improvement through all levels of organizational activity. Second, it gives your projects and/or functional groups an avenue into the SEPG so that unplanned or unscheduled issues might have a forum for air.

This liaison role should be viewed as less formal than membership on the SEPG and as requiring less time. It is important nonetheless. You should make sure your appointees are sure of their role and have been trained to work with the SEPG in an appropriate manner.

Structure Summary

For the Organization Process Focus KPA, CMM wants you to establish mechanisms for controlling software process improvement activities within your IT shop. These mechanisms will provide the foundation you need to begin your Level 3 program. Typically, the structure you will need to realize this control will shape up in one major area and one minor area. The first—and the major one—is the creation and funding of the Software Engineering Process Group, a group sponsored by executive management and charged in general with managing the organization's process improvement plans. The next area —somewhat minor in service—is the appointment of liaisons from the organization's project teams or functional areas to serve as links between development activity and process improvement initiatives.

Processes to Help Manage the Organization's SPI Focus

The SEPG manages the SPI strategy for your organization. But the strategy itself should be contained in a documented software process improvement plan. (That name comes out of CMM, but you don't have to use it. For the sake of easy reference, we'll use it here, but you can call yours anything you want.) This is a key development for Level 3. The software process improvement plan (SPI plan) is the strategy that ties your IT organization together into a coordinated whole relevant to process improvement. The Organization Process Focus KPA sets up a structure under which the SPI plan can be created, implemented, and managed. The SEPG usually authors the plan and then works with its contacts and line workers to make sure the plan rolls out smoothly. But behind this activity is a series of processes that need to be created to support this activity. In this section we'll address what kinds of processes and procedures you can develop to make sure your SPI plan becomes an effective management tool for your organization.

To help focus SPI efforts across the organization, in compliance with the OPF KPA, you might find the following processes beneficial:

- An SPI plan template
- A process to create the SPI plan
- A process to manage implementation of the SPI plan

This probably seems simple enough, but it's important to understand how critical these three areas are. The SPI strategy you devise will end up shaping how the whole organization responds to SPI objectives, and it will significantly impact how the organization meets its CMM objectives, too.

We'll begin with a look at what a typical SPI plan might cover.

The SPI Plan

Creating the SPI plan is a core effort for Level 3 shops. Once you have matured to the point where you can begin working with a standardized set of proven software development processes, you face the challenge of managing your standards in a coordinated way across the organization. Such management has now risen from the project level to the organizational level. Because all groups within your organization are now using the same processes and practices on their software projects, improvement activities need to be handled in a similar, standardized way. That is where the SPI plan comes into play. It sets in place the path to a standardized software process improvement.

As mentioned earlier, CMM is not really a software process improvement program. It is a framework on which you can build your own SPI program. It gives you the infrastructure and direction to instantiate SPI activities. And because the discipline of process improvement is complementary to but separate from CMM, a full discussion of SPI is out of the scope of this book. But we can present a template containing some basic SPI considerations that will aid you and your team in coming up with at least an initial draft of an SPI plan for your organization. (You can find a current bibliography of in-depth software process improvement materials in Appendix A of this book.)

Template for Building Your SPI Plan

Software process improvement is a discipline that is finely tailored to the environment in which it operates. Like a Saville Row suit that fits perfectly on only one person, each instance of an SPI program probably works to its fullest only in the environment it was built to manage. For that reason there is no cookie-cutter approach to creating a generic SPI plan. Look at examples of SPI plans from multiple companies, and you'll see that they are all, to one extent or another, different. They are as different as the companies themselves. For this reason it's hard to judge an SPI plan on the scale of better or worse when compared to others. SPI plans can really be judged only on their individual effectiveness. They do not stand in relation to other plans; they stand in relation to the job they have to do. If an SPI plan helps a company effectively put forth a software process improvement program, then the plan can be said to be "good." If not, call it "bad" and fix it. But just as all plans are different, you can find a core set of basic functionalities that most plans exhibit to one degree or another.

Next , I list a set of sections or chapters that you may wish to include in the SPI plan you create for your Level 3 program. Take a look at these, and judge how each relates to your organization. They may all apply, or only a few may apply. You may find that you need to expand beyond the items listed here to fully meet the needs of your environment. Take this information as a starting point, and remember that the high-level goal of process improvement consists at heart of four basic activities: reviewing processes, documenting areas for improvement, making appropriate changes, and communicating the changes to your people. However your plan shapes up, make sure this core mission remains present.

This plan can be conceived as one document or a series of multiple documents. It can be published as a traditional hard-bound volume or as an electronic resource. All options are open to you, and one is as valid as the other.

Here are the sections to consider as you build your SPI plan:

- Introduction
    - Statement of the organization's commitment to SPI
    - Statement of executive sponsorship of the SPI plan
- Description of the general goals of this SPI plan
- Description of the goals of the SPI plan as related to overall company objectives
- Description of the role of the SEPG within the organization
- Listing of SEPG membership with contact information
- Approved use of the SPI plan

- Scope of SPI activities
- Functional areas affected by SPI and the plan
- Processes open for evaluation
- Protocol for evaluations
  - Choose evaluators
  - Create evaluation forms and guidelines
  - Announce evaluations
  - Conduct evaluations to identify strengths and weaknesses
  - Document results
  - Create evaluation report
  - Distribute evaluation report
  - Review recommended improvement actions
- Coordinate improvement action integration
- Coordinate deployment of the revised (new) process assets
- Coordinate project adoption of revised material
- Coordinate training in the new changes
- Coordinate cutover to new processes
- Schedule of planned evaluations
- Definition of measurements to gauge SPI/EPG progress
- Management of the SPI plan

Let's briefly discuss each section.

Introduction

The introduction to the SPI plan should establish the general parameters under which the plan will be followed by members of the organization.

To support this, you might begin with a formal *statement of the organization's commitment to software process improvement*. A similar statement will be included in the official policy for Organization Process Focus (see the end of this chapter), so you might consider modifying the policy a little to generalize it to SPI overall and use this in the introduction. However you decide to go, the SPI plan will ultimately be used to guide all process improvement efforts, so it's best to begin with a statement that makes it clear that the organization as a whole is committed to the philosophy of process improvement.

As a complement to this, you might follow with a *statement that confirms executive sponsorship of the SPI plan*. This is an important corollary to organizational commitment. It's one thing to be committed, but for that commitment to go anywhere, to accomplish anything, executive endorsement of the direction is required. The readers of the plan should have the opportunity to appreciate this. They should come away with the understanding that this initiative is bubbling down from the highest echelons of the organization.

The first two statements (or sentences, or paragraphs, however you choose to shape them) establish the official nature of the SPI plan. With this done, you can begin to move into the plan's contents. A good first step is to *enumerate, perhaps describe, the general mission, objectives, and goals of the SPI plan.* You and your authoring team should think this section through carefully. These items will be factors that need to be addressed in detail in the heart of the plan. Here in the introduction they can be expressed in broad, nonspecific terms that will give the reader a general but accurate impression of what the plan seeks to accomplish. For example, the goal "work to improve processes to realize a 5 percent reduction in application defects within a nine-month time frame" gives the reader a feel for how the details of the plan will be used. If you can list all your SPI goals here, you'll have a solid jumping-off spot for moving deeper into SPI issues.

Another good idea for this part of the plan, especially relevant to the SPI goals, is to *describe how these goals mesh with the overall mission and goals of the corporation as a business entity.* Your IT shop, whether it's part of a larger company or whether it's a self-contained, single-focused entity, is not exclusively concerned with issues of software development. Any company must deal with a myriad of business issues: marketing strategies, capital management, human resource development, expansion, and so on. It is important to mesh the goals of software process improvement so that they *support the broader company objectives.* Your SPI work should be shaped so that it furthers the goals of the company as a whole. If you can communicate this in the introduction, you will help distribute this understanding down through the organization.

If you structure your SPI plan introduction along these lines, you'll have in place a good overview of what SPI means to your organization. Additionally, you can use this introduction as evidential support for Commitment 2 in the Operational Process Focus KPA:

> **Commitment 2:** Senior management sponsors organizational software process improvement activities.[3]

The Software Engineering Process Group

The SPI plan will be a new part of your organization's IT structure. Another new part will be the Software Engineering Process Group. You might find it beneficial to follow up the introduction with an overview of the role and composition of the SEPG (or whatever name you've elected to give to this oversight committee). This does not have to be an extensive section, but it should provide the reader with a sense of how the SEPG will support the mission of software process improvement and further the realization of SPI efforts. Two descriptive areas can help achieve this.

First, provide a brief *description of the role of the SEPG within the organization.* The beginning of this chapter dealt with the formation of the SEPG and the general responsibilities the SEPG undertakes on behalf of the organization. The specifics of the role you defined for the SEPG can be included here as a way to confirm its job and to educate your readers about what the members will be doing.

As another bit of formality (also as a way to publish the names of the members to the organization) you should consider *listing the SEPG membership* in this section of the SPI plan, along with contact information (phone number, e-mail, office location, and so on).

Approved Use of the SPI Plan

You might decide to include this section as part of the introduction. Its purpose, though, should be clear. This is where you announce up front what the SPI plan will be used for. Of course, this may already be understood by your people, but to ensure a consistent and accurate understanding, you should put the intention in writing. In a way, this is an extension of the objectives of your SPI initiative, but while the objectives are *strategic* in nature, the intention should be expressed in *tactical* terms.

For this area, you might include a description of the general *scope of SPI activities* and how they are defined in and managed by the plan. You might also list the areas within the organization—the *functional groups and/or project teams* that fall under the umbrella of the SPI initiative. This way your people will know what the SPI plan will be used for and who will be accountable to it under the SPI initiative.

Finally, you should include a brief statement as to the *ultimate authority of the SPI plan*. What this means is simply that the SPI plan is recognized across the organization as the master plan for SPI activity. No other SPI activities will compete with it; nor should any other like initiatives be permitted to percolate independently of the plan. In order for the organization to work according to the spirit of Level 3 unity, all actions that pertain to software process improvement must be centrally planned, documented, and managed.

Processes Open for Evaluation

The previous section defines the official use of the SPI plan within the organization. This section will establish the operational boundaries of the plan: that is, what processes and practices it will periodically audit. This section is important because the SPI plan will ultimately shape up to be more than just a plan for actions aimed at process improvement. It will also serve as a type of contract between management, the SEPG, and the line workers. All will have a chance to review and question the plan before it is adopted, but once it is, it will establish (for want of a better phrase) a "rule of law" for how the whole company proceeds with SPI activities. Somewhere the contract must define just what the reach of SPI authority is, who and what it impacts, and what exactly falls under its umbrella. Of course, this description is going to be strongly tied to your organization's Standardized Software Process Set (see Chapter 10 for a full discussion of the SSPS). The SSPS is the thing that is going to be audited, but not in a vacuum, in the field. The SPI plan will govern two things: how effective the processes are at managing specific software development steps and how closely groups within the organization are able to comply with the processes.

If you are going to measure both innate effectiveness and rote compliance you have to know what exactly you are going to measure. This is where you define that. Completing this section is actually pretty easy to do. Just look at the various processes and practices you have documented in your SSPS. You might even have them already listed in that document's table of contents. It might be perfectly appropriate to simply plop that table of contents into this section—you now have your boundaries established. But don't do it blindly. Look at each process and practice from the SSPS. Assess it, and then judge if it should be part of the audit realm of the SEPG and the SPI plan. If so, put it in; if not, leave it out.

Protocol for Evaluations

The CMM describes the main objective of software process improvement this way: the effort to *periodically evaluate strengths and weaknesses [Activity 2 and Verification 1 of the Organization Process Focus KPA]*. The protocol you establish for the evaluations sets the path to this objective. It will represent the heart of your SPI plan and can also be used as a standalone process, one documented and available for use by your evaluators. How you define the protocol is up to you: You should shape it for the particular needs of your organization. There are several good published programs available for conducting internally based process appraisals. The Software Engineering Institute has developed one called CBA IPI, CMM-Based Appraisal for Internal Process Improvement. This is available free from the SEI's Web site. You can also find others at your local business bookstore, or you can develop a customized one yourself. Whatever path you choose, look for a program that contains, in some form or fashion, the following steps:

1. Choose Your Evaluators

The first step you need to consider is selecting the members of your organization who will perform the evaluations. You might choose one person, or you might appoint a handful. Your evaluators, however, will need to be up to the job. They will need to know three things in detail: what your current process set contains, how the individual processes are used, and how to conduct an evaluation. For these reasons, many people select members of the SEPG to be evaluators; others select members from the software quality assurance group. Of course, you are free to appoint whomever you wish. Just make sure that they are prepared (specially trained, if necessary) and that they are free from any conflict of interest. (For example, I wouldn't appoint the software project manager of the ABC project to perform its evaluation.)

2. Create the Evaluation Forms and Guidelines

The data collected during the evaluation needs to be documented, and the best (and easiest) way to do this is with a form. You will need to develop these forms along with guidelines for using them. The forms will need to be designed in such a way that they will readily collect the compliance and performance data that you'll need to properly evaluate the effectiveness of your process set.

Because the evaluation will look at the staff activities holding up the processes as well as the work products arising from the processes, your forms should reflect this. You'll need to look for such things as the following:

- Activity issues
  - Is the team following the defined processes as documented?
  - Are the work products produced by the team created and maintained in the defined formats?
  - Does the team have access to and show familiarity with the Standardized Software Process Set?
  - Are the team's technical activities in accordance with the SSPS?
  - Are the team's management activities in accordance with the SSPS?

- Process issues
  - Are there areas where processes show definitive shortcomings?
  - Are there areas where processes need refinement, to a state of greater or less granularity?
  - Are there areas where needed processes are absent?
  - Has the work environment changed or evolved in such a way as to operate counter to the processes?
  - Do new environment characteristics call for additional or refined processes?

3. Announce the Evaluation

You shouldn't spring an evaluation on anyone. That's like a sneak attack: It's not only unfair, but it leads to distrust in the future. The evaluation should be a scheduled event, one planned well in advance of the actual event. The people or groups involved should have ample time to prepare. (They should know about the evaluation because you will have published a schedule. See the "Schedule of Planned Evaluations" section later in this chapter.) Just prior to the evaluation, you can send out an official announcement indicating the who, what, when, and where for the activity.

4. Conduct the Evaluation

The purpose of the evaluation is to identify strengths and weaknesses in your processes and in the practice of the processes. A good way to get to this goal is to perform the evaluation proper as a three-step process. First, send your evaluation forms to the parties being evaluated early, perhaps with the formal announcement. This will allow people to complete the forms on their own without the pressure of being "watched over the shoulder."

Next, collect and score the forms. How much time should pass between sending out and collecting the forms? You're the best judge of that. Workloads and other factors can all affect a person's freedom to participate in the evaluation; but if your planning has been done well beforehand and you have executive endorsement for the process, this problem should be minimized. You might allow a couple of weeks; one week can be considered as perhaps the smallest time window advisable. Once you have collected and scored the forms, you will have what I call a "hearsay account" of how things stand. I have found that usually these accounts are pretty close to the mark, but invariably some deviance occurs, typically stemming from misinterpretation. That is why you follow up with interviews. This is when the evaluators participate actively in the process.

Using the forms as a starting point, the evaluators will meet with the members being evaluated (individually or in small groups) and confirm the accuracy of the forms' answers. They can do this two ways: by going over the completed forms item by item and discussing each to confirm the responses, or by reviewing the artifacts called for in the processes to confirm compliance.

At this point, the evaluation *pro forma* ends. You should now have the data needed to summarize the outcome: You should know where your group is performing well and is in compliance with the process, and where it is performing poorly and is out of compliance with the process. This sounds like two items, but it's actually four—you should be aware of the distinction. You can perform well but still be out of compliance with

A NOTE ON THE "I'M BEING TESTED" SYNDROME

I have addressed this issue elsewhere in this book, but it bears repeating here. As you are no doubt aware, software process improvement is not about affixing blame. It's about thoughtfully and carefully becoming better at what you do. Luckily, most people understand this, too, but when anyone is being "evaluated," no matter what that term might really mean, there is a tendency to take it personally. This happens everywhere: big companies and small. People feel as if they are being tested, or they think the results might somehow get etched onto their "permanent record." It's best to assuage these feelings early, as best you can. Let your people know that an evaluation is not about people being good or bad at their jobs; it's about process. As best as it can be, it's identity-free. You can't remove all tension when you are investigating how your processes and practices are working, but you can remove most. A good basis, a starting point at least, for relaxed evaluations is to train your people in how evaluations work, so they know what to expect, and maybe even give them an orientation to CMM to help them better understand the general philosophy behind process improvement.

process, and that condition can be viewed as an activity problem (in CMM language, you've fallen back to a Level 1 characteristic). You can also be performing poorly but in compliance, in which case you probably have a process problem. Finally, if you are performing poorly and are out of compliance, you might very well have both (and then some).

5. Document the Results and Itemize the Recommendations

With the situation now investigated, you are ready to document what you have found by producing an evaluation report. There is no official format for this report; build it how you see fit. Be sure to include the kind of information and background material your readers will need to ascertain just what the report means and what impact your findings might have on the organization as a whole. Look to include data such as the following:

- The purpose of the evaluation
- The members of the evaluation team
- The date span and place(s) of the evaluation
- The teams you evaluated
- The projects you evaluated
- The processes you evaluated
- The work products you evaluated
- Areas of strength, with explanations of the likely reasons
- Areas of weakness, with explanations of the likely reasons
- A description of the action items recommended for addressing the weak areas

These action items can be grouped by order of priority with the owner, a proposed general solution/goal, dates for review, risks/assumptions associated with each action, and a brief description of how the change realigns the organization with the overall business strategy of the company. (This is in accordance with CMM Activity 3 for this KPA, establish and maintain action plans to address the findings of the software process appraisals.)

And there are two final items for consideration:

It's a good idea to close the report with a description of any lessons learned from the evaluation. This is a listing of things to do to improve the process of evaluations in the future. And you might also wish to include the raw data from the evaluation as a reference or an appendix. This could include such things as the scoring sheets, evaluator notes, lists of artifacts, and so on.

6. Distribute the Evaluation Report

You conducted the SPI evaluation and produced the evaluation report for one main purpose: to uncover ways to improve your software development processes and practices. At this point, the SPI ideas you have put into the report are just the ideas of you and your team; they are *recommendations* to move forward with specific actions. In order to move ahead, you need to distribute the evaluation report so that the organization can review what you have documented and decide which suggestions should be accepted. (If you have conducted a well-planned and thoughtfully executed evaluation, chances are—economics and politics aside—most of your suggestions will be seen as valid and will be adopted.)

You should distribute the evaluation report to three main groups within your organization: executive management, project management, and the relevant software engineering groups.

The executive audience, which will include the SEPG membership (who may have authored the report), is important because executive endorsement of all process improvement activity is absolutely required for implementation success. This audience should view the report in light of where the organization currently stands in regard to quality and where it might need to be headed. Issues of cost, resource requirements, and current commitments will come into play based on your recommendations.

The project management audience, which will include software management, is important as this is what I would call your first-line audience. The recommendations in the evaluation report will affect them directly and (should they be adopted) daily. This audience should scrutinize your recommendations for consistency, harmony with project environments, and practicality. You'll find that this audience will usually examine your report more closely than the others because project management will end up "owning" the recommendations eventually. The managers will not want to change the status willy-nilly without good reason, which always should address tangible and obtainable benefits.

The third audience I define as "relevant engineering groups." This can include a range of groups, from all groups in the organization down to selected groups you think might benefit from the report. There are several advantages to making the report generally available: (1) it gives the groups that were not evaluated a chance to see what kinds of things are involved in a process improvement evaluation and what kinds of data are relevant to the evaluation; (2) it might point out areas for improvement or examination for groups similar to the one that was evaluated; and (3) it lets other members of the organization know how different parts of the organization are performing in relation to the requirements of the standardized software process set.

You may have reasons why you want to limit this third audience or open it up. If so, follow those reasons. But at least one entity in this audience is required to be on the distribution list for each evaluation report, and that is the group you evaluated. Those who participated in the evaluation should be among the first to receive a copy of the report. The report should not be treated as a secret analysis or a private summarization. Such approaches are detrimental to any SPI program and will only foster paranoia and future noncooperation. Make the report easily and readily available to the participating group, and make sure the content for the report highlights the strengths as well as the weaknesses found.

7. Review Proposed Solutions for Agreement

When you distribute the evaluation report, you should give the audiences an adequate amount of time to review and digest its contents. That amount of time is up to you, but a work week is probably the minimum. Use this time to prepare for a formal peer review of the material (for more on peer reviews, see Chapters 7 and 11.) This will be a review session in which the report is analyzed and its recommendations are approved, tabled, or canceled.

8. Coordinate Actions for Process Improvement across the Organization

Out of the peer review should come those action items the organization wants to adopt, to incorporate into the standardized software process set. Moving on these action items needs to be managed in a coordinated effort (which is in the spirit of Activity 4 of this KPA, coordinate implementation of software process action plans across the organization. This includes assigning ownership to each action item, scheduling completion and review dates, and monitoring progress toward completion).

9. Coordinate Deployment of the New Process Assets

Once the improvement items have been individually finalized and approved, they need to be integrated into your organization's process set and then officially published in the process library. This should shape your library into two main components, the current process set and the improved process set. With this done, you should then make sure that the organization knows what has occurred. Using e-mail bulletin boards, status meetings, or some other communication form, you should let your people know what has been changed and what areas the changes affect. At this point, though, the current process set is still in use. Two further things need to happen before the improved process set can become active.

10. Coordinate Training in the New Changes

You should arrange for your people (chiefly those affected by the new changes) to be trained in the changes that have been incorporated into the process set. This is in compliance with CMM Activity 6 of this KPA, coordinate organizational learning on the software process. Give plenty of time for this training to take place. You want your team ready to use the improved set prior to the cutover date.

11. Coordinate Project Adoption
of Revised Material

In this final step, you will notify the organization as to when the improved set will become the current process set version. This is in accordance with CMM Activity 5 of this KPA, coordinate the deployment of the organization's software process assets. How you manage this cutover will depend largely on how your organization operates. You may decide on a "hot" cutover, where all at once, at an appointed time, the entire organization begins using the new set. This is an easy, clean approach if it's practical. On the other hand, for the sake of current project commitments or other internal issues, you may elect to use a staggered cut, in which different projects and/or groups adopt the improved set as the opportunity arises within their own work environments.

Schedule of Planned Evaluations

You might elect to include this section in the software process improvement plan proper or refer to it in an addendum or appendix. Either way, the point is the same: to plan for and then document when your SPI evaluations will occur. This documented intention addresses Activity 2 of the Operational Process Focus KPA, to appraise the organization's software processes to identify strengths and weaknesses periodically and as needed.

Important note: This is a good place to mention a point on the *frequency* of SPI evaluations. I don't want to give the impression that this is something the SEPG does on a regular basis or that it is some kind of ongoing police action. SPI evaluations should actually be, in my opinion, *infrequent*. The reasons are clear. First, if you are operating as a Level 3 organization you have (or should have) already spent significant time at Level 2 developing a set of proven software development processes and practices. As far as business as usual goes, you should be in pretty good shape already. (If you are not —if you are in a situation where many areas of different processes appear to be underperforming or leading you astray or if your staff seems to be consistently out of compliance—you may not have yet fulfilled all the intentions and objectives of Level 2 operations.) At Level 3, you should be moving in the direction of process refinement, not serious process correction.

Second, as you can see from the previous sections, it takes significant time and resources to conduct an SPI evaluation. It's not something you would want to do every other month, if for no other reason than you would be continually disrupting your organization's project work.

And, third, it takes time and effort to redirect efforts when you make changes to your Standardized Software Process Set. You have to document the changes, integrate them, train people on how to use them, and monitor their adoption. If you are doing this very often, your groups will be in constant shake-up mode; just when they get used to one way, they'll get hit with a new way. That you can demonstrate it's a "better" way will quickly have diminishing impact.

The schedule for evaluations is, of course, up to you and executive management. You know your groups best. From my work in the field with Level 3 shops, I would recommend implementing full SPI evaluations (which look at the full process set) no more than once a year. For many mature Level 3 shops, every two or three years is more appropriate.

Of course, you may elect to do partial evaluations (segments of the process set) on a more regular basis.

Remember: You can always do spot checks of project compliance and performance from your software quality assurance group, which should be continually monitoring such activity for each project you have underway.

A published schedule for the evaluations will serve two purposes. It will let your evaluation team members know what's up when and give them the appropriate time to plan and prepare. And, even more importantly, it will serve as a preannouncement to your group members and project managers of when they will be required to participate in the evaluation process.

When you create your evaluation schedule, think about including the following data in some way:

- Supply the date for each evaluation and allow ample time from the publication and distribution of the schedule to the first evaluation.

- Identify the organizational groups involved to let your people know who is accountable for participation in each evaluation.

- Identify the projects to be evaluated.

- Identify the processes and practices that will be included in the evaluation.

- Once the schedule is finalized make sure it gets into the hands of the people and groups it affects.

Measurements of SPI-Related Activity

This section of the SPI plan is intended to help provide improvement data that can be used to refine how you conduct SPI-related activity contained in the plan and to help you build better, more effective plans in the future. The idea here is to define a series of measurements that reflect what you have been doing from an SPI perspective and establish when these measurements will be collected and evaluated.

This section will help you meet the Measurement 1 recommendation of the Organization Process Focus KPA: define, collect, and analyze measures to provide insight into the performance of the activities for organizational software process improvement.

These measurements are related to the "Lessons Learned" section of the evaluation report, as discussed previously. The measurements will give you hard numbers from what may seem like nebulous real-life activity. The hard numbers should point out where things seem to be in balance and where things seem to be out of balance.

Here's an example of the kinds of measurements you might consider collecting to help you manage the SPI process:

- The cost of staffing and maintaining the Software Engineering Process Group over a certain period of time

- The cost associated with supplying the SEPG with needed tools and facilities

- The amount of time spent on SEPG activity during a certain period

- The number of process evaluations conducted over a certain period of time, along with the number of people, projects, and processes involved

- The number of issues that arose during the evaluation in each process/project area

- The number and types of improvement action items adopted from each evaluation

These measurements should be consistently collected and stored. They will be used to help evaluate the SPI plan and SEPG effectiveness, as discussed in the next section.

Management of the SPI Plan

This is usually the last section in an SPI plan (although it does not have to be; you could place it first if you like). This section sets up a beginning regimen for verifying the SPI and SEPG activities with different audiences internal to the organization (and maybe external to the organization, if you deem it appropriate). Using the measurement data you collected, you should periodically evaluate two things in general: the organization's adherence to the SPI plan as published and the project work products, to check that they are in compliance with the SSPS.

These verification meetings should be conducted by senior management, perhaps even with the assistance of an outside process consultant (optional) on a periodic basis. This is not an ongoing activity done, say, every month. It's a milestone check to weigh the general long-term effectiveness of the SPI efforts. I usually recommend that they be conducted no more than once every six months. And I have found that a convenient schedule is to plan them as a close-out activity every time you or your SEPG team produces a process evaluation report.

This regimen meets the CMM recommendations for verification contained in the Organization Process Focus KPA:

Verification 1: Objectively review the designated activities of organizational software process improvement for the adherence to specified requirements, plans, processes, standards, and procedures.

Verification 2: Objectively review the designated software work products of organizational software process improvements for adherence to specified standards and requirements.

Verification 3: Review the activities for organizational software process improvement, with senior management periodically and as needed.[4]

If you follow the template, you should be able to construct a valid SPI plan for your organization, one that gives you compliance with the first recommended activity of the Organization Process Focus KPA: perform the activities for organizational software process improvement according to a defined process.

This leads us to the next section in this chapter: defining a process for creating the SPI plan.

A Process for Developing the SPI Plan

The CMM's Organization Process Focus KPA is designed to help an organization take some of the first steps toward orienting its energies along common lines of conduct. The intent is to create a high-level focus on process management, use, and improvement. This KPA describes in general two entities that promote this focus. The first is the establishment of a process improvement oversight committee, often called the Software Engineering Process Group (SEPG). The second is the development of an official organizational software process improvement plan (SPI plan). The SEPG uses the SPI plan to coordinate SPI activities across the organization. In the previous sections of this chapter, we have discussed the setup and purpose of the SEPG, as well as the typical contents of an SPI plan. Now we'll take a brief look at an outline for a process that can be used by the SEPG to develop the SPI plan.

Because the SPI plan plays such a central role in shaping an organization's behavior at Level 3, it's important that a process be used to guide its creation and future management. You'll find that the members of your SEPG will appreciate having the process as a support tool; it will also prove beneficial to your team as a whole as the SPI plan evolves in the future.

You can use the following 10-step process as a starting point for your own SPI plan creation process:

1. Assign authoring responsibility
2. Align SPI objective with executive sponsorship and business goals
3. Use the SPI plan template to research and write the plan
4. Distribute drafts to affected parties
5. Review and finalize plan
6. Publish for signature
7. Train users as necessary
8. Distribute throughout the organization as applicable
9. Place under version control
10. Review and update as necessary

Let's take a quick look at each step.

Assign Authoring Responsibility

Your first step in creating the SPI plan is to appoint someone responsible for authoring it: for bringing together all the information needed for the content and then shaping this information into an organized whole. Because the SPI plan will become such an important document to your software development shop, it's important to choose an author carefully. You can go several ways on this. One way, easy but expensive, is to hire an experienced outside consultant (or team of consultants) to come in and do the work for you under your supervision. There will probably be an up-front learning curve in going this route. The consultant will need to establish contacts, learn about your business and objectives, and ascertain what your specific SPI goals are. But if the consultant is experienced in the writing and organization of such plans, you may find that the work greatly speeds up once the initial investigations are complete.

Another way is to appoint internal resources to author the plan. Many shops assign this responsibility to the members of the SEPG. If you have selected these members because of their process knowledge and business knowledge, they may be the perfect choice for authorship. But, at the same time, feel free to include others in the organization. You may know of certain people who are very strong writers or who have extensive experience with CMM or in the process improvement arena. The only real selection rule here is to appoint the strongest resources you have available in order to get the best SPI plan possible.

Once you have selected an author or authoring team, make the appointment official. This should not be a casual, off-the-cuff assignment. The appointment should be public, with the endorsement of executive management. Make sure you then provide the proper resources to develop the plan. This includes adequate monies, documentation support tools, and access to the right people in your organization. Then set a deadline for the work. How long will it take to produce the SPI plan? Naturally, that answer depends entirely on the nature of your shop, its mission, and the structure of your CMM program. A reasonable deadline might be 8 weeks; it might be 16. This is a judgment you will have to make. But whatever you decide, this is not a go-away-and-come-back-later type of project. You should monitor the progress on this effort closely. You may have appointed authors, but you will serve, in effect, as the editor of the SPI plan.

Align SPI Objective with Executive Sponsorship and Business Goals

It sounds like a statement of the obvious to mention this, but this is an area that is often overlooked. One of the first steps in authoring the SPI plan should be documenting the broad business goals of the company as a whole and then making sure to align SPI activities with those goals. Software development does not sit in isolation from the rest of the company; neither should software process improvement. The SPI plan should further the general corporate goals. Your authors should work with executive management from the outset to make sure that the direction in which your IT shop will be headed in the future is in harmony with corporate plans from a business perspective. This alignment will shape the form and contents of the rest of the plan.

Use the SPI Plan Template to Research and Write the Plan

This is the heart of the process. The authors begin to gather the data to go into the SPI plan. This is where access and resources come into play. Your authors should have the tools they need to put the plan on paper and the access they need to move about the organization gathering the data. If you are using the template provided previously, or even a rough facsimile of it, you will know generally what's going to the involved in this process. You can use the template to put together a research "map" for the authors: something that tells them who their contacts are for specific topics to be covered in the plan.

This is where the bulk of the SPI plan creation time will occur. Be sure to check in with the authoring team on a regular basis to help out with questions or access problems as they arise.

Distribute the Draft Plan to the Affected Parties

When your SPI plan authors have worked through the investigation and documentation steps, they should have a draft of the plan in place. At this time, you should plan a formal review of the draft. Before you do this, you need to identify the parties who should review the plan and distribute the draft to them so that they have time to peruse it before the formal review.

Who should review the daft? The selection of the reviewers is largely up to you, but consider including representatives from these three groups:

Executive management. Because the SPI plan will not only reflect general corporate goals but also address the accomplishment of these goals, be sure to include people from executive management on the review committee.

Group management. The SPI plan will shape how your various software development groups work within your common process set, and it will establish important standards of performance and compliance. Be sure to invite managers from the various groups to review the draft. This includes representatives from such groups as project planning, project management, software quality assurance, documentation, configuration management, and software design.

Line worker representation. Finally, you might consider inviting a select group of line workers to review the SPI plan. I consider this an optional audience, but you may feel that, given the nature of your shop, it's important that they are included. There is no such thing as too much input on the SPI plan or too much circulation of the plan. Select this audience as you deem proper.

Once you have identified the review audience, send the draft out to them with a notification of the formal review date. Make sure there is ample time between draft dissemination and the review date for the audience to be able to go over the document thoroughly. (For more detail on this review procedure, see the information in this book on peer reviews.)

Review and Finalize the Draft

Once distribution is complete and the target audience has been given time to look through the plan, a formal review of the plan should be scheduled. This review should be treated as a standard peer review in which the plan is inspected for defects, conflicts, and inconsistencies. From this review should emerge a series of recommendations for content improvement, refinement, and basic editing. Record the changes, and then make them to the document as appropriate. If the changes are significant, you may want to have a re-review to go over the document again. If they are not major, you may be able to distribute the edited content for a final offline checkout. The result of this review should be a document that receives everyone's approval for implementation. Your audience's acceptance of the SPI plan should be interpreted as approval (and they should be informed of this) and acceptance of the contents. You and your SEPG group are, in fact, making an implied contract with the audience, one in which it is understood that once implemented the plan will be honored by all parties.

Publish for Signature

With the SPI plan reviewed and revised to the satisfaction of the organization, it is ready to be signed into work. This is the point at which executive management will place its imprimatur on the document. This gesture is more than a mere sign-off. It's an official adoption of the document as company policy. This step is important: The entire organization should view the SPI plan as The Way. It must be seen as containing not a series of desirable ideas or idle constructs, but rather a set of definitions and policies that will guide the IT arm of the organization toward the realization of tangible and valuable goals. Such a position within the bounds of authority requires the signature of and public endorsement by executive management. Without executive backing, the plan may end up carrying little weight when it comes to the work of implementation.

Train Users as Necessary

Once the plan has been reviewed, approved, and officially adopted, you are ready for implementation. To facilitate full and effective implementation, you should train the people who will be implementing the plan in the philosophies and contents of the plan. If the authors are the ones who will be handling implementation, this training could be minimal. But if the implementers are dealing with someone else's work, the training might be extensive. In addition to this, you may also wish to host interorganizational training on the SPI plan, offering training and orientation to your managers and line workers about the scope and intent of the organization's SPI plan. (See the training sections that follow for some recommended training sessions.)

Distribute throughout the Organization as Applicable

At this point, the SPI is ready for implementation. Its contents have been reviewed and approved, and the people who must work the plan have been trained to do so. You can now distribute the plan within the organization. You should think of this step from two perspectives: how do you distribute the plan and to whom do you distribute it.

The SPI plan can be published in any format you wish. It can be a traditional paper document or an electronic file. It can be a single collection of chapters, or it can be a series of linked yet independent reports. Its form will, in part, determine how you distribute it. The important thing to remember here is that the term "distribute" implies access. You do not have to physically place the plan into the hands of a certain set of people, but you should make sure that these people have easy access to it. This might mean printing X number of copies and placing them on everyone's desks. It can also mean locating the plan in a hardcopy library and simply telling people where it is and explaining the checkout procedures for it. Or you can place the plan's electronic files in a common directory and then e-mail the files to your audience. Your options here are wide and varied. Choose any distribution path that suits you and your people best.

Place under Version Control

The previous steps have produced an approved SPI plan ready for implementation. You should now place the plan under version control. The SPI plan will be a living document for your organization. It is not a set of static rules and policies carved in stone. The plan you created is version 1.0. Expect it to evolve over time, to change as your organization changes. Placing the document under version control will help you manage the changes that will be introduced over time.

Review and Update as Necessary

Now that the SPI plan has been adopted and implemented, you should periodically review it to keep it current with the goals of your company and with the current state of practice in your IT shop. (See the last section on the SPI plan template.)

Training to Support the Organization's Focus on Process

Training is one of the least appreciated facets of the Capability Maturity Model. And, in my opinion, it is one of the most important. The issue of training is introduced at Level 2 and can be found in each of the six KPAs for that level. Training at Level 2 is not what we would call a formal process. Its primary intention is to prepare the members of the project team to perform their duties competently and to do so within the framework of a process-driven management methodology. Training at Level 2 is a project responsibility.

At Level 3, training becomes an organizational responsibility. This being the Defined level, the organization has a set of processes and practices that is used for all projects. The organization has become unified enough in its software management operations that it may now begin to train its people in a common manner, along common lines. That's why, at Level 3, training becomes its own Key Process Area training program. We will take an in-depth look at the role of training at Level 3 (see Chapter 13), but we will begin by touching on it briefly here as it relates to creating an organizational focus on process. The reason for this split is pretty clear when you look at the various KPAs at Level 3. The training that the Training Program KPA deals with (and this is a generalization, but one that works) is chiefly concerned with educating the members of the organization to use and manage the Standard Software Process Set, that collection of software development processes and practices that the organization has defined as its official way of doing business. But that's not the only training required at Level 3. You might consider that training to be "operational." There is another level: "preparatory." As you are first creating the Level 3 structures within your organization to support the use of the SSPS, you will need to train a select group of people to operate within the structure. This is first-step training. Until you have taken this first step successfully, you can't spread your Level 3 program to broader reaches of the organization. We'll address this preparatory training in this chapter and in the following one on creating the defined process set.

When a software organization elects to institutionalize its development and management processes, it becomes in many ways a *centralized* operation. You can think of Level 2 as decentralized in that each project is free to operate in its own way within the general boundaries of the Level 2 KPAs. Becoming centralized at Level 3 requires some mechanism for centralized management, and this usually takes shape in the form of the Software Engineering Process Group. In addition to the members of the SEPG, you will also appoint certain members of the organization (either from a project perspective or from a functional area perspective) as supporting players who provide input and feedback to the SEPG.

To launch your Organization Process Focus plans properly, you will need to train the members of the SEPG in their general role and specific duties, and you will need to train the SEPG support contacts in their responsibilities. Additionally, you will need to orient the workers in your organization about the role and value of the SEPG as well as the general structure and intention of the organization's process improvement initiative.

When we discussed training for Level 2, we talked about the various kinds of training that were needed for a project to run smoothly. Training tended to fall into one of two categories: structural training (instructions on how we do things) and application domain orientation (overviews to orient us to the nature of the business/project). (For details, see Chapter 5.) We defined four kinds of structural training: direct process training, indirect process training, tool training, and role training. And we defined two kinds of application domain orientation: business/operations orientation and technical/architecture orientation. We'll keep these definitions for this chapter and the subsequent dealing with the CMM Training Program KPA. You'll see that they apply at Level 3 just as they did at Level 2.

Before You Begin Training

For the Organization Process Focus KPA, the issue of training is covered under a single key practice ability.

> **Ability 4:** Train the people performing or supporting organizational software
> process improvement as required and needed.[5]

That's a pretty benign statement; it implies a lot more that it says. But there is an important character to this ability that needs to be emphasized—the phrase "as required and needed." Here's what it means. CMM does not expect you to carry out formal OPF-related training activities if your OPF group (the SEPG, the support contacts, and so on) is already up to speed on its duties and responsibilities. As long as you can demonstrate in an assessment that your people in this area are up to snuff on your SPI plans and management processes, you should be OK.

For many organizations just moving into Level 3 operations, however, formal and careful training might indeed be the best course. The inner workings of process improvement, CMM, and process management might be very new to you and your team members. In this case, thorough training will only make your program stronger. For this reason, we'll now take a look at what training areas you might consider implementing to prepare your group to initiate and manage an effective organization-wide process focus.

SEPG Training

The Software Engineering Process Group has, for all practicality, a threefold duty:

- To manage the company's software process improvement plan
- To manage the company's CMM compliance efforts
- To oversee the activities of company workers in relation to process improvement

You might find it profitable to provide training for the SEPG in each of these areas.

The most important is training the SEPG to understand, use, and manage the organization's software process improvement plan. The heart of the Organization Process Focus KPA is the SPI plan. Depending on your company (its size, culture, and market focus), your SPI plan may be a far-reaching, complex document, or it may be comparatively straightforward. But, big or small, it will serve as the guiding principle behind how you operate. Because the SEPG serves as caretaker of the SPI plan, the members of the SEPG must be intimately familiar with the spirit and contents of the plan. If they are not, your Level 3 quality efforts will stall before they can get started.

Who: Members of the SEPG

What: Training on the content, scope, execution, and management of the organization's software process improvement plan

When: When a member is appointed; as membership changes; as the SPI plan is revised

Scope: Training that prepares the members of the SEPG to use the SPI plan and manage its evolution within the organization

Type: Direct process training

To support the management and use of the SPI plan, you should consider training members of the SEPG in the structure and philosophy of the Capability Maturity Model, with emphasis on Levels 2 and 3. Naturally, you can implement a sound and effective process improvement program within your organization without the use of CMM, but if you are reading through this chapter right now, we can assume that you are approaching process improvement with a view of doing it through the Capability Maturity Model. That being the case, your Level 3 organization will need some knowledge of the model to help guide its actions and assess its progress. In particular, your SEPG will need a comfortable understanding of the Key Process Areas and key practices that shape CMM. This training need not be official Software Engineering Institute training, but it does need to be thorough enough to support your SPI efforts under CMM.

What I have seen from companies that have successfully moved into operating as Level 3 organizations is that the SEPG has the following depth of knowledge concerning CMM:

- Knowledge of the spirit of CMM and its practical implementation
- A basic and broad understanding of the KPAs for Level 2
- A basic and broad understanding of the KPAs for Level 3
- A detailed knowledge of the implementation and management of the KPAs' Integrated Software Management, Software Product Engineering, Integroup Coordination, and Peer Review

The fourth item is the critical training item from the perspective of managing your Level 3 program. The first three prepare your SEPG to work within the guidelines of CMM. The fourth is the knowledge base that will enable the SEPG to manage process improvement activities. These KPAs are the "shared" KPAs of Level 3, the ones that are dynamically implemented for all projects and thus shape project management and provide the mechanisms for feedback to measure and refine your organization's Standard Software Process Set. (See Chapter 7 for a general overview of these KPAs.)

Who: Members of the SEPG

What: Training on CMM in general and specifically on those Level 3 KPAs (ISM, SPE, IC, PR) the members may need to monitor

When: When membership is appointed; as membership changes; as the SPI plan is revised

Scope: Training that prepares the members of the SEPG to understand SPI under CMM and to be able to help others in the organization work within specific Key Process Areas of the model

Type: Tool training

The Software Engineering Process Group will support your process improvement efforts across all levels of the organization. The members of the group will do this by conducting themselves along two management lines: process management and people management. CMM recognizes this and so suggests that it might be beneficial for your SEPG members to receive general training in these two areas, especially if some of the members have not been formally exposed to either discipline. You'll find that even a basic understanding of each makes for smoother progress in your process improvement efforts.

Who: Members of the SEPG

What: General/generic training in the fields of personnel and process management

When: When a member is appointed; as membership changes; as the SPI plan is revised

Scope: Training that prepares the members of the SEPG to effectively manage SPI activities within the organization

Type: Role training

Orienting SEPG Support Contacts

As we discussed at the start of this chapter, the SEPG works as a kind of centralized controlling body for your organization's SPI efforts. The SEPG manages the plan, oversees CMM compliance matters, and works with the organization to coordinate appropriate SPI activities. This last item is important; this is the way that the SEPG gets feedback from the organization, feedback that is used to refine the process activities of the company. But in order for this to happen, the SEPG needs to have appointed links to the various arms of the software development environment. To facilitate this, you should appoint people within your organization to serve as those links. Which people and the number of people you appoint will depend on your own organizational structure. You may elect to base it on functional areas, appointing someone from the coding, design, and test teams. Or you may elect to do it based on projects, appointing people to represent each project. Or you may do it based on KPA knowledge, appointing people to manage at the line level the Integrated Software Management, Software Product Engineering, Integroup Coordination, and Peer Review KPAs.

However you choose to proceed, you should consider some light training—orientations—for these SEPG support contacts in three areas: the role and value of the SEPG, how to support the SPI plan at the line level, and how to work intelligently under the specific KPA areas that shape your Level 3 program.

The first orientation should serve to introduce the SEPG contacts to the scope and direction of the SPI plan. Software process improvement efforts are efforts carried out at every level of the organization. For them to be especially effective, they must be properly implemented by the average line worker, at the point where the activity is initiated. The people you appoint to link from this level to the SEPG need to know what the SPI plan is about so that they can help relate it to the general workers within the organization.

Who: SEPG support contacts from the Software Engineering Group

What: The SPI plan

When: As appointed; as the SPI plan is revised

Scope: Training on the KPAs and processes of Level 3 as they relate to the operation of the organization

Type: Orientation

The support contacts should also receive orientation in the purpose, scope, and spirit of CMM. This is not as critical as their understanding the intentions of the SPI plan, but it does provide valuable background knowledge about how the organization is structured and operates. The SPI plan will, in all likelihood, reflect CMM to a degree, but if you are going to operate as an "official" CMM shop, then your people should have at least a working knowledge of what CMM, at Levels 2 and 3, is all about.

Who: SEPG support contacts from the Software Engineering Group

What: CMM orientation

When: As appointed; as the SPI plan is revised

Scope: Training on the KPAs and processes of Level 3 as they relate to the operation of the organization

Type: Orientation

Finally, you should consider giving your support contacts an orientation as to the general role and value of the Software Engineering Process Group. This orientation should also include an overview detailing how the contacts should interface and work with the SEPG.

Who: SEPG support contacts from the Software Engineering Group

What: Role and value of the SEPG

When: As appointed; as the SPI plan is revised

Scope: Training on the KPAs and processes of Level 3 as they relate to the operation of the organization

Type: Orientation

Orienting Your Workforce to the Focus on Process Improvement

Focusing your organization on the path to coordinated process improvement involves the participation of many groups: requirements management, project planning, project management, configuration management, software quality assurance, executive management, and potentially many others. In order for these groups to participate fully in the process, it is advisable to give all the workers in your organization a basic overview of several areas of your SPI program. Two that will bring distinct benefits are an orientation to the organization's SPI plan and an orientation to the basics of CMM Levels 2 and 3.

Giving general workers an orientation to the scope and spirit of the SPI plan prepares them to view their daily tasks within the boundaries of process awareness and process improvement.

Who:	General workforce
What:	The SPI plan
When:	As hired; as needed
Scope:	Training on the KPAs and processes of Level 3 as they relate to the operation of the organization
Type:	Orientation

Who:	General workforce
What:	CMM orientation
When:	As hired; as needed
Scope:	Training on the KPAs and processes of Level 3 as they relate to the operation of the organization
Type:	Orientation

Training Related to Evaluations

Formal process improvement evaluations within your organization will probably take place (major ones, that is) only every one to three years. That's what you might call a low-density schedule. Properly conducting these periodic evaluations is one of the most important process improvement tasks your organization will undertake. It's important to make sure that the people who will be conducting the evaluations are trained to carry them out in an effective and efficient manner. It's also important to make sure that the people who are on the other end of the evaluation—those working with the processes or projects being evaluated—are oriented as to what can be expected from the evaluation process. Two training sessions can help address this.

The training session for your evaluators should cover three broad areas: (1) how to conduct the evaluation proper—that is, how to plan one, how to use the correct forms, how to follow the protocol; (2) how to use the resulting data to formulate recommendations and create the evaluation report; and (3) how to work with the various members of the evaluation population to communicate the importance of participation in the process while stressing its "nonjudgmental" qualities.

Who: Your appointed evaluators

What: Training on the purpose, process, and practicalities of conducting evaluations

When: When an evaluator is appointed; as the evaluation process is revised

Scope: Training that prepares the evaluators to execute a thorough evaluation according to process, and to do so within the context of open communication and personnel support

Type: Direct process training

To support the process of periodic evaluations, it is also a good idea to give your software managers and general staff an orientation as to the purpose, process, and practicalities of conducting evaluations. This orientation will help them prepare for evaluations and participate fully in the process. The session can also be used to alleviate any feelings of being judged that can stem naturally from the process of evaluation.

Who: General members of the organization

What: Orientation as to the purpose, process, and practicalities of conducting evaluations

When: As members are hired; as the evaluation process is significantly revised

Scope: An overview of the evaluation process designed to help members prepare for an evaluation and to understand its true purpose and intention within the organization

Type: Orientation

OPF Training as Preparation

Your efforts to train the members of the SEPG, their support contacts, and the general worker in the approach your organization is taking toward process improvement can be seen as preparatory for the subsequent tasks of implementing SPI activities throughout the shop.

The training that I have recommended need not be taken as a rule, but as a series of suggestions. You should bear in the mind that your people will need knowledge of these areas if they are to be conscientious contributors to the corporate mission of process improvement. But if they come to the table with this knowledge intact, you need not feel the obligation to train them anyway, just to follow convention. The idea behind this training (and we'll touch on this further in Chapter 13) is to make sure your people are ready to participate. If you can accomplish this through formal training, go ahead. If you can do it through informal sessions, that's fine, too. If you judge that you don't need it at all, OK. Your professional judgment will guide the level of OPF training needed for your different teams.

A Policy for Organization Process Focus

In this chapter we have looked at what an organization might set into place in order to prepare IT operations to focus on process improvement formally. We discussed a practical structure, a series of supporting processes and procedures, and specific training needs that would prepare your team to implement these ideas. At this point then, we'll look at a final, but critical, ingredient for the Operational Process Focus area. This is the use of an executive policy that will guide the organization's adoption of your OPF initiative.

You'll remember that we took a specific look at CMM policies in Chapter 6, their purpose within CMM, and how to create them. We won't cover that here, so recheck that chapter for a look at those areas. Here we'll simply discuss the contents of your policy, presenting you with a series of items you might wish to include in yours.

Let's begin with this basic point: The OPF policy will serve as an example of executive sponsorship of your OPF activities. Without this, your OPF program is unanchored; it is adrift. The policy, because it comes from the highest point in the organization, sets a standard for performance that must be accounted for at all levels of the organization. This makes it an invaluable tool for pushing forward your CMM program.

The need for an OPF policy is cited as Commitment 1 for this Key Process Area.

> **Commitment 1:** Senior management establishes and maintains the written organizational policy for organizational software process improvement.[6]

As with all CMM-related policies (and a good general rule for policies of all kinds), your OPF policy will be best built when it is short and to the point. That said, consider building your policy around these five statements. They set the path, in a broad way, for the strategic management of software process improvement activities.

This policy calls for an organizational commitment to the following goals:

- Periodically evaluate the organization's processes and practices as related to software development in order to determine strengths and weaknesses

- Based on the results of the evaluation, establish plans for improving the processes and practices

- Make the improvements available to the organization through publication and distribution

- Coordinate implementation of the improvement actions across the organization

- Educate members of the organization in the proper use of the revised processes and practices

A policy created from these goals should adequately meet the general goals you set forth in your Organization Process Focus area. Once the policy is written, make sure to have it signed by executive management and then, just as importantly, make sure to distribute it (through any mechanism you deem best) to all groups throughout the organization.

Supporting Organizational Focus on Process

As we've noted, establishing a focus on process in your organization requires a series of steps that will result in some form or fashion as a structure to support this focus, some processes to follow to manage the focus, training to get your people up to speed on how to use the processes, and a policy to guide all this from the executive level. Out of your efforts to establish this will arise artifacts that you can use during an assessment to demonstrate both adherence to your own organizational standards and compliance with CMM Level 3 recommendations. Following is a brief description of some of the artifacts you might have. Keep in mind that these are just examples. What you end up with may be quite different but just as valid.

Structure

For the Organization Process Focus KPA, you can show that you created a group responsible for managing process improvement activities for the organization as a whole. This is usually called the Software Engineering Process Group, but you can call it anything you want. You might also demonstrate that you have appointed members of the software engineering group to act in a support/liaison role between the SEPG and the various development groups in your shop. For all of the above, you can use organization charts that show the presence of the SEPG, job descriptions that detail the definition of the SEPG and support positions, and staff assignment forms that show you have officially filled the defined positions.

You might also want to show that you have provided the appropriate tools and facilities to help carry out the process improvement management activities. You can do this with a list of the tools you have acquired and deployed for the purpose of process improvement for use by the SEPG or support players. You might also show any rooms or workstations you have dedicated for the use of SPI activities.

Finally, you should be able to show that you have funded all of these to the appropriate level. You can demonstrate this with organizational budget allocations and capital expense items. You can also show this with items in your project plans or on your project budgets if these items are reflected there.

For more on Level 3 structural elements and the kinds of artifacts that will help support a proper Level 3 structure, see Chapter 11.

Processes

To manage your organization's software process improvement activities, you'll need a documented plan in place. This is the software process improvement plan. And in order to derive this you'll need a documented process that guides you from researching the contents to creating a draft, to receiving final approval to publish it. Some of the artifacts you can use to show that you have done all this are the following: an official copy of the SPI plan, along with any early drafts of it, review notes from groups within the organization, and any input notes that were collected early in the process and incorporated into the document. You might also show the SPI plan template, the approved table of contents outline that guides what the authors need to think about and ultimately include in the plan.

In addition to the plan, you should have a documented copy of the plan development process you used to get the plan to the point of publication—that is, the plan that outlines all the steps the authors must take from concept to official adoption.

Finally, you can demonstrate that the plan is actively managed by the SEPG by showing any version control records you have kept, any records of revisions and updates you have done, as well as the distribution avenue you have used to make the plan available to the rest of the organization.

For more on Level 3 processes and procedures, see Chapter 12.

Training

It's a good idea to be able to show that in addition to setting up the structure and getting your processes in place for process focus, you have also trained your people to operate in the new environment. To demonstrate this, gather any training materials and training records you have to show that you provided some form of training in the following areas: training the members of the SEPG and the support players in their specific job roles, training selected group members in the spirit and use of the SPI plan and perhaps in the philosophy and structure of the CMM, orientation for the support players in working with the SEPG, and perhaps general workforce orientation in the spirit and value of software process improvement. For more on Level 3 training, see Chapter 13.

Policy

To show that you have executive endorsement for establishing the process focus environment in your organization and that you have a commitment to this endorsements you should be able to show the executive policy that documents this endorsement and commitment. In addition to the policy itself, you might want to gather any early drafts of the statement, any review notes associated with it, and an explanation of the distribution avenue you used to disseminate the policy to your workers. For more on Level 3 policies, see Chapter 14; for policy creation in general, see Chapter 6. Table 9.1 presents examples of the kinds of artifacts you might develop in order to show that you have worked through the recommendations contained in the Level 3 KPA, Organization Process Focus. As with other artifact descriptions in this book, these are just suggestions. You may have a different set you use, but these have been presented as typical examples of what other companies produce.

Table 9.1 Evidence of Organization Process Focus Activity

KEY PROCESS AREA	EXAMPLE ARTIFACTS
Structure	Organization chart with SEPG, appointment/assignment forms, capital budget, job descriptions
Processes	SPI plan development process, SPI plan template
Training	For each course: Training scope sheet, training invitation, training course material, student hand-out material, completion certificate
Policy	Policy statement, early drafts of statement

Summary

The first step toward CMM Level 3 compliance (assuming the existence of a mature Level 2 operation) is aligning the whole organization in a common direction for software process improvement. In CMM this is called Organization Process Focus, and it's the first KPA defined for Level 3. In this chapter we've discussed ways to set up this Key Process Area and prepare your people to operate under it. But you can't really separate OPF from the thing that OPF is charged to manage, and that is the organization's Standard Software Process Set (SSPS). The SSPS is that set of proven software development and management processes that your team developed during its Level 2 efforts. At Level 3 you collect those proven processes, and then you define them as the way the organization as a whole will operate relative to software development. The Key Process Area OPF is designed to manage the evolution of the SSPS over time. But, in order to do this, the SSPS must exist.

That is why the ideas and concepts concerning OPF cannot be fully expressed until you have an understanding of the KPA Organization Process Definition, the KPA that deals with establishing the SSPS within your organization. We'll discuss this KPA in the next chapter, and for all purposes you should think of OPD as a companion KPA to OPF; they support and define each other.

Implementing the concepts in this chapter takes you to (about) 15 percent compliance with Level 3 recommendations.

Table 9.2 Key Practices Fulfilled by Implementing the Concepts in This Chapter

MANAGEMENT AREA	ACTION	KEY PRACTICE
Structure	Create the SEPG, fFund the SEPG, appoint SEP contacts	Commitment 1, Ability 1, Ability 2, Ability 3
Process	Create SPI plan development process, create SPI plan template	Activity 1, Activity 2, Activity 3, Activity 4, Activity 5, Activity 6, Measurement 1, Verification 1, Verification 2, Verification 3
Training	Train SEPG in: use of SPI plan, use of CMM, process management Train SEPG contacts: use of SPI plan, working with SEPG, CMM orientation, Train workforce in: SPI plan orientation, CMM orientation	Ability 4
Policy	Create OPF policy	Commitment 1

Organization Process Definition

The entry point for Level 3 is a degree of maturity marked by an already present focus on process improvement. The move to Level 3—the organization's adoption of a common set of software development processes and practices—is almost always accompanied by a depth of experience that provides a benchmark for what works well. At Level 3, that knowledge is formally defined.
Booch Kasadian, Process Development Enterprises

There are two kick-off KPAs for CMM Level 3. We talked about the first one, Organization Process Focus, in Chapter 8. Now we will deal with the second one, Organization Process Definition. From these two KPAs, the other five KPAs of Level 3 emerge. This is different from the Level 2 structure. At Level 2 we could see how all six of those KPAs (from Requirements Management to Project Tracking to Configuration Management) could have arisen together, parallel to each other in many ways. But at Level 3 something happens to change that parallel nature. Your organization comes together—and intersects—in its process improvement activities. Two big changes herald this: First, you set up an organization-wide process improvement group (the SEPG) to oversee and coordinate SPI activity; second, and perhaps more important, you establish a common set of software development processes and practices that are adopted for use by the whole organization for every project.

You will begin moving in this direction by focusing on establishing the organization's process focus (Chapter 9) and then by defining your organization's Standard Software Process Set. From there, the rest of Level 3 can come into play. In a very real way, our discussion here of Organization Process Definition is an extension of the previous chapter's material. Both are shaped to provide a common management direction for process improvement and to bring your IT shop into harmony in the way it develops software systems. And in a very real way, it is the ultimate achievement of your Level 2 work. It's what Level 2 leads to.

At Level 2, the Repeatable level of the CMM, you were in a discovery mode: trying out different processes and practices to see which worked best, discarding those that didn't work out at all, and repeating the winners to fine-tune them even more. With consistent attention to the effort, you should end up with a collection of the best processes and practices, those that have been proven to work well across a wide variety of project types. Now the diverse search can stop. At this point, you can institutionalize these processes and practices, making them the gold standard by which all projects are developed. They become the way the whole organization conducts its software development business. The process improvement focus hasn't ended, but it has shifted. It is no longer diverse. It reaches a level of maturity where at last it can become unified. At the last step of Level 2 you are ready to define this standard. At the start of Level 3 you do it.

Creating a Defined Way of Doing Business

Level 3 is called the Defined level because it's the first stage at which you can define an official way for your IT shop to develop software systems. It's a common definition, one adhered to by all groups within your shop and one supported by a centralized authority within the organization. You can attach many names to the collection of processes and practices that you decide to adopt for organizational use. Some people call it the Defined Software Process Set (DSPS); others call it the Organization Process Standard. I call it, for no other reason than the sake of convenience, the Standard Software Process Set (SSPS). You are naturally free to label it whatever you wish. The important thing is that we establish a common understanding of what it is. This understanding will arise out of what we accomplished at Level 2 and what we should think about adding to it at Level 3. We'll start with a broad view.

At the highest level the SSPS comprises five assets. Two (perhaps the major ones) are carry-overs from Level 2. These are the documented processes and practices that you have elected to institutionalize across the organization and the descriptions of the software development life cycles you have elected to allow for use on your projects. (You'll have to add a few new processes here to support some new Level 3 activity, but the bulk of it comes from Level 2.)

Three new assets emerge from Level 3 to support the Level 2 assets. The first is a set of tailoring guidelines that helps your people fine-tune the SSPS to the unique needs of a specific project. The second is the establishment of a common measurement database used as a repository for all project-level process and practice measurements. Finally, you establish a centralized process library that is used to manage and version control the contents of the SSPS. In this chapter we'll look at what's involved in each of these areas.

Goals of the Organization Process Definition KPA

The main goals of the activities built into the Organization Process Definition KPA are as follows:

Goal 1: The activities for organizational software process definition are institutionalized to support a defined process.

Goal 2: A set of standard software processes for the organization is established and maintained.

Goal 3: Assets related to the organization's set of standard software processes are available to software projects.[1]

NOTE I have chosen to include the goals as defined in draft C of Version 2 of the CMM specification. There is no essential difference between this draft and the published 1.1 spec, and I think the draft additions make the general purpose of OPD clearer.

These goals call out for four basic and somewhat generic activities:

Define the SSPS. The SSPS must be a *documented* collection of processes and practices, and it must be unified in some way. It doesn't have to be found in one big book, but it should be logically accessible as a whole. It (being all its parts) needs to be separated out from what was used and discarded in the past; it needs to be current.

Centralize its use. Once the SSPS is defined, it should be brought into the center of the organization. The entire organization must know its purpose and its makeup, and to control its use and evolution, it needs to be centrally managed.

Make it available to the whole organization. Once the SSPS is defined and centralized, it needs to be made available to all groups within the organization whose work it shapes. It's one thing to have a standard, but if no one has access to it (and this includes providing for training and operating resources), then the standard might as well be nonexistent.

Provide an avenue for feedback. Finally, to foster a continuing focus on process improvement, the organization should provide a way to elicit feedback from the users of the SSPS.

These goals bear a direct relation to the goals of the Organization Process Focus KPA. There the Software Engineering Process Group (SEPG) is created to manage the implementation of these goals. The Organization Process Definition KPA is all about amassing the SSPS and then maintaining it.

We'll begin our look at this KPA with a brief discussion of the kind of organizational structure you might elect to put in place to support the recommended activities of this KPA.

A Structure to Support Organization Process Definition

The Organization Process Focus KPA and the Organization Process Definition KPA can be thought of as two sides of the same coin. They complement one another. Together, they bring centralized process management into your organization. For the Organization Process Focus KPA, you established the Software Engineering Process Group, and

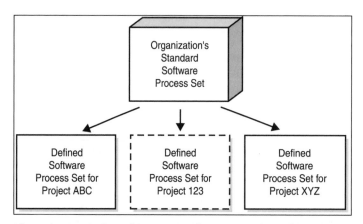

Figure 10.1 Project planners use the SSPS to draw the source process steps required for their projects. Each project in the organization is free to take the SSPS and tailor it to the project's specific needs. The guidelines for tailoring should in fact be a part of the SSPS.

you appointed support contacts as a liaison to the SEPG. You created a software process improvement plan to guide SPI activities, and you set in place the authority, funding, and facilities to support these groups over the long run.

The Organization Process Definition KPA uses the same structure to serve the needs of process definition, with a few extensions. There are three key practices for this KPA that suggest a structure to support the KPA's specific activities:

Ability 1: Establish and maintain the plan for organizational software process definition (that is, perform the activities for organizational software process definition according to a defined process).

Ability 2: Obtain adequate resources and funding for organizational software process definition.

Ability 3: Assign responsibility and authority for organizational software process definition.[2]

You may notice that Organization Process Focus has already given you a structure to handle each activity. What's new here are the job roles. For Organization Process Focus, you set up the SEPG and the support contacts and you charged these people with creating the SPI plan. In that sense, most of Process Focus was focused on Level 3 setup activities: getting things in place to operate at the defined level. For Organization Process Definition, we expand the roles created in Organization Process Focus. We now add the daily management duties required to keep SPI activities ongoing in the organization in an organized manner. These new activities include the following:

- Define the Standard Software Process Set
- Identify approved software development life cycles

- Create and maintain SSPS tailoring guidelines

- Create and maintain an SSPS repository

- Create and maintain a centralized measurement database

These new activities will need to be integrated into job roles of the SEPG, the support contacts, or perhaps into a new series of positions you create. However you structure it, responsibility for the activities should remain with the SEPG. These are centralized activities as defined previously and need to be centrally controlled by the governing SPI body.

What you will need to consider is the extension of activity. From the activities mentioned, your process definition structure will require three tangibles:

- Documented Standard Software Process Set

- Centralized measurement database

- SSPS repository/library system

This structure may call for increasing the operating budget for the group and perhaps adding new facilities, tools, and other resources. The structure you set into place to support the expanded roles will depend in large part on how you set up the SEPG and its supports, as described in Chapter 9. To help you consider how best to support these new activities, we'll take a brief look at the scope of each in the next section.

Processes for OPD

For the Organization Process Definition KPA, you will need to define how the SSPS will be used and managed within the organization. Organization Process Focus established the mission and the teams responsible for this. Here we establish what the teams should be charged with. In essence, there are five activities to undertake. In this section we'll look at the following:

- Steps to establish the SSPS

- Steps to identify approved software development life cycles

- Steps to define SSPS tailoring guidelines

- Step to create an SSPS repository

- Steps to create a centralized measurement database

We'll begin with the SSPS.

Establishing the Standard Software Process Set

The central control point of your Level 3 CMM program is your core process set. Out of this you manage your software development activities. In this section we talk about putting the SSPS together, but it's really not an assembly process. You should actually amass the SSPS over time. Working at Level 2 will expose you to the processes and practices that work best for your organization across a broad spectrum of tasks. You'll discover what works best for estimating, what works best for SQA, and so on. By conscientiously moving through Level 2 you should, by natural accretion, begin to collect the components of your organization's standard process set. Almost by definition, you will have reached Level 3 when the set is complete.

The act of defining the SSPS is of central importance to successful CMM implementation. Yet it is also pretty wobbly. And by wobbly I mean that I can't (and the SEI can't and your consultants can't) direct you on how to do it. As central as it is to the framework of the CMM, the SSPS is even more a reflection of your shop's business flow, and so only you and your people, those who know how your shop works, can adequately define it. In fact, the CMM seems to acknowledge this by its straightforward way of expressing the task in Activity 2 of Organization Process Definition KPA:

> Establish and maintain the organization's set of standard software processes.

That single activity will go a long way to helping you become a cohesive, process-centered software development shop. And we could no doubt write an entire book on this activity alone. In practicality, though, it's a task that comes down to your hands or the hands of your process teams.

With this in mind, I present the following steps as a series of considerations you might undertake when moving to define the SSPS within your shop. These steps can be used to move through the definition process so that you end up with a collected process set that meets the needs of your organization while positioning it for further process improvement efforts:

1. Review available SSPS materials

2. Select the contents of the SSPS

3. Generalize the SSPS

4. Peer review the SSPS

5. Publish the SSPS

6. Configuration manage the SSPS

7. Revise the SSPS as necessary

We will now cover each of these steps in more depth.

Review Available SSPS Materials

This step is actually embedded in Level 2 activities. As a Level 2 shop, you do this as part of your regular process improvement activities. When you are preparing to move from Level 2 to Level 3, you will have on hand a series of different processes and practices developed across multiple projects over time. Through a period of refinement, you should at some point be able to identify the best of all these. This will require you and your people—perhaps as one of the first jobs of the Software Engineering Process Group —to examine what is in use in your shop carefully and to evaluate its effectiveness.

I don't mean to make this step sound discrete, as if it is something that happens over the course of an appointed week. I define it as a single step only for convenience's sake.

This step might actually be called "work at Level 2 until . . . " The point is to give your-self ample time to review what has been tried out in your shop and see what works, and not only what works for the product but especially what works for your people. In the experimentation stage of Level 2 you should be constantly reviewing and assessing the different avenues and refinements you try out. When you come to the point where you want to institutionalize things, you want to be ready and able to select the wheat from the chaff.

Select the Contents of the SSPS

Software process improvement is a continuous commitment, one that aims for consis-tent and measurable advances. But it's not about perfection per se, getting things absolutely right, right from the start. The SSPS you choose to begin with will not be the answer to all your development issues from the get-go, but it will be an ordered start. So at step 2, after careful review of all the available materials you have worked with, you'll bring together the best of what you have and begin to shape this into a corporate stan-dard.

In Chapters 3 and 4 in the first part of this book, we looked at various processes and practices that you might adopt. Taken together, these might make up part of your SSPS. Table 10.1 shows a sample of some of what an organization's SSPS might contain.

Of course, your processes and practices may be organized differently, with different names, some grouped together or divided further. What you should see is that the full scope of your CMM Level 2 activities is included in the SSPS. In addition, you'll be adding some support processes that we talk about in Chapter 12.

The objective of step 2 is to collect all the defined processes and practices and begin to organize them into a cohesive unit, one that you will be able to publish as a stan-dardized set. You'll need to keep CMM compliance in mind as you do this. As you begin to put the SSPS elements together, make sure to check them against what you have set-tled on regarding CMM requirements. You will want to continually ensure that the set that rises up out of this effort not only addresses your development needs, but also cov-ers what you have decided to adhere to as far as CMM goes.

Generalize the Elements of the SSPS

When you select the contents of the SSPS, you'll be pulling in processes and practices that have proven themselves worthwhile through use on varied projects. Because of this, some of these may still carry project-specific characteristics. An important step in establishing the SSPS is to make the processes and practices as generic as possible, to make them extensible to any project within the organization. To do this, you will have to examine each closely and smooth them out for common use, removing steps or forms or actions that reflect the specific needs of a single project. You'll be able to account for the unique needs of individual projects later, when you devise guidelines to tailor these generic SSPS to specific projects.

The objective in this step is to make the individual components of the SSPS as broadly applicable across the organization as possible while still retaining the effective-ness of each.

Table 10.1 Sample Level 2 Processes Typical in an SPSS

REQUIREMENTS MANAGEMENT	REQUIREMENTS ANALYSIS PROCESS
Software Project Planning:	Software development plan creation/approval process, estimating procedure for work products size, estimating procedure for work product effort/cost, estimating procedure for defining critical computer resources, estimating procedure for scheduling, estimating procedure for risk assessment, software development plan template
Software Project Tracking and Oversight:	Software project tracking process, software development plan revision process, commitment review procedure, status review procedure
Software Configuration Management:	SCM plan creation/approval process, SCM plan template, SCM baseline management process, SCM baseline audit process, change control process
Software Quality Assurance:	SQA plan creation/approval process, SQA plan template, SQA audit process, SQA compliance escalation process
Software Subcontractor Management:	Vendor selection process, contract development process, work plan development process, work plan template, vendor sdp review and approval procedure, work plan change procedure, subcontractor scm review procedure, subcontractor sqa review procedure, acceptance verification procedure

Peer Review the SSPS

After you have established the set of processes and practices that will make up the SSPS, you should review them with the shop to confirm their suitability. Peer review can be formal or informal. We talk more about peer reviews in Chapters 12, 13, and 14. In essence, a peer review is a review of documented material by the team affected by the contents of the document. The idea is to create a session in which the contents can be queried for clarity and inspected for any possible defects. To conduct a peer review, make sure the material is ready for review; then you identify the people who should review it. You send them advance copies for inspection. You schedule a meeting and invite the reviewers. You hold the review meeting and take change notes. You revise the material as needed; and then you publish it.

A peer review of the entire SSPS can be a big process, and so it is usually best carried out in pieces, perhaps over time using several review teams. Naturally, parts of the SSPS will affect different parts of your organization so it's a pretty straightforward process to align reviews with those people affected by the various segments.

The point of the peer review should be fairly obvious. If you are going to go to the trouble of setting up an organizational standard, it's a good idea to give the organization a chance to take a look at the standard. Most of your people should know the material well: They will have been working with it in various forms for some time now. The peer review will serve three purposes:

- It will give your people a chance to understand what will be included in the standard.

- It will give them a chance to shape the standard to more suitable ends.

- It will provide a sense of buy-in to the whole effort of institutionalizing your software development practices.

Publish the SSPS

With the SSPS assessed, collected, and reviewed for organizational acceptance, it can now be published. Published in this sense really means to be made accessible to the organization as a whole, to be designated for use by the organization as a whole. We'll take a look later in this chapter at setting up a repository for the SSPS. This is a location where the published (the official version) SSPS will reside. From this location, it is accessed by the organization in a controlled manner.

Configuration Manage the SSPS

The SSPS is the key management tool to manage in the organization's resource repository. Key to its successful use is its uniform and consistent application within the organization. Changes to the base standard cannot be made willy-nilly, nor should you allow for the possible alteration of the assets without some form of due process. That's why it's important to place the published version of the SSPS under the controls of configuration management. This will help ensure that everyone in the organization is working with the same assets throughout project development.

Revise the SSPS as Necessary

The SSPS is the starting point for coordinated process improvement within your organization. In Chapter 9, we looked at how this coordination gets its focus. Part of it comes through the implementation of a software process improvement plan, the SPI plan. This plan will contain a management approach for periodically examining the SSPS. Like your operations at Level 2, Level 3 is not a static plateau of fixed conduct. Refinement and improvement continue onward. Once the SSPS is in place and you have had time to roll it out in your organization and use it under a variety of circumstances, you should establish checkpoints to inspect it for efficiencies and effectiveness. The SPI plan will map out these checkpoints and provide a process for revising the SSPS as necessary.

Defining the Approved Software Life Cycles

A software life cycle is a series of steps undertaken to develop a software system. Most of the time it's represented as a work breakdown structure (WBS): the steps ordered with indications of time durations, the resources required, and the costs associated with each step. You can see it as one of the central tools for both project planning and project management. When a project planner begins to develop a software development plan, one of the first things to consider is the life cycle that will be used. An organization using a centralized process library should be able to help the person make that choice. The CMM phrases it as an Organization Process Definition key practice this way:

> [The organization will] establish and maintain descriptions of the software life cycle models approved for use by the projects.

Identifying and defining these choices usually consists of five steps:

1. Study and select the life cycles
2. Define them and their steps for all to use
3. Peer review them for approval
4. Configuration manage the results
5. Revise them as necessary

Let's take a quick look at each.

Selecting the Software Life Cycle Models

There are many established and industry-accepted software development life cycles available for use by software shops. There's the waterfall, in which you develop the full section of one aspect of the project (like requirements) before handing off to the next effort (requirements handing off to analysis). There's the evolutionary methodology in which a system is built in pieces; first, the core pieces are put into place, then the process starts over to add more sophisticated features, and so on as the system grows. There are many other methodologies. Some software shops have their own work breakdown structures, their own life cycle models.

What your SEPG needs to be aware of is that your SSPS will need a selection of models for your people to choose from for project management. A single life cycle will probably not be enough to accommodate all project types (but if you can justify that it is, that's fine, too). You and your SEPG members need to look closely at what life cycles you want to work with, which ones fit your needs, and which ones don't.

Documenting the Life Cycle Models

The step above—selecting the life cycles—involves a dose of steady research and intelligent analysis. Once you have selected the set of life cycles your organization will use, you can set about posting these into the SSPS. The descriptions you come up will be used by the organization as a basis for project planning and project management. The descriptions then should be adequate for those two tasks and should contain detailed steps and definitions on each activity included in the work breakdown structure. If you are using an industry standard life cycle model, like the waterfall or spiral methods, then you will be readily able to find the detailed descriptions you need. If you are using your own custom life cycle methodology, then you will need to make sure that the documentation available on it is suitable for the needs of the organization.

Peer Review the Life Cycle Descriptions

After you have selected the family of life cycles you'll support in your SSPS and defined them for use by your shop, you should have a review of the descriptions with the shop to confirm their appropriateness. The process of peer review can be a formal or informal one. We talk more about peer reviews in Chapter 12, 13, and 14. In essence, a peer review is a review of documented material by the team affected by the contents of the document. The idea is to create a session in which the contents can be queried for clarity and inspected for any possible defects. To conduct a peer review, you make sure the material is ready for review. Then you identify the people who should review it. You send them advance copies for inspection. You schedule a meeting and invite the reviewers; you hold the review meeting and take change notes. You revise the material as needed; and then you publish it.

It's important to peer review the descriptions of the selected life cycles because the life cycle will rest at the heart of every software development plan. The range you select and the descriptions of each will bear a large impact on the capability of the SSPS to address a range of IT needs. The review and approval of these by the organization is important to the mission of organized process improvement.

Configuration Manage the Life Cycle Descriptions

The software life cycles (and their descriptions) that you end up with through the peer review process now become a hard asset within your organization. By "hard," I mean that they are fixed; no other choices are available other than them. They represent the set of life cycles available for project planning and project management. To protect the integrity of these assets, their descriptions (detailed definitions on how each works) need to be configuration managed. This way you can ensure that the version of the life cycles in the current SSP repository is current for the organization. Revisions to the life cycle descriptions should come through the change control process, and new versions should be made available—be published—only through a document base line control process within configuration management.

Revising the Life Cycle Descriptions

Over time, the nature of business changes, sometimes in small ways, other times in big ways. You may find that your shop is moving more and more toward handling very large projects, or you may find that your shop is beginning to deal with software systems pertaining to a specialized segment of industry. Business also changes as new tools and technologies become available to industry as a whole. As things change, you'll want to keep an eye on your life cycle descriptions. You may find that from time to time you have a need to modify to stay current with business needs. You may need to add new life cycles or to retire old ones. You may want to change some of the elements of another.

It's a good idea then to schedule periodic peer reviews of the life cycles you are using in your shop. The reviews don't have to be frequent, and they may not even have to start out being very formal. But the regular attention you give to them will help ensure their suitability to your needs without major interruptions.

Creating the SSPS Library/Repository

The organization's library of software process-related documentation is used to collect, store, and make available the process documentation that it uses for current and future project management. In the preceding section, we discussed how to amass and build the Standard Software Process Set. This central effort at Level 3 is important because it defines how the organization will work to produce software systems. Once you have formulated the contents of the SSPS, you must now make it available to the organization as a whole. And not just make it available. You should make it available in a manageable way—that is, in a way that will protect its integrity.

At this juncture, you should consider creating an SSPS repository. This is some form of library system that houses the contents of the SSPS in a central place for use by the whole organization.

The CMM describes this activity in the Organization Process Definition KPA as:

> [The organization] establishes and maintains the organization's library of software process-related documentation.[3]

The SSPS will in all likelihood contain a collection of documented processes and procedures that touch on most groups in the organization and shape how software projects are managed. The SSPS may contain such items as software process descriptions, procedures for scheduling and estimating, templates for software development plans, templates for software quality assurance plans, training materials, process aids, and other support tools.

All of these will need to be collected and organized as a whole. They all relate to one another, and they potentially affect one another. The repository then will serve as a centralized management environment in which the individual elements of the SSPS can be version controlled and accessed.

You have a lot of choices when it comes to configuring the repository. You may elect to set up a basic hardcopy library, or you may choose to implement some form of automated software management tool. In either case, the goals will be the same: to keep the contents of the SSPS current, avoid data corruption, and provide ready access to the members of the organization.

In order to set up the repository, you should consider the following four general steps:

Design the repository for your environment. You and perhaps your SEPG should design the way the repository will work in your environment. You will want to come up with a series of controls for it. For example, you will need to define how documents become a part of the repository, how items are removed from the repository, and how your people access the contents of the repository. A lot of this can be based on your change control and version control processes, but the approach will have to be well managed. Issues such as access rights, repository reports, repository management responsibility, and repository reviews will all need to be documented.

Peer review repository design and functionality. Once you have decided how the repository will be set up, you will need to review the design with members of your organization. The review—a formal peer review if possible (see Chapters 8 and 12 for more details on peer reviews)—will give your people the opportunity to understand the purpose and use of the repository and to question any details concerning its use that might be unclear or perhaps in need of adjustment. Involve those people in your organization who will be using the repository most often, and then solicit their feedback on its design. It will be important that there is a consensus of opinion on the structure of the repository. Try to ensure through the peer review and to as great an extent as possible that the repository fits the day-to-day business needs of the organization.

Implementing use of the repository. Once the structure of the repository has been designed and reviewed by the organization, it can be implemented in your shop. The repository will hold the contents of the SSPS as well as some other supporting materials, like the tailoring guidelines. Implementing the repository will involve several steps, including technical setup and training. Take time to make the setup and the training as thorough as possible. This repository will become the central management tool for the SSPS in your organization. If it works well, you will find that it provides a smooth avenue to the tools of project management for all the projects ongoing in your shop. Provide ample support to the organization on its use and regular maintenance.

Revising the repository's framework. You will need to periodically take a close look at the workings of the repository with two things in mind. First, you will want to examine the contents of the repository. As the SSPS changes—when new process assets are added or when process assets are retired—you will have to make sure that these changes are reflected in the repository. Because one of the main purposes is to keep the SSPS current for all members of your shop, this will become an important duty. Second, you will want to periodically assess how well the repository is working for your organization. Here you want to make sure that the repository (and the processes and procedures governing its use) are well suited to how your people work. From time to time you may need to refine how the repository works, to bring it closer in line with how your people work.

Defining the Tailoring Guidelines

At Level 3, your organization adopts a Standard Software Process Set. The SSPS becomes the central project management tool used for software development in your shop. Everyone uses it. As a complete set, though, it might not be right for all projects. The idea of the SSPS is that it is a superset of development processes and practices. Sometimes (perhaps often) you will find that all of them don't always apply to the needs of each project. Small projects might not need to be so comprehensively managed.

Other projects—those very constrained in scope—may require only a slice of the SSPS. Each project, after all, is its own thing. Very rarely will you find that two projects are exactly alike, that they require the same management and oversight steps. The value of the SSPS in your shop is not that it is applied in full for each project in your shop. Its value comes from the fact that it is robust enough to be tailored to the needs of each project. Each project can adapt the SSPS for its unique needs, in order to be optimally managed. That is why it is important at Level 3 to create a series of guidelines that help your people tailor the SSPS to the needs of each project.

This is a very important element of Level 3 operations. The tailoring guidelines will be continually referenced and used as projects are introduced into the organization. The tailoring guidelines will become a source for project planning, estimating, team assignment, project tracking, configuration management, and most of the other elements of development. For this reason you will need to prepare the guidelines carefully and with consideration.

Your guidelines should provide for a range of tailoring options. Reasons why your staff may want to tailor the SSPS include the following situations:

- The project's technical approach may require a specific blend of SSPS elements.

- The project may not represent a full-life cycle effort, and so it requires only a streamlined version of the SSPS.

- The project may be of such a nature that some acceptable SSPS processes can be appropriately waived.

The CMM calls for tailoring guidelines in the Organization Process Definition KPA this way:

Activity 4: [The organization will] establish and maintain tailoring guidelines for the organization's set of standard software processes.[4]

This can typically be performed in six steps:

1. Study and select the tailoring steps
2. Document the steps for all to use
3. Establish the procedures to waive certain SSPS steps
4. Peer review the guidelines for approval
5. Configuration manage the results
6. Revise the guidelines as necessary

Let's take a quick look at each.

Establish the Tailoring Criteria

To start this process, your SSPS should be in place and you should know its contents. Your tailoring guidelines should cover a range of customization options. For example, you should specify the selection criteria for choosing a software life cycle from the acceptable choices. You should also specify the criteria for identifying which process steps will be included in the project's development plan. A good idea here is to identify which steps are mandatory for all projects—that is, which ones cannot be waived. A minimal set of process steps may be used as a good starting point for project planning. From this, needed processes can be added. In your SSPS, you will have a series of processes, a series of reports, perhaps pre-identified milestones, perhaps pre-identified work products. All these are items that will need to be considered for inclusion in a project.

Some organizations begin the tailoring process (which will naturally grow and develop over time) by creating three or more classes of projects. The classes represent project size and/or scope. The largest class gets a certain prepackaged SSPS treatment, the next gets a different treatment, and so on. This may be a good way for you to start. Or you may elect to establish a set of individual rules that can be considered for each component of the project's SDP. However you approach it, make sure the tailoring guidelines are clear and can be easily implemented by your planners and managers.

Documenting the Project's Software Process

The tailoring guidelines you create will be used in the project planning effort to create the framework for the project's software development plan. We've discussed the contents of a software development plan in Part One of this book. The tailoring guidelines will be used to flesh out the SDP, to give it the detail it needs. You may wish at this point to establish the minimum contents of a software development plan—that is, a minimum set of sections to the SDP. This minimum set will complement the tailoring guidelines, providing a template for decision making against the guidelines.

Waiver Procedure

Part of the initial approval process for each project's SDP should be a review of waivers developed to address the tailored SSPS for the project. At the time it may be necessary to go beyond the normal bounds for typical SSPS customization, and these cases may require special review before they are officially allowed. In this case, you might consider the use of waivers. Here a waiver is a form (backed by a series of steps) that the planner (or some other participant) fills out to indicate why certain normally accepted steps are being omitted from the project. The waiver will typically identify the project, the steps omitted, and the reasons for the omissions. These forms become part of the SDP, usually part of the front matter or perhaps an appendix. The waivers should be reviewed and approved by management before the SDP is reviewed and approved.

Peer Review the Tailoring Guidelines

It's important to peer review the tailoring guidelines and the waiver procedures because these will shape the structure of the software development plan. The choices you establish will bear a large impact on the ability of the SSPS to address a range of IT needs. The review and approval of these by the organization is important to the mission of organized process improvement.

Configuration Manage the Tailoring Guidelines

The tailoring guidelines and waiver procedures that you end up with through the peer review process now become hard assets within your organization. By "hard," I mean that they are fixed; no other choices are available other than them. They represent the set of process choices available for project planning and project management. To protect the integrity of these assets, they need to be configuration managed. This way you can ensure that the versions open for use by your people are current for the organization. Revisions should come through the change control process, and new versions should be made available—be published—only through a document base line control process within configuration management.

Revising the Tailoring Guidelines

Your SSPS will, over time and as the nature of your business changes, need to change itself. As your shop grows or your industry focus shifts, you may find the need to add, retire, or enhance your set of tailoring guidelines and waiver procedures. In fact, this is the norm in a program of software process improvement. All things will change. So, as things change, you'll want to keep an eye on your tailoring guidelines. You may find that from time to time you need to modify them to stay current with the contents of your SSPS.

It's a good idea then to schedule periodic peer reviews of the guidelines you are using in your shop. The reviews don't have to be frequent, and they may not even have to start out being very formal. The regular attention you give to them, though, will help ensure their suitability to your needs without major interruption.

Measurement Database

You began your software process improvement program at Level 2 by repeating the steps you use to create software from project to project. You studied that repetition by taking measurements of what worked well and what didn't. Based on the measurements you could then refine the steps, making them more effective with each iteration. That's the essence of software process improvement. Use, measure, refine, reuse. At Level 2 you will have spent time defining and collecting a series of different measurements for each of your projects. You will have taken measurements in the areas of project planning (like the raw data for estimates), measurements for project tracking (like the number of schedule variances), measurements for configuration management (like the number of change requests), and so on.

At first, these measurements might have seemed a little superfluous, not much help. And that's true early in the collection process. When you are just starting, the measurements won't tell you a whole lot. Over time their value will become apparent. In fact, time is essential for measurements; that is how trend lines will become established. You'll begin to see patterns emerging from the data, data that tells you, for example, that you are consistently overestimating in this area or that you are regularly dealing with a large amount of change requests.

More and more, you will manage your process improvement efforts based on your measurements. And at Level 3 this effort becomes even more important. At Level 3 you make the measurement-taking process standard across the organization. All your projects begin to collect the same kinds of measurements, and these measurements are predefined so that everyone knows what they are. These centralized, predefined measurements represent the organization's measurement database. It's described in the Organization Process Definition KPA as this:

Activity 5: [The organization] establishes and maintains the organization's software measurement database.[5]

As part of the Organization Process Definition, you and your SEPG (or whoever you designate) should create this centralized measurement management tool and make it available for use by the whole organization. You can approach this task using the following general 10-step process:

1. Define the measurements
2. Design the database
3. Peer review the definitions and the design
4. Create the database
5. Configuration manage the database
6. Version control the measurement definitions
7. Maintain the database for integrity
8. Manage proper use of the database
9. Release measurement data to the organization as needed or requested
10. Revise the measurements and the database as necessary

Let's take a brief look at each step.

Define the Measurements

There's no standard set of measurements you should collect for your organization. Every organization is different. What is a useful measurement one place might not be so useful someplace else. But if you conducted your Level 2 program appropriately, you should by now be pretty familiar with the use of measurements on your projects. I hope that you already have a set of measurements you have been using for some time. The first step in the process then is to define what these measurements are, to codify them in a sense. This will then become the set of measurements that will be collected on every project.

We've talked about measurements in Part One of this book, and we mention them again in Chapter 12. You should expect to define a somewhat broad series of measurements. You'll probably have a few for requirements management, project planning, project tracking and oversight, and perhaps some for subcontractor management, some for software configuration management, software quality assurance, software product engineering, training, peer review, intergroup coordination, and so on. There's no limit on what you collect, but don't define measurements just to have them. Make sure each serves a specific purpose in your process improvement efforts.

For each measurement definition provide a description of the measurement, an indication of the measurement unit to be used, the measurement formula if one is needed, an owner responsible for collection, and a collection frequency. Also, note that you may not require all measurements to be collected for all projects. If this is the case, you may wish to tag each measurement as mandatory or optional or to code for the kind of project for which it needs to be collected.

Design the Database

For the sake of consistency and coordinated management, the measurements should be centrally located. Here I use the term "measurement database," and what I mean is a typical database, one in which the measurements are entered as a series of individual records. But you don't have to automate this if you don't want to. The objective is to manage the measurements centrally. How you accomplish that is up to you. A relational database is a handy, common way to do it, and it's the way I'll assume here.

You should design the measurement database to reflect the needs of your organization. The DBMS you select, the environment it runs under, and the amount of support it requires will need to be carefully thought out. Part of the design will emerge from your definitions. These will help you with the structure and formats of the tables. But you will also need to consider other aspects, such as user access rights, entry edit criteria, and measurement reports. All these considerations must be weighed against the needs of your users and the maintenance of the database itself.

Peer Review the Definitions and the Design

In steps 1 and 2, you defined a series of measurements to be collected for each project, and you designed a database to store the measurements. At this point, you get a buy-in to what you have created from the rest of the organization. To do this, you should consider holding a peer review on the measurement database. This is a process in which you gather together representative users of the database and go over the definitions and the operations of the database itself. This will give the reviewers a chance to study each in detail and to submit ideas for clarification or modification. The processes associated with a peer review are discussed in Chapters 8 and 12, but in essence it's built as a review meeting. You select the participants, send them the measurement definitions and database information to study, schedule a meeting, hold the meeting, take notes, and then revise the material as requested. The peer review will help cement a common understanding of the purpose and use of the measurement database across the organization.

Create the Database

Now that the organization has had a chance to review the measurements you have designed, you can proceed with the process of creating the database and implementing it within the organization. A note at this point: Don't worry about making the database perfect from the start. Just make it useful from the start. You'll have time to refine it the more it is used. The process of creating and implementing the database may be somewhat technical in nature, and you may need technical assistance for this step. Of course, it all depends on the complexity of your design and the database tool you have chosen. Set the system up, and then make it available to your staff. Be sure to provide any training and documentation that might be helpful for using the database.

Configuration Manage the Database

The measurement database is an organizational tool, to be used by people within the organization. But it's not intended for common management. You want to avoid the possibility that people can alter it on the fly or add their own measurements when the whim strikes them. The integrity of the database—its structure and its contents—has to be protected. The best way to do this is to place the database system under the care of configuration management. An appointed configuration manager can take charge to maintain the database, keep it running for the shop, and shield it from unapproved changes or corruption.

Version Control the Measurement Definitions

In the previous step, you locked in the safe-keeping of the measurement database by placing it under configuration management. You need to protect the measurement definitions in the same way. You went to the trouble of defining the measurements in the first place in order to provide measurement standards for the organization. Projects will collect measurements according to specific measurement definitions. That way the measurements will share a common background. But if the measurement definitions begin to shift over time in a this-way/that-way flux, their meanings will begin to be lost. There will cease to be a common background that gives the measurements applicability across projects and for future projects. That's why it's important to version control (or configuration manage) the measurement definitions. Only authorized people should have access to the core definitions, and changes to the definitions should be introduced only in an organized manner and through a define change control process.

Maintain the Database for Integrity

Part of the job for configuration management is to care for the integrity of the data in the measurement database. To address this, from time to time, the configuration manager should review the data entered into the measurement database to ensure its completeness, accuracy, and currency. This is really a maintenance focus. You want to take care to keep the data in the database as clean and current as possible. You may find the need to delete old measurements that have lost their relevance. You may want to remove incomplete records or records that appear to have been incorrectly entered. For the data to have its most use, it will need to be as clean as possible. Regular inspections of the database contents will help ensure this.

Manage Proper Use of the Database

This is an important item, one that shares a concept I have stressed elsewhere in this book. The software CMM is not about judging people, their skills, or their value to the organization. It is not a basis for collecting performance data on software workers. It is solely concerned with software processes and the improvement of those processes. You shouldn't use CMM as an avenue to enhance human resource management. That's not what CMM is about.

One thing about the measurement database is that some people in your organization might think it's a good tool for extracting performance data. They might think that they can use it to tell which groups are doing well, which are doing poorly. Curtail that endeavor from the start. Measurements in the database are useful for many things but not that. Measurement data on its own is a poor pointer to performance indicators. Out of the context of daily flows, the data tells you little about performance causes, factors, and indicators. To use the data in that way is to use it inappropriately.

Make sure that the people in your organization understand the real use and purpose of the measurement data: to help you analyze process functionality, improve it, and enhance planning overall.

Releasing Measurement Data

The data you amass over time in the measurement database will be used mainly for two purposes:

- The first purpose is to provide performance data on the processes and practices contained in the SSPS. Over time, you'll collect such kinds of data as the number of requirement changes, the types of schedule deviations over the course of a project, resource effectiveness, and so on. This kind of data can be used to analyze the effectiveness of the SSPS and to point to areas of strength and areas of weakness within the SSPS. The database is a great source for beginning process improvement analysis.

- The second purpose is to increase the effectiveness and accuracy of planning efforts. The database will accrue over time a wealth of trend line data, data that shows how estimates turned into actuals, how forecasts faired in reality. This data can be used to help make future predictions better by basing them on similar examples from the past.

Such data can help serve the needs of the people at work in your organization. You need to provide a mechanism to get data analyses and summaries to those people who can use them. This includes SEPG members who are planning process improvements and project planners and estimators who are shaping the future work for the organization.

Revise the Measurements

Over time your measurement needs will probably change, so you should keep an eye on the measurement database and work to keep it current. The database may need to be revised when new measures are added, when measures are retired, or when the definitions of measures need to be changed. It's a good idea to manage all database changes through your internal change control process and to peer review changes as they are documented and made ready for implementation.

Training for Organization Process Definition

To properly use, manage, and refine the organization's Standard Software Process Set plans, you will need to train the members of the SEPG in their extended role and specific duties, and you will need to train the SEPG support contacts in their enhanced responsibilities. Additionally, you will need to orient the workers in your organization to the nature and use of the SSPS and its related tools.

When we discussed training for Level 2, we talked about the various kinds of training that were needed for a project to run smoothly. Training tended to fall into one of two categories: structural training (instructions on how we do things) and application domain orientation (overviews to orient us to the nature of the business/project). (For details, see Chapter 5.) We defined four kinds of structural training: direct process training, indirect process training, tool training, and role training. And we defined two kinds of application domain orientation: business/operations orientation and technical/architecture orientation. We'll keep these definitions for this chapter and the subsequent dealing with the CMM Training Program KPA. You'll see that they apply at Level 3 just as they did at 2.

For the Organization Process Definition KPA, the issue of training is covered under a single key practice ability. It reads as follows:

> **Ability 4:** Train the people performing or supporting organizational software process definition as required and needed.[6]

The phrase "as required and needed" is important. It means that the CMM recommends a considered approach to job execution preparation, training the people who need to be trained, preparing people to work in their specific job roles. The proper use and management of the SSPS is so central to success at Level 3 that training takes on special importance. You will need to employ care so that your people are demonstrably up to speed on their duties and responsibilities. We'll now take a look at what training areas you might consider implementing in order to prepare your group to use and manage software project development under the broad umbrella of the SSPS.

Potential Training Courses for the SEPG and Contacts

Three courses relate to training for the Organization Process Definition KPA. They all have a few things in common. They are all forms of preparatory training; that is, they prepare your process managers to create the core Level 3 components of your process improvement program. From this, they are all what I call one-time classes; your people need to take them only once, or until they change significantly. And they are all specialized courses; they are specific to the role of process management and not general courses in the sense that they apply to everyone. For these reasons you may find that regulated self-training or group mentoring is the best way to impart the training material. Here's a quick look at each course.

One of the first things you'll have to do when you begin to move from Level 2 to Level 3 is to define and publish the SSPS. You'll need a plan for doing this, a process to follow that can be repeated when you need to enhance the SSPS. Once you have created a plan to produce the SSPS, you will need to train your people on how to go about it. They will need to know the process: what to include in the SSPS, how to amass it, how to review it, how to get it approved. This is the beginning of your Level 3 activities, and you will need to have people ready and in the know for it.

Who: Members of the SEPG and support contacts

What: Training on the process to define/publish the SSPS

When: Early in the Level 3 effort

Scope: Training that prepares the members of the SEPG (and support contacts as needed) to create the SSPS. This covers collecting, merging, reviewing, and publishing the SSPS.

Type: Direct process training; one time

Part of the process of developing a centralized SSPS is to identify which software development life cycles can be included in the SSPS, which ones can be endorsed by the organization as acceptable for us on its various projects. You will have developed a series of consideration steps for this selection and definition, and so your process managers need to trained on how these steps work and how they apply to the SSPS (its definition and use) overall.

Who: Members of the SEPG and support contacts

What: Training on the process to identify acceptable software development life cycles for inclusion in the SSPS

When: Early in the Level 3 effort

Scope: Training that prepares the members of the SEPG (and support contacts as needed) to identify acceptable software development life cycles for use by the organization.

Type: Direct process training; one time

One of the main management responsibilities of the SEPG is to oversee the creation of process tailoring guidelines. These guidelines are used by project planners and other members of the organization to customize the SSPS to the needs of each project. Once you have the SSPS in place, you will need to follow a set of steps to define the tailoring guidelines. You will have to know what these steps are (see the previous section on tailoring processes) and train designated people in them.

Who: Members of the SEPG and support contacts

What: Training on the process to define SSPS tailoring guidelines

When: Early in the Level 3 effort

Scope: Training that prepares the members of the SEPG (and support contacts as needed) to create guidelines to tailor the SSPS for individual project needs

Type: Direct process training; one time

Potential Training Courses for Managers and Line Workers

What you'll notice about these four process definition courses for the managers and line workers is that they are, by and large, one-time courses, just like the previous ones. They will need to be repeated only when the processes are significantly changed. The idea with these courses is to train the software development practitioners in the organization to work with the Level 3 processes and tools put in place by the SEPG, as described in the previous courses. There are four areas where training might be considered.

The first is obvious: training on the SSPS. Your organization has moved from Level 2 to Level 3 by carefully defining a core set of common processes and procedures that can be used across all projects, in one form or another. You have collected these into a centralized software process set. But at this time there may be many people in the organization who have not been exposed to one or more areas of the set. That is why, once the SSPS has been collected, reviewed, and approved, your shop should be trained on how to use it. This training would include things like an overview of the purpose and scope of the SSPS, the relationship to the SSPS and process improvement, and the day-to-day use of the SSPS. If this is to be the core software development management tool in your organization, the whole group will need to be comfortably familiar with it.

Who: Work group managers and members

What: Training on how to use the SSPS

When: As hired or on assignment

Scope: Training that prepares people to understand and use the processes and practices contained in the SSPS

Type: Direct process training; one time

Next is training on the use of the SSPS repository. The repository is your main SSPS management tool. It oversees access to the SSPS as well as changes to the SSPS. It's the mechanism by which the SSPS is kept current and clean. In addition to your people knowing how to use the SSPS as a process tool, they will also have to be trained on how to work with the SSPS in its management environment. This calls for some training on using the SSPS repository.

Who: Work group managers and members

What: Training on how to use the SSPS repository

When: As hired or on assignment

Scope: Training that prepares people to understand and use the organization's SSPS repository/documentation library

Type: Direct process training; one time

One of the main tools you'll set into place for Level 3 compliance is a measurement database. The database will be used as a central storage site for project performance data. The data you collect will be used for two purposes: as an historical foundation for future planning (trend line planning) and as a basis for process improvement analysis. Everyone in your shop will probably need to participate in measurement collection in one way or another at one time or another. To give them a foundation in this effort, they will need to be trained on your measurement database: what to collect, how to record it, how to use the database, and so on.

Who: Work group managers and members

What: Training on how to use the measurement database

When: As hired or on assignment

Scope: Training that prepares people to understand and use the measurement database

Type: Direct process training; one time

A select group of your people will also need to know how to tailor the SSPS during project planning so that the resulting software development plan meets the needs of the project being managed. These people will need to be trained in the guidelines used to tailor the SSPS. You can consider this a course as complementary to the course on the use of the SSPS itself.

Who: Work group managers and members; project planners

What: Training on how to use the SSPS tailoring guidelines

When: As hired or on assignment

Scope: Training that prepares people to use the tailoring guidelines to shape the SSPS to individual project needs

Type: Direct process training; one time

Process Definition Training as Preparation

I mentioned this at the end of Chapter 9, but it bears repeating:

Your efforts to train the members of the SEPG, their support contacts, and the general worker in the approach your organization is taking to centralized process management can be seen as preparatory for the subsequent tasks of disseminating SPI activities throughout your shop.

In light of this, the training courses that I have recommended need not be taken as a rule, but as a series of suggestions. You should bear in mind that your people will need knowledge of these areas if they are to be conscientious contributors to the corporate mission of defined process management. But if they come to the table with this knowledge intact, you need not feel the obligation to train them, just to follow convention. The idea behind this training (and we'll touch on this further in Chapter 13) is to make sure your people are ready to participate. If you can accomplish this through formal training, go ahead. If you can do it through informal training, that's fine, too. If you judge that you don't need it altogether, OK. Your professional judgment will guide the level of process definition training needed for your different teams.

A Level 3 Policy for Organization Process Definition

In this chapter we have looked at what assets an organization can set into place to manage the ongoing tasks central to both quality software development and software process improvement. We discussed how the structure from Organization Process Focus might be extended. We looked at a series of processes and procedures used to support the SSPS. And we reviewed potential training needs to help prepare your team to implement these ideas. At this point then—as we did with Organization Process Focus—we'll look at a final ingredient for the Operational Process Definition area. This is the use of an executive policy that will guide the organization's adoption of your OPD initiative.

NOTE We took a specific look at CMM policies in Chapter 6: their purpose within CMM and how to create them. We won't repeat that here, so recheck that chapter for another look at those areas. Here we'll simply discuss the contents of your process definition policy and present you with a series of items you might wish to include in yours.

A beginning basic point here holds true for all CMM policies: the process definition policy will serve as an example of the executive sponsorship of your OPD activities. Without a formal policy, your OPD program will be unanchored, adrift. A policy, because it comes from the highest point in the organization, sets a standard for performance that must be accounted for at all levels of the organization. This makes it an invaluable tool for pushing your CMM program forward.

The need for some form of process definition policy is cited as Commitment 1 for this Key Process Area :

The organization follows a written policy for developing and maintaining a standard software process and related process assets.[7]

As with all CMM-related policies (see the policy descriptions in Chapter 6 and at the end of Chapter 9), your Organization Process Definition policy will serve best when it is short and to the point. Less than a page will usually accommodate any policy. That said, consider building your policy around the following four objectives. They set the path, in a broad way, for the strategic management of the Standard Software Process Set.

The Standard Software Process Set is defined for the organization. What this means is that your software development processes and practices have been committed to paper (or disk, CD, and so on). Further, this process set is recognized as the major tool used by the whole organization for software development. It's a *centralized* software process set.

The SSPS is maintained and periodically evaluated. It's not enough to define the SSPS and leave it alone. Regular maintenance is required. The goal in an SPI environment is to use, measure, refine, and repeat. Your SSPS is no exception. For it to grow in value and applicability, it needs to be conscientiously maintained (kept current with business needs) and evaluated for improvement.

Projects use a tailored version of the SSPS. The SSPS can be thought of as a superset of the development processes. But in its pure on-the-shelf form, it might not perfectly fit different kinds of projects. It might be too broad, or it might call for steps that don't apply to a certain kind of project. To address this, you should create a series of documented tailoring guidelines that allow your people to fine-tune the process set to the exact needs of a project.

Projects and other uses of SSPS report back measurements as data for future improvement considerations. This is a key SPI commitment. Use, measure, refine, use again. That's how to work toward regular improvement. The organization must make a commitment to learning lessons, to analyzing its actions. By collecting and reporting measurements over the course of its projects, the organization can build a repository of valuable performance data.

A policy created from these four concepts should adequately meet the general goals you set forth for Organization Process Definition. As with all CMM policies, once it's written, make sure to have it reviewed, approved, and signed by executive management and then, just as importantly, make sure to distribute it (through any mechanism you see as best) to all groups throughout the organization.

Supporting Organization Process Definition

As we've noted, establishing a program to manage and maintain a process definition for your organization requires a series of steps that will result in a structure to support this focus, some processes used to manage the definitions, training to get your people up to speed on how to use the defined set, and a policy that endorses all this from the executive level. Out of your efforts to establish this program will come certain artifacts that you can use during an assessment (or just to keep on record) to demonstrate both adherence to your own organizational standards and compliance with CMM Level 3 recommendations. Following is a brief description of some of the artifacts you might see coming out of your process definition management/maintenance program. Keep in mind that these are just examples. What you end up with may be quite different but just as valid.

Structure

For the Organization Process Focus KPA, you created a group responsible for managing process improvement activities for the organization as a whole: the Software Engineering Process Group. All the artifacts that rise up from this area can be used in conjunction to support Organization Process Definition. You probably also appointed members of the software engineering group to act in a support/liaison role between the SEPG and the various development groups in your shop. For all of these, you should have things like organizational charts that show the presence of the SEPG, job descriptions that detail the definition of the SEPG and support positions, and staff assignment forms that show you have officially filled the defined positions.

You are probably also able to show that you have provided the appropriate tools and facilities to help carry out the process improvement management activities. This might be a list of the tools you have acquired and deployed for the purpose of process improvement for use by the SEPG or support players. You might also have dedicated facilities to support SPI activities.

You might also show that you have funded all of these items to the appropriate level. You can demonstrate this with organizational budget allocations and capital expense items. You can also show this with items in your project plans or on your project budgets if these items are reflected there.

Finally, you can show the existence of these items in direct support of organizational process definition activities:

- The SSPS itself
- The SSPS repository
- The SSPS tailoring guidelines
- The centralized measurement database

For more on Level 3 structural elements and the kinds of artifacts that will help support a proper Level 3 structure, see Chapter 11.

Processes

To demonstrate your conscientious support of an organizational process definition program within your organization, you can show the various documented process and procedures you have developed and set into place within your shop. We've talked about the major processes for the following:

- Creating the organization's SSPS
- Identifying the organization's approved software development life cycles
- Using the software development life cycles
- Defining the SSPS tailoring guidelines
- Using the SSPS tailoring guidelines
- Creating the measurement database
- Using the measurement database
- Creating the SSPS repository
- Using the SSPS repository

For more on Level 3 processes and procedures, see Chapter 12.

Training

It's a good idea to b able to show that in addition to setting up the structure and getting your processes in place for managing a process definition you have also trained your people to operate in the new environment. To demonstrate this, gather any training materials and training records you have to show that you provided some form of training in the following areas: training the members of the SEPG and the support players in their specific job roles, and training various groups the spirit and use of the various SSPS management processes. For more on CMM Level 3 training, see Chapter 13.

Policy

To show that you have executive endorsement for establishing and managing defined processes in your organization and that you have a commitment to this endorsement, you should be able to show the executive policy that documents this endorsement and commitment. In addition to the policy itself, you might want to gather any early drafts of the statement, any review notes associated with it, and an explanation of the distribution avenue you used to disseminate the policy to your workers. For more on Level 3 policies, see Chapter 14; for policy creation in general, see Chapter 6.

Table 10.2 presents examples of the kinds of artifacts you might develop in order to show that you have worked through the recommendations contained in the Level 3 KPA, Organization Process Definition. As with other artifact descriptions in this book, these are just suggestions. You may have a different set you use, but these have been presented as typical examples of what other companies produce.

Summary

Beginning a CMM Level 3 program takes your organization into the business of centralized process management. This move requires you to create a focus on process man-

Table 10.2 Evidence of Program Compliance

KEY PROCESS AREA	EXAMPLE ARTIFACTS
Structure	(Same as Process Focus with . . .), SSPS repository, measurement database
Processes	Defining SSPS, defining life cycles, defining tailoring guidelines
Training	For each course: training scope sheet, training invitation, training course material, student hand-out material, completion certificate
Policy	Policy statement, early drafts of statement

agement within your organization, which you do with the help of a Software Engineering Process Group and an organizational software process improvement plan. These two elements guide the organization in its process management and use activities.

At the same time, you define for the organization a common set of software processes and practices to be used on software development efforts. This Standard Software Process Set is used and managed by the organization across all software development efforts. To support the SSPS, you establish a set of tailoring guidelines used to fine-tune the SSPS to the needs of each project. And you introduce all of this into the organization with the support of training and feedback avenues defined for use by your work force. A sharply defined process focus and a central set of common practices will serve as the foundation of your developing Level 3 activities. They will help you move in an organized manner toward increased development efficiencies within your project activities and enhanced product quality overall.

In the next chapter we'll take a look at some of the processes you might consider adding to your SSPS to support centralized process management and software development within your organization.

Implementing the recommendations in this chapter takes you to about 15 percent Level 3 compliance, and together with the recommendation in Chapter 9, to about 30 percent Level 3 compliance.

Table 10.3　Key Practices Fulfilled by Implementing the Concepts in Chapter 10

MANAGEMENT AREA	ACTION	KEY PRACTICE
Structure	(Same as for Process Focus)	Ability 1
Process	Create process to define the SSPS, define approved life cycles, define tailoring guidelines, create measurement database, create SSPS repository	Activity 1, Activity 2, Activity 3, Activity 4, Activity 5, Activity 6, Measurement 1, Verification 1
Training	Train SEPG/contacts in: defining SSPS, defining life cycles, defining tailoring guidelines Train workforce in: using the SSPS, using the life cycles, using the tailoring guidelines, using the measurements/ database, using the SSPS repository	Ability 2
Policy	Create OPD policy	Commitment 1

Creating Level 3 Structures

The structures that are put into place at Level 3 are there, ultimately, to help you communicate. There is an organizational need to share a common body of knowledge with the workforce. There are also specific communication needs within each project—sharing information on progress, status, and the risks each group needs to be aware of.
Dan Payne, Senior Analyst, Lockheed-Martin Corp.

Throughout Levels 2 and 3 of CMM, you'll find recommendations that encourage you to add new positions or functional areas to the existing structure of your organization. When you understand the spirit of CMM—that its goal is to help you shape the tools you need for process improvement and, ultimately, quality improvement—it's easy to understand why. The details that make up conscious process improvement require consistent attention and distinct action. Both are needed. Consistent attention without the action results in nothing better than lip service; action without consistent attention is a recipe for energetic disaster. At Level 2 you begin to put in place the enhanced structure needed to focus attention on process improvement and to direct project actions along defined lines. You will continue this at Level 3.

Organizations that would rate at "Initial" on the maturity scale lack the built-in structure that promotes process awareness and improvement. In these shops, especially the rawest ones, the only measure of performance is getting to the finish line. That may be a good measure for a sprinter in a 100-yard dash (a 9.X seconds effort), but it's not so good for more complex operations. A ship that sets out for New York from London had better be concerned with more than docking. There will be engines to maintain, navigational tactics to address and adjust, weather issues to be aware of, a crew that needs to be fed and rested. The ship (the crew that runs it, at least) needs to be self-aware, and it needs to tend to itself during the voyage. Docking may be the final measure of performance, but it is not the ultimate measure, and neither is it the best.

Building a software system is much more like running a ship at sea than it is like running the 100-yard dash. It's a complex enterprise, a calculated construct, not a single burst of energy. Immature shops tend to operate in bursts, as you probably know. That's the makeup of what is often called "organized-chaos," only it's usually more chaos than it is organized, and the attention it is given is akin to looking up to see if you are at the finish line, seeing you are not, and then sprinting harder. I know because I ran a Level 1 shop for years. I not only ran it, I led it. I was the chief sprinter. It was exhausting.

More mature organizations pay attention to what they're doing. These shops know that the sprinter analogy quickly runs out of steam in practical application. Sticking with the ship analogy, they add a crew to help manage the voyage that is the project life cycle. This crew (and you'll realize it as people, tools, and funding) gives you the structure you need to manage the trip. This structure will carry some degree of overhead and cost with it. That's the reality of quality. But without it, a ship pointed in the direction of New York could easily drift to Newfoundland, and the cost of fixing that error would greatly outweigh the overhead of putting on the right crew.

Review of Typical Level 2 Structure Elements

When you choose to move your shop from the Initial level to the Repeatable level, from Level 1 to Level 2, you begin to add increasing degrees of self-awareness to the organization. You put into place mechanisms that help you progress from being solely product focused, a "come hell or high water" focus, to being process focused also, a focus that will gradually help you avoid both the hell and the high water.

Moving to Level 2 is usually initiated by the voluntary, conscious realization that software systems are best built in an organized environment. You and your team should be willing then to add the framework that holds up this organized approach. The structure of this framework will necessitate adopting a new way of doing business. (The degree of newness will depend on how close to Level 2 your Level 1 business is operating.) This structure will set up boundaries in which your teams will work. Level 1 shops are usually pretty much unbounded: Efforts are free to wander all over the place, to drift wherever the tide of urgency takes them. At Level 2 you establish boundaries that corral and thus focus efforts. You'll find, and your people will find too, that these boundaries more and more bring a level of stability into your environment. Over time, you'll see that the stability will foster consistency, the consistency will increase predictability, and the rise in predictability will lower overall risk.

CMM begins the process improvement at Level 2 by beginning with how projects are managed. Level 2 has little to do with the organization as a unified entity. Your process practices are probably not developed enough to be unified. Instead, the aim is to develop effective processes independently, across projects, with each project free to try out different things. At the same time the CMM recognizes the need for some common structural elements to support this independent approach. The idea is similar to framing a house. Houses come in a wide variety of shapes and sizes, but some common construction techniques governing foundations and exterior wall design apply to all. Same here with Level 2. Just about any software development project that truly seeks the rewards of diligent management and conscientious control will need to operate under a minimum set of management criteria. The CMM calls these the Key Process Areas, the KPAs.

At Level 2 you'll introduce structures into your organization that touch on six areas of project development and management. These are Requirements Management, Software Project Planning, Software Project Tracking and Oversight, Software Configuration Management, Software Quality Assurance, and (if you use outside vendors or integrate third-party products) Subcontractor Management. If your shop currently has the areas operational you are a step ahead; if not, you'll need to build them in. At any rate, you'll probably have to tailor how they work to facilitate CMM's proactive management approach. To support these areas you'll have to make commitments (what level depends on your shop and the size and type of your projects) along three lines: resources, funding, and tools (see Figure 11.1). Resources involve staffing your projects with individuals who are skilled to work in these six areas and who are prepared to carry out their responsibilities according to your published standards. To do this, adequate funding is required. Each project needs to allocate an appropriate slice of its budget and schedule to allow the resources to operate accordingly.

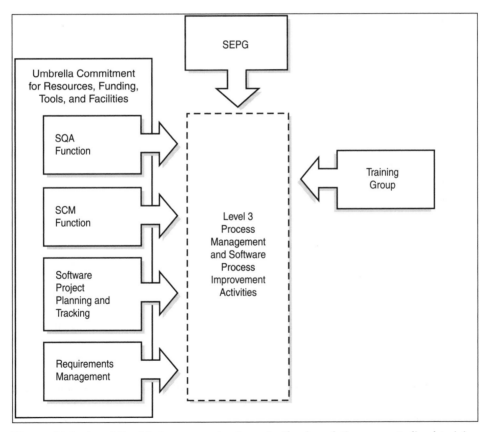

Figure 11.1 Level 3 adds two new structures to the foundation: a centralized training program and a centralized process management team, the SEPG. These support the infrastructure set into place at Level 2.

Finally, you'll need to provide these resources with any tools or facilities they require for performing their jobs in each project environment.

Three items make up the structural characteristics of every KPA at Level 2 and Level 3):

- Resources

- Funding

- Tools

Here's a brief overview of what's usually put in place for each KPA at Level 2. (For more detail on this, see Chapter 5).

For the Requirements Management KPA you'll put in place a structure that includes a person or team appointed to review the requirements and allocate them hardware, software, and so on. You'll provide funding for this team so that it can properly perform this task on the project, and you'll give the team any allocation or analysis it needs to examine the requirements properly. These elements will help the project begin its planning efforts with a clean slate of solid and sound requirements.

For Software Project Planning you'll put in much the same structure. You'll appoint a qualified person or team to produce a software development plan for the project, based on the requirements and the statement of work (and any other available preproject data). You'll fund this position proportionate to the size of the job, and you'll allow an adequate amount of time to carry it out. You'll also provide any planning tools or facilities required to produce the SDP in its expected form. These elements will help ensure that the project is started with as much foresight as is available and with lines of activity defined as clearly as possible.

For Software Project Tracking and Oversight you'll implement a structure that facilitates tracking the progress of the project against the plan. This encompasses the traditional project management job functions. You'll appoint a software project manager to do the tracking, and you'll fund this position to the level required for the project and for the full course of the project. And you'll provide any tools needed to track project activity against what's been defined in the plan. These elements will allow the course of the project life cycle to be monitored at regular and defined points and adjusted as necessary before any large, serious deviations occur.

For Software Configuration Management you'll fill two roles. First, you'll set up a Software Configuration Control Board (called Change Control in many organizations), and you'll appoint members to it. You'll then fund this board to the level required for each project. In addition, you'll appoint a configuration manager to manage base line production for each project and fund this position as required. You'll also set up a configuration management library system, or repository, under which the base lines and other CM material are managed. These elements will help ensure the integrity of base line releases as the various work products and software code versions evolve over time.

You'll do pretty much the same for software quality assurance. For each project you'll make sure that someone or some group has been appointed to carry out the auditing and oversight duties of SQA. You'll fund these positions so that the people can indeed work as expected, and you'll provide any tools they need to work as the projects need them to work. These elements will provide a foundation for feedback that helps realign team activity should it begin to deviate from what's been described in the project plan.

For those projects that use subcontractors external to the organization for various aspects of project development, you'll need to appoint someone on the project team to control and monitor the contractual obligations of the subcontractor and fund this role to support the appropriate level of involvement. These elements will help add visibility to external activities that might have been out of your control or out of your domain of experience.

As you move into Level 3, that is structure you should have in place. Of course, your structure might not be so distinct and segmented as these descriptions. Job roles may mingle, and lines of responsibility may cross. How you set up this structure will depend on the size, culture, and mission of your organization. But somehow these elements will need to work to a recognizable and demonstrable level of productivity.

At the highest level of abstraction, what the Level 2 structural elements support is enhanced project management. They help the software project manager track and correct as necessary conditions that affect the cost, schedule, and integrity of the project's defined work product. This structure has, in effect, expanded the *breadth* of project management and increased its *reach*. As you move into Level 3 you'll see that you now need to move in a different direction structurally. The Level 2 elements stay in place and continue to perform their defined roles, but you now add to them. From this point on you are not just supporting the traditional project values of cost, schedule, and product integrity. You now have to support the unified efforts of the entire organization along the lines of software product development. At Level 3 you need to establish structural elements that increase the *depth* of your process improvement activities.

Level 3 Structural Elements

If you can think of operating at CMM Level 3 as a solid cube, then you put up the six sides of the cube at Level 2. This is a major portion of the structure required to operate at Level 3. In fact, most people who manage to get their Level 2 structures in place over time find it relatively easy to set up the structures for Level 3. With Level 2 you put the people, budgets, and tools in place to carry out project-focused process improvement activities. At Level 3 you begin to fill up the cube, to make it a solid, an integrated whole. You'll find that the structure requirements here do not really introduce new positions or teams (except for one, the Training Program area). Instead it expands the responsibilities of the teams you have in place. At Level 2 your people were charged with performing certain tasks in specific areas with only the project in mind. Now at Level 3 you expand those duties in order to bridge project activities to corporate standards.

Accountability is expanded at Level 3. To accommodate this, the roles of your groups and teams should address the needs of corporate unity and consistency.

You should consider providing supporting structures to seven areas of your organization at Level 3. These areas are Organization Process Focus, Organization Process Definition, Training Program, Integrated Software Management, Software Product Engineering, Intergroup Coordination, and Peer Review. We've already discussed the structures helpful to fulfilling the missions of Organization Process Focus and Organization Process Definition (see Chapters 10 and 11). For this chapter, we'll focus on the remaining five.

Throughout this review you'll see the same three common elements. Each area requires adequate resources, funding, and tools. But don't feel you have to set your structures up exactly as they are outlined in the CMM specification or as I have described them here. How you structure your structure is entirely up to you. If a blend of areas fulfills the purpose and works best within your environment, then go ahead and approach it that way. If you find that further segmentation is in order, then go that way. If you consider the intention and purpose of each of the following items and then accommodate those in your structures you'll be well on your way to CMM compliance.

Training Program

The main new structural area that CMM introduces at Level 3 is the KPA labeled Training Program. At Level 2 training activities were introduced through all the KPAs. Management had to make sure that the members of the project teams were trained to perform their assigned duties in specific areas. For example, the people responsible for turning in estimates to the project planner had to know how to derive those estimates; likewise, planners who were responsible for creating the final project plan had to be trained in the acceptable content and format of a software development plan. Each KPA had its own training and orientation needs. At Level 2, however, the training was really the responsibility of the project or, more specifically, project management. Because each project might have its own processes and practices, training was project specific: "Here's how you do things for this project." Take a look at Chapter 6 in Part 2 for an overview of the kinds of training typically required across the Level 2 KPAs. You won't abandon these at Level 3. Instead, you'll consolidate them. We discuss this in depth in Chapter 14 when we look at Training for Level 3 overall, but here we'll simply reinforce the idea that at Level 3 you will have defined a common set of software development processes and practices for use across the organization for all projects. This reduces, except for the freedom to tailor, project independence with regard to process. That being the case, training becomes a consolidated effort. Your people, no matter what project team they are on, need to be trained in the same things. This consolidation *centralizes* training, and CMM proposes a structure that helps support this centralization.

At Level 3 you will build a training program that serves the training needs of the entire software development shop. You are free to shape this program in any way that best serves your specific training needs. You'll get a good guide for where to start by reviewing the three Training Program abilities that support this structure.

Ability 1: A group responsible for fulfilling the training needs of the organization exists.

Ability 2: Adequate resources and funding for organizational software training are allocated.

Ability 3: Members of the training group have the necessary skills and knowledge to perform their training activities.[1]

NOTE In the new draft of the revised CMM specification (still under review), these numbers shift down as a new first ability is inserted. It calls for the existence of a Training Program plan. We'll look at this plan in Chapter 13, but as far as the structure goes these concepts remain intact.

Establishing a Training Group

This ability calls for you to establish a training arm within your organization. At Level 2 you probably set up a few new groups like SQA or configuration management. It's the same thing here. With common training needs across all projects you'll have to appoint someone or some group to be responsible for addressing these needs. The key term here is "responsibility." Call it training manager or group instructor or the training division, but this will have to be an official assignment, one endorsed and supported by senior management within the organization.

This assignment may be doled out as a full-time or part-time position. It might involve one person or a group of people. You should use your professional judgment in developing the scope and shape of this training function. If you keep it consistent with your training needs you'll be in compliance with the intention of this CMM KPA.

The training group (we'll refer to it as a group from here on as a matter of convenience) will be responsible for performing a series of duties. Understanding these duties may help you decide on a scope and shape for the group. First, the group will need the time, tools, and access to identify the training needs of the organization as a whole. This may involve analyzing in-depth your shop's Standard Software Process Set. It may also involve working with your software managers and line workers to ascertain skill levels and individual project demands. (This effort, as we'll see later, is an important step in developing the Training plan.) The training group will then take this information and create a series of courses that meet the needs uncovered by the analysis. Once this is done (or even as it is being done) the group will have to make a decision on how to deliver the training. It might elect to develop the facilities to handle it in-house exclusively, or it might choose to use the services of an outside training company. Often, it will select a blend of the two.

The group will not only create the training program for your organization and ensure its delivery, it will also have to take an active role in monitoring its progress and effectiveness over time. It will have to keep the training program on track with the evolving needs of the organization and so take regular measurements to produce this visibility. Finally, the group should be required to provide reports on these activities to both senior management and project management on a periodic basis.

Funding and Supporting the Training Group

It's one thing to set up a training group on paper, even to walk around making staff appointments. But if you don't give the group the funding and resources it needs to operate, none of the other stuff counts. If you're going to make a commitment to training it's best if it's a full commitment. The preceding section gave you an idea of what your training group will have to focus on, with what tasks it will probably be charged. As you design the scope and shape of your training group, keep in mind that you will have to fund it and give it the tools needed to carry out its responsibilities.

The funding and support you give to the group should be realistic; that is, it should be proportionate to its tasks. This is an area that needs to be carefully considered. You can find in many organizations that the training program exists on paper but that in practice it is weakly supported and only sparsely funded. I can appreciate the temptation to ignore this area. Busy shops might feel the need to focus all their time and energies on the work at hand. They give only short shrift to their training program, employing what they call on-the-job training that is really no training at all or slim mentoring programs that really amount to ask-me-when-you're-in-trouble programs. As easy or tempting as these alternatives might be, they really don't help an IT shop move along the road of process improvement, and they don't cleanly fit the bill for CMM compliance. You'll need to fund your program to the level that brings about both stability and demonstrable results. When you think about funding, thinking about filling needs in four areas: staff appointment, tools purchase, tool maintenance, and facility design.

You'll have to fund the hiring or contracting of those responsible for training design and execution. This will involve appointing a training manager (in some form or fashion) and perhaps a support staff, too. (The assignment of a training manager has been proposed as an official addition to the next version of the CMM.) Next, you'll need to give these people the resources to carry out their jobs. This includes such things as tools for developing course material, databases for record keeping, training analysis systems, training workstations, and packages for developing presentation materials. You might also consider funding for the purchase of existing course materials and learning programs.

You should also fund so that appropriate training facilities can be established within your organization. The extent of these facilities will depend on the design of your program, but some of the setups you might want to consider are learning centers for self-paced instruction using computer-aided instruction and/or multimedia instruction, ergonomically designed classrooms configurable to suit various learning styles, and workstations equipped for instructional delivery (e.g., online access to training sessions or CD-ROM multimedia training). At the very least, you'll probably have to budget for enough dedicated space so that the training group can conduct its analysis, design, monitoring, and reporting duties.

Choosing Members with Adequate Skill Sets

The final item that will influence the structure of your training program is the need to hire people who are adequately skilled to join your shop as effective contributors. You should be careful to hire people who are up to the job at hand. Staffing the training group shouldn't be a willy-nilly appointment. The importance of training in shaping organizational conduct along consistent lines is so significant that if you treat it mildly or as a side issue it may lead to problems later in many different areas of your operations. When you begin the process of staffing the training group you may choose to appoint from your internal resources or you may choose to hire from the outside.

Whichever way you go, look for a blend of experience in three areas. Each person you bring on doesn't have to show this blend, but when you team is assembled as a whole, it should demonstrate some level of competence in the areas of subject matter expertise, courseware design and development, and general management planning.

Subject matter expertise may be readily in place if you appoint from within. This is knowledge of and familiarity with your Standard Software Process Set. The training mission, after all, is to prepare your people to follow your established processes and practices. If your trainers know them well they will have a head start of preparing the training regimen needed to fulfill this mission. To complement a firm foundation in the content and workings of the SSPS, you might look for people who have general experience in software development and people with an understanding of the scope and philosophy of the CMM.

In addition to subject matter expertise, you should look for people who have training in designing, developing, and delivering course material. This is a specialized area, one that requires a specific set of talents: organizational skills, an appreciation of instructional disciplines, practical experience teaching, and even a sense of art direction and art design skills. Look for people who are either experienced in or have an affinity for needs analysis, courseware design, and educational materials management.

Finally, you'll need people with some level of general management planning experience. A lot of the work in developing and then maintaining an effective, well-focused training program will require this kind of experience. Someone on the team will need to spearhead the development of project training plans, as well as track progress measurements and issue training program status and management reports.

If you combine all three of these structural attributes you'll end up with a competent staff, officially set up within your organization and ready with the tools and the facilities to support the training needs of all the software engineering groups within the organization.

At Level 3, this KPA is the only one that requires such a significant structural addition. The remaining ones, which we'll look at now, are really responsibility extensions that deepen the accountability and scope of some of your current structures.

Integrated Software Management

The Integrated Software Management KPA of the CMM is in many ways an extension of the Software Project Planning and Software Project Tracking and Oversight KPAs from Level 2. Those two KPAs deal with how to plan a software project and then how to track project activity against the plan. But those two KPAs were exclusively project focused. At Level 3 the focus of Software Project Planning and Software Project Tracking and Oversight changes; it expands, and necessarily so. At Level 3, the entire organization has adopted a common set of software processes and practices, and every project is expected to plan and track according to the dictates of these processes and practices. In short, the management of software development has now become integrated at the organizational level. In light of this, project management must now extend past the bounds of the project. The common use of the organization's Standard Software Process Set places two new responsibility elements on project management, and these must be supported by the organization. First, project management must receive support to plan the project using the SSPS, and it must be given guidelines it can use to tailor the SSPS according to the unique needs of each project. Second, project management must be given the time and funds needed to manage the project to include new organizational activities such as Software Product Engineering, Intergroup Coordination, and Peer Reviews.

All of this is implied in the first ability for the Integrated Software Management KPA:

Ability 1: Adequate resources and funding are provided for managing the software project using the project's defined software process.[2]

NOTE There is a draft of CMM still under review that breaks this ability out in more detail, calling for specific assignment of a project manager to manage the project through the plan. We'll account for that in our discussion here.

This is a function for either senior management or high-level project management. It should be accounted for in the overall infrastructure of the organization. The idea is pretty straightforward and ties in with the organization's commitment to process management and improvement. At Level 3, the organization has made a commitment to planning and managing projects in a specific way. This way has been documented in the SSPS, and executive policy says that with only limited exceptions it must be followed. Because there is more involved in project planning and development at Level 3 than there was at Level 2, senior management must allow software project management the extra time and resources it needs to follow the expanded responsibilities in the SSPS.

For example, a Level 3 project will usually feature several new activities not typically included in Level 2 activities, like meetings and milestones for accommodating the specific steps required for software product engineering. Senior management can't mandate that these activities be followed without acknowledging the time and cost they'll require and then allowing these to be built into the project plan and management activities.

Providing adequate resources and funding generally affects two distinct areas:

Providing Support for Tailoring the SSPS

First, resources and funding should be made available so that the software project planner can tailor the SSPS to the specific and unique needs of the project. This usually involves setting up tailoring guidelines that are then made available to the planner (with training potentially included in this) and then the allocation of an appropriate amount of time for the planner to create the plan according to the enhanced elements found in the SSPS.

Providing Support for Managing the Project

Second, resources and funding should be available to allow software project management to include the overhead of centralized control in its management activities. This involves allowing time in the schedule and funding to support such activities as intergroup communications and peer reviews.

Unlike the Training Program KPA, which introduces funding and resources to support a new functional area within the organization, the resources and funding for Integrated Software Management are used to expand the Level 2 roles of software project planing and software project tracking and oversight.

Software Product Engineering

Software Product Engineering is related to Integrated Software Management in that both are extensions of the Software Project Planning and Software Project Tracking and Oversight KPAs of Level 2. Integrated Software Management extended these KPAs to take into account the need to tailor the SSPS and then track the project to include expanded Level 3 activities such as intergroup coordination and peer reviews. Software Product Engineering expands these KPAs in another direction. This KPA sets up a series of defined work steps (or work breakdowns, if you prefer) through which every project should pass. It's a way to set up a series of standardized development and review steps for all projects.

At Level 2 the project planner was pretty much free to develop a software development plan in any way that was acceptable with the project management overall. In Chapter 6, we looked at what might go into a typical SDP, but this template conspicuously lacked a detailed work breakdown structure (WBS). The plan's contents focused more on things like budgets, schedules, work product identification, status checkpoints, and progress milestones. These items remain intact in a Level 3-compliant plan, but the planning is taken a step deeper to include some very specific development activities that all projects should adopt (unless there's a documented reason not to). Naturally, the addition of these steps requires two things: the ability to plan for and manage them and the ability to execute them.

This is reflected in the CMM ability for this KPA:

> **Ability 1:** Adequate resources and funding are available for performing the software engineering tasks.[3]

NOTE The new draft version of the CMM that is currently under review expands this ability by recommending the specific appointment of someone responsible for managing the software engineering activities. This is usually the software project manager, and we'll include this in our discussion here.

For more detail you can also refer to Chapter 4 for the structure recommended for Software Project Tracking and Oversight.

How do you "adequately" provide resources and funding for this KPA? Start off by considering what areas need the support. The details of software product engineering require your project to engage in a series of engineering activities. This will require you to have someone to oversee these activities, people qualified to conduct the activities, and perhaps some tools needed to carry out the activities. Let's take a brief look at each area.

Assigning Responsibility for Managing the Engineering Tasks

The software engineering tasks your project will follow will be detailed in the software development plan (or in some related document). It's one thing to have them defined in the plan, but it's another to make sure they are carried out in the appropriate manner. To ensure this, you need to appoint someone to monitor the engineering activity over the life of the project. There are several ways to accomplish this. The way you elect will shape the manner in which you fund this area.

One way is assign this responsibility to the software project manager. This might be the best choice for your organization. The software project is the point of contact for most tracking and review efforts on the software development activities, so why not have this person track the detail of the engineering activity? It's a logical appointment, but in some cases it might not be ideal. The software project manager begins with the large responsibility of tracking the schedule, costs, and product integrity on a software project. Those are big items. On big development projects it might be asking too much for this person to track the detail of defined engineering tasks as well.

You could decide instead to assign this responsibility to someone on the SQA team. SQA will have someone looking over your project activity for compliance anyway. It might be logical to have that person also audit the performance of the engineering tasks and report on this to project management. This choice would work for many projects. Yet you might decide that this also is not quite ideal. You may want your SQA analysts to focus solely on process and practice, and while they may need to gather independent feedback on how the engineering tasks are being handled, you may want them to remain in that independent role, officially apart from the project team.

A third alternative would be to appoint a special assistant to the software project manager who provides some auxiliary tracking and oversight services that focus especially on the engineering activities.

As you can see, you can take care of this appointment in many ways. Your choice should be based on the needs of your project and the potential resources you have available. However you handle the appointment, make sure that it is done officially, not casually, and make sure that the person or people you select are skilled in the ways required to handle the job. For more on this, see the following section.

Appointing People with the Skills and Expertise Needed

As seen previously, it's important to appoint someone for each project who will be responsible for ensuring that the software engineering tasks defined in the SDP are carried out over the course of the project's life. This sets up the structure to monitor the engineering activities. You need a complementary structure in place, though, for this one to have any purpose. You need to assign skilled workers across the project team who are capable of carrying out the defined software engineering activities. In other words, if you are going to go to the trouble of tracking the jobs you're going to need some people who can do the jobs.

That's the structure you need in place for your Level 3 projects: a skilled team explicitly appointed to perform the work as defined in the plan and to be responsible for its end products. Of course, this can touch on every part of your project team, depending on the scope of the project. In a typical full life cycle software development project, you would have to make official appointments to establish responsible leads in the following areas: requirements management, design, coding, testing, measurement, documentation, software maintenance, and so on. And you should make sure that you are appointing people who have the skill and experience in each of these areas to meet the demands of the plan. Finally, it's best to make the appointments early in the project so they can all participate in the planning and scope analysis efforts.

Acquiring and Deploying Tools

Your structure for Software Product Engineering is now almost complete. You have appointed people to track the engineering activities, and you have appointed people to perform the engineering activities. The final element comes with providing the workers with any tools they may need to perform the activities. This is a broad area, and you'll have to look at your projects to determine what tools should be acquired and deployed. This can include a wide array of products: workstations, database management systems, application software, requirements tracking tools, modeling tools, compilers, test generators, and so on. You'll need to get these tools in place in time for the teams to use them, and you should consider also placing them under version control if they are of the type that might undergo revisions and changes over time.

Intergroup Coordination

Intergroup Coordination is a way of establishing project interface channels, and in the new draft (Craft C) of the CMM this KPA is renamed Project Interface Coordination. The intent and the purpose, though, remain intact. This KPA puts a structure in place within the organization that allows the various teams working on various phases of a development project to regularly communicate with each other in order to coordinate activities and plans for upcoming work. This is an important function for any software development project (for *any* effort within an organization, many would say). At Level 2, this communication and coordination are implied in the activities Of Software Project Tracking and Oversight. But here these activities become more formalized, and a plan is put together for each project that details how Intergroup Coordination will be handled. For this to take place, you'll need a structure that supports the effort. The following abilities from the CMM expresses this clearly:

Ability 1: Adequate resources and funding are provided for coordinating the software engineering activities with other engineering groups.

Ability 2: The tools available for use by the different groups are compatible to promote communications.[4]

The amount of coordination you'll want to account for will depend, of course, on the size and scope of each project. You'll use an organizational standard for planning the coordination activities, but you're free to tailor this to the needs of each project. Some may require extensive coordination; others may require much less. In any event, you'll have to manage the coordination with a structure that has three elements to it: a person responsible for managing the coordination, tools to facilitate the smooth exchange of information, and the funding necessary to bring these people and tools about. Let's take a brief look at each.

Assigning Responsibility for Managing the Coordination Tasks

Someone (or some group) on each project team needs to be appointed to make sure that Intergroup Coordination is actively practiced on each project. Who you choose for this role is up to you and will reflect the culture and shape of your shop. You might select the software project manager or an assistant to the software project manager. Or the person may come out of the ranks of high-level project management. The latitude you have in assigning this position will be balanced by the functions this person must manage. The role will call for someone to prepare the coordination plan for the project, help integrate that plan into the overall software development plan, and then track project activity against the detail of the plan. This might be a full-time role or a part-time role, but be sure to select a person who can take on the responsibilities and devote the proper amount of time to them without a conflict of interest with other areas of the project.

Acquiring and Deploying Tools

Intergroup Coordination is an effort that will bring all of the groups working on a project together at selected times over the life of the project. This coming together may be literal or figurative. You might schedule meetings where representatives from each group get together to review progress, pending issues, and identified risks. You might instead use communication and status tools in a defined manner in order to exchange information electronically, without having to actually come together in one place. Most of the time a combination of the two are used, regular group meetings and e-communications. Whatever blend you decide on, you'll need to ensure that you have the proper tools in place to carry off both.

There are lots of tools you can consider to help out in this area. There are scheduling programs that let you coordinate meetings based on people's personal calendars, e-mail systems that let you send messages to individuals and groups, defect tracking systems that help you consolidate reporting across groups, and library management systems that help you version control documents important to many groups working on the project. These kinds of tools should be deployed with one purpose on mind, to promote communications. To do this, you should make sure that the tools you select (and identify in the coordination plan) are acceptable to all groups within the project team, that they are, to as great an extent as practical, compatible with each other, and that the members of the various groups who will be actively participating in the coordination activities are trained in how these tools work.

Providing Resources and Funding

Once you establish the coordination plan for the project and decide on the tools you set in place to facilitate communications across groups, you should make sure that you give the project the proper amount of funding required to support the coordination activities. This may be in several areas: monies and time for a person to develop the project's Intergroup Coordination plan; monies for a person to manage the activities for the life of the project; monies to procure and deploy the selected tools; and monies and time to train project members on how to use the tools and how to participate in coordination activities.

The scope of your coordination plan will influence how you fund this area. But keep in mind that this will involve members from various groups within the organization. Representatives from requirements management, software quality assurance, documentation, testing, software design, and project management may all, at one time or another, be involved in the coordination activities. The main idea is to put a structure in place that lets all these groups keep one another informed as the various pieces of the project puzzle start to fall into place. Intergroup Coordination, like the use of peer reviews (see the following section), is used to help the project stay on track and to avoid small problems or delays from turning into larger ones. Frequent and open communications is one of the best ways to achieve this. If you keep this central concept in mind and build for it, you'll end up with an effective Intergroup Coordination structure in place.

Peer Review

At this stage in your understanding of CMM Level 3 you've probably come to the conclusion that one of the chief traits of this level is a focus on communication. And that's quite right. Three of the seven KPAs at this level are devoted to communications explicitly (Training Program, Intergroup Coordination, and this one, Peer Review), and the other four actively promote it as part and parcel of their structures. Peer Review is an important part of the communication mix at Level 3. The main purpose of peer reviews is to provide a means for intelligently inspecting work products that emerge from various stages of the project life cycle. The inspections are conducted by a cross-section membership of the project's subgroups, and the aim is twofold: (1) to provide an opportunity for discussion and learning and (2) to look for defects, inconsistencies, and other trouble spots in the products that might affect quality when they are passed down the line. The inspections are usually technical in nature and are typically conducted by technical members of the project teams. (Managerial issues are usually handled through the activities of Intergroup Coordination.) The CMM recommends a structure that supports peer reviews in the following ability:

> **Ability 1:** Adequate resources and funding are provided for performing peer
> reviews on each software work product to be reviewed.[5]

Usually peer reviews are included as an integral part of the software development plan for each project. The plan will hold the schedule for each peer review, it will note the work products that will be reviewed, and it will identify what groups will participate in each review. Perhaps more so than any of the other KPAs at Level 3, the structure for supporting peer reviews is a bit nebulous. It's evidenced as a set of abilities shared throughout the project team. Let's look now at what you might consider when you are setting up an environment that will support peer reviews for your projects.

To set up an effective Peer Review operation in your shop you'll need to make sure that you allocate sufficient funds to each project for the purposes of preparing your people to conduct the reviews and then actually making them happen. To do this, consider these five lines of structural preparation.

Assigning Responsibility for Coordinating Peer Review Activity

As mentioned, Peer Review activity is usually reflected in the project's SDP. If it's not there, then it should be in some related document. (If it's not documented somewhere, then some additional planning might be required before the project starts.) Peer reviews are important enough that you should be sure to appoint someone on the project team to monitor them over the course of the project. Most of the time this is handled by the software project manager as part of regular project tracking, but it might be assigned to anyone on the team you think can best carry out the function. This individual will be charged with three things in general: (1) making sure peer review materials and facilities are ready as scheduled, (2) making sure each review event occurs as scheduled, and (3) making sure proper feedback emerges from each review meeting. Keep these things in mind when you are considering the appointment.

Assigning a Peer Review Leader for Each Software Work Product

Peer reviews are formal meetings and need to be managed as such. It's important that you appoint a leader to conduct the meeting, to make sure it follows process, and to make sure it stays on track (a peril for nearly all meetings). One structure that I have seen practiced in the field with much success is what I call the ARM structure. Each work product review meeting is managed by three people. The first, A, is the main author of the work product (or a representative of the author). This person is present as the meeting's subject matter expert, the person who can answer questions concerning the work product and clarify any ambiguous understandings. The next person, R, is the recorder. This is the person who documents any changes, issues, or action items that arise out of the review. The third person, M, is the official meeting leader, the monitor who guides the participants through an organized review of the work product.

Assigning Specific Roles for the Peer Review Participants

For each work product review, you'll need to decide who should be in attendance. Different kinds of work products may require different kinds of main audiences. Some companies I have worked with divide the peer reviewers into two categories: primary and secondary. The primaries are those people who will be directly affected by the work product or who have provided content items for the work product. These people will need to be very comfortable with the work product as it may affect their future work. Therefore, they need to be very active reviewers, or primary reviewers. The secondary reviewer is a person on the project team tangentially connected but not directly linked to the work product. That person's general feedback is usually solicited but not required for the review. To support peer reviews in your organization you should consider identifying which job roles will be considered for your traditional series of work products and which might be considered secondary. You should then get consensus from the different project teams that this assignment is appropriate and will be supported.

Obtaining Appropriate Tools

You may find that using some specific tools will help you better manage the peer review process. For example, you might use a multiuser calendar system to schedule peer reviews and coordinate attendance. You might want to use a database management system to track issues raised during the review. And then you might simply rely on word processing to help manage these tasks. Whatever tool set you decide on (if, indeed, any) make sure that it is acquired in time for effective use on the project, then deployed in an organized manner throughout the project's infrastructure. Finally, make sure that your peer review managers and leaders are trained on how to use each package in the set.

Providing Funding to Support the Process

Finally, you should ensure that the project has been allocated enough funding to cover the costs of executing the peer review process (for more on this, see Chapter 13). People, time, and materials are needed to carry out peer reviews, and these should be accounted for up front in each project plan. The funding will typically support, at a minimum, the following five steps:

1. Distributing the work products to be reviewed
2. Gathering the author, recorder, moderator, and the primary and secondary reviewers
3. Conducting the reviews
4. Reporting on the results
5. Acting on the results

These structural items are spread across the organization, reaching into every team participating in peer reviews. In many ways, this function is an extension of project tracking and control. In other ways, it is a technical arm of Intergroup Coordination. All groups must take responsibility to support the process, allocating their people with the proper amount of resources and time to make sure the peer reviews make the contributions to common understanding and quality that they are intended to do.

Demonstrating Level 3 Structures

At Level 2, you built up in your organization a series of functional areas that helped support project management and process commitment for your software development efforts. These areas included such functions as software quality assurance, requirements management, and software configuration management. These are usually what I call highly visible functions; that is, they are typically set up as distinct groups, separate (to one extent or another) from each other, at least in terms of task assignment. For this reason, demonstrating compliance with CMM at Level 2 along the lines of having the right structures in place is something of a straightforward process. The organization itself should be evidence enough that you have these areas set up and working. But at Level 3, the structures tend to be less visible. As mentioned at the start of this chapter, the structures you implement are really functional extensions of what you put in place at Level 2. With the single exception of Training Program, the KPAs at Level 3 do not lead to the establishment of any new organizational entities (unless you elect to shape them so). Rather, the abilities of these KPAs lead you to enhance existing functions. Demonstrating that you have done this in compliance with the CMM recommendations may be less obvious at Level 3, but there are lots of artifacts you can use to readily show it nonetheless. Let's take a look at a sample of artifacts that might arise naturally out of your Level 3 environment. These can all be used for internal assessments or for formal external appraisals to show that you have been operating within the Level 3 bounds of the CMM.

People on Your Project Teams

For Level 3 you'll want to show that you have the right people in place for a series of jobs. Your people, obvious as it may sound, can be pretty good evidence of this. You'll want to show that you have people in place to manage and deliver training, people who are able to tailor the organization's SSPS to the needs of each project, people who can track project progress according to organizational standards, qualified people in place to carry out the technical tasks for each project, and people who will manage and facilitate Intergroup Coordination and Peer Review. Your people who carry out these functions should know their job roles and how they integrate with the rest of the project team, and they should be able to intelligently discuss how they carry out their jobs and how they support the project efforts as a whole.

Resumes, Job Descriptions, Staff Assignment Forms

These items complement the presence of your people on the project teams. Individual resumes can demonstrate the experience and educational background needed to carry out specific jobs. Job descriptions can be used to show that the organization has designed its staffing needs along CMM-compliant lines and that the roles have been shaped to fit in with a software process improvement program. Staff assignment forms can show that for each project you have officially appointed people to carry out specific job functions. For each project at Level 3, you should show that you have appointed someone to plan the project using a tailored version of the SSPS, that you have appointed someone to track the project against organizational standards, that someone is responsible for the training needs of the project team, that project team members are qualified to carry out software engineering activities, and that specific people on the team have been appointed to coordinate group communications and peer reviews. These artifacts can help support all of this.

Training Materials

The organizational training program you develop at Level 3 is probably the most obvious new structure you'll set into place. If you do it properly you should have plenty of artifacts on hand to demonstrate its active existence. In addition to your training people, you should be able to show some form of training facilities. You will probably also have a training plan that outlines the training mission for the organization and details available training resources. In addition, you may also have documents that demonstrate the scope of your training offerings. These can include things like course listings and course descriptions, course signup sheets, training schedules, and organizational training requirements. You should also be able to show training plans for each of the projects underway in your shop. Finally, you should be able to show some evidence of class activity. This includes things like examples of textbooks, hand-out materials, and presentation materials. You can also use things like course completion certificates and your own repository of student scores/records to substantiate the activity of your training program.

Lists of Tools

As you set your Level 3 structures in place across the various groups in your organization, you'll probably acquire and deploy a series of tools to help with the new functions you create. These can be used as artifacts to support the existence of the functions. For example, for your training program you might show the use of computer-based training aids, the existence of training workstations, or the use of automated course design software. For intergroup communications you might show the use of common e-mail programs, event scheduling programs, or defect tracking programs. For peer reviews you might show the use of an active issues database, status tracking software, or meeting management systems. All these tools will help show that you have actively implemented Level 3 structural support elements.

Presence on the Organization Chart

One of the cleanest artifacts for structural support is an organization chart showing distinct groups or positions within the organization or within the project that addresses Level 3 recommendations. Organization charts can be for the organization as a whole or for each project. Both would be helpful during an assessment. The organization chart will typically show the various groups set up within the organization. Such a chart might feature such groups as requirements analysis, project management, software quality assurance, technical documentation, testing, and so on. For Level 3 you should probably have a training group on the chart, or at least a box that can hold the training function. More structural evidence can be found on the project team chart. This is typically a chart that shows what functional positions have been assigned to a project, and it may or may not have individual names associated with each position. Here is a good place to show that you have assigned positions to cover things like project planning and process tailoring, team training, group coordination management, and peer review management.

Funding and Budget Allocation

All of the KPAs at Level 3 lead you to perform certain tasks and appoint certain people to manage the tasks. This will necessitate the freeing up funds to cover the costs associated with such activity. A good way to show that you have allocated appropriate funds for these activities and positions is to account for them in formal organizational budgets and individual project budgets. All organizations budget in their own way, but the idea here is to show that you have recognized the costs associated with operating in a quality improvement environment and you have made the commitment to support the environment from a fiscal perspective. For evidence of this you can show staff estimate forms, capital set-asides for equipment purchase, cost reports from the various project areas that relate to the KPA activities, and final project cost reports.

These artifacts are just examples of what might be used to help demonstrate CMM Level 3 compliance during an assessment. They are summarized in Table 11.1. Usually the artifacts one organization produces are very different from what another organization might produce. The forms, management tools, and staffing positions you use within your IT shop may prove very effective in demonstrating the desired level of compliance. As long as you can show that your structures are active, consistently deployed, and operating within the spirit of CMM, you should be fine as far as an assessment goes. You might it find it beneficial to look at the different forms and documents that you produce in the different groups in your organization. You might already be producing many of these artifacts now and will need only to gather them together or tag them for consistent collection.

Summary

At CMM Level 3, you bring about a new dimension to the structures you set up at Level 2. You introduce into the organization a coordinated training program. You set up the bounds and rules for integrated software management. You establish considerations for software product engineering. And you set up formal communications through intergroup coordination and peer reviews. All of these areas need to be supported. They each call for a degree of formalized structure. The same categories we discussed for

Table 11.1   Evidence of Program Compliance

KEY PROCESS AREA	EXAMPLE ARTIFACTS
Training Program	Staff assignment form, general organizational chart, job description, budget allocation/capital account
Integrated Software Management	Staff assignment form, general organizational chart, job description, budget allocation/capital account
Software Product Engineering	Staff assignment form, general organizational chart, job description, budget allocation/capital account
Intergroup Coordination	Staff assignment form, general organizational chart, job description, budget allocation/capital account
Peer Review	Staff assignment form, general organizational chart, job description, budget allocation/capital account

Level 2 structures hold true here. You will need the right people, tools, facilities, and funding in place to support a new series of plans and activities. The organization will need to support both the setup of these areas as well as the on-going operation of these areas. Further, the organization should make a long-term commitment to growing these areas under its umbrella of coordinated software process improvement.

Implementing the structural recommendations in this chapter for CMM Level 3 will take you to about 20 percent program compliance. Together with the recommendations in Chapters 9 and 10 you should be at about 50 percent compliance.

In the next chapter we'll look at how you'll set your new structures into motion through Level 3 plans, processes, and practices.

Table 11.2 Key Practices Fulfilled by Implementing the Lessons in This Chapter

KEY PROCESS AREA	CHAPTER TASK	KEY PRACTICE
Training Program	Assign responsibility, provide funding and resources	Ability 1, ability 2
Integrated Software Management	Assign responsibility, provide funding and resources	Commitment 1, ability 3
Software Product Engineering	Assign responsibility, provide funding and resources	Ability 3
Integroup Coordination	Assign responsibility, provide funding and resources	Ability 1, activity 3
Peer Review	Assign responsibility, provide funding and resources	Ability 1, ability 2

Creating Level 3 Processes

Effective process management at Level 3 requires the extension of what you have built at Level 2. At Level 2 you set the pillars in place for process improvement. At Level 3 you strengthen them, and the foundation for process improvement settles into place.
Ransom Day, Public Health Software Systems

The CMM is all about establishing a framework for software process improvement in your software development shop. Part of this framework comes in the form of certain structures, staff and facilities to carry out the SPI activities. Part of the framework centers on training, making sure your people are prepared to work in a process improvement environment. And part comes from the creation of formal policies that shape and demonstrate your organization's commitment to process focus. But the part that stands for most is the collection of documented processes and practices that you employ to manage your software development activities.

For CMM Level 2, you'll set up processes for requirements management, software project planning, project tracking, SQA, configuration management, and vendor management. Each of these areas can be seen as existing in many ways apart from each other. Each addresses a specific functional area along the development chain. But at Level 3 things change. The CMM introduces only one more independent KPA, Training Program. The others-Organization Process Focus, Organization Process Definition, Integrated Software Management, Software Product Engineering, Intergroup Coordination, and Peer Review—all serve to expand the Level 2 processes, to deepen their reach within the organization, to crystallize tracking elements down to finer detail.

You'll find that the Level 3 processes especially impact (by adding new control elements) the activities for Software Project Planning and Project Tracking and Oversight. The processes and practices of Level 3, like many of those at Level 2, are chiefly project management centered, expanding job role awareness and responsibility for project management. These processes can be seen as the active heart of your SPI program.

They spell out the actions you and your team will take to develop software systems at a new tier of maturity. They are your control mechanisms.

Because they are important they require careful development and documentation, with all the material (forms, applications, Web sites) in place for your people to use them. They require review, approval, and then (with executive endorsement) integration into your Standard Software Process Set. Most importantly, all parties should be trained in their use and objectives. Finally, they can be conscientiously implemented and then measured to test their usefulness and effectiveness in your environment.

In this section we'll go through some basic process elements you might want to include in your Level 3 program. We'll take a look at these by each Level 3 KPA.

Peer Review Process

The purpose of a peer review is twofold: (1) to pass essential system elements down the line of project activity, and (2) to provide an opportunity to inspect the elements for defects. In short, a peer review is both a learning opportunity and an inspection opportunity. Both are essential to quality management. In a peer review members of the project team who are affected by the product in question take the product, study it, then get together to discuss its readiness and integrity. The peer review is a chance to understand the product so that it can be further developed in accordance with the project plan and to question any parts of it that might seem vague or in conflict with other project elements. The objective of the process is to ultimately emerge with a version of the product that all parties agree is in solid shape for further activity.

In Chapter 11 we looked at what kind of structure you should consider having in place to support peer reviews. This includes the ability to identify owner groups, primary reviewer groups, and secondary reviewers. In the owner group you should be able to appoint an official author responsible for the content of the product. (This can even be multiple authors, but for accountability's sake try to keep the total number under four.) Within the owner group you should also be able to appoint a moderator to facilitate the meeting and a recorder to take notes at the meeting. All three should be trained in peer review processes and practices. You should also have established an official approval chain, knowing what sign-offs from what people are needed to signal that a product is ready to be baselined. Third, you should have some kind of version control or configuration management library system in place to be used to maintain the integrity of the baselined product.

Basically, you can peer review two main kinds of project products: management products and technical products. Management products are usually plans, and technical products are usually results documents that reflect some component of the completed project (see Table 12.1).

You can also use peer review for other elements of a project, such as estimates, decision packages, change control assessments, and so on. You can use peer review for any plan or any document that affects others. It's a very versatile quality control tool, and there are no hard rules on what can be peer reviewed and what should not be peer reviewed. In this regard, a degree of professional judgment comes into play. Reviewing everything would become tedious and time-consuming. Review too little, and you could be inadvertently introducing avoidable problems into the project. The decision should

Table 12.1 Some Project Products That Might Be Peer Reviewed

MANAGEMENT PRODUCTS	TECHNICAL PRODUCTS
SPI plan	System designs
Project contract	Integration test plans
Software development plan	Acceptance test plans
SQA plan	User documentation
SCM plan	Technical documentation
Training plan	Requirements specifications
Intergroup Coordination plan	
Subcontractor Management plan	

eventually center on the question of impact. If the product has enough impact as to directly affect project quality or the ability of project work to proceed, it should probably be peer reviewed. In the following sections then we'll take a look at a peer review plan template you can use to plan peer review activity, and steps for a general peer review process.

A Peer Review Plan Template

The Peer Review, the way most places use it, is a natural byproduct of a well-designed software development plan. The goal of the peer review plan is to identify what project products (documents, code, and plans) need to be reviewed prior to approval and when. Common to many software development plans is a Gantt chart that details the project schedule against what work steps have to occur. You'll usually find that included in this detail is a series of progress benchmarks, milestones along the development timeline in which certain products are released to the team for analysis and further work. These milestones are usually good indicators of what needs to be peer reviewed.

For your shop you may assign a specialist to produce a peer review plan for the project, or you may simply assign that responsibility to the project plan. However it's handled, and whether the peer review plan is part of the SDP or a standalone plan, it's important to identify what needs to be peer reviewed in adequate detail. The following basic peer review plan template can be used to help with this:

- Work products for review
- Peer review dates
- Peer review participants
- SQA quality control points
- Metrics collection

Let's take a brief look at each.

Work Products for Review

The first step is to identify the work products to be peer reviewed. A work product is typically a document (such as the requirements document) or a plan (such as the system test plan). The person identifying these products must know the project and know what will be produced during the course of the project. Usually a project will produce a series of management products and technical products, any of which may need to be peer reviewed.

Typical management products include such items as the requirements document, the software development plan, the SQA plan, and the configuration management plan. Examples of technical products include the system design and the various project test plans.

Not every product that comes out of a project need be peer reviewed. But if the product represents a major milestone in progress or if subsequent groups will rely on its integrity for further progress, then it probably should be reviewed.

For each product to be reviewed, you should also consider identifying the following items.

Peer Review Dates

There are usually a series of dates related to each peer review. Three are most commonly identified. The first is the draft ready date. This is the date that really lets the product author (or authors) know when a first draft of the product should be completed. Next is the review date. This is the date (typically about two weeks out from the draft ready date) identifying when the review will be held. Finally, there is the date (perhaps 2 or 3 weeks out from the review date) identifying when the draft should be clean and complete enough to be baselined.

These dates are initial targets to shoot for, and while important they can be adjusted as needed.

Peer Review Participants

Together with the product and its review dates, it is also important to identify the review participants. You need not be so specific here as to cite names, though if you can that detail would be welcomed. But you should at least be able to cite the various groups that will be involved in the process. They should be categorized into three groups.

First is the owner group, the group responsible for authoring the product and arranging and managing the review meeting. Next are the primary receivers, those groups who will be primary reviewers, reviewers whose input and implied approval are necessary for the product's official approval. Finally, the secondary receivers, those groups who are invited to provide input but who are not directly responsible for the progress and approval of the product.

SQA Quality Control Points

Because the peer review plan will guide some degree of management activity on the project, and because it will result at certain points in progress moving forward on the project you should also identify in it at what points SQA should conduct audits of its progress. It's usual to ask SQA to check up on things at the three main peer review dates —the draft ready date, the review date, and the baseline ready date. You can decide which dates or which activity points work best for your shop.

Here you might also cite an end-of-project date in which project management and SQA (and whoever else you choose) get together to discuss how the peer review process went for the overall project.

Metrics Collection

Part of your organization's Level 3 process improvement activities will include the consistent collection of metrics across the various processes and activities you undertake for software development. With this in mind your peer review plan should identify which metrics you'll be gathering from each review. (And they should be close to the same for each review, and almost always the same for each of the same kind of review.) Some organizations track items such as: average prep time by each reviewer. number of critical, major, and minor defects, defect density per page, and number of issues needing further investigation. The measurements identified will be collected and then ultimately entered into the organization's central measurement database.

A final thought here: Should you peer review the peer review plan?

You can, of course, but you'll probably find it easier just to treat it as part of the software development plan and review its contents when the SDP itself is reviewed.

In the next section we'll look at a process to follow for managing execution of the peer review plan.

A Peer Review Process

The peer review plan will set the documents and work products that will need to be peer reviewed before they can be approved and passed onto the next stage in development. A companion to the plan then is a process that can be followed when peer reviews are initiated. Companies will usually come up with their own process, one tailored to their needs and structure, but the following one can be thought of as a generic example of the peer review process, one with steps common to most peer review activities.

1. Draft Ready Date Arrives
2. Draft Author Assigns Review Moderator and Recorder
3. Draft Confirmed to Be Ready for Review
4. Meeting Facilities Prepared
5. Material Distributed and Meeting Announced
6. Review Period
7. Review Meeting Occurs
8. Meeting Notes Distributed
9. Revisions Made as Requested.
10. Revised Document Redistributed

11. Product Submitted for Signature/Approval

12. Product Baselined

13. Process Metrics Collected

Let's begin with Step 1.

Draft Ready Date Arrives

The project plan will usually include a benchmark date for each work product that has been identified for peer review. These dates and work product IDs may come from the peer review plan that has been integrated with the general software development plan, or they might come from other sources, like the SQA plan or the SCM plan. They might even show up as milestones set into the project planner's project schedule. However they appear, it is important that these review dates are documented. The dates give your workers the deadlines they need to shoot for and allow for the organization of related resources in advance.

As a regular project management activity, you should regularly check the progress of a scheduled draft document or product (such as code or compiler versions) prior to the draft due date arriving. But in any regard, the peer review process formally begins when this draft date arrives.

Draft Author Assigns Review Moderator and Recorder

It's typical to assign the author as the one responsible for organizing the peer review effort. The "author" might or might not be the chief creator of the product for review. This person will need to be a representative authority for the product, one who can vouch for its contents and answer questions that might address or help clarify content. You may elect to appoint a single author to a product if it has emerged from a team, or you may assign a few. Keep in mind that assigning more than three authors to a single work product usually results in diminished effectiveness. Keep the author team small.

When the draft date arrives, the author could assign two major roles to the peer review team: review moderator and recorder. The moderator is the person who will lead the review meeting, facilitating the smooth and organized exchange of comments. The recorder is the person who will record the comments made during the review, identifying issues, resolutions, and action items.

The author should have prepared these two selections prior to the due date, being able to request this participation from a list of people available. Each type of work product will probably have its own list of potential moderators and recorders. Setting these lists up in advance and securing support for the process will help ensure smooth selection.

Draft Confirmed to Be Ready for Review

Before the details of the review meeting are set, the author and moderator should perform a basic inspection of the work product up for review. They will look at it to confirm a single trait: Is the planned draft indeed ready for review? Unless it is there is no reason to hold the review. The author and moderator can answer this question on two readiness-criteria fronts: Is the content of the work product complete? That is, does it address the full range of functionality it intended to address? Next, does it conform in layout and presentation to established template and format standards? Has the author followed the proper conventions in presenting the material? You may decide to include your own readiness criteria (and indeed many others might be valid), but these two will serve as an entry point for making a readiness decision.

Of course, the author will come into this step knowing the true condition of the product. It's up to the moderator to look over the document and then confer with the author to arrive at a go/no-go decision.

If the author and moderator agree that the draft is ready for review, then the process can proceed. If they decide that it is not, then they usually initiate a change request to reschedule the draft ready date for a determined time in the future. An announcement might also be made to the expected participants of the review or the issue raised in a regular project status meeting.

Meeting Facilities Prepared

With the draft product ready for review, the author (perhaps with the help of the moderator) sets about preparing the details of the meeting. This usually involves about four basic activities; first are the physical arrangements. The author should schedule a meeting room adequate for the number of attendees (in both size and location). The author should also arrange for any telephone conference bridges necessary as well as any special presentation equipment needed (like overhead projectors, white boards, or video phones).

Next, the author should identify the individual participants who will be part of the review. Many companies use a primary/secondary designation for identifying review participants. A "primary" reviewer is one who needs to be present at the review, one whose input is vital to approval of the work product. A "secondary" reviewer is one whose input is desired but will not detain product approval. Secondary reviewers usually don't have to be present at the reviews. They may submit comments offline.

Third, the author should prepare the review materials that will need to be distributed in advance to the participants. This may involve copying documents or creating overheads, whatever is necessary to present the material at the meeting.

Finally the author should prepare an agenda for the meeting.

Material Distributed and Meeting Announced

With all pertinent information now ready, the author can send out a notice to the participants regarding the scheduled meeting. This is a basic what, who, where, when notice. Together with this notice the author can attach a copy of the agenda and a copy of the material that will be reviewed. You should set a time span that the author can use to set up the meeting dates. A typical period is 2 weeks; that is, the notice for the meeting goes out 2 weeks prior to the meeting occurring. Select a time span that works for your organization and then standardize on it.

Review Period

The purpose of distributing the review material with the meeting notice is to give your reviewers an opportunity to go over the material and organize their comments prior to the meeting. This is also a chance for people to turn in comments to the author prior to the meeting. A person who will be unable to attend the meeting can also use this time to make sure that his or her comments have been registered and that his or her issues will be addressed. Those who can't attend the meeting need only document their comments and then either get them to the author or perhaps pass them to others who can then raise them at the meeting.

This period is very important. If you make it short, say a day or two, your attendees may not have time to adequately prepare for the review, and that might impede the review's effectiveness. But make the period too long (say a month or more), and you may risk having the material set on a back burner, ignored until the last minute, which will bring its own effectiveness compromises.

The path here is to make the time period fit the material. If it is long or complex, extend the time; if it's simple and straightforward, feel free to reduce it.

Review Meeting Occurs

When the review meeting begins the moderator will usually handle its management and flow. The author will be present to answer questions and help clarify discussion content, and the recorder will be on hand to take the necessary notes.

Before the meeting can officially begin, the moderator will have to make a judgment as to whether things are in order to move ahead. This entails establishing two basic conditions. First, are the necessary attendees present? If the acceptable number of attendees is not met or if the group lacks the necessary technical expertise, the moderator may elect to delay or reschedule the meeting. Likewise, if the right people are there but they report that they have not had time to prepare adequately, the moderator may also choose to reschedule the meeting.

If the meeting needs to be rescheduled, the moderator should make sure that proper notification is given to the software project manager so that any other necessary adjustments can be made. Otherwise, the meeting can move ahead.

The moderator will guide the review team through a presentation of the material. The recorder will take notes, being especially diligent to record defects or issues that require further action. You may wish to establish a severity index for each item recorded. Many companies assign an M for an issue that's minor, MJ for major, and C for critical. Usually MJ and C issues will have to be fully adjusted in the product before approval can be granted.

After the review is complete the moderator may have the recorder recount the recorded items to ensure that all have been properly identified. As a final step, the moderator may take a vote to see if another peer review of the material is required or if changes can be incorporated for a simple confirmation read. If the changes are complex, unclear, or extensive, a re-review may be called for. If not, the changes should be made and then the document redistributed for the confirmation read.

Meeting Notes Distributed

As quickly as possible after the meeting, the recorder should prepare the meeting notes for distribution to the attendees. These notes will further confirm what changes are being made to the product. The notes might also be accompanied by a "last chance" notice that says in effect, "Here are the changes we are making; if you anything further to add let us know by X date." The X date is usually about a week out; it's close to the date when the author plans to release the revised draft. This is a final chance to make sure the product will be in acceptable condition for the next phase of the project.

Revisions Made as Requested

As the attendees are off considering any last-minute changes to the product, the author will be busy revising the documented with the necessary corrections, clarifications, and amplifications. During this time some new changes may come in, and the moderator and author will need to review these for appropriateness, perhaps investigating them further.

When the revision date arrives, no more new changes should be made to the document. The author should also confirm that all approved changes have been incorporated.

Revised Document Redistributed

The revised product, now serving as a corrected proof, is redistributed to the review team so that all may confirm that the necessary changes have been made. This should be a fairly clean read for most of the reviewers. Usually a week or two is granted for this confirmation read, with a notice as to the anticipated date of publication.

If the re-read results in any new changes being requested, the moderator may have to work that issue with the help of the author and any review team members who may be affected by the change. One of the advantages to following a peer review process, though, is that it will help avoid the submission of unforeseen or last-minute changes. In the business world, however, these have been known to occur under even the best of circumstances and so they will always have to be dealt with.

Product Submitted for Signature/Approval

With all revisions made to the document, and the document recirculated to the review team, there should come a point where you are comfortable that the document is ready to be approved. Within your organization there should be a managerial/executive level responsible for officially adopting a document. This may the SEPG or the Change Control Committee or a certain group of managers. However you plan to handle this in your shop, you should submit the product to the right authorities for approval. This approval, in the form of signatures or some other official mark, is important. It communicates endorsement from high levels in the organization and lends credibility to the product itself. This approval paves the way for the product to become baselined.

Product Baselined

Now that the product has been reviewed, revised, and approved, you should control its contents by placing it under version control or by baselining it under formal configuration management. The choice depends on what the product is and what your configuration management policies are. All subsequent changes to the product should now come through your shop's change control process.

Process Metrics Collected

At this point, the peer review process is complete. A final step then is to take a look at how the process went. All along the author, moderator, or recorder should have been collecting a series of measurements that indicate activity during the process. These measures will be a source for process improvement decisions and actions in the future, and for use in future project planning. A wide variety of measurements can be collected. Define ones that have meaning for you and your team. Some organizations track items such as average prep time by each reviewer, number of critical, major, and minor defects, defect density per page, and number of issues needing further investigation. The measurements should be entered into the organization's central measurement database for use by others.

Training Program Processes

In the next chapter, we'll take a look at the general working of the Level 3 Training Program KPA. We've already talked a little about the training program in Chapter 11, going over some of the structural elements you may want to get into place to support training activities. The purpose of establishing a training operation within your organization is really twofold: (1) to train your people in a common way on the workings of the organization's SSPS, and (2) to provide any other skill set training that may be required for your people to perform their managerial and technical duties on software development projects.

Your training operation will encompass a series of activities, including appointing people responsible for planning and conducting the training, setting up training facilities, and acquiring the equipment and course materials necessary to hold class. In this section we'll look at the processes associated with the training program. These processes can be used to manage the three major duties of training: defining the courses that the training program will offer, creating a training plan specific to the needs of each project and reflective of the program's offerings, and giving the project team a chance to review and approve the training plan. These three duties fall into two broad categories of activity:

- **Preparing a syllabus for each training course you are offering.** The syllabus presents overview and summary information for each course offered. The use of a standardized syllabus template will help you manage this process.

- **Preparing a training plan for each project being initiated in your shop.** In order to ensure that all team members assigned to a specific project are prepared to carry out their process practices and technical duties, an appointed training manager will usually prepare a training plan for the project that details any training requirements for members of the team in accordance with project business and technical needs. The use of a standardized training plan template will help ensure that all plans share a consistent format and content. And the use of a standardized plan review process will help ensure the smooth review and approval of the plan for the project.

Let's begin with a look at a template for a generic training course syllabus.

A Training Course Syllabus Template

One of the chief jobs in the area of coordinated training management is to develop a series of training courses that address the ongoing needs of the organization. Training may occur in a variety of areas: process training, tool training, job skill training, and so on. As you identify and define each course for the program you'll need a way to keep the content organized and consistent across offerings. A good way to do this is to create a course syllabus for each class your program is prepared to offer (or sponsor you to take). Using a standard syllabus form will help ensure two things: (1) that you consider and identify a fixed set of variables for each course, and (2) that you are able to present to your organization course offering descriptions that are concise, formatted in a standard manner, and readily organized.

You should consider creating a syllabus for each course you have selected to include in your training program. You can use the following list as a basis for the kind of information you might want to include in your course descriptions.

Course Syllabus Format:

1. Course Number
2. Course Title and Subtitle
3. Course Description
4. Textbook and Required Materials
5. Learning Objectives
6. Content Outline
7. Course Length
8. Audience; Enrollment Criteria
9. Waiver Criteria
10. Instructor/Sponsor
11. Location/Classroom
12. Cost Per Attendee
13. Review Cycle
14. Scheduling Point of Contact

Let's take a brief look at each of these items.

Course Number

You may or may not elect to assign course numbers to your courses. Depending on how you choose to catalog your offerings, you might find course numbers useful for a number of reasons. First, if you select a logical nomenclature, the course number can be used to indicate the general nature of the class. For example, one could easily tell that course PM301 is a project management course and that PRG100 is a programming course. The numerical part can also be used to indicate series order. It'd be obvious that PM301 is a course that probably follows PM201. The use of course numbers can also be used as a sorting key if your listing is contained in and managed by a database system. This way you could send to project management team members a listing of all PM courses without having to include unneeded listings.

Course Title and Subtitle

The use of a course title and a subtitle can serve as the chief way to identify each course. If you define your titles carefully, they can go a long way to communicating course intent as well as content. The title should impart a feeling for the focus, scope, and level of the course without moving into wordiness. Subtitles of longer length can help pad out the meanings if necessary. For example, the title "Introduction to Visual Basic" followed by the subtitle "A 2-day lab for programmers with little to no Visual Basic experience" remains concise yet imparts basic decision points about the course. Thoughtfully designed titles and subtitles can serve as a high-level step in course selection, giving readers a first-take from which they can drill down for further information.

Course Description

This is really an extension of the course title—or you could think of the title as a summary of this description. The course description is a more detailed account of the focus, scope, and level of the course. Course descriptions are typically (but there's no rule for this) kept between 50 and 120 words, enough to fully reveal the nature and value of the course without getting into specific course content.

Textbooks and Required Materials

For each class you offer, you'll probably use a specific set of presentation materials, and you may give out to the students, or require them to purchase, some special course material. This might include textbooks or study guides or hand-out materials. If this is the case you can identify this material here. This serves both an informative purpose as well as a management purpose. It tells your readers what documentation they'll be using, and it helps your course designers keep a specific record of what material goes with what courses.

Learning Objectives

This description provides a concrete statement of the value of the course. A learning objective is a statement about the practical, applicable, and demonstrable knowledge/skills that will be imparted to the student during the course. It's a "what you will learn" statement. Usually students will learn a lot of different things during a course, so the learning objectives shouldn't be too specific. A good rule is to identify the top three to five objectives and to phrase them in a way that communicates what the students will have accomplished by the conclusion of the course.

Content Outline

We've been drilling down the syllabus to this point: an outline of course content. This is a detailed summary or depiction of what will be covered during the run of the course. The content outline is usually culled from instructor material and may or may not be included in all course-offering hand-outs. This outline can be used to manage the current content of the course; it can also be distributed to potential students who need specific information before enrolling in a class. The outline can also be used as a stage-one review step when beginning to analyze a course for appropriateness, currency, and completeness.

Course Length

This is an indication of the time commitment required for each course. The length is usually stipulated in days, such a half day, 3 days, or 10 days. Managers who will commit their people to class participation will need to know for how long they're committed. The course length will tell them this as well as give them an idea of the general intensity of the course.

Audience

Here you can indicate for whom the course is designed. Some classes may require students to possess special experience or technical skills prior to enrollment. Any specific entry criteria or participation requirements should be identified here. This will prevent enrollment by students who are ill-prepared to absorb the class material.

Waiver Criteria

Part of the standard training program management will be the consideration and application of training waivers. Sometimes a certain employee may be officially required to undergo a certain regimen of training, yet that person's experience or prior training already accounts for what is expected. In cases like this, when a person has for all practicality undergone necessary training, you may elect to issue an official waiver for a certain course for that person. Each class may have its own set of waiver criteria that you may wish to stipulate. The waiver criteria is usually linked to the learning objectives. Citing the waiver criteria for each course lets the organization know who can be pre-counted as already trained for each area.

Instructor/Sponsor

This is simply an identifier for the instructor of the course. If you use an outside vendor for the class you might also cite the vendor's name.

Location/Classroom

This is an indication of the classroom or location of the training. This might be an entry as plain as Room 201 or as fancy as Ace Ballroom, Mariott Hotel, 112 Fearson Drive, Tempe, AZ.

Review Cycle

It's a good idea to periodically review the content of each course. This review point may be once a year, every quarter, or whatever time span you decide. The point is to take a look at each course to make sure its content is current and that it continues to address the knowledge/skill needs of the organization. You night choose to code each course to indicate its review cycle. You can code a course C if it has been recently updated and is now current; M if it has been reviewed and is being changed, but the material in use until the new stuff is available may not be completely current; and R if the material is current but has reached the point where a content review is due.

Cost per Attendee

Use this item to link participation to fee amounts. The typical costs should be itemized, and can include such things as enrollment, books/materials/ travel, per diem, and more.

Scheduling Contact Info

This is the name and contact information to be used to get more information on training courses or to schedule class enrollment.

A Training Plan Template

You should probably develop a training plan as part of the preparation for every project your shop undertakes. We've talked about other kinds of plans related to CMM in this book, and a few of them can be pretty extensive. The software development plan, for example, usually contains an extensive amount of project detail, things like budgets, schedules, team assignment, work product definitions, and so on. The training plan is likewise an important tool for project management, but it need not be such an extensive document. In actuality, the plan need cover only a handful of items. We'll look at these more closely, but first a point as to the general purpose of the training plan.

The training plan is usually created by someone appointed as a training planner within your organization. This can be a full-time or a part-time role, but it is a specialized role and needs to be conducted in a consistent manner. The planner's main job is to assess the readiness of the team to begin work on the project. This involves looking into several areas of preparedness. One involves the organization's SSPS. Do the individual members of the team have the training or experience they need to work with the SSPS processes and practices relevant to their jobs? Another area involves basic skill set assessment. Do the members of the team have the technical skills sufficient to the technical demands of the project? For example, if you have decided to design this project using industry standard object-oriented analysis and design methodologies, do your people have adequate OOA&D exposure? Finally, practical business orientation should be assessed. Do the members of the project team have an adequate understanding of the application's business mission, one that sits the products from the project within a real-world business environment?

Process skills, technical skills, and business orientation. These three items form the core considerations for the project planner. With this in mind, and with a full understanding of the courses that your training program currently offers or sponsors, the planner takes a look at the team and begins to formulate the training blend that will address any deficiencies in readiness that might hinder project work. The plan that emerges from this analysis is in essence a series of training recommendations. Here's what a basic training plan template might contain:

1. Courses to be taught
2. Recommended participants
3. Rationale
4. Training duration and cost
5. Available training dates
6. Preparation tasks
7. Waiver option

Let's take a brief look at each.

Courses to Be Taught

This is an identification of the courses recommended to be taken prior to certain benchmarks in project progress. It is entirely possible that sometimes a training plan ends up empty. That is, the planner's analysis revealed no real training needs at all. This is common in shops with very experienced, long-term personnel, and in shops that tend to specialize in certain industries or technologies. But chances are, some kind of training will be recommended, even if it is just a business orientation session, in which the team meets to get a presentation on the business aspects of the project. Whether the recommendations are few or many, the key is to identify each course required individually. To do this, you might simply cite the course number and the course title (and subtitle), or you might go further and include some of the course description detail available from the course syllabi.

Recommended Participants

This is related to rationale and is, of course, central to the training plan. In the plan you need to clearly identify who it is that needs to be trained for each course you have recommended. The rationale should be used as an expansion of this identification.

Rationale

For each training course you recommend you should include a rationale with it. This is a brief explanation as to why you are recommending this particular training. This explanation need not be long or extensive, but it should give the project manager and the other team members enough data to ascertain the appropriateness of the recommendation. The rationale will usually be person specific in some way, such as "John Adams and Cindy Goodhew have not yet undergone training in our processes to manage software requirements." You might also state in your rationale until when the training can be delayed, if indeed it can. If you need to train a team member in how to develop an acceptance test plan there is no reason for the project not to start and the training to wait until that step on the project draws nearer.

Training Duration and Cost

These items are useful for project management in terms of scheduling and budgeting. For each course you recommend consider including an indication of the length of the training and the cost of the training. These items can usually be pulled right from the course syllabus.

Available Training Dates

When you decide to recommend a certain training course for members of a project team, you should be sure to include as many available training dates as possible. The objective here is to give project management some choices and perhaps some flexibility as to when they will need to commit their people to training. If this training is delivered in-house, you will need to know the schedule that is currently supported. If you use an outside source, then you'll need to coordinate this information with them first. Try to provide as much choice here as is practical while still meeting the needs of the project.

Preparation Tasks

You may find that you don't have to use this item a lot. It's simply a description of any preparatory actions the participants need to undertake prior to the start of class. For example, they may need to acquire certain textbooks, or they might need to attend a special sign-up session. The objective here is to identify anything that the student will need in advance in order to participate fully in the course.

Waiver Option

A waiver option, in this case, is usually a form that is completed to excuse someone from training for some specific reason. There is also another use of the waiver option: to document why a person does not need to undergo recommended training. This use is usually for people who already meet the requirements that the training would address. For example, you might issue a waiver for a C++ programmer you just hired to skip the company's required training in C++ programming. If the person has 10 years' experience using C++, there might be little value in going through the training. A waiver in this case implies demonstrable competence. But the first case is different. It's more a waiver of convenience. Here's how it's used:

In creating the training plan, the planner will have analyzed the skill levels of your team members. During this process it will become apparent who has the demonstrable skills necessary for the project and who might lack them. The only people who show up on the training plan are those people who the planner has assessed to lack certain needed knowledge. If the planner has overlooked something here it can be addressed during the peer review of the plan (see the next section), but usually it should be pretty close to being right. But a waiver still might be requested. A waiver for the sake of convenience (or perhaps "hardship" might be a better word) is used when the team acknowledges that the person does indeed need the training but for some compelling reason cannot be removed from the project in order to receive it.

Your organization will need to think through what reasons would justify this type of a waiver, but in any event it should be an option made available to project management and the team.

Other General Items

There are a few other items that you might also want to include in your training plan. These items have less to do with training activity than with the objective review and measurement of that activity. These items—there are four of them—are usually included in a section on their own at the end of the training plan. Take a look at them, and decide how they might enhance your plan.

Results and recommendations report. A training representative should be assigned to each project, at least for the duration of the training needs. Usually this is the planner, and the assignment need not be full-time. But the official attachment—the window into the project—is important. Your training program should be always working toward currency; that is, working to keep its curriculum up to date concerning class needs and improving its ability to deliver training services. That's why metrics are important. The project's training appointee, at the end of the training activities, should produce a report that summarizes training activity as compared to what was recommended in the plan and then make recommendations, if any, as to how the process might be improved. This report is often a part of a project's end-analysis, and it can be used as the foundation for the project management and software project management review.

SQA review windows. It's a general (though unstated) rule within CMM project management that the SQA function has a window into every activity on a project for which a plan has been created. This applies to the training plan. What's important to ensure is that what gets approved in the training plan is actually carried out. The project's software quality assurance resources can help you track this. The training plan then should identify several SQA checkpoints in which the plan's execution is assessed. This might happen for such training milestones as plan approval, training start and training end, and final training review. The training planner should work with the SQA planner to make sure the training process audit points are also included in the project's overall SQA plan.

Final SPM review and final PM review. These are akin to what I like to call satisfaction review meetings. Your Training Program, after all, can be thought of as a project service, and as a service you should probably want to measure customer satisfaction from time to time. I recommend it for every project, to be conducted with software project management as well as executive project management. This can be conducted as an end-of-project review meeting in which the pluses and minuses of the project's training activities are discussed, documented, and acted on. This is part of your overall software process improvement activities and goes a long way to shaping the quality and effectiveness of your training program. In the training plan the dates for these meetings can be identified as well as the logical participants.

Training Plan Approval Process

The training plan for each project will become an official part of the overall project plan, and as such it will be closely monitored. But before the plan is officially adopted for the project it should be carefully reviewed by members of the project team. You can assign anyone you think best to be involved in the training plan review and approval process, but it's best to select those people who are immediately affected by the training recommendations contained in the plan.

The people in this group usually include the software project manager, the project's training planner, leaders or appointees from those groups who will need to participate in the identified training regimen, and perhaps leaders or appointees from other groups (in case they have been inadvertently) excluded from training. Identify these people up front, at project initiation or as they are assigned, and be sure to include them on the review team.

The process to follow for reviewing and approving the training plan could well be the peer review, which is described at the start of this chapter. This general review/approval is suitable for any process or plan that identifies, describes, or is used to manage activity for a development project.

Software Product Engineering Processes

The Software Product Engineering KPA of the CMM is a different kind of KPA. Think back to the six KPAs at Level 2: Requirements Management, Software Project Planning, Software Project Tracking and Oversight, Software Configuration Management, Software Quality Assurance, and Subcontractor Management. These can be thought of as managerial KPAs in the sense that they put into place the structures and regimens that govern broad areas of project activities. Beginning with a broad approach is a logical way to move out of Level 1, in which even the broad approach is often absent. When you move into Level 3 the granularity of your focus shifts, becomes finer. You enhance your Level 2 structures through such new KPAs as Peer Reviews, Intergroup Coordination, and Integrated Software Management. But it's only with Software Product Engineering that the CMM begins to address direct intervention into the rote technical activities involved in software development.

The idea of a software product engineering KPA lies pretty much in its name: improved technical performance through the administration of process measures. In practical terms, what software product engineering is really about is making sure that the organization has the technical tools it needs to produce software products as technically spec'd, to make sure that the people charged with carrying out technical roles for the project have the skills necessary to do so, and to facilitate both of these by supporting them with project management controls. In Chapter 11 we looked at the structural recommendations the CMM makes regarding software product engineering, and in Chapter 13 we'll look at the kinds of training for software product engineering that helps prepare your technical people for their technical jobs. In this section we'll look at the new kinds of activities that the software project managers should considering folding into their work to help the engineering complete in a smooth and predictable manner.

Stages of the Development Life Cycle

You probably already know a lot about software product engineering. After all, yours is a software development shop. It's what you and your team work at every day. So you'll know that it's a big discipline. It covers a lot of activities. In fact, software product engineering isn't really one thing at all; it's a collection of specialties. It covers the range of software development phases from requirements specification to final acceptance testing and product turnover. In descriptions of traditional system development life cycles a series of 10 basic steps is usually identified: requirements gathering, system analysis, system design, coding, unit testing, system testing, integration testing, documentation, acceptance testing, and maintenance. For the Software Product Engineering KPA, the CMM is not concerned with all 10 of these. It omits system analysis (lumping that in with design, as is commonly done). It also treats system and unit test as one contiguous activity, and it leaves off maintenance as being out of the realm of software engineering (categorizing it under support).

Software product engineering focuses on requirements management, software design, coding, unit testing, Integration testing, acceptance testing, and documentation. To this the CMM also adds the control of development tools and the manner in which defect data (metrics) is gathered and managed. To paraphrase the CMM, here's what the SPE KPA recommends:

1. Software development tools are integrated into the project's Defined Software Process Set (this is the DSPS, the tailored version of the SSPS) and kept consistent across the life of the project.

2. Requirements are managed according to the DSPS.

3. The software design is managed according to the DSPS.

4. System code is managed according to the DSPS.

5. Unit/system testing is performed according to the DSPS.

6. Integration testing is performed according to the DSPS.

7. Acceptance testing is performed according to the DSPS.

8. Project documentation is created according to the DSPS.

9. Defect data is gathered according to the DSPS.[1]

Those items touch on most areas of software development. But the phrasing here introduces a question: What is the CMM getting at when it says "managed according to or performed according to the DSPS"?

First a note on the DSPS, the Defined Software Process Set. What this is (how I use the term) is a subset of the organization's SSPS, the Standard Software Process Set. The SSPS is, of course, the superset of software processes and practices that the Level 3 organization has centrally adopted for use on all its software development projects. And yet the entire SSPS need not be applied to every project. The size and scope of the SSPS is buffered by a series of tailoring guidelines (see Chapter 10) used to pull out those processes and practices most appropriate for use on the project. This subset, which becomes in effect an extension of the project plan, represents the *project's* SSPS, or the DSPS, the Defined Software Process Set.

So the CMM is indicating that in order to see the engineering activities through in a controlled and predictable manner they need to be subject to the same kind of process management activities that you apply to such things as the budget, the schedule, the SQA plan, and so on. The latter things you did as a matter of course at Level 2. Here at Level 3 you're going deeper. In each of the nine engineering areas you should consider tracking four stages. These four stages are development, maintenance, documentation, and verification. Here's how that translates into specifics:

For the system code, for example, you should consider including in the software project plan, by way of the DSPS, activities to track how the code is developed, maintained, documented, and verified.

And it's the same for each of the items. You should follow the development, maintenance, documentation, and verification of the requirements, the code, the design, the three test areas, the project defect metrics, and the definition of acceptable project tools. This process of managing software product engineering begins in the realm of software project planning. Let's take a look.

Extending Software Project Planning

Managing software product engineering begins in the project planning stages. In Chapter 4, we looked at the processes involved in software project planning. Activities to gather data, create estimates, and assign resources result in the creation of a software development plan (SDP). The SDP is used to manage the software portion of the project. The use of the SDP is introduced at Level 2, but its use continues through the other tiers of the CMM maturity scale. At Level 2, however, the SDP is focused mainly on the management of broad issues and work products. A typical Level 2 SDP might include the following sections:

- Statement of work
- Introduction/overview
- Life cycle adopted
- Standards and procedures
- A list of the work products to be developed
- Scope projections

- Schedule
- Measurements to be made
- Facilities and support tools available
- Risks and assumptions
- Any related appendixes

You'll notice that the presence of software engineering activities is not explicit in the template. That's fine. At Level 2 you are just beginning to amass the components of overall quality management. But at Level 3, the focus changes. It grows finer, sharper in a sense. The activities and work products that make up the software engineering effort become explicit management items, items that need to be identified, assessed, and included in the software development plan and then tracked in a coordinated manner.

There are two general ways of doing this. You can use one or the other, or a combination of both. In general I find that most shops use a combination of both.

The first approach is to manage the development, maintenance, documentation, and verification of the project's engineering activities through the creation of a specific set of engineering processes and practices. Usually most development shops serious enough about quality to adopt the CMM already have in place some of these processes and practices. This includes things like an established standard for the way programmers comment code, a template that test analysts can use to create consistent test plans, and page layout rules that govern the presentation of documentation.

These items should be made a part of your organization's standard software process set. When you're working on a Level 3 program you should include these in your steps to investigate, document, and review material for the SSPS. This book, however, can't really address this approach in depth. The reason is twofold. First, I haven't space enough (and you probably don't have time enough) to look at every possible blend of processes and practices we can adopt for the management of software engineering activities. The discipline is too broad. Second, this is an area that is highly specialized to the company. The blend you have developed over time is probably quite different from what others have done. There's no recognized leading standard.

The point is that your approach no doubt has value, especially if you consistently work to improve it. You can use it to address the recommendations of software product engineering contained in the CMM by comparing what you are doing against what you read in the CMM (see the next section for an overview). If you match closely you may be all right. If not, you may need to adjust.

The second approach is less original, but it'll probably fit the bill for most organizations. It is to apply the CMM's recommendations for project planning, together with management recommendations from Level 3, in order to predictably control the engineering activities. This begins, of course, in the planning stages and results in the development of a true Level 3 software development plan. Let's go over this approach now.

Software Engineering Additions to the SDP

At Level 3, the software project planner will inherit the management of software product engineering. The management items that will account for this will need to be defined and planned for. As the software project planner now begins to formulate a Level 3 SDP for the project the Level 2 template can still be used, but various sections of it will need to be enhanced to account for the added focus on engineering. Here are eight main planning areas you'll now need to consider:

- Identify major engineering milestones
- Budget and schedule resources
- Assess risks
- Create a software quality assurance plan
- Create a software configuration management plan
- Create an intergroup coordination plan
- Conduct peer reviews
- Add Integrated Software Management practices

Let's take a quick look at each.

Identify Major Engineering Milestones

The main development phases that the CMM looks at for software product engineering include requirements management, software design, coding, code testing, integration testing, acceptance testing, documentation, and metrics (defect) collection. Within each of these phases the planner must work with the technical groups within the team to identify what work products will be created through the engineering activities.

For example, your test members might indicate that a formal integration test plan will be developed and executed in order to measure how the various components of the system work together as a whole. This should lead you to a handful of engineering milestone conclusions. You'll know that certain information will need to be available to the test team for the members to develop the test plan. There will be a draft date for the first version of the plan. There will be a review date, approval of the revised plan, a date for test execution to begin, and a date for it to end. These can then become the engineering milestones for the integration test phase of the project.

Looking at each of the other areas will reveal milestones for all the engineering activities we are managing.

Budget and Schedule Resources

The additional milestones you identify from the engineering activities will be added to the other milestones in the project, and from these the project's budget and schedule will begin to emerge. The project's overall budget and schedule should not be calculated to accommodate the engineering activities. This does not mean that the Level 3 budget/schedule should be larger than a Level 2 budget/schedule for the same project. You would hope that they would be similar, that the end numbers would closely match. But with Level 3 you'll have a finer view of the expenses and the time requirements, both broken down to a greater level of detail. In the planning stages then you'll be scheduling and budgeting in finer increments, which should lead to greater accuracy.

Assess Risks

The detailed look you take on a project in the Level 3 planning effort is going to take you down to finer detail in the exploration of risks and assumptions that might affect overall project activities. As you begin to define and plan for the engineering activities that will become part of the software development efforts you'll need to consider any risks that might exist to change the shape of the product as you have defined it. You'll also need to explore any assumptions that might have a similar impact.

Consider the risks and assumptions that surround the activities in each of the eight engineering areas. Document these and be sure to include them in the SDP.

Create a Software Quality Assurance Plan

In order to objectively verify the proper development, maintenance, and documentation of each of the engineering work products and their supporting activities, project management should provide an SQA window into the engineering activities. An enhanced SQA plan, one that now includes engineering audit points, should be developed for the project and carried out in a conscientious manner. The kick-off point for the SQA plan can be the definition of the engineering milestones. There the quality assurance analysts can establish at what points quality checks should be made to confirm that the activities are being conducted according to plan.

Create a Software Configuration Management Plan

Just as the SQA plan is enhanced at Level 3 to include engineering activities, so the configuration management plan is enhanced to include the maintenance and documentation of selected engineering work products. Software project management should work with the engineering groups and the SCM group to establish SCM participation points in the engineering activities. An SCM plan should be developed to manage this. As with SQA, the kick-off point for the SCM plan can be the definition of the engineering milestones, specifically the tangible work products. From there the CM analysts can establish at what points documents will need to be baselined and version controlled to protect their distribution, use, and integrity.

Create an Intergroup Coordination Plan

New for Level 3 software development plans is the intergroup coordination plan (described later in this chapter). This is a plan that outlines how the various groups within the project team will coordinate communications and activities among themselves. The purpose of intergroup coordination is to provide a forum for exchange between groups. Such an exchange will facilitate a consistent understanding within the team of all phases of project activity. The coordination plan should include coordination of engineering activity interfacing across the project life cycle.

Conduct Peer Reviews

The products that you identify as emerging from the software engineering activities should be included within the project's peer review plan (we looked at the peer review process at the start of this chapter). The peer review steps should be the same for the engineering products as for other project products.

Add ISM Practices and Processes

Finally, you should consider applying some of the new Level 3 procedures from the Integrated Software Management KPA (see the next section for a fuller discussion of ISM recommendations). This is an extension of project planning and rolls actively into project tracking and oversight. The idea here is to identify all work products for a project, including the software engineering work products, and then actively manage their evolutions in terms of work product size, effort and costs, use of critical computer resources, timelines for critical paths and dependencies, and assumptions and risks.

Applying these eight items should help you manage the engineering activities with the same degree of detail and predictability with which you manage the other facets of a software development project.

Extending Software Project Tracking and Oversight

By introducing software product engineering considerations into the software development plan the project team is able to identify a finer detail of activity across the life cycle of the project. The activities specific to software engineering will be managed just like the other activities, and so the introduction of software engineering concerns extends to the activities for project tracking and oversight. When you develop a Level 3 SDP for your project you'll very likely end up with a plan that contains the following items blended together in some fashion:

- Software development plan
- Software quality assurance plan
- Configuration management plan
- Intergroup coordination LAN
- Peer review plan

These plans, enhanced in terms of depth and reach over what you might expect to see in a Level 2 plan, will guide your tracking and oversight activities. Not only will the definition and identification of the engineering activities become a formal part of the project's scope, but you will have designated members of the team ready to assist the engineering activities in terms of quality checks and the application of monitoring and control tools.

Software product engineering then extends both software project planning and software project tracking and oversight into new areas of responsibility, accountability, and effectiveness.

Integrated Software Management Processes

The Integrated Software Management KPA is in place to help coordinate the use of the organization's Standard Software Process Set across the projects within the organization. The beginnings of integrated software management lie in software project planning. Here the planners tailor the SSPS to the needs of the project, pulling in some elements of the SSPS, leaving out others. What they end up with is an SSPS subset for the project, what I call the Defined Software Process Set. (The CMM uses that term—DSPS—for both the full set as well as the project set, but I find that can be a little confusing.)

Once the integrated nature of the organization's process definition has been reflected in the plan, integrated software management then moves into the realm of software project tracking and oversight, extending the role and responsibilities of the software project manager. It's akin to software product engineering (discussed previously). Software product engineering brings into play the specific engineering activities required to produce software products. It then applies formal definitions and management stakes for each. Integrated software management works in the same way. Here the software project manager uses the DSPS to shape and control various elements of project progress and activity results. These include work product size, cost and effort, critical paths and dependencies, critical resources, and risks.

We'll begin with a look at a process that project planners might consider using when tailoring the SSPS to extract the project's DSPS.

Guidelines for Tailoring the SSPS

In Chapter 10, in our discussion of organizational process, we looked at steps to create the Standard Software Process Set for the organization. The SSPS is the centralized, documented, and collected processes, practices, and procedures that your people use to plan for and manage a software project. The SSPS is meant to be used on all your software projects, but that's not to say that it works in the same way across all projects.

Every project is different. Each has its own mission, its own scope, and its own functional characteristics. The SSPS then can be thought of as a superset of management tools that the planner can look to create a development plan specially tailored for the project. This way the SSPS serves as a base for tailoring activities, increasing its flexibility and applicability.

Key to this type of generalized use, however, is the creation of guidelines for tailoring the SSPS to create the DSPS. As we mentioned in Chapter 9, you will need to develop these guidelines for your shop. To do so you can follow these six broad steps:

1. Study and then define the tailoring steps.
2. Document the guidelines for all to use.
3. Establish the procedures to waive certain SSPS steps.
4. Peer review the guidelines for approval.
5. Configuration manage the resulting guidelines documents.
6. Revise the guidelines over time as necessary[2].

Naturally, the tailoring guidelines will emerge from the process set you have accumulated in your shop. But most guidelines will share a few features in common. Take a look at the following items. You may find that they are helpful to you for creating your own tailoring guidelines.

First, give your planner some guidelines in choosing a software development life cycle. Your SSPS will contain a series of approved life cycles around which your people can wrap project management. Examples of life cycles include spiral, waterfall, and evolutionary. You may have your own. Different life cycles work well for different kinds of projects. Define which life cycles you'll allow for the different kinds of projects you undertake. This will help your planner choose appropriately.

Next, prepare some general guidelines for modify the selected life cycle, if needed. Your planners should have some leeway in using a life cycle model, as a way of further tailoring it. But make sure you set the limits, indicating what is optional and what must be included.

With a life cycle selected your planners can then begin to assimilate the processes and practices that will be followed for the project. Start out by defining a minimum set. These are the base elements each project must contain. For example, you'd probably consider the creation and use of a software quality assurance plan as being part of the minimum set. Same with procedures for estimating cost and effort and work product size. Provide the flexibility then to choose from the remaining items by providing definitions of how each selection can support project activity. These definitions will help the planners choose according to their needs. But it will be important, prior to SDP approval, that the process omissions have been documented with reasons attached. These should be assessed in relation to the scope of the overall plan.

The Level 3 Software Development Plan

In Chapter 4 we discussed the creation of the software development plan. And we presented a template that could be used to forge a Level 2-compliant SDP. That template is expanded at Level 3. You begin to introduce new items, such as training program plans, intergroup coordination activities, peer review activities, software product engineering activities, and integrated management activities. Here's a cursory list of some major elements that most comprehensive software development plans will either include or link to at Level 3:

- Statement of work
- Introduction/overview
- Life cycle adopted
- Standards and procedures
- A list of the work products to be developed
    - The work products include requirements, the software design, system code, unit/system testing, integration testing, acceptance testing, and project documentation. This includes both plans and activities for each.
    - Also included with these are size estimates, effort and cost estimates, critical resources required, critical paths or dependencies, and identified risks/assumptions.

- Scope projections
- Schedule
- Measurements to be made
- Facilities and support tools available
- Risks and assumptions
- Any related appendixes
- Software quality assurance plan
- Software configuration management plan
- Intergroup coordination plan
- Vendor management plan (if you're contracting with outside services)
- Peer review plan
- Training plan
- Risk management plan
- Any relevant appendices
- The project's Defined Software Process Set (by way of reference)

SDP Approval Procedure

The software development plan will emerge as the chief project management tool for each project under the roof of your shop. You can use the peer review process (see the start of this chapter) to review and approve the SDP, along with the ancillary plans it contains. This general review/approval is suitable for any process or plan that identifies, describes, or is used to manage activity for a development project.

Managing the SDP

Integrated software management is in place within the CMM to provide tools to two areas of management: software project planning and project tracking and oversight. We have seen how the software development plan is expanded at Level 3 and how it includes provisions for new detail and new performance and progress measures.

As you'll recall, managing the SDP at Level 2 involved status tracking at identified milestones and with a view toward a specific granularity. You can continue this practice at Level 3, but you'll find the management reach is broader (through the addition of such functions as peer reviews, intergroup coordination, and formal training plans) as well as deeper. The detail gets finer.

The CMM's Integrated Software Management KPA introduces some new recommendations for managing this enhanced management view. Specifically the recommendations call for you to manage by key tasks and work products, define entry and exit criteria for task and product readiness, collect measurement data to asses status, and at the end, prepare analysis of lessons learned for reference by others.

Those concepts can be reduced to these four management views:

- Define the prime tasks and products that will emerge.
- Define entry and exit criteria to each task and product.
- Measure to assess current conditions.
- Record lessons learned for reference by others.

These views work best when centered on the multiple traits of each task or activity. Think back to Level 2 software project planning. One of the main activities there is to plan the project through a series of project estimates. In this effort you define a series of work products that would emerge as various phases of the project completed. The point of emergence for these products could be used as project milestones, stages where progress and issues can be somewhat cleanly assessed.

For planning purposes you put together (by soliciting data from relevant project team members) estimates for each product. This included estimates of the product's final size, effort and costs to produce that product, estimates of the critical computer resources needed in the process, estimates of anticipated critical paths and dependencies that might affect product production, and estimates of any risks to any of the facets.

The approach of integrated software management is to define and then track these items closely across the life of the project. We'll look at both steps next.

Planning

Careful planning up front will help you control the size, cost, and integrity of each work product you define for a project. For each product, consider the following planning approach.

First, for each product you define add a contingency buffer to its size estimate. A common range is 10 to 20 percent . Anything lower, and you're left with not much protection; anything larger, and you're probably planning with a wait-and-see attitude in mind. The buffer will flow down to affect cost and effort and time.

Second, you should work to identify reusable material up front. This is another form of buffering. Items like reusable code, boilerplate documentation material, and the like can be valuable in increasing efficiencies on a project.

Third, you should identify any outstanding risks that might creep up and affect your progress. Documenting these helps you keep an eye out for their appearance.

Finally, with all this in place the estimates should be reviewed and approved by the project team, management, and perhaps even the customer to confirm that they are reasonable and that commitments can be made to them.

Once approved, the items can be tracked. The next four items cover the tracking activity.

Tracking

When you begin to enter the tracking part of the project you can manage the work products' evolutions using another short four-step process.

First you begin by establishing not-to-exceed limits for the critical element of each product. For some, size might be the threshold factor. For others, effort could be key. The point is to set a limit here beyond which lies problem territory. You want to keep the products out of this territory.

Second, you should establish options that you can set into motion should you notice any of the products approaching its threshold.

Third, with the thresholds defined and options to deal with variances, you can begin to track the products at your regular status meetings, at certain project milestone points, or at both. Make adjusts as needed well in advance of the problem territory, and you'll go far to keep the project on track.

Finally, for the sake of future process improvement directives, be sure to define and collect measurements on work product evolution across the life of the project. These measurements can be used to help you plan and track more effectively in the future.

Intergroup Coordination Processes

Software development can involve many different groups. The process of creating the tangible software alone can run through a requirements group, a design group, a coding group, a test group, and a documentation group. And that doesn't even include management and service groups such as project management, configuration management, and quality assurance. And then this universe is made even larger when you begin to add other potential system groups, like hardware architecture, contract management, and vendor management. For very large systems development projects you can have multiple teams within groups until the final number of people actively working on a project at one time can run in the many hundreds. When you look to the highest-end technical projects, like a space shuttle launch, it can go to the thousands.

That's why effective and coordinated communication is so important to quality software development. If you have a large collection of talented and motivated individuals but they are working along divergent paths, their efforts may amount to little. Coordination of effort, whether the team is large or small, is key. In fact, we might say that the CMM is all about coordination. The plans, processes, and practices employed to create a product are there as a way to coordinate activity in a predictable and trackable manner. Software project coordination activities are introduced in the CMM at Level 2. The recommendations for requirements management, project planning, project tracking, SQA, configuration management, and vendor management all involve to one extent or another the coordination of activities within and across groups. At Level 2, the project status meeting is probably the clearest evidence of an emerging intergroup coordination formality. At Level 3 considerations for intergroup coordination become a dedicated Key Process Area of the CMM. Activities are defined to a deeper level to strengthen them into a dependable communication tool.

Is Intergroup Coordination then different from regular project status meetings?

Yes and no. No in the sense that any exchange between groups can be seen as a status meeting of sorts, and the format that you'll use for the exchanges will be probably be for all practical matters the same as for regular status meetings. There's no reason to do things much differently. But yes in the sense that these exchanges, the intergroup coordination "events," will be individually planned in advance. They will be anticipated in the project plan and recognized as perhaps "formal" status meetings where specific items, not just project progress in general, need to be addressed.

The conditions that can help you decide when you want to hold a coordination meeting can be summarized along two lines: when the project is reaching a stage where knowledge needs to be transferred (an intergroup movement) or when significant plans or activities are being carried out in one group that might impact others (an intragroup movement). In the first condition one group needs to prepare the other group for subsequent work, passing the baton, so to speak. In the other condition the one group needs to make sure others have no objection to a path of action being considered. The use of the CMM's Intergroup Coordination recommendations helps manage these conditions through communications and product exchanges across the project team.

As you begin to develop your shop's strategy for dealing with IGC issues, you'll have to think about what project groups you'll include in the mix. There's no pat answer for that. It will depend on the makeup of your teams. The groups can be as extensive as or as or as compact and focused as you'd like. Select the range with the goal in mind. Make your decision based on the extent you think will be required for smooth and proactive communications across the life of the project. IGC activities will help set up formal exchanges between the groups, with an established agenda ready at each exchange.

Extending the Role of Software Planning and Software Tracking

It usually falls to the software project manager to take on the responsibilities for Intergroup Coordination activities. In many practical ways, this KPA can be thought of as an extension of the CMM's Software Project Planning and Software Project Tracking and Oversight KPAs. At the heart of IGC is a formalization of Level 2 status meetings, an extension of status reporting. Formal communications are now planned.

Because of this, you might consider augmenting each project's software development plan with an intergroup coordination plan. This plan identifies the who, what, where, and when of the communication exchanges.

NOTE ON INFORMAL INTERGROUP COORDINATION

Software development usually fares poorly in an isolationist environment. Communication is vital for any project, not just within teams but between teams, too. In this section on Intergroup Coordination we'll be discussing the formal approach to the CMM recommendations. But it's important to remember that you should also promote casual communications as much as possible. These casual exchanges are used not to shape direction but as a way to bubble up ideas and recommendations and to expose unanticipated problems and risks. Set up a project environment that supports free exchange across teams, and you'll find that you forge teams that are better prepared to meet the objectives of the project.

The project planner will need to plan up front for these exchanges and then track the contents of the plan across the life of the project.

In the following sections we'll discuss what can go into an intergroup coordination plan, and we'll mention how the peer review process (discussed earlier in this chapter) can be used as a tool to review and approve the plan prior to adoption.

A Template for the Intergroup Coordination Plan

At CMM Level 2, when your project planner created the software development plan, a series of status checkpoints was probably included in the schedule or in the work product descriptions. Such status meeting checkpoints are probably peppered through any SDP. That slice of the SDP is in a way an intergroup coordination plan. But at Level 3 the detail is refined. You have to consider more for each event, formalizing it into part of a practical plan.

For each project you might decide to mesh creation of the intergroup coordination plan with other software planning activities. Or you may elect to create an independent IGC plan that you can follow and manage apart from the SDP. Whichever way you go, consider identifying the following kinds of data for each IGC milestone you define for the project:

- The milestone
- The participating groups
- The agenda
- Event date
- Event location (if available)
- SQA review points
- SCM review points
- Coordination measurements

Let's take a brief look at each section.

The Milestone

Intergroup coordination should occur naturally across the various stages of software development. But to manage this communication you should define certain points in the project life cycle in which a coordination meeting should occur. The event is usually timed around an anticipated product hand-off. For example, a good point for an IGC meeting would be just prior to the point where the requirements analysts hand the approved software requirements over to the design team. This is the point of a knowledge transfer.

Another good point for an IGC meeting might be the point at which the design team has drafted an initial technical approach and wishes to inform other groups about it to avoid any unforeseen problems the choice might entail. This is an internal group movement that might affect other groups.

Try to plan for as many IGC meetings as you can define up front. You can always hold special or emergency meetings if a need for them arises. To repeat, two good identifiers for holding an IGC meeting is to prepare in advance one group to receive the work products from another group and to inform a group (or groups) of a decision that might affect it later.

The Participating Groups

For each IGC event it's important to identify, at least from the group level, who will be participating. In terms of knowledge transfer there is almost always a transferring group and a receiving group. In terms of plan communications there is usually an originating group and one or more affected groups. Try to identify each and include them in the plan.

The Agenda

During each IGC meeting the participants should explore three areas of activity:

- Technical issues
- Critical dependencies
- Overall status

The agenda for each event should allow for these three dimensions of discussion. It's important that the receiving group (or the impacted group) come away with a firm understanding of the condition of the incoming product, what its technical issues are. This should involve a discussion of the scope and integrity of the product with the intention of familiarizing the receiving team with its details. Likewise, a discussion of critical dependencies that may affect transfer or resulting actions should be discussed. This helps both teams prepare for contingencies. And from these two an overall picture of stage status should emerge.

Event Date

For each event you should attach a meeting date, a start time, and the expected duration of the meeting.

Location

In the planning stages, data on the physical meeting details may not be available. But if it is, or if you have a standing location, you will want to indicate the meeting place (room, floor, building, city, etc.), conference bridge numbers, and any other connecting data you might have.

Metrics Collection

Your intergroup coordination plan should identify which metrics you'll be gathering from each event. (And for consistency's sake, they should be close to the same for each event.) Some organizations track items such as types of issues raised, length of meeting, number of participants, and the number of action items identified. The measurements identified will be collected and then ultimately entered into the organization's central measurement database.

Other IGC Plan Items

There are a few other items that you might also want to include in your intergroup coordination plan. These items deal with the objective review and measurement of the coordination activities. These items—there are three of them—are usually included in a section on their own at the end of the plan. Take a look at them and decide how they might enhance your plan.

SQA review windows. It's a general rule within CMM project management that the SQA function has a window into every activity on a project for which a plan has been created. This applies to the IGC plan. What's important to ensure is that what gets approved in the plan is actually carried out. The project's software quality assurance resources can help you track this. The IGC plan then should identify several SQA checkpoints in which the plan's execution is assessed. This might happen for such milestones as plan approval, meeting points, follow-up on action items, and more. Software project management should work with the SQA planner to make sure the intergroup coordination audit points are also included in the project's overall SQA plan.

Final SPM review and final PM review. These items will help ascertain the effectiveness of your project's coordination actions. This constitutes a review meeting conducted with software project management as well as executive project management. This can be done at the end of the project in which the pluses and minuses of the project's coordination activities are discussed, documented, and acted on. This is part of your overall software process improvement activities and goes a long way to shaping the quality and effectiveness of your processes. In the intergroup coordination plan the dates for these meetings can be identified as well as the logical participants.

Intergroup Coordination Plan Approval Process

The IGC plan for each project should become an official part of the overall project plan, and as such it can be closely monitored by project management. But before the plan is officially adopted for the project it should be carefully reviewed by members of the project team. Feel free to assign anyone you think best to be involved in the review of coordination commitments and approval, but it's best to select those people who are immediately affected by the meetings and coordination points identified in the plan.

The people in this group will usually include the software project manager, the project's leads from the different development groups, and the appointees from those groups who will need to participate in coordination efforts. Identify these people up front, at project initiation or as they are assigned, and be sure to include them on the review team.

You can use the peer review process (see the start of this chapter) to review and approve the IGC plan. This general review/approval is suitable for any process or plan that identifies, describes, or is used to manage activity for a development project.

Artifacts to Support Your Use of Level 3 Processes

In reviewing this chapter you may have noticed that the plans, processes, and practices that help your Level 3 program jell in your organization are in many ways extensions of your Level 2 program. That is especially true for the Level 3 KPAs Integrated Software Management, Software Product Engineering, Intergroup Coordination, and even Training Program. In fact, you can view Level 3 as a logical extension of Level 2. For this reason you will find a distinct similarity between the types of artifacts you designed at Level 2 and those you are thinking about at Level 3. They fall into the six broad categories described below and then pointed out as specific examples in Table 12.2.

Table 12.2 Evidence of Program Compliance

KEY PROCESS AREA	ARTIFACTS
Organization Process Focus	See Chapter 9
Organization Process Definition	Chapter 10
Training Program	Training course syllabi, training plan template, training plan for project
Integrated Software Management	ISM activities as reflected in the project's software development plan and in the defined software process set
Software Product Engineering	SPE activities as reflected in the project's software development plan and in the defined software process set
Intergroup Coordination	Intergroup coordination plan template, intergroup coordination plan for project
Peer Review	Peer review plan template, peer review process, peer review plan for project
Executive Review Process	Meeting minutes review with project team, meeting minutes review with SQA, meeting minutes review with SCM, meeting minutes review with requirements management

Plan Templates

In order to manage your CMM program well at Level 3 you'll need to conduct the same kind of upfront planning you did at Level 2. You should, to a large or small degree, prepare a series of plans for each project that will define, among other things, how the organization's Standardized Software Process Set will be tailored to the needs of the project, how specific software engineering activities will be monitored (usually an extension of the Software Development Plan), what training needs the project calls for, what intergroup coordination activities will be carried out over the course of the project, and what products will be peer reviewed. In order to prepare these plans effectively and consistently across projects, you may have elected to created plan templates to address each. These templates serve as valid artifacts demonstrating your activities in the Level 3 Key Process Areas.

Plan Review and Approval Procedure

Another valid series of artifacts are the review and approval processes you use for moving these plans from draft to baseline. In this chapter I have suggested that you can adopt the Peer Review process to manage this path for each plan you propose for a project. Of course you are free to use any defined procedure you feel meets the needs of your organization. The procedure itself serves as solid evidence that you are conducting the activity in a defined and considered manner.

Project Plans

Of course some of the best kinds of artifacts to show Level 3 compliance are the actual Level 3 plans you develop for each project. In reviewing this chapter you'll see that a series of plans are recommended. For each product you'll need to consider developing a training plan, a peer review plan, an intergroup coordination plan, an SSPS tailoring plan, and a software development plan that includes the management of specific software product engineering activities. Each of these plans serves as demonstrable evidence of your organization's efforts in specific Level 3 KPA areas.

You should also have developed for the organization as a whole, a unified Software Process Improvement Plan (for more on this, see Chapters 9 and 10).

Processes

The processes you use to manage plans and activity at Level 3 are also excellent components of compliance. These processes, which were discussed in this chapter, work hand in hand with the plans you develop in each of the KPA areas. The processes are your tools to manage how the plans are implemented and adjusted over the course of a project. If you adopt the recommendations for process development described in this chapter, you will produce a series that includes: a process to create a training plan for each project, a process to create an organizational training course regimen, a process to tailor the SSPS to the needs of each project, a process to track the software product engineering activities for the project, a process to manage intergroup coordination across the life of the project, and a process to conduct and manage peer reviews according to plan.

All of these are excellent indicators of Level 3 compliance.

Activity Artifacts

At Level 2 you set into place a series of structures and project practices that governed how the phases of a project life cycle would be managed. Out of this management there arises a series of activity artifacts that can be seen as tangible corroboration of Level 2 compliance. These activity artifacts include such things as status meeting minutes, staff assignment forms, project resource allocations, SQA reports, SCM audit reports, and so forth.

These same activity artifacts will arise out of your Level 3 activities. By following the plans and processes you design for each project you should amass many examples of these over time. In addition to those cited above, you'll collect items like peer review announcements and results reports, minutes from intergroup meetings, training certificates, training waiver forms, and a host of other items. These serve as solid evidence that you are not only planning activities but that you are following through on the plans.

Measurements and Refinements

Finally, in order to demonstrate that you are consciously working through your software process improvement program you can show the series of measurements (and the measurement data) you collect for each of the Level 3 activities you have defined. Measurements serve as a key basis for making process refinement decisions, so they are an important part of any compliance effort. To support these measurements you may also want to show the evolution—through a series of revised baselines—of any of the documents you have been refining over time.

Summary

The new processes introduced in the CMM at Level 3 can be seen in large part as extensions of Level 2 processes. Level 2 processes focused mainly on management activities concerning software development. Software Project Planning and Software Project Tracking and Oversight were supplemented by activities under Software Quality Assurance, Software Configuration Management, and Requirements Management. At Level 3 these areas are expanded and deepened. Processes to structure and manage peer reviews, integrated software management, software product engineering, and intergroup coordination serve to focus the reach of project management along sharper lines. Only the Training Program KPA rises as a new independent process arm (akin to SQA and SCM).

There are two common elements to each of the areas we've discussed in this chapter. First is the need to create a plan of action for each of the KPAs: peer reviews, integrated software management, software product engineering, intergroup coordination, and the training program. Then there is the need of a process to follow to review and approve each plan. After that, these elements are usually integrated into the overall software development plan (SDP).

Implementing the recommendations in this chapter takes you to about 30 percent of Level 3 compliance. If you implement these recommendations together with those in Chapters 9, 10, and 11 you should be at about 80 percent Level 3 compliance. (Naturally, and in all of these percent benchmarks, it's assumed you have a compliant Level 2 program in place.)

In the next chapter, we'll taker a look at Level 3's independent KPA, Training Program.

Table 12.3 Key Practices Fulfilled by Implementing the Lessons in This Chapter

KEY PROCESS AREA	CHAPTER TASK	KEY PRACTICE OBLIGATION
Organization Process Focus	See Chapter 9	
Organization Process Definition	See Chapter 10	
Training Program	Create training plan template, create training course syllabi	Activity 1, activity 2, activity 3, activity 4, activity 5, measurement 1, verification 1, verification 2
Integrated Software Management	Integrate ISM activities into the SDP and the project's DSPS	Activity 1, activity 2, activity 3, activity 4, activity 5, activity 6, activity 7, activity 8, activity 9, activity 10, activity 11, measurement 1, verification 2, verification 3
Software Product Engineering	Integrate SPE activities into the SDP and the project's DSPS	Activity 1, activity 2, activity 3, activity 4, activity 5, activity 6, activity 7, activity 8, activity 9, activity 10, measurement 1, verification 2, verification 3
Intergroup Coordination	Create IGC plan template	Activity 3, activity 4, activity 5, activity 6, activity 7, measurement 1, verification 2, verification 3
Peer Review	Create peer review plan template, create peer review process	Activity 1, activity 2, activity 3, measurement 1, verification 1

Creating a Level 3 Training Program

Training is an important long-term success factor in organizations. Personnel management studies point out an interesting correlation— companies that invest in training show a lower level of turnover than companies that don't. Training not only brings needed skills and knowledge to the workforce, but it in many other ways reinforces the workforce, imparting both a sense of individual growth and a sense of common mission.
Makie May, Quality Assurance Consultant

We discussed training in Part 2 of this book (see Chapter 5), but training in CMM is very different at Level 3 than at Level 2. Training at Level 2 plays an important role in project management and touches on most areas of project activity. But because each project is free to work with its own set of processes and practices, training at this level is very customized for each project. At Level 3, you have taken the time to consolidate your processes and practices into a collected set—the Standard Software Process Set—that is used by the whole organization for all projects. In this environment, training becomes standardized and centralized, two of the major reasons that training becomes its own KPA training program at Level 3.

At Level 3 you need to organize your training efforts in a tighter fashion, but you'll also find that your training needs, time, and overall costs diminish. How's that? Well, you should now have reached the point in process maturity where economies of scale come into play. At Level 2 you had no consistent approach to project management; you were in experimentation mode, so for every unique process or practice that touched on certain areas of the software development life cycle you had to somehow make sure that your team was prepared to exercise each. No matter if your team members have been with you, say, eight years, if they're put on a new project with refined processes, they'll have to undergo training. What I have found at Level 2 is that training is usually an ad hoc affair, not well practiced and often ignored with a panacea of on-the-job-training. The time it takes, the materials, the planning, the tracking, all of these are necessary but, when compared to what happens at Level 3, relatively burdensome.

At Level 3 your organization adopts a common set of processes and practices, so your training demands greatly diminish. You can now establish curricula, plan course schedules, and prepare materials in a more orderly fashion.

In this chapter we'll look at how you might set up a Level 3 training program and what kinds of courses you could consider adopting in order to meet CMM recommendations for this KPA. To begin this, most Level 3 organizations will create some form of training group: an independent group within the organization or a subgroup within an existing block on the organization chart. For example, I have seen some organizations that will group technical documentation, Web content design, and training operations into a single unit. The structure you decide on will be shaped by your shop's industry focus, culture, and executive mission. We talked about a basic structure for a CMM-compliant training program in Chapter 11. Its duties usually focus on three areas:

- Identifying the range of courses needed across the organization

- Developing class material and/or establishing class access for all the courses

- Delivering the courses to the organization in a timely manner

These duties represent an ongoing cycle of evolution. The training program should always be current with the SSPS and with the technical and business directions of the organization as a whole. All will change over time. Let's take a look at some general aspects of training that solidify its value for an organization.

Costs and Benefits of a Training Program

Training turns out to be a difficult concept to put across to many organizations. The arguments *for* it are so intuitive that many managers think they are already doing it. And when they realize the scope of a well-rounded training program, they think "luxury" or "Hey, one day, when things slow down around here, we should look into that." Developing a training program requires a significant investment in structural and ongoing expenses, although it is a critical element in any effort to achieve both Level 2 and then Level 3 of the CMM.

If the money doesn't throw you, then maybe the time investment will. Successful IT shops (and if you're serious about CMM, you're probably one of these) are almost by definition "too busy." How is it possible that you could somehow find the time, and then find the time for other people, to design, develop, and implement a training program that has any degree of validity?

Additionally, most managers know very little about the discipline of training and its formalities. Having to acknowledge this deficit and then go about developing expertise in this area might seem like more of a headache than it is worth.

But expense, time, and expertise (ETE) are the three ingredients that make any IT shop go. You deal with them everyday. You're building a type of perpetual motion machine in this business, one in which the amount of SPG that comes out (success, profitability, growth) should be significantly higher than the ETE that went in. When you've got this ratio going, your prospects are bright. In my opinion, you should think of training as ETE kernels with the ability to burn brightly.

The benefits of a well-played training program are some of the most tangible ones and among the first to surface in any process improvement program. Here's a quick look at six major ones:

Centralized accountability. With a Level 3 training program, the responsibility for training shifts from the project to the organization. As a result, there is less pressure on project management to take on training activities. You now have people appointed to assist project management in planning training needs, scheduling courses, and delivering content. With these duties assigned to a specific group, the organization can plan for and develop its training regimes with much greater focus.

Consistency of understanding. Centralized training that is based on the SSPS and on the technical foundation of the shop will lead to the delivery of highly consistent course material to training participants. This is one of the strongest benefits. In any process improvement program, it is critical that everyone shares, to as great an extent as possible, a common understanding of the way business is conducted. This commonality helps ensure that processes are followed and that practices are adhered to. Without this, with training delivered in a customized or ad hoc manner, the commonality drifts from person to person over time, until eventually people are far apart on how this or that works.

Reduced learning curves. For new employees or employees with new assignments, a formal training program can greatly reduce the learning curves on new applications or cognitive skill sets. You can set new people loose in an environment and let them pick up on the whys and whens at their own pace, but you'll probably find that their productivity levels are low. They'll be low because they were launched into the environment unprepared. Now they are having to spend much of their time training themselves, usually by a combination of seeking out help and trial and error. If people's training needs are identified up front with training delivered at the onset of the new work assignment, you'll find that (all things being equal) your people become significantly more productive early in the process. They come into the new assignments prepared to carry out their duties, and so they do.

Central knowledge repository. A Level 3 training program will also give your organization a central repository for its library of training material. This knowledge repository will facilitate the process of identifying future training needs and planning effectively for them. It might also serve as a base for a check-in/check-out self-learning educational initiative for members of your organization.

Philosophical osmosis. This training benefit comes to your people quietly, but chances are, it will last. During training, especially over a defined curriculum, not only will your people acquire the tactical knowledge of how to follow the SSPS and how to work within the bounds of the organization, they will also begin to absorb the organization's philosophy on software process improvement. The steps and methods of process improvement will already be built into your way of doing business. As the students learn this way, they will also pick up on the theme and direction of your process improvement program. Its philosophy will become part of their habits.

Just-in-time readiness. Finally, you'll find that a formalized training program should be able to anticipate your knowledge needs, especially if the program is well connected with your various projects. This advantage should help you be ready to adopt new advances as you evaluate them and to be able to work with them faster than if adoption issues had not been preconsidered.

Of course, for these benefits to become real you've got to make a commitment to training. That commitment will include the structural elements we looked at in Chapter 11, but it will also include the management of a series of courses. Look back at Chapter 5 on Level 2 training in Part One of this book. There we saw how you might need to account for as many as 18 separate training courses. In this chapter we'll look at about 16 additional Level 3 training recommendations. That's 34 courses right there. Many may be combined and consolidated, but the point remains: You'll have to commit to what they require, which is planning and investigation, preparation, materials production, and presentation. Plus you'll have to follow this up with regular evaluation and needs projections (see Figure 13.1).

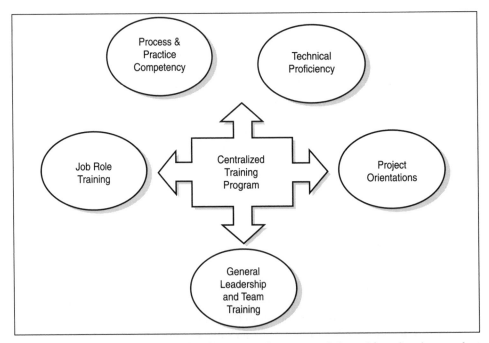

Figure 13.1   Your Level 3 shop should create a focus on training with a view into project readiness. This involves preparing your project teams to follow your defined processes and practices, to prepare them to carry out their technical assignments, to train them in their job roles, to orient them to each project mission, and to provide an avenue for professional growth.

Balancing the Load

I want to continue to emphasize the importance of training for any shop seeking general process improvement gains or specific CMM-compliance certification. But I don't want to make the job sound bigger than it might be for you. There's a *lot* you can put into a training program, and in this book I've tried to point out as much of it for you as I could. But you needn't consider it all. If something doesn't fit for you, feel free to leave it aside. There are only three goals for the CMM Level 3 Training Program KPA (and they would fit for just about any training program): plan the training, provide technical training, and provide process-and-practice training. In other words, make sure your technical people are trained in the technical tools and development methodologies you are fixed on for a project, then make sure everyone on the team has been trained in the processes and practices they need to follow in their job roles, and finally, make this happen in a smooth manner; plan it all out. This is what you should be aiming for.

Make your training program fit your organization and its needs. Meet the intention and spirit of the three goals, and you'll be on solid ground. Determining this will take your professional judgment and objective evaluation abilities. Training is something of an amorphous entity. Maybe that's why it can appear to be an underassessed area: Like a gas, it will assume the shape of its container. That makes it something of a personal KPA, an expression of the organization at large. A valid training program will reflect the structure of your Level 3 organization, and it will address its knowledge needs. As there are so many options available for meeting this end, the flexibility in your practical approach is great.

However you set up your program, remember that all your courses—no matter how many you elect to support—will typically fall into one of four categories. We discussed these in Chapter 5, but we'll take a brief look at them here. The four categories are as follows:

Direct process training. This is training that teaches the participant how to follow the processes and practices from the SSPS that directly affect the job role the participant will fill.

Indirect process training. This is training to teach the participant how to interface with other groups and process areas during the course of project activity. It is a tie-in to other processes that indirectly affect the participant's job role.

Tool training. This is training in any physical tools you may be using on a project. This might include JavaScript training, training in the use of MS-Project, or training in how to use your organization's defect-tracking system.

Orientation. This is a session that devotes its energies to a broad overview of a specific topic. It's a few steps under the intensity of regular training. You'll generally have two orientations scheduled for each project: one as an overview of the technical approach chosen, and the other as an overview of the business domain in which the projected system will operate.

By now it's apparent that there are many possible training courses to offer in four broad categories. It can seem like a lot, but one factor mitigates the size: training frequency. Most of the training you will need to offer to employees is what I call one-timing. In other words, once they're trained, they rarely need to be trained again.

Your training will tend to fall into one of two types: one-timing and repeatable. Most of your training will be one-timing because this type tends to impart *hard content*, content that does not change much over time. Train a person once in how your change control process works, and that person is set for a while. Likewise, train a person to program using the C++ language, and those skills are going to be valid for the life of the project effort, at the very least. Direct process training, indirect process training, and tool training are usually all hard content, one-timing courses.

The repeatable type is not really training at all. It's most usually an orientation. It's a *soft content* course. The information changes from project to project and so must be repeated for each project. Your two orientations for each project (the overview of the technical approach and the overview of the business domain in which the projected system will operate) are examples of repeatable training sessions. Table 13.1 details the frequency of these training sessions.

What this table demonstrates is that, over time, your training loads will stabilize. Orientations will be ongoing, but you'll only have to revisit the hard content courses when significant revisions are made to your tools or processes and when new hires are brought in or people are promoted to new areas of responsibility.

In this chapter we'll discuss Level 3 training from three views. First, we'll look at some training courses you might consider adding to support the Level 3 KPAs. Next, we'll present a brief overview of the scope and curriculum that might make up a Level 3 training program. Third, we'll look at some of the different training approaches that are open to you and can be readily adopted by your organization.

Let's begin with a review of some new Level 3 courses suggested by the activities in each of the Level 3 KPAs.

Level 3 Training Courses

When you move from CMM Level 2 to Level 3, you will expand the operations that support project management and process improvement. You'll develop new capabilities for training in general, you'll establish finer project management guidelines, and you'll initiate new intergroup coordination and review procedures. All these new areas will require a level of training. In this section we'll look at potential training needs for each

Table 13.1 Training Frequency

TYPE	FREQUENCY	CONTENT
Direct process training	One time	Hard
Indirect process training	One time	Hard
Tool training	One time	Hard
Orientation	Many times	Soft

Level 3 KPA. This will cover course preparation and thoughts for training in such areas as integrated software management, software product engineering, intergroup coordination, and peer review.

> **NOTE** We've omitted training for the Organization Process Focus and Organization Process Definition KPAs here because they are individually covered in Chapters 9 and 10 of this book.

Training Programs

The people in your training group will at one time or another need to be trained in how to carry out their specific job roles. At the same time, members of the software development groups will need a basic understanding of how the training group works in the company and how it's set up to serve project teams. Three courses can help with this.

Course Preparation Training

You'll probably offer a series of courses in your training program. Some may be technical, such as how to program using Java. Others might be process-oriented, such as how to use the company's change control process. As you assign instructors in your group to teach these various courses, you will have to make sure that they are competent to do so. If they have a professional history in the areas or have been certified or trained in the past, then their competence can be readily demonstrated. But if they are new to the organizations or new to some of the technical areas of your operations, they may need to be trained in these areas so that they are able to train in these areas.

Who: Members of the training group

Course: Course material as assigned

When: As hired or on assignment

Scope: Any training needed for the instructors to be able to effectively and competently deliver the materials for the various courses they are assigned

Type: Direct tool training

Waiver: Adequate experience; certification as applies

Training Plan Management

In addition to subject matter expertise training, the members of the training group may need to be trained in the process of creating, approving, and managing a project training plan. Each Level 3 project you undertake will require the development of a training plan. This plan will emerge from an analysis of the training needs of the team members as related to project requirements. The training planner will need to work with the project's software managers in order to derive much of the strategy in the plan. The planner will therefore need to be trained in the contents of a software project training plan and the steps taken to create, review, approve, and manage it.

Who: Members of the training group

Course: Training plan management

When: As hired or on assignment

Scope: Training in the processes to create, review, and approve a training plan for a specific project

Type: Direct process training

Waiver: Adequate experience; prior attendance

Training Program Orientation

With your internal training group members trained in their planning duties and in the courses they will teach, one final effort is recommended. This is an orientation that presents an overview of how the training group works and what services it can offer to the various project teams. The software managers will need to know such things as what contributions they will have to make to the shaping of a project training plan, what training courses the program can offer them, how to identify the right courses for a particular student, how to enroll participants, and what time/cost commitments the various courses may require. This overview will typically be a high-level look at the program, usually accomplished in a single session of perhaps a few hours.

Who: Software managers as designated

Course: Orientation to the training program

When: As hired or on project startup

Scope: An overview of the training program that enables the project's software managers to manage the training needs on the project

Type: Orientation

Waiver: Adequate experience; prior attendance

Integrated Software Management

The Integrated Software Management KPA is chiefly concerned with the way project management uses the Standard Software Process Set for individual projects within the organization. At Level 3, all projects must follow the SSPS, but not all projects are alike. Some are big; some are small. Some are full life cycle efforts; others address only certain stages of the life cycle. To address this, the organization establishes guidelines at Level 3 that tell a software project planner how to tailor the SSPS to the needs of the project. In addition, the guidelines may also address the required steps all projects must include (the mandatory activities, such as status reviews and measurements).

This requires that your software project planners and software project managers receive training in these areas so that they are able to plan in accordance with standards and are then able to manage in accordance with standards. Three training sessions can address this need.

Using and Tailoring the SSPS

The organization's Standard Software Process Set is its central project management mechanism. All project planning and project management efforts need to be derived within its boundaries. Your SSPS may be detailed and extensive, or it may be relatively small. But whatever its makeup, your planners and software project managers are going to have to know two things about it: what it is made of and how to tailor it for specific projects. Training in this area then will involve two things: going over the major areas of the SSPS that impact project planning and tracking so that the participants emerge able to work according to the SSPS, and reviewing the guidelines that control how the SSPS can be tailored for each project. Both of these areas are of significant importance. Any planning and tracking activities that deviate in an unrecognized manner from the SSPS will impede the progress you are making in your software process improvement efforts. At Level 2, both Software Project Planning and Software Project Tracking and Oversight emerged as critical management areas with regard to process improvement and quality control. At Level 3 that importance is amplified.

Who: Software planners and project managers

Course: How to use and tailor the SSPS

When: As hired or on assignment

Scope: In-depth training that instructs the participants in the scope and details of the organization's SSPS and then instructs on the guidelines used to tailor the SSPS to individual projects

Type: Direct process training

Waiver: Adequate experience; prior attendance

Managing with the Tailored SSPS

In the preceding session the software planners were trained in how to develop a software development plan using the SSPS and how to tailor it to the needs of their particular project. Here the software project managers are trained in how to manage the project using the custom-tailored SDP. This function is really an extension of the Software Project Tracking and Oversight KPA of Level 2, but because the management scope has expanded, additional training is required, too. Here the goal is to train the managers in how to manage at the Level 3 tier, which includes such new Software Project Tracking and Oversight items as peer review, intergroup coordination, and enhanced software product engineering steps. All this requires instruction in what to expect and how to manage each of these new entities.

Who: Software project managers
           Group managers as designated

Course: How to manage with the tailored SSPS

When: As hired or on assignment

Scope: In-depth training that instructs the participants in how to manage a project using the project plan as derived from the SSPS

Type: Direct process training

Waiver: Adequate experience; prior attendance

Using the Software Process Database

One of the new project management tools at Level 3 is the organization's centralized software process database. This database is a repository for the measurements and the lessons learned that arise out of every project. These are collected in the database and then used as accumulated historical data, as a tool for better planning in the future, and as a mechanism for analyzing process improvement progress and activity. The type of SPDB you set up will depend on your organization. It might be something as sophisticated as relational Oracle database tables accessed through custom windows, or it may be something as simple as an Excel spreadsheet. How you set it up is up to you (for more on this, see Chapter 12), but whatever you end up with you'll have to teach people how to use it. This training is usually given to the software project planners and the software project managers, as they will have to work directly with the tool, identifying measurements and collecting them. But you might also find it useful to include other software managers in your group, as some of their team members may be required to assist in this area, especially for group-specific measurements.

Who: Software planners and project managers
Software managers as designated

Course: How to use the software process database

When: As hired or on assignment

Scope: Training on how to use the software process database tool (with usage rules) to store and analyze the various measurements taken on a project

Type: Tool training

Waiver: Adequate experience; prior attendance

Software Product Engineering

Software product engineering is an expansion of the role of software project management at Level 2. It recommends project tracking at a finer granularity than at Level 2. At this finer level, the project is managed with very specific products in mind, such as the software requirements, the software design, testing, and documentation. All of this is now followed in greater detail. Because of this, software product engineering calls for demonstrable competence in job role performance. The members of the project teams must be able to carry out their specific duties, especially in the technical realms, in order to support this finer level of granularity. The training in this area is important, but it can be interpreted in many ways. The chief goal here is to make sure your project team members have been trained in the technical and administrative duties they perform. This covers a wide range of possibilities. If your shop codes exclusively in C++, you must make sure your people are competent C++ programmers; if they are not, train them to get them up to speed. Likewise, these people will need to know how to conduct their coding activities in your shop: what reports they must make or what measurements they might have to take. They may need training for this, too. In addition, to facilitate the smooth workings between groups, it's a good idea to give your group managers some form of orientation in how the other groups in the shop work: what their roles are, how they interface, and more. Finally, and this is usually done for each new project, the project managers and the software managers (perhaps with the whole team, if preferable) should receive an orientation at the start of the project as to the general technical approach the project will use. Let's look briefly at each.

Technical Job Training

There is probably a large collection of somewhat independent groups working within your IT shop. Requirements, software design, coding, testing, documentation, technical support, SQA, and configuration management are just a few that you might have set and working. Each group makes a specific contribution to each project, sometimes large, sometimes small, but always to some extent critical. If you throw members of a group at a project and they are not equipped to carry out their duties in a manner that reflects the cost , time, and quality expectations in the SDP, the project may be forced off course, and it may fall into jeopardy. That's why it's important to make sure your people are qualified to work in their specific job roles. It's usually easy to gauge this: A person will have had a certain amount of experience you deem acceptable, or he or she may have had some formal training elsewhere that makes him or her qualified with limited experience. But take care with those who have neither. Train them first before you place them in a project into which they might (through no fault of their own) introduce unnecessary bumps and hurdles.

Who: Members of the project teams as designated

Course: Technical job role training

When: As hired or on assignment

Scope: Training in the technical aspects of their job; training in the administrative/process aspects of their jobs

Type: Direct process training/tool training

Waiver: Adequate experience; prior attendance

Job Role Orientation

Naturally, it's important that each member of your project team is qualified to carry out a technical role on the project. These people must, in effect, know their job in order to best perform their job. But an additional dimension will augment this job performance. This is an orientation for the workers in how the *other* groups on a project work. No group can work in isolation. Software development is a cumulative, interactive effort. While job competence is important, so is an awareness of what all the other job functions are and how they all fit together in the software development landscape. You'll find that a general high-level orientation covering the makeup of your organization and the function of its defined group will help your people better understand their place in the whole. And this should enhance their ability to work within the whole.

Who:	Members of the project teams as designated
Course:	Organization job role orientation
When:	As hired or on assignment
Scope:	An orientation on how the various groups in the organization work. This gives people outside of the groups a feeling for the contribution and value each provides, and it provides an understanding for how to work with each group during a project.
Type:	Tool training
Waiver:	Adequate experience; prior attendance

Technical Orientation for Project Managers

Every project you'll undertake is unique—we've mentioned that a few times already. Because each project is unique, the solution you come up with for making the thing real is going to vary from project to project. You may use different tools and methodologies, different kinds of work products, schedules with new milestones, and so on. All this will be reflected in the project's software development plan. And the SDP will get into the hands of your various project managers. But in the interest of smooth and efficient project management, it's not a good idea to start your project without first going over the SDP with them. This is a technical orientation for your managers. During this session you go over all the critical points in the plan: schedules, tools, and work products, as you see fit. The idea is to establish a common understanding among all your groups as to how the work will proceed and what is expected from each group, each step of the way.

Who:	Project and group managers
Course:	Technical orientation to the project
When:	Project startup
Scope:	A technical overview presented to the managers assigned to the project in order to give them all a common understanding of the technical makeup of the project
Type:	Orientation
Waiver:	Usually no waiver

Intergroup Coordination

Intergroup Coordination is all about creating the kinds of interteam interfaces the project needs for open communications. The groups may be set up as independent units, but only very rarely should they operate as independent units. The various teams need to work together. Because one's work can have a critical impact on the work of another, a formal and open channel of communication between teams must be in place for every project. As important as communication is, be aware that it comes in two flavors: raw and refined. As much as possible, the goals of the Intergroup Coordination KPA are in place to foster refined communications. The raw stuff might be honest and accurate, but by definition it is unshaped and not well organized. Find yourself stuck in any ill-managed business meeting, and you'll know what I mean. Intergroup Coordination is put in place to allow for refined communications between development groups. To build these avenues you will usually find it helpful to train some of your team members in the philosophy and discipline of teamwork.

Teamwork Training for Group Managers

Effective intergroup coordination is going to require effective team management within groups and between groups. For this reason, you may want to have your group managers formally trained in the discipline of teamwork. Such training usually includes instruction on how to manage individuals, how to design for effective group dynamics, how to build teams, how to manage teams, and what type of planning is useful for team management and growth. You'll have to know your managers to decide to what extent you want to take this training. Some managers seem to have natural abilities in this area. Others seem to have a difficult time with it. Your approach will depend on your own needs.

Who: Group managers

Course: Teamwork training

When: As hired; on assignment

Scope: Training in such teamwork disciplines as team building, team management, group dynamics, and teamwork planning

Type: Training

Waiver: Adequate experience or certification

Group Orientation

This is a session used to give the task leaders on all the teams a chance to better understand what roles the other groups in the organization play in the process of software development. This orientation will serve to accomplish two things. First, it should give the participants a broad overview on how to work with the other groups. Second, it should give them an appreciation for how each group contributes to the project and how each group must interface with others to help ensure consistent product quality.

Who: Group managers and team members

Course: Group orientation

When: As hired or at project startup

Scope: An orientation that gives workers a general understanding as to what roles the other groups in the organization play in software development

Type: Orientation

Waiver: Adequate experience, prior attendance

Teamwork Orientation for the Teams

Finally, to foster the ability for the different teams to work together in an organized and efficient manner, you may find it helpful to give your group members an orientation in the general field of teamwork. You might cover such topics as the philosophy of teamwork, aspects of group dynamics, teamwork tools, and teamwork objectives. This type of high-level session should make your people more aware that software development really is a team effort and that coordinated, facilitated work and communication between teams will lead to a better product in the end.

Who:	Task leaders, group members
Course:	Orientation on teamwork
When:	As hired or on project startup
Scope:	An overview on the tools, techniques, objectives, and purpose of teamwork
Type:	Orientation
Waiver:	Adequate experience, prior attendance

Peer Review

Training in the area of peer review is important because peer review, if not managed well, can take on a judgmental form that it was never designed to have. Peer reviews are in place to review work products to understand content and to inspect them for any potential defects. Peer reviews should have nothing to do with personal performance or individual skill sets. Those issues fall outside the CMM. You might readily agree with this assessment of peer reviews, but to manage them in the right way takes either a solid amount of intuitive people skills or a degree of formal training. You should assess your teams in two areas concerning peer reviews: Are my peer review facilitators (those people who will organize and lead the peer reviews) prepared to begin peer reviews according to organizational standards? And are the people who may be called on to participate in peer reviews prepared to do so in the appropriate way? Two courses may help you answer these questions "yes."

Facilitator Training in Peer Review Process

Your peer review facilitators need to be trained in the full process of peer reviews. (For more on this, see Chapter 12.) This type of training will usually include such things as these:

- The objectives, methods, and philosophy of peer reviews
- The different types of peer reviews (test, requirements, design, and so on)
- How to plan and organize a peer review
- How to evaluate entrance and exit criteria for a peer review
- How to conduct a peer review

- How to report on review results
- How to collect measurement data from peer reviews

Who: Peer review facilitators

Course: How to conduct a peer review

When: As hired or on project startup

Scope: Training on the tools, techniques, objectives, and purpose of peer reviews

Type: Direct process training

Waiver: Adequate experience, prior attendance

Participant Training in Peer Review Process

This final piece of training is for the members of your groups who may be called on to participate in a peer review, either as an author or as a reviewer. This session is usually shaped as a scaled-down version of the preceding one. The objective here is twofold: first, to leave the participant with an impression of the purpose and use of peer reviews and, second, to inform the participant about the specific duties that will be expected of them, and in what form, for the peer review in which they participate.

Who: Peer review participants

Course: How to participate in a peer review

When: As hired or on project startup

Scope: Training on the tools, techniques, objectives, and purpose of peer reviews

Type: Direct process training

Waiver: Adequate experience, prior attendance

A List of Potential Courses

In Chapter 5 we looked at the kind of training your people might need in order to operate in your Level 2 development environment. Here, in Chapter 13, we've done the same for Level 3. Many of the courses we've discussed can be addressed pretty much as described. Others can be combined, further delineated, and merged with other courses. The key to planning your training program and to shaping the curriculum it contains is knowing how your development shop operates and then finding out if everyone else knows, too. Table 13.2 contains a listing of all the courses we have talked about in this book. Most of these have been recommended in the CMM; others are simply logical selections it would seem that almost any training should have. The list is here for your review. If you decide to use it as the basis for building your own training program you'll find it to be fairly complete. On the other hand, you might simply want to review the table to get a feel for what might be contained in a generic training program. Naturally, as we've said for most of the things in the CMM, the kind of training program you build will depend on your organizational structure, the details of your SSPS, and the experience and skill base of your team members.

Table 13.2   Collection of Potential Courses

COURSE	WHAT	WHO	FREQUENCY	TYPE	WAIVER
Requirements Analysis and Allocation Process	The methodology, rules, and tools used to allocate requirements to hardware, software, and other project elements	Requirements analysts	One time	Direct process training	Yes
Orientation to the Business Background of the Project	An orientation to the business solution that the project will address, expressed in terms of real-world applications	Requirements analysts	Many times	Orientation	No
Project Planning Methods and Processes	The methodology and rules used to plan a software project and create a software development plan	Project managers	One time	Direct process training	Yes
Project Planning Rule for Estimating	The contacts and rules applied to the process of estimating costs, schedules, and resources for a project	Project managers	One time	Direct process training	Yes
Project Planning Tools and Utilities	Training on the system tools and applications used to develop the software development plan	Project managers	One time	Direct process training	Yes

continued

Table 13.2   Collection of Potential Courses (*continued*)

COURSE	WHAT	WHO	FREQUENCY	TYPE	WAIVER
Project Planning Rule for Estimating	The contacts and rules applied to the process of estimating costs, schedules, and resources for a project	Software engineering group	One time	Indirect process training	Yes
Project Tracking Processes	Training in the steps and activities defined in the software tracking process	Project managers	One time	Direct process training	Yes
Project Tracking Tools	Training in the system tools and applications used to track the software project	Project managers	One time	Direct process training	Yes
Orientation to the Technical Aspects of the Project	A presentation of the architecture, tools, and technical approach the project will take	Software engineering group	Many times	Orientation	No
Configuration Management Methods and Processes	The methodology and rules used to conduct version control activities across a project	Configuration managers	One time	Direct process training	Yes
CM Tools and Utilities	Training on the system tools and applications used for version control during the project	Configuration managers	One time	Direct process training	Yes

continued

Table 13.2   Collection of Potential Courses (*continued*)

COURSE	WHAT	WHO	FREQUENCY	TYPE	WAIVER
CCB Rules and Procedures	Training as to the rules and processes that must be followed by members of the CCB when performing their duties	Members of the Configuration Control Board	One time	Direct process training	Yes
Processes Required to Participate in CM Activities	The steps and rules applied to the process of configuration management as well as training on the general role and value of CM within the organization	Members of the SEG	One time	Indirect process training	Yes
SQA Methods and Processes	The methodology and rules used to conduct SQA activities across a project	SQA managers	One time	Direct process training	Yes
SQA Tools and Utilities	Training on the system tools and applications used for SQA during the project	SQA managers	One time	Direct process training	Yes
Processes Required to Participate in SQA Activities	The steps and rules applied to the process of configuration management as well as training on the general role and value of SQA within the organization	Members of the SEG	One time	Indirect process training	Yes

continued

Table 13.2 Collection of Potential Courses (*continued*)

COURSE	WHAT	WHO	FREQUENCY	TYPE	WAIVER
Course Material as Assigned	Any training needed for the instructors to be able to effectively and competently deliver the materials for the various courses they are assigned	Members of the training group	One time	Tool training	Yes
Training Plan Management	Training in the processes to create, review, and approve a training plan for a specific project	Members of the training group	One time	Direct process training	Yes
Orientation to the Training Program	An overview of the training program that enables the project's software managers to manage the training needs on the project	Software managers as designated	One time	Orientation	Yes
How to Use and Tailor the SSPS	In-depth training that instructs the participants in the scope and details of the organization's SSPS and then instructs on the guidelines used to tailor the SSPS to individual projects	Software planners and project managers	One time	Direct process training	Yes

continued

Table 13.2 Collection of Potential Courses (*continued*)

COURSE	WHAT	WHO	FREQUENCY	TYPE	WAIVER
How to Manage with the Tailored SSPS	In-depth training that instructs the participants in how to manage a project using the project plan as derived from the SSPS	Software project managers and group managers as designated	One time	Direct process training	Yes
How to Use the Software Process Database	Training on how to use the software process database tool (with usage rules) to store and analyze the various measurements taken on a project	Software planners and project managers, software managers as designated	One time	Direct process training	Yes
Technical Job Role Training	Training in the technical aspects of their job; training in the administrative/ process aspects of their jobs	Members of the project teams as designated	One time	Tool training	Yes
Organization Job Role Orientation	An orientation on how the various groups in the organization work. This gives people outside of the groups a feeling for the contribution and value each provides, and it provides an understanding for how to work with each group during a project.	Members of the project teams as designated	One time	Orientation	Yes

continued

Table 13.2 Collection of Potential Courses (*continued*)

COURSE	WHAT	WHO	FREQUENCY	TYPE	WAIVER
Technical Orientation to the Project	A technical overview presented to the managers assigned to the project in order to give them all a common understanding of the technical makeup of the project	Project and group managers	Many times	Orientation	No
Teamwork Training	Training in such teamwork disciplines as team building, team management, group dynamics, and teamwork planning	Group managers	One time	Direct process training	Yes
Group Orientation	An orientation that gives workers a general understanding as to what roles the other groups in the organization play in software development	Group managers and team members	One time	Orientation	Yes
Orientation on Teamwork	An overview on the tools, techniques, objectives, and purpose of teamwork	Task leaders, group members	One time	Orientation	Yes
How to Conduct a Peer Review	Training on the tools, techniques, objectives, and purpose of peer reviews	Peer review facilitators	One time	Direct process training	Yes
How to Participate in a Peer Review	Training on the tools, techniques, objectives, and purpose of peer reviews	Peer review participants	One time	Direct process training	Yes

Implementing Your Training Program

There are many ways to implement a training program in your organization. One option is to simply outsource it all, providing you can find the right classes. Another approach is to do it all in-house, to build a totally self-sufficient training operation. Because training is such a strong reflection of your team and the experience in your shop, you'll have to design a training program that best fits your needs. In this section we'll look at some of the forms of training you might want to consider for your shop. Chances are, you will not be able to farm out everything; neither will you be able to accommodate everything in-house. Here we'll look at the general types of training available so that you'll at least know what options are open to you.

Basically, there are two categories of training. They can be called in-house training and out-of-house training. Each carries a unique blend of considerations. For example, with in-house training you must set up a mini-school on the premises, then you must staff it, prepare course curricula and student material, and buy equipment and supplies. On the other hand, this choice puts you in complete control of your course content. It can be tailored to your exact needs. Further, you can schedule the training activity when it suits you best. And you have a great degree of flexibility in adjusting the course content as your needs change.

With out-of-house training you don't have to set up school. You can send out for the school. You don't have to worry about staffing or materials other than as expense items. You can go a la carte or prix fixe. But for the ease of going out, you will sacrifice a degree of content control and access control. The material may be not ideally suited to your needs, just close enough to help. And you'll have to accommodate outside schedules to meet your needs. And in the end, you'll have little choice over content or material updates.

Out-of-house training is typically viewed as cheaper in the short term and more expensive in the long term. In-house training is typically considered cheaper in the long term and more expensive in the short term. Most companies use a blend of both, balancing cost efficiencies as their program changes. This is summarized in Table 13.3.

Table 13.3 Category Benefits

IN-HOUSE	BENEFITS
Control	Complete control
Content	Tailored/custom
Expense	Cheaper long term
OUT-OF-HOUSE	**BENEFITS**
Control	Little control other than choice
Content	Generic
Expense	Cheaper short term

Most companies offer at least some form of in-house training. Even the basic process of training a new hire on the front door security system can be considered in-house training. But internal training as far as CMM (and process improvement) goes actually means more; as a management tool, its purpose is to enhance potential and performance, to further the mission of the company and the achievement of its goals.

Internal Training

Management decisions regarding the implementation of internal training programs must weigh the frequency of required training with the resources required to support it. The possible implementation formats that arise from this analysis can cover a wide spectrum of plan structures, ranging in a continuum from elementary training, like team assimilation, to the formalized training structure of a fully staffed, in-house training department. Following is a brief description of each segment of in-house training.

Training through Team Assimilation

At one end of the training spectrum is team assimilation. This form is often overlooked because it exists as a natural characteristic of the business environment: An employee who joins an organization trains on the job simply by becoming a member of a team. Many managers consider this merely "socialization" and not a form of training. A strong argument can be made that this is the most pervasive and enduring form of training in use today.

Team assimilation may be one of the most effective ways to train an employee. People tend to adopt workplace practices and performance standards from those team members around them. Socialized learning of this type has a high rate of endurance; because the training information is saturated in the environment, the learner tends to integrate the knowledge into his or her general approach to work. Endurance and retention, as a result, tend to be high.

This adaptive process encourages learning by trial and error. And progress is measured by a common team standard of performance. Because people learn most by performing actions themselves, and by acting in an environment where there are real consequences and outcomes to actions, team assimilation is a form of training that leads to very high retention.

Team assimilation is, however, a slow process, with an intensity level rated low. In this training form, knowledge is not directly pushed to the trainee; rather, it must be absorbed from the environment at the initiative of the trainee. The trainee must "pull" the knowledge from the other members of the team. In this regard, the learning curve is steep. Management must provide very little commitment to endorse and support team assimilation. It is a natural byproduct of the work environment. Because of this, you might consider team assimilation as an adjunct form of training. It's not the primary kind that CMM has in mind, nor is it widely recognized for its efficiency. It's a form of "throw 'em-in-the-fire" training, ill conducive to the planning and preparation foundations found in CMM. Team assimilation works best when it is combined with some of the older, more formal modes of training. Table 13.4 lists some of the attributes and traits of team assimilation.

Table 13.4 Training Form—Team Assimilation

RESOURCE	MEASURE	RESULT	MEASURE	QUALITY	MEASURE
Commitment	*Low*	Endurance	*High*	Efficiency	*Low*
Intensity	*Low*	Retention	*High*	Consistency	*Low*

Most new hires will respond well to team assimilation. The key is that the individual must have a basic skill set enabling him or her to function as a team player. Rare is the opportunity to completely train an unskilled worker in a functioning role (this approach is not only expensive, but slow). Team assimilation is most effective for junior workers, those less experienced trainees who do not yet have a backlog of processes and approaches gained from prior experience.

Management's main concern with this format is to make sure the trainee is exposed to sound learning and avoids exposure to bad work habits or work philosophies that do not blend well into the overall environment. This is the chief risk of team assimilation: Trainees will absorb both the good and the bad in the environment. But as long as management understands that mistakes will be made and progress will be slow, team assimilation can play an important part in the training mix.

Training with Mentoring

Up the scale from team assimilation is the training process termed mentoring. Mentoring is a much overused, little understood term. Despite a run of popularity in the 1980s, formal mentoring programs have not been widely adopted in the corporate training mix. Mentoring's lack of success is due not to a fundamental flaw in its approach or design, but rather in management's thin understanding of its use and purpose.

In its most elemental sense, mentoring is the focused act of placing a junior employee under the guidance of a senior employee for the purpose of achieving both growth and functional improvement. In many formal mentoring programs, the commitment made is akin to corporate "adoption:" A manager (typically one with executive authority and designated seniority) "adopts" a junior-level employee (typically one being groomed for executive status) and shows him or her the ropes.

But there are many other forms of mentoring, some formal, most casual. Often in its less formal form it is called directed guidance or directed feedback. In this form, mentoring is not a fixed one-to-one process. It is a corporate-sponsored "outreach" effort in which senior management supports the growth and development of junior management.

Mentoring in all its forms is good at imparting the following:

- Interpersonal skills
- Communication skills
- Technical expertise

- Conflict resolution skills
- Time management acumen
- Goal-setting skills
- Management preparation
- Executive development

Mentoring can be considered in intensity a moderate form of training. Because it is an extended, personalized form of team assimilation, its endurance and levels of retention are moderate in nature. And because this form of training is, at best, a part-time effort, the knowledge imparted must compete with other forms of training and environmental influences. Mentoring, in its part-time nature, is also moderately intensive, characterized by brief sessions separated by dormant periods of time.

Mentoring also requires a moderate commitment on the part of management. Little overhead and practically no capital resources are required, but there must be a dedication on the part of the executive branch of management to deliver the minimum amount of time to making mentoring work and to provide a good-faith effort toward the growth and development of the individual. Table 13.5 lists some of the attributes and traits of mentoring.

The single biggest consideration for the implementation of a mentoring program is who decides on the appropriate candidate. Mentoring is an exclusive form of training. It is not doled out to the masses at large (although this might prove to be an innovative if exhaustive concept). It is carefully targeted to a select few.

What qualities should the select few exhibit? Several are immediately apparent. First, as the candidate will be occupying the valuable time of an executive member, the person should demonstrate a level of performance that warrants such attention. Second, the candidate should become a part of the program-shaping process; that is, a mentoring program should be a path of knowledge shaped by the participation of human resources, the executive, and the training candidate.

But be careful here. Many companies adopt a mentoring-type training program with the feeling that, unsupervised, it will meet their CMM expectations. Mentoring activity, like all forms of training, should be closely monitored and tracked.

Using Focused Seminars

This option is the first step into classroom instruction. Seminars are usually short, high-level orientations to a particular topic or issue. Their length (usually a half day or so) makes them ideal for introducing common information to a collection of people. Here

Table 13.5 Training Form—Mentoring

RESOURCE	MEASURE	RESULT	MEASURE	QUALITY	MEASURE
Commitment	*Medium*	Endurance	*High*	Efficiency	*Medium*
Intensity	*Medium*	Retention	*Medium*	Consistency	*Low/medium*

you bring people together into a group and make a presentation to them. If you have ever attended a new hire orientation or a benefits-explanation meeting, you know what this type of training is good for. For CMM purposes, you'll find that seminars are great for project introductory training, business orientations, process change updates, and other types of instruction that do not involve a lot of detail. Table 13.6 lists some of the attributes and traits of focused seminars.

Formal In-House Training

At the far end of the internal training spectrum is the formation and support of an in-house training department offering full-blown training classes across a spectrum of topics. Many large companies feature in-house training departments. These companies typically have large human resource needs, many new hires, and a promote-from-within policy that focuses on employee growth.

But in-house training departments are not just for large companies. The Bureau of Labor Statistics reported in 1998 that 91 percent of all companies included in a recent study used in-house staff for at least some training, most often on an informal basis.

In-house training is different from the more casual programs of mentoring and team assimilation. In-house training involves the establishment of training facilities, the development and maintenance of specific training courses, and the support of an in-house training staff.

A commitment to in-house training represents a dedication to long-term employee development. In today's era of come-and-go employees and revolving-door hiring policies, this form of training is less and less common. In addition, the impact of in-house training on the corporate bottom line is hard to measure (unless you simply directly compare hard costs to sending trainees to off-site training groups). But in-house training does offer some major benefits.

Quality, duration, support materials, course refinement, and evaluation are all under direct control when training efforts are managed in-house. Plus, in-house training supports a wider spectrum of training programs, programs that must be selected a la carte from out-of-house training organizations.

Through in-house training, management has a single source for a wide array of both growth and development training and functional improvement training. In-house training can support such diverse needs as employee orientation, benefits reviews, job training, dealer support, technical and product overviews, and others. Because in-house training provides a dedicated staff and dedicated resources targeted at the student, it is the most intensive form of employee training. It represents a focused effort at educa-

Table 13.6   Training Form–Focused Seminar

RESOURCE	MEASURE	RESULT	MEASURE	QUALITY	MEASURE
Commitment	*Medium*	Endurance	*Low*	Efficiency	*High*
Intensity	*Medium*	Retention	*Medium*	Consistency	*High*

tion, over a fixed period of time, typically a few days, usually in a classroom setting, away from the daily work environment, where the attendees can concentrate. Training in this manner is usually very orderly, with established learning goals and custom-designed support material.

In-house training requires a firm commitment on the part of management. The organization needs proper space: Some form of classroom setting must be specially designed. Management must be willing to purchase and maintain training equipment: computers, projectors, and audio/visual equipment. Management must also support and fund the efforts to create and maintain updated learning plans, course outlines, and course materials. Most importantly, management must hire and maintain a training staff with the skills and experience necessary to the tasks at hand.

In-house training can be made readily available to all employees, but it is best for use in long-term development programs where the employee receives not just spot training here and there, but instead a series of training, in a planned format, over a long period of time.

In-house training is also effective for technical training used to solve short-term problems. Here the student's learning will be put to immediate use in the business world.

Of course, the high commitment required of in-house training programs requires a comparable level of activity within the organization. Table 13.7 identifies some of the attributes of dedicated in-house training.

The internal forms of training represent, to greater or lesser degree, a form of overhead that management must recognize and accurately cost out. Perhaps for this reason the most common type of training used in corporations is, according to the Bureau of Labor Statistics (1998), off-site training. Over 80 percent of business establishments with more than 50 employees report using off-site training. In fact, many corporations with established in-house training programs use off-site training as well, as an integral part of the training mix.

External Training

Of course, there is sometimes a distinct benefit for going outside the company to receive training: to receive a different world-view of things as a form of added enlightenment. While we learn mostly from experience and the other people in our environment, it could help to get away from our day-to-day work environment to get new perspectives. That is why it's recommended to take advantage of both internal and external training programs. It helps to get the stimulation of other, external sources to maximize the usefulness and effectiveness of all-round training.

Table 13.7 Training Form—Dedicated In-House Training

RESOURCE	MEASURE	RESULT	MEASURE	QUALITY	MEASURE
Commitment	*High*	Endurance	*Medium*	Efficiency	*High*
Intensity	*High*	Retention	*High*	Consistency	*High*

The next category is taking the classroom outside the organization: out-of-house training. There are essentially two types of this training: professional/corporate training and traditional academic training.

Professional or Corporate Training

This is an area that has grown exponentially into an industry all its own. Professional or corporate training is a type of training focused on specific skill set improvement, offering training in very specific and practical subjects. You'll find many companies that provide this type of service; most have campus-based learning facilities, and most will also make arrangements to come to your site.

This type of training is recognized as an effective means of imparting what I call generic information, or industry-common information. For example, if you are a C++ shop and some of your new hires lack C++ skills, you might find it a good option to send them to a C++ class at a professional learning center. Because C++ coding regimens are basically followed in the same way, most places, you know your people will, in all likelihood, be trained properly. You don't *have to have* a C++ course in your in-house program because it is commonly offered outside.

On the other hand, professional/corporate training is not so well suited to custom practices unique to your own shop. For example, you probably couldn't find an outside training company that could train your people on your process for building a software development plan. That would probably have to come from inside your shop.

Off-site training is usually a service contracted for between the company and an outside training organization. Many well-established training organizations exist for a wide range of industries and disciplines. Training companies offer formal courses in topics ranging from OSHA safety training for industrial factories to computer training on WordPerfect, Excel, or other popular business software packages.

Academic Training

A different type of external, out-of-house training is formal academic training, the kind offered by established colleges and universities either as part of their normal curriculum or as part of continuing and extended education programs. Academic training is usually included in the training to provide a form of growth and development training. In its most basic form, a company may cosponsor an employee's education efforts, paying a portion of tuition for courses that both agree to fill the professional or degree needs of the employee as well as the business needs of the corporation.

Many colleges are beginning to recognize the need to fill a training role within the corporate community. The boundaries are beginning to blur between the college's more traditional mission of educating learners who are yet to be employed and its expanding mission of educating fully employed learners in the workplace. Enlightened companies have begun to see the instructional role as a continuum, with the traditional student on one end and the business clients who contract for training their employees on the other end. Indeed, if you look closely you'll see that colleges and universities are now beginning to take on some of the shape of corporate/professional training enterprises. They are focusing a bit less on the traditional range of courses and more on a select, a la carte approach. This is especially true in these schools' night course programs, which are by and large geared to the needs of people with day jobs looking for new skills or career advancement. In fact, many of our most prestigious universities, such as Emory and Perdue, are offering select evening and weekend courses specifically targeted to the working professional.

Supporting Your Level 3 Training Program

The following list of artifacts will help you demonstrate CMM compliance for the Training Program KPA and the other training areas recommended at Level 3. Don't worry if your actual artifacts are different from these. As long as yours are helpful and in active use, they'll probably do fine:

Training group on organization chart. To show that you have set up a training function in your company, whether it handles everything in-house or farms everything out, it helps to have the group officially recognized on organization charts, company directories, and other such visual references.

Training program policy. Having a copy of the training program policy on hand helps demonstrate that the group has been established and has an executive endorsement for its activities.

Training group staff assignment forms. Because every project has to consider its training needs at the outset, a training analyst (full- or part-time) should be assigned to every project. You can demonstrate this with the use of staff assignment forms, or assignment e-mails, or a project team list that includes the training planner. The key is to show that for each project, and for the training program group as well, you have appointed the people necessary to do the planning and course delivery work for the organization.

Training facilities and equipment. Your training program cannot exist solely on paper. It must be a real, physical, ongoing enterprise. It need not be as large as a series of dedicated classrooms and instruction terminals and administrative offices, but it should fit your shop's needs and at least have the part-time tools or facilities it needs to prepare training plans and program announcement material and keep student records.

Corporate budget for training activities and project budget allocation for training activities. In addition to assigning people and facilities to your training program, you will need to provide the budgetary resources required for its ongoing activity. In order for the function to operate properly, and to address the needs of your shop, you'll have to make some form of capital commitment to it.

Training plan template process. To demonstrate that you are considering the issue of training on all projects, you might want to keep a copy of your training plan template handy, along with a copy of the training plan development process. This will show that you have prepared for training analysis on each project. A copy of a completed training plan for a project will also help show that you followed through with the process.

Course syllabi. A listing of all the courses your program offers, both in-house and outsourced, will help show that you have thought out your training program and implemented it in a specific way. This will also show the level of commitment your organization has made to a training program, and it will demonstrate the scope of thought and planning that has gone into your course designs.

Training schedule or course presentation schedule. This schedule will further substantiate the existence of your training program. It helps demonstrate the management of a core curriculum of courses and shows formally when they are being made available to the organization. The schedule will also help show the scope and depth of your program and will verify a look at the needs of the organization as a whole.

Instructor material for each course and student material for each course. These artifacts can be used to represent the core of your training program. The material for each course need not be extensive or published in an elaborate manner. Instead, it should be cleanly presented, well organized, and comprehensive to the topic. Many organizations that provide your out-of-house training will be able to give you, for your office records, copies of the training materials in some form or fashion.

Student records. This is an important management activity for your training program. It's useful in keeping track of who in your shop is prepared to do what, and it also provides a great base for taking training program measurements.

Training measurements. Keeping an active series of measurements on your training activity is one of the best ways to show a focus on process improvement. These measurements might be such things as the number of people trained per course, the frequency of certain courses, the demand level for certain courses, student satisfaction with the presentation, manager feedback, and more.

Training program status reports and training program review reports. From time to time, in the interest of process improvement, the training program group should review its activities and strategies with other groups within the organization, opening up a channel for feedback. Naturally, this will result in a series of status reports and/or review reports. For each project or for each class initiative, you should look to get documented feedback from the SQA team, software project management, and the various development groups.

You can use as many of these artifacts as you wish. They are summarized in Table 13.8. The key to remember is that the value of your Level 3 training program is immense. It's your first path to a consistency of understanding and uniform conduct on your development projects.

Table 13.8 Evidence of Program Compliance

KEY PROCESS AREA	ARTIFACTS
Training Program courses	Training scope sheet, training invitation, training course material, student hand-out material, completion certificate
Integrated Software Management courses	Training scope sheet, training invitation, training course material, student hand-out material, completion certificate
Software Product Engineering courses	Training scope sheet, training invitation, training course material, student hand-out material, completion certificate
Intergroup Coordination courses	Training scope sheet, training invitation, training course material, student hand-out material, completion certificate
Peer Review courses	Training scope sheet, training invitation, training course material, ctudent hand-out material, completion certificate

Summary

You should think through your program design carefully, not just in view of CMM recommendations but more so in view of your real and practical needs. Training needs should be investigated and documented, and then a fixed plan should be developed to address what has been discovered. You should view training as an organizational tool for growth and as a distinct corporate benefit. You should also view your training program as a group that serves your projects; it is also a benefit for projects. Your project managers should be able to count on your training regimen to help foster the skills and the competence that are part and parcel of developing and delivering quality software applications (see Table 13.9).

Attention paid to this area, which is so often neglected even by mature organizations, can lead to significant benefits early in the CMM adoption process. But more than that, it can help make sure that your people are as productive as they can be and that they are prepared to take on the tasks that in the end will grow your business.

This chapter has covered recommendations for organization process focus and definitions, structures and processes for Level 3, and Level 3 training considerations. Implementing the recommendations in this chapter should take you to about 15 percent compliance with CMM Level 3. Together with the recommendations in Chapters 9, 10, 11, and 12, you should be close to 95 percent compliance. We'll take a look at that last 5 percent in the next chapter on Level 3 policies.

Table 13.9 Key Practices Fulfilled by Implementing the Training Lessons in This Chapter

KEY PROCESS AREA	CHAPTER TASK	KEY PRACTICE OBLIGATION
Training Program	Course material as assigned, training plan management, orientation to the training program	Ability 4
Integrated Software Management	How to use and tailor the SSPS, how to manage with the tailored SSPS, how to use the software process database	Ability 4
Software Product Engineering	Technical job role training, organization job role orientation, technical orientation to the project	Ability 4
Intergroup Coordination	Teamwork training, group orientation, orientation on teamwork	Ability 4
Peer Review	How to conduct a peer review, how to participate in a peer review	Ability 4

Creating Level 3 Policies

At Level 3 the entire organized becomes focused on process improvement. It's an important step up the maturity scale. At this point your teams have developed a set of proven processes and practices that have been shown to work over time and across a wide variety of projects. The challenge now is to gather these into a single program and then to implement it across the organization, with the idea of measurement and improvement still in mind.
Peter Dillon, Staffing Resources Inc.

In this section we'll discuss creating policies for five of the Key Process Areas of Level 3. To operate at Level 3 you'll need to implement the functionality described in these KPAs in some form or fashion. How you do it is up to you and the workings of your IT shop. But the expression of these functionalities as you have implemented them should ultimately be reflected in a series of documented policy statements. The five KPAs are Training Program, Integrated Software Management, Software Product Engineering, Intergroup Coordination, and Peer Review.

We have already discussed creating policies for the Organization Process Focus and Organization Process Definition KPAs in Chapters 8 and 9. These KPAs are basically two sides of the same coin, and together they form the foundation for the Level 3 program off which the remaining five KPAs work. That's why we treated them separately.

We also looked at CMM policies in the first part of this book. In Chapter 6 we discussed the purpose and use of policies in general, and we looked at a seven-step process for creating policies. We won't repeat that here. What's there applies here as well, so if you need a refresher on those concepts, go back and take a quick look at Chapter 6.

Many organizations I work with start off thinking that policy creation should be one of the first things that gets done when adapting a CMM program to the workplace. You can see why they would think that: The CMM begins each KPA with a recommendation to manage each KPA with a written policy. It's one of the first things described, so why not make it one of the first things implemented? Also, it starts off looking like an easy first step, something you can accomplish pretty quickly, so why not get it out of the way? I usually take a different approach, and I think most people well versed in CMM and the discipline of process management would probably take a similar approach. Policies should be one of the *last* items you create for a process improvement program. The reason is pretty clear to grasp. Each policy should be a succinct expression of a manner of conduct already in place (or ready to be put in place). You can't really create a good policy until you know what you will be supporting or promoting in it. If you can first finalize your operating structures, establish your processes and practices, and define your training needs relevant to the preceding, then you will be in a position to summarize what you have created. At that point you can express it in a policy in such a way that the purpose and directives you seek to communicate are clear and well shaped.

Carrying Over Policies from Level 2

In shaping your Level 2 program you created a series of policies for the six Level 2 KPAs. At a minimum here is a summary of what you probably created:

- A requirements management policy directing the conditions and use of requirements within a project

- A project planning policy governing how project planning materials are developed and approved, and how formal commitments are made concerning the project

- A project tracking policy directing the manner in which project resources and commitments are kept consistent with project progress

- A subcontractor management policy on the use of overseeing subcontractor work

- A configuration management policy describing the use and availability of configuration management resources and tools for each project

- A software quality assurance policy governing the oversight and reporting duties particular to the SQA mission

Did you create just six policies in your Level 2 program? Probably not. If you worked your program following in the true spirit of CMM Level 2, it is more likely you created 24, 30, even 50 policies. Over your course of operating at Level 2 you were consistently learning, repeating what worked well, and refining it over time from project to project. Across all your projects at Level 2, you were probably refining your policies in the six areas, adjusting them with each new project or as your process needs changed. At some point in your term working at Level 2 you would have established a legacy of evolving policy statements. Additionally, because projects are managed independently at Level 2, you would have, at any one time, a series of active policy statements in effect, a collection of at least six for each project. If you had five projects going on at the same time, you may easily have had 30 policies in effect, all valid, with each set pertaining to specific project.

Juggling many ways of doing business is a characteristic of Level 2. It's the way you learn the best way to do business. When you move to Level 3, you'll be dealing with fewer policies. You'll have to add some new ones for the new KPAs you'll be addressing, but you'll reduce the 20, 30, or 40 from Level 2 down to a core of about six.

Policies Required in a Level 3 CMM Program

Operations at Level 3 are an extension of what you were doing at Level 2. When you move to Level 3 you'll still be doing requirements management, project planning, configuration management, and the other KPA activities of Level 2. You'll still need to use the policies in place for these areas. At Level 3 you'll be adding the infrastructure required to support the centralized management of these activities, so you'll need to add a series of policies that support this infrastructure. CMM introduces six new KPAs at Level 3. Each of those key process areas requires a specific governing policy. In this chapter we'll discuss the following five:

> **Training Program.** A policy enforcing the maintenance and support of an organization-wide training program designed to support the use of common practices and processes.
>
> **Integrated Software Management.** A policy governing how project planning materials are tailored and developed to reflect the standards documented in the Standard Software Process Set.
>
> **Software Product Engineering.** A policy directing the manner in which project resources and commitments are kept consistent with project progress.
>
> **Intergroup Coordination.** A policy describing the tools and standards used to promote communication and coordination between various groups working on disparate elements of a common project.
>
> **Peer Review.** A policy governing the purpose and approach of peer reviews.

NOTE We discuss the policies for Organization Process Focus and Organization Process Definition in Chapters 8 and 9.

Quick Review of Policy Basics

Four qualities are basic to all well-designed policies. They need to be written, committed, brief, and distributed. The written part is obvious. Policies can't exist only in the ether. If they are to bear any weight, they need to be made real: You've got to write them down. Next, they need to be committed. This means they need to be backed up by executive authority. Your policies must express the mandates of senior management and reflect the highest missions and goals of the organization. The next quality is brevity. Think of your policies as executive summaries of your positions in certain operational areas. Policies should not be designed as handbooks on conduct or as educational material in the sense that they instruct. They are high-level tools of communication, imparting directives in a general sense. They accomplish this best when they are short and to the point. Finally, and perhaps most importantly, the policies need to be distributed to those people they impact. It's one thing to create a perfectly phrased policy statement, but if it doesn't get to the intended audience, it's as if it doesn't exist. Make sure to plan a distribution avenue for each of your policies. This can be done any number of ways: inclusion in employee handbooks or via training material, e-mail, or even a posting in the employee break room.

A review of the processes outlined in Chapter 6 to create your policies covers seven steps:

1. **Identify the owners.** These are the managers (usually senior) who will sign the policies.

2. **Think it through.** The policy must accurately reflect two things: the items that help support CMM Level 2 compliance and the operational characteristics unique to your program.

3. **Write the policy.** With the content of the policy in fairly solid shape, the author should commit the information to final form: a policy statement.

4. **Review the policy.** Each draft policy needs to be reviewed by two main audiences, the senior managers who own the policies and the line managers, and the people on the front line of the work who will be responsible for implementing and following the policies.

5. **Approve the policy.** With final forms of the policies in place, you can either re-review them or submit them to executive management for approval.

6. **Publish the policy.** With the policies approved and signed, they are ready for publication and organizational-wide distribution.

7. **Maintain the policy.** Treat policies as living documents, with regular reviews to help keep them current.

In this section, we'll look at what the CMM recommends for each policy at Level 3. Remember, like many of the facets of the CMM program, these points are not dictums. They are not rules or commands; they are suggestions. Your policies should be carefully thought out to reflect the inherent needs of the program. You do not have to include each of the items cited here in your policies if you have a good reason not to, and if the absence does not result—later down the line—in a deviation from generally accepted CMM practices. You'll probably find though that the following suggestions help you create a series of policies that promote a consistent effort toward process improvement and compliance with CMM guidelines.

Training Program Policy

The Level 3 Training Program is put into place as a mechanism to impart knowledge within the organization in a consistent and well-planned manner. The training regimens are designed to educate the workforce on the standard processes and practices that have been adopted by the organization for software development. They are also designed to enhance the workers' skills in areas of teamwork, technical skill development, project and process management, and personnel management. A policy for the Training Program addresses this mission from a high level and typically covers four points:

- A training curriculum is developed to address the managerial and technical needs existing within the organization.

- Effective training vehicles are identified and approved.

- Training is provided to build the skill base of the organization, support the specific needs of the projects, and enhance the skills of the individual.

- Training is developed within the organization or obtained from outside resources as appropriate.

The idea here is to support and promote the goals of organizational training. To do this, the training group within the company must begin by determining the training needs of the organization: what skills are needed, and what curriculum will address these needs. With the scope of training identified, the training group should then decide which training vehicles would prove most effective for imparting knowledge. These could be formal classroom training, one-on-one mentoring, on-the-job training, computer-based instruction, videotaped instruction, and guided self-study, among others. With the scope and direction established, the group can then decide how to deliver the course material, either through internal resources or by contracting for external training services.

Integrated Software Management Policy

The Integrated Software Management KPA helps establish the boundaries for using the organization's Defined Software Process Set. Each project will use the DSPS, but because all projects are different the project planners may tailor the DSPS to the unique needs of each project. The integrated software management policy sets this direction from the executive level and may do SP with four basic points:

- Each project tailors the organization's Defined Software Process Set to the scope and needs of the project.
- Deviations from the Defined Software Process Set are documented and approved.
- Each project performs its activities according to the project's defined processes.
- Each project collects and stores appropriate and defined measurements in the organization's central measurement database.

The first item makes it clear that project management and project planning can tailor the DSPS to the needs of the project. This is supported in the ISM KPA by the establishment of guidelines that instruct project planners on the acceptable ways in which the processes can be tailored to custom fit a project. The next item enforces the requirement that any deviations—the reasons for expanding or streamlining the process set—are documented and reviewed before adoption. This serves to prevent casual or careless tailoring or tailoring that inadvertently subverts the quality process. The third item promotes adherence to the tailored process set, and the final item promotes the collection of measurements against the tailored processes for use in later process improvement initiatives and activities.

Software Product Engineering Policy

As we mentioned in Chapter 13, Software Product Engineering is a direct evolution of the Level 2 KPA, Project Tracking and Oversight. Project Tracking and Oversight set into place a series of recommendations for controlling the activities that go into creating a software system. Software Product Engineering takes this a step further, providing additional guidelines for managing projects in an institutionalized atmosphere of process and performance. Your policy for Software Product Engineering should express this, and it could do so by emphasizing three points:

- Software engineering tasks are designed and defined to follow the organization's Defined Software Process Set.

- Appropriate methods and tools are used to build and maintain the software products.

- The software plans, activities, and products are traceable to the documented system requirements.

The first item endorses the organization's institutionalization of its software management and development processes. All activities planned and carried out for the project should be derived from the organization's Defined Software Process Set, the standard set of software processes used by the entire organization for all projects.

The next item helps ensure that the project will use the tools and development methods appropriate to its scale and scope and in harmony with organizational standards. And the final item, perhaps the most important, establishes the responsibility of being able to trace all work products, plans, and activities of the project back to the documented, agreed-on system requirements.

Intergroup Coordination Policy

This KPA is used to coordinate the activities of various groups working on a project. It is used to manage the interface between the groups. The CMM recommends that the policy you create for this area feature three main ideas:

- For each project, the objectives and system requirements are reviewed up front by all affected parties.

- The affected parties coordinate their plans and activities.

- Management will foster an environment that promotes communication and coordination between the affected parties throughout the course of the project life cycle.

The concept behind this policy is clear: The groups that participate in the development of a software system should coordinate their activities and communicate their plans and progressions in a manner that supports the objectives of the project and ensures consistent quality.

All of these items you have encountered earlier, in your Level 2 program, but in a less formal way. Here the concepts become institutionalized. The first item is there to make sure all groups start out with a common understanding of the mission, objectives, scope, and requirements of the project. The term "affected parties" usually refers to the development groups you have established for the project: design, coding, documentation, test, SQA, configuration management, and project management. All these groups will be contributing their piece to the project puzzle, so they must all begin with a common understanding of the eventual shape of the puzzle.

Items two and three are in place to support this common understanding. Once the project kicks off, the groups should not simply go off and work on their own, isolated from the other groups. They must communicate with each other, coordinating planned activity and sharing data on progress, problems, and issues. Management must make a commitment to make sure that this environment of communication and coordination is maintained for all groups working on the project as well as for executive management and the customer (as needs dictate).

Peer Review Policy

Your Peer Review activities should support the free exchange of ideas and investigations that lead to the discovery of defects and potential problems embedded in the various work products that are created during the project. The CMM suggests a peer review policy that covers five aspects of peer review activity:

- The work products that are open for peer review, from the organizational perspective, are defined up front.
- The work products that will be peer reviewed for each project are defined for that project.
- Peer reviews are led by trained facilitators.
- The reviews will focus on the content of the work products, not on the producers.
- The results of the peer reviews are used only to improve the work products, not as a measurement of individual performance.

You probably recognize these concepts from the discussion in Chapter 12 on the processes that can be used for managing peer reviews. The policy statement should encapsulate your organization's philosophy regarding peer reviews, and these five statements can help forge that philosophy for your workers.

The first statement supports what will probably be in your software process improvement (SPI) plan. But even if not, the idea is the same: For the sake of consistency and commonality, the work products that the organization will allow to be peer reviewed will be officially identified someplace. A good place for this could be in the SPI plan, but you might elect to define this set of work products in the peer review process itself or in some other document. Just make sure that the set is defined somewhere, and that your people know what this master set contains.

The next statement is derived from the first. Each project needs to define what work products it will peer review, and this set is usually found in the software development plan (SDP). This set is not independent of the first; it is a subset of the first. This subset is defined based on the scope of the project. Any one project might not produce all the work products for peer review defined in the master set; the project need review only those products relevant to its scope.

The third item is there to make sure the peer reviews are conducted in an effective and efficient manner, one that promotes productivity. To accomplish this, it is important that your peer review leaders know how to conduct a review session. They need to be trained to manage the meeting, facilitate the material review, record comments and action items, and identify further actions needed to integrate improvement recommendations.

The fourth and fifth items protect the tone of the peer reviews. A peer review can occur in such a way that it resembles a personal critique, but that is not its purpose. The review is undertaken to spot potential defects in a work product and remove them. The review should not be used as a basis to judge the author's ability or skills; neither should the documented results of the review be used to judge the author's performance on the whole. This is very important to the integrity of peer reviews. For them to exist as an open forum for the free exchange of ideas and information, this quality of "non-judgment" must be openly communicated and endorsed by senior management.

Use and Care of Your Executive Policies

Policies are an underappreciated element of the CMM, and probably an underappreciated element of IT management in general. More often than not, they are seen as necessary, but more from a documentation, ducks-in-a-row perspective. Their practical value is rarely considered. That's too bad, too, because the *active* use of policies in your organization can help bring forth ready and tangible benefits. Consider these obvious four:

Policies serve as an effective communication medium within your organization. They can quickly and easily establish the high-level direction your company has adopted for specific areas of operation. They are vehicles for disseminating strategic highlights.

Related to this is the fact that policies are also effective at establishing executive priorities. Of course, there are numerous directives within any IT shop, all vying for different levels of attention. A policy can help pull up those directives that are critical to the mission of an organization and help to give it the weight it needs to be noticed and followed. It's a way to segment the big picture from the detail. And it does so in a manner that shows executive endorsement of the statements—an imprimatur of the organization's official position.

Next, the active use of policies fosters consistency across groups. Different groups can have different local missions in any organization. That being the case, they often move in their own directions. But when these directions come together at the macro level they need to be pushing in the same general direction. Policies can help accomplish this. It gives the various groups a high-level target to shoot for, and so it promotes consistency across the efforts of all groups.

You can use policies as a first-line defense in CMM and process compliance in your organization. Before a group or team can be in compliance at the micro detail level, they need to be in compliance at the macro level, the level of mission, objectives, and broad conduct. Policies can spell this out in executive-summary type terms.

When you are operating at Level 3 you'll probably be managing at least 13 policies. Six are from the KPAs of CMM Level 2, and seven are from the KPAs of Level 3. But you don't really have to build your policies along these segmented lines if you don't want to. There's nothing in the CMM that compels you to follow this structure. If you find it more suitable to your operations, you could combine two or more policies into one. Just be careful not to forge a consolidated policy statement that's overly long, cumbersome, or convoluted. Clarity and conciseness should always rule the day. You might also elect to create a finer level of policy statements than is recommended in the CMM. That's OK, too. For example, you might find it practical in your shop to issue a policy regarding the practice of project estimating. The CMM rolls this into the project planning policy, but that might be the most effective path for you. Feel free to create as many policy statements as you need to establish the broad directives of your organization. Just refrain from going too granular. I doubt if you would want to actively manage dozens of policies, and I doubt if that fine detail would prove any more effective than what is generally recommended in the CMM.

The term used here—active management—is important to your policies. Some people in the industry settle into the process of creating their series of policies—doing a very good job of it—but once they're done, the policies are posted with a finality that dooms them to turning yellow around the edges. That approach is like taking a step in the right direction and then stopping. Instead, treat your policies as living documents. If you go to the trouble of creating and disseminating them but then effectively shelve and forget them, they lose any power and influence they may have had with respect to your process improvement program. Your policies need to avoid two fates: getting out of date and (as a result) being ignored. To circumvent this, keep your policies as current as you keep your process program. Pull them and inspect them periodically, perhaps once a year, perhaps with each major SPI evaluation you perform. Make it a regular practice.

Policy reviews should involve at least two parties: senior managers and software managers. Senior management owns the policies. They are the true authors no matter who created them. The policies should always reflect senior management's intended objectives and goals, so these managers need to take a periodic look at the policies to see if their contents match what senior management is working toward. Software managers should also be involved in the review. These managers work within the guidelines of the policies everyday. They will know from a practical, hands-on standpoint when a policy has become out of sync with what is really going on in the organization. Software management can provide valuable feedback to senior management as to the condition of the policies and can help realign them as appropriate.

To facilitate the policy reviews, you might it helpful to involve the Software Engineering Process Group. Often it's advantageous for the SEPG to coordinate the policy reviews. They can work through the process of scheduling meetings, conducting the review, taking notes, and working on a consensus for refinements. Such a process could involve a series of 11 sequential steps:

1. **Review notification.** A meeting invitation is sent out to designated senior managers and software managers, notifying them of the date, place, and time of the review.

2. **Distribution of policies under review.** Usually sent with the meeting invitation, the policies that will be reviewed are also sent to the meeting invitees.

3. **Individual review preparation.** There should be ample time before the meeting for the managers to be able to review the policies on their own, giving them time to prepare for the meeting.

4. **Review meeting and discussion.** This is the actual review meeting, conducted in essence like a peer review.

5. **Recording of action items/recommended edits.** During the meeting, the moderator or recorder takes notes from the discussion and identifies action items and proposed edits.

6. **Distribution of action items/recommended edits.** After the meeting, the action items and proposed edits are distributed to the participants for review and confirmation.

7. **Approval of action items/recommended edits.** Those items to be acted on are approved by the participants.

8. **Making of revisions as necessary.** Based on the approved action items and edits, the policies are revised.

9. **Approval of revisions.** The revised policies are distributed to the participants for final review. Upon final acceptance, senior management signs the policies, in effect "officializing" them.

10. **Notification to organization of new policy changes.** The organization is notified that new policies will be going into effect on X date.

11. **Distribution of new policies.** The new policies are distributed to the organization.

Of course, this process is just an example, a sample you cab choose to adapt or modify. Whatever approach you take, keeping your policies current will help them remain active and effective process improvement tools.

Supporting Policies

When you built your Level 2 program you had to create policies for requirements management, software project planning, project tracking and oversight, configuration management, subcontractor management, and software quality assurance. The process of creating your Level 3 policies is very much the same. If you choose to be formally assessed at some time during your Level 3 operations, you will need the same kinds of artifacts to support your compliance with CMM policy recommendations that you used at Level 2. Basically, you'll want to be able to show an assessment team that you created the policies, that you disseminated them throughout the organization, and that you periodically review them to make sure they are still current with operations and continue to address the mission of the organization.

For all this you should gather the following: the documented policies themselves, early drafts of each policy, any review notes related to each policy, any policy revisions you might have made, and a description of the distribution avenue you used to disseminate the policies to your workforce. This is summarized in Table 14.1.

Table 14.1   Evidence of Program Compliance

KEY PROCESS AREA	ARTIFACTS
Integrated Software Management	The policy, any policy drafts or notes, distribution avenue, assessment or change notes or memos
Software Product Engineering	The policy, any policy drafts or notes, distribution avenue, assessment or change notes or memos
Training Program	The policy, any policy drafts or notes, distribution avenue, assessment or change notes or memos
Intergroup Coordination	The policy, any policy drafts or notes, distribution avenue, assessment or change notes or memos
Peer Review	The policy, any policy drafts or notes, distribution avenue, assessment or change notes or memos

Summary

Though we discussed policies last for both Level 2 and Level 3, they are really the beginning of your CMM program. They establish the commitment and set the direction for process improvement, first at the project level and then for the software development organization as a whole. For these reasons your policies, while they should be short, concise, and easily absorbed, are of critical importance and so should be seriously considered and carefully crafted. Your executive managers should also have an appreciation of what it is they are committing to when they set these policies into place. Well-informed managers will set into policies that lead their organizations into the realm of solid software process improvement. The work you define for organization process focus and definition, integrated software management, software product engineering, intergroup coordination, and peer reviews will all flow out of these high-level directives.

Implementing the recommendations in this chapter takes you to about 5 percent Level 3 compliance. By implementing the recommendations in Chapters 9 through 13 together with Chapter 14, you should be at about 99 percent Level 3 compliance. Of course, the key to compliance is consistent and regular use, so in Part 4 we'll look at how you can begin to spread your CMM program throughout your organization in a smooth manner. Finally we'll look at what you can expect in general should you elect to perform an internal assessment of your CMM program in order to document the progress you have made.

Table 14.2 Key Practices Fulfilled by Implementing the Lessons in This Chapter

KEY PROCESS AREA	CHAPTER TASK	KEY PRACTICE OBLIGATION
Training Program	Write a Training Program policy	Commitment 1
Integrated Software Management	Write an Integrated Software Management policy	Commitment 1
Software Product Engineering	Write a Software Product Engineering policy	Commitment 1
Intergroup Coordination	Write an Intergroup Coordination policy	Commitment 1
Peer Review	Write a Peer Review policy	Commitment 1

Implementation
and Assessment

CHAPTER 15

Implementing the CMM in a Smooth Manner

When we go in for an implementation, we set up what we call "cooperation channels" first and move on from there. Considering the flexibility at hand, implementing CMM really starts best with that free exchange of informed opinion. It's a good way to get the team on board. And it's even better for learning the best way to go forward from there.
Jenna Doelux, SSAC International

So far we've looked at the philosophy and recommendations behind Level 2 and 3 of the SEI's Capability Maturity Model. Now we will turn to implementation. Many IT organizations have already begun to adopt the CMM—in fact, it has become one of the mainstay process management programs in the software industry, here and abroad. Most companies currently affiliated with the CMM began at Level 1 or 2 and moved through the tiered scale as assessments confirmed. All faced the question, how do we get from here to there? And each company answered in its own way.

In Chapters 1 and 8 we discussed software process improvement and the CMM as if they were separate things. And to be truthful, they are. Software process improvement is bigger than the CMM. It's a widely layered concept. CMM is an action map to put SPI into motion. Our discussion of implementation (in the next chapter) will really be talking about implementing the CMM in an official way—that is, with a view toward eventual industry assessment. How you ultimately implement your CMM program is largely dependent on what you need to do, so this process will *always* need some customization.

But there are steps that will work in almost any implementation environment, which we'll call *key success factors*. These key success factors are a set of steps you move through in implementing a CMM program. You might decide that some of these steps are optional. For others you might see the order as varying. But because implementation is so critical to any organization's CMM program, each step will be briefly described in this chapter. Here's a quick list:

- Know the mission.
- Establish the mission.
- Create knowledge base.
- Orient your organization.
- Develop a plan.
- Preassess.
- Refine your processes.
- Train your people.
- Use the program.
- Support your people.
- Assess your progress.

These success factors can be used as tools to make your work with the CMM become a visible part of your organization's way of doing business.

Making Implementation Work

Careful, thoughtful implementation is a critical component to any successful CMM program. To help your program roll out to a smooth start, it's important to prepare your staff, educate them on the mission and objectives of your CMM program, and then support them in the various implementation stages. In previous chapters (Chapters 3, 4, 5, 6, 7, 8, 9, 10, 11, 12, 13, and 14) we looked at the structures, processes, policies, and training requirements you need to have in place in order to address the recommendations of CMM Level 2 and 3, the Repeatable level and the Defined level. If you've been able to fit these recommendations into a program for your organization, you will be well on your way to meeting CMM compliance.

But it is not enough to just get your program in place in order for it to work. Just as important is the care you take to implement CMM in your environment. In fact, a well-ordered, smooth implementation may be the single biggest success factor for any CMM program. In this chapter we'll touch on a series of mechanisms for introducing your Level 2 and 3 programs into the work place. To start with a broad objective, you should think about implementation along the lines of preparation, education, and implementation

Your staff will play a major role in the success of your CMM program. The manner in which it is introduced into the environment and supported from the level of the line worker on up will determine its overall effectiveness. By preparing carefully up front, educating your people on the mission and structure of the program, and then implementing with them in mind, you can expect that adoption of the program will go more smoothly (much more smoothly) than if you were to simply drop it into the workplace.

That last phrase may sound like an overstatement, but I have seen many instances where management has done just that: They designed a CMM program and then more or less unobtrusively planted it in the environment. The hope was that it would somehow take hold from that point on, like kudzu, and spread enthusiastically on its own. But to achieve full-breadth, long-term use, you'll need to be more proactive in your implementation.

Key Success Factors

Now let's turn our attention to 11 key success factors that influence areas of implementation readiness. These items are not all inclusive. That is, this is not an exhaustive list. These are items that can make solid contributions to your implementation efforts. We'll begin with a basic one, knowing the mission of your CMM initiative.

Know the Mission

Adopting the CMM means you are choosing to become a different kind of IT shop, one focused on itself now as well as on its products. You seek to become a process-centered shop instead of a talent-centered shop, a practice-centered shop instead of a product-centered shop. Think of a factory. You shouldn't have to worry about the end product too much if you know that the various machines are doing their piece of the job right. What comes out at the end ought to be fine.

The first step in implementing CMM is to know the mission that you are setting out on. Usually the *idea* of being CMM compliant comes into the organization from the executive level. This decision is usually based on a summary of the CMM benefits: reduced rework, better planning, increased efficiencies, greater customer satisfaction, monies saved, and so on. But CMM won't take root at this level. Rather, it will require a deep familiarity with CMM for the program to begin to take shape. Your CMM lead will need to understand the real mission of CMM implementation, formulate a high-level summary of what that mission will entail, and present it to management for what I call "tangible" buy-in (step 2 following). Knowing the mission may require that you take time to become trained in CMM and take time to study the specification and support materials—in short, to become the in-house expert. From that you should then summarize the mission for your executives based on the spec and how you want your business to work. This summary (and you can use the steps here as a high-level summary if you like) should help the executive move from benefit to commitment, from strategy to tactics. It should give your decision makers the ability to take it to the next step with the understanding that the next step will bring a lower-level plan for action, time, and money.

Step 1:   Know the mission.

Who: CMM program manager

Resources: Executive management; CMM materials

Time: As needed up front

Establish the Mission within the Organization

Your executive community may know what it wants to get out of CMM, but it probably won't know what it has to give to get it. For an implementation to be successful you've got to take the strategic goal of the mission (see step 1) and break it down into tangible, tactical terms. You won't need a firm plan yet. That comes in step 4. But you will need to put into place a broad description of what it will take to get from point A (where you are) to point B, where you want CMM to take you. This kind of detail will help establish the CMM mission within the organization by giving the top-tier level of the company the broad strokes of the commitments it will take to make the program work. Realistically defining these commitments is the true beginning of your CMM program.

You should look to define four things out of this effort:

- Time commitment
- General budget commitment
- Commitment of resources
- Commitment to rewards

The time commitment, which may span 12 to 20 months, will give management a feeling for the general length of time required to bring a CMM program into place. It will serve to set expectations on progress and rates of movement. The budget commitment will attach a value to the time efforts and will also include a nod to some expenses that may not always be understood up front, such as training, materials development, consulting, and so on. A general budget will place the implementation effort within a financial frame of reference. A general "use-of-resources" commitment will define what and how many people in the organization, perhaps varying over time, will be required to bring about the program. And, finally, a realistic rewards commitment will show what milestone benefits can be expected at major points along the implementation road.

Step 2:	Establish the mission.
Who:	CMM program manager
Resources:	Executive management
Time:	As needed up front

Create an In-House Knowledge Base

Steps 1 and 2 give you the go-ahead for CMM activity. You've defined in broad terms where the organizations needs to be, why it needs to be there, and what approach you'll take to move it in that direction. From this point on you'll need help. Depending on the size of your IT shop, you'll need to assemble a team of people, full-time or part-time, who will work with you to push the CMM initiative forward. You'll know best how many people you need. The parts of CMM you want to implement, the timeline you've been given, the size and scope of your projects, and the amount of work you think you have in store will all help you make the decision.

The goal is establishing a knowledge base to gather together a team of people who can initiate CMM, getting it working in the environment, and then keep it working smoothly. Your team will act as liaison to the worker in the organization, providing help and support and facilitating feedback and refinement. Your team should be knowledgeable about CMM and the philosophy of process improvement. Its members should be good team players, with the ability to work within all areas of your shop. And they should have had ample experience working in the shop. The better they are at knowing how you do business now, the better they'll be at advancing your shop toward its new objectives.

Step 3:	Create an in-house CMM team.
Who:	CMM program manager; team members
Resources:	Group management; line workers
Time:	2–4 weeks

Create an Implementation Plan

Use Chapters 15 and 16 to create an implementation plan. This will be a guide that the whole organization can follow for the course of the implementation effort. Your plan should contain a timeline, resources commitments, expense identifications, and progress milestones. The plan should also address the following broad activities:

- Mission definition
- Program commitments
- CMM team formation and identification
- Workforce orientation
- Reassessment planning
- Assessment activity
- Process refinement and publication
- Organization training
- Program use
- Program support
- Reassessment milestones

Step 4:	Create an implementation plan.
Who:	CMM program manager; team members
Resources:	Group management; line workers
Time:	3–5 weeks

Orient the Organization's Managers and Line Workers to CMM

Most problems that crop up during an implementation come from lack of knowledge, from not knowing what to do or not knowing why certain things ought to be done. Both of these can be overcome with training, and I usually try to encourage thorough training in two areas. The first is CMM training, and the second in training in your shop's own processes and procedures. I talk about the second one in Step 8. I'd like to talk about the first one here.

To initiate the implementation process, you began with executive buy-in to the procedures and benefits of CMM. You followed by establishing a CMM knowledge base in your shop and then assembling a team of people to help you roll the program out. But you need to take care so that rolling out the program doesn't roll over the company. I have actually seen this happen in a big way on two separate occasions, both with major telecommunications companies. In both cases, management set CMM as a goal for the IT organization and tied this goal to IT management's compensation package. The first shop had 1,200 workers; the second had more than 6,000. The message was clear: Get to CMM Level X by Y date, or wave your bonus goodbye. Both companies had executive buy-in, both assembled an impressive knowledge base, and both made sure that plenty of funding was in place to let the teams do their work.

In both cases, the programs steamrolled right over both shops. The managers and workers found themselves in a wash of unexpected, uninformed changes. They knew what the mission was by way of general dissemination, but they had no knowledge of their parts in it, what it was all about, why this was being adopted, or why it really mattered in the long run. Needless to say, the implementations failed in both shops.

Failure can also occur on a smaller scale, in ways that don't necessarily derail the effort but stretch it out longer than necessary. The CMM management approach is a front-line way to manage software development; it's a framework for active participation on all levels, and much of it takes place at the line level. It's not enough to take care of just the executive nature of CMM. Your people need to be given a thorough orientation to what it's all about. In the long run, they will be your main players, and they will be the ones who will ultimately make the effort a success.

I recommend a series of orientations. These do not have to be in-depth training sessions, just orientations. The idea here is to bring the people in on the organization's mission and to give them the background needed to appreciate the goals of the mission and to know what their part in the mission will be. One orientation session introduces workers to CMM as a philosophy and as a practical, hands-on model. Another introduces the workers to the general software process improvement mission within the company. And a third spells out the role each group will play in carrying out the mission.

This orientation will prepare your people to participate in the implementation in an informed and well-organized manner.

Step 5:	Orient the workforce to CMM.
Who:	Managers; leads; line workers
Resources:	Training services, facilities
Time:	3 weeks; includes prep and planning

Preassess Your Current Work Habits

The previous steps have all been preparatory. You've been smoothing the way for implementation activity to start. It's been pretty much a people effort, too. You've defined the mission. You've got executive management on board. You've assembled a knowledge force. You've informed the people in the organization about what will be happening. Now you and your team are ready to begin the implementation proper. The first step I usually recommend is what I call a preassessment. I talk about assessments in depth in the following chapter and also in step 11. I'll keep it brief here. Refer to Chapter 16 for a detailed look at the things I'll be talking about.

A preassessment is simply an analysis of how your current work habits (your shop's software development methodology) match up against what's in the CMM. If it turns out that you're close, your implementation may be a simple matter. If you're far apart, you may have a bit more work to do. The key is to know where you stand, and to know precisely where you stand.

By now you'll already know what you want to use of the CMM. You decided that in steps 1 and 2, when you defined the mission. You ought to be able to list out of this the specific processes, procedures, forms, tools, and other program bits you'll want to have eventually.

You probably also have a general feeling for how close you already are to matching that list, but you'll need to go a step deeper. Before you can really shape your approach, you'll want conduct an in-depth audit of the processes and practices in place in your shop. That's what a preassessment does for you. Here's a high-level take on how it works.

You assign areas of investigation to your process team members. This assignment is based on the scope of CMM KPAs that you will be adopting for your shop. Next you inform key people within your shop about the audit, what it will involve, and what material will need to be looked at. Your process team will then work with certain project teams or with certain software groups to check what is currently happening against what you ideally want to happen. The team will look at several areas within the organization. It will look at the documented processes and compare these with what is recommended in the CMM. It will also look at the various artifacts that tend to rise up from development activities. They includes things like status reports, project plans, staff assignment forms, and more. The idea is to see if the projects are creating a trail that shows they are following published processes. The team will also look at individual areas of development activity, what the people on the projects or in the groups are doing. This will help point to areas of process management that may be missing in relation to the CMM.

From this preassessment your team will develop an assessment report. The assessment report will identify your areas of CMM strength as well as areas of CMM weakness. You'll know what is CMM compliant and what is not. You can use the assessment report as a map to be used to adjust where you are so you can get where you ought to be. The report will indicate the amount of work involved in the next step, refining your processes to get them in line with CMM recommendations.

You'll find the preassessment and the assessment report to be valuable tools in your implementation effort. But don't keep these to yourself. They should be broadly circulated throughout the organization so that everyone knows where they stand and everyone has a feeling for what will be coming next.

Step 6: Preassess.

Who: CMM team

Resources: Access to organization

Time: 4–8 weeks

Refine Your Processes

In the previous steps, you completed a series of steps in preparation for implementation. You've brought the mission into the organization; you've gathered together a process team; and you've examined the organization in order to determine where it stands in relation to your CMM goals.

Now that you know where you stand, you're able to point the organization in the direction of your goals; you can align the shop with CMM recommendations. This is a major step in CMM implementation. Here you fill in the gaps between what you are doing and what you and the organization have determined it ought to be doing. The major task in this step—and the most visible one—is to refine your documented processes and procedures to encompass your goals.

To accomplish this, your team members should work with the organization's managers and line workers to modify existing processes or create new ones. This is an important step. You're documenting how business will be run. It's important to understand up front that it's not *too* important. What I mean by this is that your processes don't have to be perfect. This is especially true if you are just starting down the CMM trail (or any process improvement trail, for that matter). It could take your team many months to analyze and investigate everything that might go into a set of project management processes. And by the time the team members had thought it all through, new elements would likely have appeared in the environment. Your processes don't have to be perfect—the idea is to set the boundaries in place within which process-analysis can occur. You want a set of rules that will allow you to measure what you are doing and repeat it.

I have found that this concept is often misunderstood in the field, usually by people who take the CMM for a book of law. But software process improvement is not about maximum efficiency or quality saturation; it's not about perfection. Those may be goals that SPI can help point you toward, but SPI is really about improvement. It's about taking one way of conduct and making it better, and not better for everyone—not generically better—but better for you, for your shop, for your people. It's not a competitive system or a scoring system.

If you can impart this understanding to your process team and to other members of your organization, you will have given them an important perspective on CMM implementation as a whole: that no one is being judged; that no one is being scored; that it's OK to make mistakes. Improvement—thoughtful, methodical, perhaps slow improvement—is the mission here. Work your processes with these concepts in mind, and you'll find that the definition effort goes a lot more smoothly than if it's seen as a do-or-die effort.

Nevertheless, this will be a big job. Process refinement may touch many areas within your organization. If you are new to Level 2, you may have to create processes within all six KPAs; if you are working toward Level 3, you may to consider an additional seven KPAs. You may have to look closely at many independent processes and procedures, so you should be sure that your team and your shop's managers and line workers will be able to set aside time for this. The job will require focus and investigation, review and adjustment, and all along you must aim to strike a blend. What you end up with in the way of documented processes and procedures must fit two bills. They should be in harmony with CMM, and more importantly, they must work for your organization. There's no sense in creating great CMM-type processes if they won't work well in your shop. Working well should be your overriding concern. You'll find that processes that work well tend to be used; processes that don't work well tend to be shelved.

Fortunately you have a lot of flexibility in this area. CMM is not what I would call a "demanding" spec; rather, it suggests a broad avenue you can use to get to a place you know you probably want to be. This should make it easy to create processes that get you to CMM compliance while meeting the specific needs of your organization.

The timeline for this phase is flexible. Some companies implement it piecemeal, one KPA at a time, others jump in all at once. Either way is fine as long as the support is there. Chapters 3, 4, 9, 11, and 12 offer advice on how to create your processes and structures for a CMM program, so you can refer to them for more information on this step of implementation. But let's close this step with what may be a reminder to some, news to others. The heart of CMM implementation rests not in the documentation you prepare. It rests in how well your people are prepared to carry out the documentation.

Many people view CMM as simply documentation: a series of written processes and procedures; you follow them and you are CMM compliant. In my view, the documentation should be more like cue cards, prompts to help your people stick to the script. CMM implementation is really about people joining you in a coordinated process improvement. Make your documentation good, refine the processes and procedures to align with CMM, but don't forget the reason for it all: to provide your people with useful, valuable tools. That's why the next step, training, is so important. In my view it's the single most critical step in the whole implementation process.

Step 7: Refine processes.

Who: CMM team; managers; line workers

Resources: Access to input and review with workers

Time: 6–12 weeks

Train Your Staff

The CMM specification mentions training throughout its structure, and I emphasize it in my work with corporations. A cornerstone of CMM effectiveness is shared knowledge, the dissemination of what I call commonalities. For your program to work at its peak, your people need to understand and use it in a consistent manner. They should have a common understanding of what it's all about. The best way to do this is with training and on-the-job support. (We look at support in step 10.)

After you have assessed your organization's operating patterns and modified them to be compliant with your CMM goals, you need to introduce the new patterns into the shop. In step 5, you provided general training in CMM. This gave your people a knowledge base and strategic viewpoint. Here you need to train your people in the processes and practices you have revised for your program. Most of the time this will be a modification of what they've already been doing; sometimes you may have to introduce whole new concepts to the group.

Take care to train carefully here, and well. This is really the beginning point of your program, where you pass the knowledge on to the people who will be expected to act on it. To simply throw the new stuff at them in the work environment is to beg for confusion, frustration, and disuse. Up-front training will relieve you of this problem as much as possible. Your people will get a chance to review and understand the scope of the new material; they will have a chance to question it, to ascertain how it fits into their individual roles. Thorough training will also prepare them to carry out their assignments once on the job, with learning curves being reduced over cold introduction. And finally, sound training will give your people the understanding they need to critically evaluate how the processes and practices serve the needs of the organization from the line level. Partnership is important with the CMM, and training is one of the ways to bring your people into a partnership relationship with you and your CMM program.

Step 8:	Train organization in new processes.
Who:	Managers; leads; line workers
Resources:	Training services, facilities
Time:	3 weeks; includes prep and planning

Use the Program in the Workplace

You can define and document the best process improvement program in the world, but it's nothing if it's not used. Sounds obvious, right? Many people, however, want to practically skip this step altogether. To them this step is anticlimactic: the thinking done, the doing seems banal. Until now they have been studying shop practices, refining processes, training users, and setting executive expectations. When they release the program into the environment they can have the feeling that the job is done. These people probably know that the program is right on the money with CMM, and what they want to jump to next is the assessment. They see that as the test that will confirm their success. But for all their enthusiasm things haven't ended here. They've really only just begun.

The whole key to CMM—to any process improvement effort—is *measured use*. What that means is you must use something over time in order to know well how to improve it. A journeyman chef might follow a master's recipe for an apple torte a hundred times before starting to tinker with it. Columbus made three trips across the Atlantic before he finally knew where he was going and could chart how to get there. Measured use in software development is important in the same way. Here are three reasons to consider:

- First, you need time to cycle your processes and practices through the various phases of multiple projects. You can't introduce new processes and then assess them 2 months later. There probably has not been enough time to test them thoroughly, to see how they work in different circumstances. Many of them probably haven't even had a chance to be put to a full test. Your processes need to live in your environment in order to become fully productive, just as a new employee needs time to get used to how you do business and learn the lay of the land.

- Second, the evidence you need to assess your processes, and to help prove that you are following them, will bubble up to the surface over time. It's not enough to have one example of some process or activity. You can't evaluate a single example of anything; there's nothing to compare it to. What you need is a history that will support a trend line. To gather a line of artifacts that supports consistent and constant use will require that you move past established stages of software development several times, across different projects ideally.

- Third, your people will require ample time to absorb the work patterns of your CMM environment. This will take a while. You'll want your people sufficiently immersed in the new way that they can demonstrate that they have been trained to follow the processes, that they are following them automatically, and that they can articulate what they are doing relative to established processes. They won't need to be CMM fluent as long as they can recount what they are doing and that that is in harmony with the CMM program you have set up.

This kind of familiarity takes time. Your people, in big ways or in small ways, will be working in a new job environment. They'll need to get acclimated, then up to speed, and finally fully comfortable with their responsibilities.

Repetition is the key to effective use, and repetition takes its own time. From the time you implement your program to the time you decide to assess how well it is working, you should be prepared to live with your program as it is, and you should provide the atmosphere in which your people can live with it, too. Don't rush in to tweak it every time a problem pops up, and don't try to make major adjustments to it during the saturation period. Let it be; let your people move through its use. Most importantly, support them with ample attention, guidance, and patience.

Step 9:	Use the program.
Who:	Whole organization
Resources:	Business as usual
Time:	18 weeks and on

Support Your People

Once the organization begins to use the processes it has worked to develop, your job will change somewhat. In fact, it should stabilize into what it should be 80 percent of the time, a support arm of the company. In this role you will be required to walk a delicate line, but I don't want it to come across as being *too* delicate. You will know where this line falls if you begin the support effort with one acceptable assumption: Mistakes will be made.

In this role your job is to keep the shop on track with CMM. You'll want to make sure that your people are using the processes as described and that they are acting in ways harmonious to your shop's CMM goals. If not, you'll need to intervene; you'll need to realign. Just understand that 100 percent is probably a long way off. If you are just starting out on the CMM trail, the amount of change you introduce to the organization may appear to be substantial. Change needs time to be fully absorbed into any environment. Strict adherence is not as important as firm dedication. Stick to your program over time, and it will eventually jell. Many mistakes will be made up front. People will forget what they ought to do now, or they'll fall back to Level 1 shortcuts, or they'll proceed only partway down new paths.

Don't let it get to you. And don't let it get to the team either. Do not equate noncompliance with failure. Look at it simply as lack of practice. Early on most everyone will be new to the game, so mistakes will probably come from everywhere. Gently adjust, and soon you'll find the missteps diminishing. As the processes (and the process oversight) become more and more a part of daily business life, you'll see that the habit of quality begins to take root, and then to grow almost unnoticed. Quiet, graceful alignment is almost always preferable to sharp, abrupt alignment. Your uncritical help and support, along with your patience, are required for this new way to become the standard way in your company.

If your organization puts forth CMM expectations with tight deadlines or with a view toward Pass/Fail, you may encounter a beginning passion that is quickly squelched by the frustrations of cold reality. This takes us back to step 1, know your mission. By shaping a carefully thought-out CMM program you are making an effort to usher your shop into a new realm of software development. Your people will need the time, resources, and support to follow you. If you provide these to them, the process should go smoothly.

For this role, you should see that people have been appointed as CMM contacts. These people may specialize in certain KPAs, or they may be overall experts. Use them for what I call passive and active support. Passive support simply means that these people are available for questions and casual consulting. They may have other primary jobs and work on CMM only as a sideline assignment, but they should be a presence in the organization, identified to all, and ready to help in their areas of specialty. You'll find that this passive support goes a long way to making active support much easier.

Active support is your team taking on the role of compliance auditors. From time to time on projects (as alluded to in the SQA role of Level 2 and the SEPG role of Level 3) your CMM contacts should perform process and activity checks to measure compliance, problem areas, and areas of strength more formally. These two together should provide your shop with the foundation to move forward in the direction of process improvement.

Step 10:	Support the program.
Who:	CMM team
Resources:	Business as usual
Time:	18 weeks and on

Assess Your Progress

In the next chapter we will discuss what typically happens during a CMM assessment. There are two ways to approach an assessment: officially or unofficially. An official assessment involves the services of an authorized lead assessor, investigations along a series of defined lines, and carefully reported results that can then be recognized by the Software Engineering Institute. Official assessments of this nature take time, call for the dedication of internal resources, and require a certain financial commitment. The nature of an official assessment ensures to a large degree that you will get good results, results you can depend on to be accurate. An official CMM assessment is the ultimate verification of your shop's compliance with CMM guidelines.

I don't recommend this kind of assessment at this point. Here I'm referring to an unofficial assessment—one you conduct internally in your organization, without the services of a lead assessor and without the formal constraints that a regulated assessment calls for. The reasons for starting with an unofficial assessment are pretty clear. First, you might as well know where you stand unofficially before you make it public. If you have studied CMM and followed the general tenants of this book in preparation for implementation, you should have the knowledge base in-house to assess yourself. An unofficial assessment is also less expensive and time-consuming than a formal assessment, so it will be less disruptive to your shop. Plus, if this your first real look at your progress, you might find it managed more easily with familiar people, not with some outside consultants.

For a collection of ideas on how to conduct an assessment, see Chapter 16. Here we'll just briefly note that the assessment will serve as an audit of your program. It's a close look at your processes and practices as compared to the CMM. The purpose of the assessment is to find areas where you are in strong compliance with the CMM and areas where you are in weak compliance or no compliance. Based on the results of the assessment you then refine your program to align more closely with the CMM and you move on from there. Based on the assessment you'll know how closely your program matches your CMM goals. And then, after you already know pretty much where you stand, might you then go forward with a formal assessment.

But official or unofficial, partial or full, the concept of periodic assessments is crucial to the CMM and to software process improvement in general. An assessment is the end and the beginning of your cycle of improvement, and it should be continually recurring. It is the end because it comes when you have worked with a set of tools long enough to collect enough data to see how well they work. It is the beginning because it's the starting point for refining the tools to make them even better.

Your assessment of where your shop stands should be conducted as a careful review, free of judgment, exclusively focused on process and practice. (It's important to remember that assessments have nothing to do with the skills, talents, or performance of your people.) The result should be shared with the whole shop and used to form the basis for improvements. This will take you back to step 7, refinement. Based on the assessment, you'll refine the processes as needed, train your people in the changes, and then begin their use all over again. Use, measure, refine, reuse: That's the essence of process improvement and the key to successful CMM implementation.

Step 11:	Assess progress.
Who:	CMM team
Resources:	Managers and line workers; CMM users
Time:	As planned

Summary

One of the main keys to any successful CMM-compliant process improvement program is a careful and thoughtful implementation. Each CMM implementation shares some commonalities, but how you choose to implement CMM will depend on many things: your shop's industry focus, its experience with process management and process improvement, the slice of CMM you have elected to follow, and so on. Your thoughtful implementation should lead you to the stage where you are ready, if you so choose, for a formal assessment of your progress. We'll take a look at the assessment process in the final chapter of this book.

IMPLEMENTATION STEPS

Step1: **Know the Mission.**

Who: CMM program manager

Resources: Executive management; CMM materials

Time: As needed up front

Step 2: **Establish the Mission.**

Who: CMM program manager

Resources: Executive management

Time: As needed up front

Step 3: **Create an In-house CMM Team.**

Who: CMM program manager; team members

Resources: Group management; line workers

Time: 2–4 weeks

Step 4: **Create an Implementation Plan.**

Who: CMM program manager; team members

Resources: Group management; line workers

Time: 3–5 weeks

Step 5: **Orient the Workforce to CMM.**

Who: Managers; leads; line workers

Resources: Training services, facilities

Time: 3 weeks; includes prep and planning

Step 6: **Pre-Assess.**

Who: CMM team

Resources: Access to organization

Time: 4–8 weeks

Step 7: **Refine Processes.**

Who: CMM team; managers; line workers

Resources: Access to input and review with workers

Time: 6–12 weeks

Step 8: **Train Organization in New Processes.**

Who: Managers; leads; line workers

Resources: Training services, facilities

Time: 3 weeks; includes prep and planning

Step 9:	**Use the Program.**
Who:	Whole organization
Resources:	Business as usual
Time:	18 weeks and on
Step 10:	**Support the Program.**
Who:	CMM team
Resources:	Business as usual
Time:	18 weeks and on
Step 11:	**Assess Progress.**
Who:	CMM team
Resources:	Managers and line workers; CMM users
Time:	Flexible

Applying these steps to your implementation makes the process more orderly. Over time, you will begin to notice the success factors paying off. Your planing will improve. Management will become streamlined. Work efforts will be better defined. And you'll be able to predict the path your projects will take more accurately than in the past. As a result, you should see a distinct rise in the one thing you got into this for in the first place: You'll be building software products of increased quality, and you'll be doing it at reduced risk, with better controls in every niche of your organization.

CHAPTER 16

Understanding the Assessment Process

You may run a process improvement program for years, and it may bolster your operations in a multitude of areas. But you'll still be in the dark about it all until you make a formal assessment of where you are, measure it from where you started, and use it as a benchmark to sight where you want to go.
Kendell Reese, Quality Improvement Consultant

All organizations involved in the mission of process improvement will, from time to time, want to take a measure of where they stand with regard to their SPI activities. Process improvement programs in the software industry usually start off as big programs (as in coming down from the executive branch of the company), but they more than often end up small, that is, practiced by the workforce in the trenches of project development. Because of this common trait, process improvement comes in small steps over time, sometimes unnoticed in pieces of activity that by and by become habit. Many people in your workforce may be directly responsible for a large amount of the improvement change, but as it happens on a daily basis, ongoing over time, they may be only vaguely aware of how the big picture is shaping up. Likewise executive management, perhaps removed from the regular tussle of development practice, may also share but a vague idea of the progress being made at the line level. Of course, you will have plenty of micro detail that you can use to measure performance in the program. Your projects will be steadily amassing a wealth of such data. But, too, this may give you only a part of the picture for a given time. What's needed for most process improvement programs, at certain times in their evolutions, are full-blown program assessments, detailed looks across an organization that identifies the progress, strengths, and weaknesses that have found a place within your program's practice.

You may think of this assessment as an audit. And in many ways it is an audit. In fact, the process shares many similarities with audits in the accounting field, as when a recognized firm produces an official report on the financial position of a corporation. A software process improvement audit produces similar results for your SPI program. The Software Engineering Institute recognized the need to support some form of audit process for its Capability Maturity Model: You shouldn't have a performance spec without a way to measure the spec. As a complement to the CMM, the SEI developed what it calls the CMM-based Appraisal for Internal Process Improvement, or CBA IPI for short. Organizations that have adopted the CMM can use the CBA IPI as one way to measure their conformance with the recommendations contained in the model. We'll address the issue of assessment in this chapter, but my aim is not to teach you everything you need to know about conducting an SEI-sanctioned CBA IPI assessment. Rather, I will try instead to give you a broad understanding of the process so when (and if) you decide to conduct an assessment within your organization, you'll understand the breadth of the process and recognize the structure and use of each of the steps of the process.

What Is an Assessment?

You can assess your software development organization at any time you like, and in whatever manner you choose. There's no one way to do it. If you want your assessment energies and results to be recognized by the SEI, however, you will need to conduct the assessment in a manner recognized by the SEI. In this chapter we'll be referring to the SEI's CBA IPI process when we talk about assessments, audits, and appraisals.

Basically, an assessment is a coordinated and objective measure of the strengths and weaknesses found in your software process improvement program. The high-level goal of most assessments is to identify which CMM KPAs you are in compliance with and which ones you are not, and why. Contrary to popular belief, the chief goal of the assessment is not to rate a group on the CMM scale (the five tiers). That comes about almost as a side effect: If you satisfy the six specific KPAs at Level 2, then by default, you can call yourself a Level 2 shop; the same with Level 3 and 4 and so on. The main purpose of the assessment is actually to identify areas for improvement focus, areas where you may need to shore up resources or redefine how things work. To do this for you, the assessment process will need to look at your processes and practices in working condition, usually across select projects in your organization. The goal is to get a *representative* picture of your program (akin to a statistical sample) and then, based on that picture, document observations, make conclusions, and propose recommendations.

Because an assessment can be a big undertaking it is not something to enter into lightly. Many organizations space them out over time, with maybe 18 or 24 months between assessments. The reasons for such spacing are pretty obvious. The assessment proper may take several weeks, involve potentially dozens of people, and require the purchasing of outside services. Do that every 6 months or so, and you'll have little time to get back to work. But all organizations engaged in SPI initiatives should probably assess its program every one to three years or so, at least as a self-checkup.

When you decide to assess your program you can select from two general approaches: what I call internal or external assessments. An internal assessment is a true self-checkup. You perform the assessment on your own, using your own resources and your own methodology to arrive at a final picture of your program. An internal assessment may follow the typical CMM CBA-IPI process or some variant of it. It will be of value as long as the process provides for an objective comparison of your processes and practices with the CMM (given that's the model you will be using). There are advantages to performing an internal assessment. Typically they are cheaper than external assessments: You don't bring in outside help, and you are in direct control of the assessment activity. For these same reasons you may be able to conduct an internal assessment more quickly than an external assessment. But there are drawbacks as well. If you don't already have the in-house knowledge of the CMM and the assessment process, your people may not be able to design and execute a very effective assessment effort. But even if they do have the knowledge and skills required, you should understand that internal assessments are typically "unofficial" assessments. What I mean by this is that internal assessments are usually geared to detailing an organization's process maturity, and that is the chief (and usually only) goal. But if this effort is not coordinated by a CMM authorized lead assessor, and does not follow in the accepted flow of a general CMM assessment, the results you end up with will, in all likelihood, not be accepted as "good and true" by the SEI or CMM-affiliated organizations. While an internal assessment may very well give you the main benefit of a well-enacted assessment (that is, a true picture of where you stand process-wise), you can't use the results to documents for the world that you have reached a specific CMM maturity goal. To do that—to give the results the power to stick—you'll need to conduct an external assessment.

Now, by external I don't mean you have to hire an outside CMM consulting organization to manage things for you. What I do mean is that you will have to engage someone *external to your business mission* to manage things for you, and that someone will adhere to a formalized assessment process, one recognized by the SEI. Many large organizations train members of their staff in CMM methodologies and in the process of SEI-sanctioned assessments. And these people can then become authorized assessors who work internal to a company. But the process is still external in the sense that it is conducted by a set of external standards (from the SEI) and must follow certain steps and objectives that are independent of the organization being assessed. You may have the inside expertise to handle this for you, or you may have to purchase it from the outside. Because an external assessment is conducted in a formalized way, its results are "official." The SEI will recognize them. In order to achieve this, you may find that an external assessment takes more time than an internal assessment, and though you may be its sponsor, you are not really in direct control over the activities of the external assessment. You may also find that the monies you pay for an external assessment are more than for an internal one. But you may feel that the extra expense is justified in light of the results: thorough, objective, official, and recognized.

Either way, internal or external, an SPI assessment is an undertaking that requires a conscious commitment of time and resources on the part of your organization. Because an assessment requires a significant effort it will help your organization if you know how a typical assessment is structured and conducted. You'll be able to better manage your end of things when you know what to expect from all ends. For the sake of convenience we'll treat the following steps as if you had elected to do a formal, external assessment. The steps hold true, though, for internal assessments as well.

Steps for Conducting an Assessment

When you begin to consider the value and merits of a CMM assessment, you should approach the topic with an idea of its scope and requirements. In this section we'll look at what steps are typically followed in an assessment. There are 20 steps:

1. Decide to conduct an assessment.
2. Contract a lead assessor.
3. Select the assessment team.
4. Choose the projects.
5. Choose the [participants.
6. Create the assessment plan.
7. Determine Plan review and approval.
8. Train the team.
9. Prepare the team.
10. Hold kick-off meeting.
11. Administer the maturity questionnaire.
12. Examine questionnaire results.
13. Examine process and practice documents.
14. Conduct on-site interviews.
15. Consolidate information.
16. Prepare draft findings.
17. Present draft findings.
18. Publish assessment findings.
19. Hold executive session.
20. Deliver report.

Deciding to Conduct an Assessment

To do an assessment, you've got to have something to assess. That may sound facetious, but it's a point that's often ignored. Ideally an assessment will measure how well your full life cycle processes are working across many projects. Such a comprehensive look will give you comprehensive results. We'll discuss the particulars in the following sections, but right now let's just mention a few boundary points you may want to remember when the question comes your way, when can we get a CMM assessment?

Assessments deliver the best results when the following conditions exist:

Your processes have been in place long enough for your project teams to have been actively using them. Whether you are doing a Level 2 assessment (project focused) or a Level 3 assessment (more organization focused) you are going to need the artifacts and the activities that demonstrate process compliance. If you have just introduced key processes into the work place it is entirely possible that your team hasn't had time to work with them. No matter how CMM compliant the documented processes are, if you haven't had ample time to exercise them across your projects, an assessment would almost be pointless. Make sure that you have reached a point in your organization's working ways where your processes are not just documented, but well in practice across the projects in your organization. Your people will need to be very familiar with them if an assessment will hope to measure their effectiveness.

Assessments deliver the best results when you look at projects well underway in their life cycle. A project that is just starting out, say at the very early stages of design, will have such a scant history of process compliance that any measures you take will be incomplete at best. Projects that are well underway should give you what you need: a detailed audit trail that touches on the major areas of your process map.

Assessments that seek to address the organization as a whole should look at projects that represent the organization as a whole. A typical assessment will take a close look at four or so projects in your organization in order to get a composite picture of the whole. Because of this you should be sure that the projects that are to be assessed are typical of the kind of work you do most of the time. You want to select typical projects, not the smoothest-running ones, or the littlest ones, or the freshest ones. Be sure that the projects that are typical of your organization are at a stage in their progress where they can be included in the assessment without unnecessary risk to the project itself.

Assessments require executive sponsorship. The assessment, being the major piece of work that it is, requires sponsorship from the highest levels within the organization, what I call the ownership level. This is the executive branch that has direct ownership of the results of the assessment. This will vary, of course, from organization to organization.

Once you have considered these four factors you may determine that your group is indeed assessment ready. The next step is to contract a lead assessor to coordinate the effort for you.

Contracting a Lead Assessor

Not just anyone can officially assess your organization. For your assessment to be recognized and recorded by the SEI, you will need to use one of the institute's authorized assessors. These are individuals—sometimes outside consultants, sometimes corporate employees—who have undergone a series of CMM training courses and have also participated in a series of assessments. These people are then registered with the SEI and are recognized as being qualified to conduct assessments according to SEI standards.

The SEI publishes a semi-annual list of its authorized assessors. You can find this list at the SEI Web site (www.sei.cmu.edu), by contacting the SEI customer service line, or by doing an Internet search using keywords like "CMM Assessors," and "Lead Assessors." You'll quickly find a list of businesses in your area that offer assessment services.

When you are thinking about contracting for an assessment service, you should keep in mind that the assessment process, as it stands today, is to a degree subjective in nature. True, the assessors are trained in common rules and procedures, but because the CMM can be implemented in so many ways and in so many environments, assessments require a certain amount of personal judgment on the part of the assessor. A practice that one might acknowledge as being CMM compliant might not be recognized in the same way by another. Although this tends to happen only in very ambiguous situations (where good arguments exist for either decision), the subjective elements remain. The SEI is aware that this potential dichotomy exists in the area of assessments, and it's working to refine the process even more, making it as uniform and as structured as such an undertaking can be. But while the SEI is trying to make assessments consistent, remember they are still, even to a slight degree, interpretive. Because of this you should carefully interview and screen the organizations you consider hiring as assessment consultants. Here are some screening tips that might help your assessment go smoothly right from the start:

Remember, you are the customer. The assessor—whoever you choose—will be working for you. True, the assessment will be conducted under SEI guidelines, but you want an assessor who is going to work closely with your organization during the assessment. It is not a passive process; it should (and is designed to) involve you and your team at almost every step of the way.

During your interviews, judge the assessor's feeling for the latitude and flexibility inherent in the CMM. All IT shops are different, and the CMM was designed to be implemented in a flexible way to accommodate these differences. The assessor should be acutely aware of this and appreciative of the different ways many of the CMM recommendations can be put into practice.

You might also find it beneficial to select an assessor that has had experience assessing IT shops similar to yours, in size or in industry focus. If the assessor knows something about your business focus or has worked with shops that are similarly structured, you might find an enhanced ability to understand how you have implemented CMM in your organization.

Ask for a list of references, and then talk to those organizations that have had previous experience with the assessor. This is one of the best ways to gather data and make a decision about which assessor to select.

Finally, ask the assessor what services will be provided to your organization. Some assessors come in with a complete assessment team; others let you help shape the team. Some will produce an extensive results report; others may offer a different type. Some may provide some forms of required CMM training; others do not. You'll want to be able to make a consistent comparison of offers before you finally choose an assessor.

Select the Assessment Team

Your assessor may work closely with you on this task. An assessment team, as defined by the CMM, should be composed of no fewer than 4 and no more than 10 members. The size of your team will depend on a few factors: who's available in your group, the people the assessor may bring in, the number of projects being assessed, the size of the projects being assessed, and the assessment schedule. The SEI itself recommends eight team members, but there's no indisputable logic to this number. The size ultimately is up to you. Work with your lead assessor to come up with a size appropriate to the scope of the job.

However you shape your team, *at least one* person on it has to be from your shop. I think it's usually best that you have as many people on the team from your own shop as possible. If your people are already experienced in assessments, so much the better; if not, then you might strike a balance between inside appointments and outside expertise. Ultimately, however you shape it, your team will have to meet certain minimal qualifications in order for it to be recognized as adequate by the SEI. I break these qualifications up into groups: hard composition and soft composition. The hard composition qualities are readily identifiable tangibles. Here is what they are:

- All members of the team must have received CMM training in two areas: the SEI's *Introduction to the CMM* course (3 days) and *CBA IPI Team Training* course (also 3 days). This training must have been delivered by a group authorized by the SEI to provide such training. Usually, your lead assessor's company can provide this training if your people need it. The training is a one-time requirement. You don't have to repeat it for each assessment.

- Your team must have at least 25 years of combined software engineering experience. This gives you room to appoint some novices and some experienced folks. But you can't have too many fresh faces: The overall (combined) average for each member must be at least 6 years, and no one individual on the team can have less than 3 years' experience.

- Your team must also have at least 10 years of combined management experience, and one of the members individually needs to have at least 6 years' experience.

- Here's something of a tricky requirement (but only in how it sounds): 75 percent of the team needs to be experienced in at least one-third of the shop's development life cycles. Let's look at an example of this. Say your team is composed of eight people and you are assessing a shop that uses either the waterfall methodology, the modified waterfall, or the spiral methodology to development software. In this case, at least six people on the team (75 percent) need to be experienced with using at least one of these methodologies. Further, at least two members of the team should be experienced in all the life cycles used. Appointing people from your own shop is a good way to get this familiarity on board.

- At least one member of the team has to have deep familiarity with the organization structure, workings, and culture of the entity being assessed. At the same time, that person cannot have a vested interest in the assessment outcome. This is important. It is tempting to place people on the assessment team who know the projects and company well and who are also very active in the mission of SPI and CMM compliance. But you have to balance appointment of these people against the objectivity required to work through an assessment appropriately. You probably know that it would be a conflict of interest to make a project manager part of the team assessing that project. Keep that level of consideration open when thinking about other potential appointees.

Those five items constitute the hard composition qualities of the assessment team. The soft composition qualities are less tangible but just as important.

- To begin with, your team members must have knowledge of the CMM KPA areas being assessed. It also helps if they are familiar with software process improvement philosophies and approaches.

- Finally, the team members must have the motivation, abilities, and objectivity required to carry out an assessment.

These qualities help ensure that the assessment team is a capable body, one that is well prepared for the tasks of investigation, analysis, and recommendation. Once you have selected a lead assessor and an assessment team you can begin the process of selecting the projects to review.

Choose the Projects

Implied at this step is the decision on the assessment scope. What will you be assessing exactly? The central purpose of a CMM assessment is to measure your shop's compliance with specific CMM Key Process Areas, or KPAs. You'll recall that there are six KPAs at Level 2, and seven at Level 3. You can assess any range of KPAs you want. As an extreme example, you could formally assess your organization's compliance with only the Requirements Management KPA of Level 2. Such an assessment would be completely valid, even though it is quite limited. Most organizations assess a range of KPAs, and most do it by CMM level. If the organization wants to be recognized as a Level 2 shop, it will usually assess for all the KPAs at Level 2. If the organization wants to be recognized as a Level 3 shop, it will usually assess for the KPAs at both Level 2 and Level 3.

Once the KPA scope is defined, you can then select the projects that will come to the forefront in the assessment effort. But don't misunderstand this (many people do). Just because you choose several projects for the assessment those are not the only ones that the assessment team may look at or discuss. Only if your organization seeks CMM recognition for the workings of a selected project (and this is almost exclusively for Level 2) will the investigation be confined. The idea most of the time is to find out if the shop is performing overall at a certain CMM level. The projects you pick to help uncover this are really just standout examples the assessment team can use. These projects will provide the sources needed for artifacts, documentation, and general activity reviews. But the assessment team may well look into other projects or investigate the workings of other organizational teams. When it comes to choosing the projects for an assessment consider the following:

- The projects should be representative of the entity being assessed. Choose projects that give the team a valid feel for the size, scope, and type of projects the organization typically undertakes. This may not be the "average" project. If your shop has 75 projects underway, but eight of them require 70 percent of your resources, the average would not turn out to be representative. The idea is to choose the projects that will help the assessment give you a true picture of where your organization stands regarding process compliance.

- When possible, choose projects that have been underway at least 6 months and try to include full life cycle projects. To measure your processes you need to look where they have been in practice for some time. The SEI recommends picking four projects to focus on during an assessment, but the actual number will probably be influenced by what's going on in your shop at the time. Choosing brand new projects can be problematic: They may not be far enough along to have touched on many of your Level 2/3 processes. The mix in your shop of early stage versus late stage projects will shape the blend you pick for the assessment. Look for a blend that gives you ample history for those KPAs you have elected to assess. If you are doing a full Level 2 assessment, you'll need to look at projects (and these are just the focal points, not the boundaries) that assess requirements management, project planning, project tracking, software configuration management, software quality assurance, and perhaps subcontractor management. The blend for a full Level 3 assessment will be more demanding. You'll have to choose projects that guide you through the Level 2 KPAs as well as the Level 3 KPAs: organizational process focus, organizational process definition, training program, integrated software management, software product engineering, intergroup coordination, and peer review.

This step may be the single most important one in the assessment process. If you choose wisely the blend should mirror your organization as a whole, and your assessment results should have great applicability. If not, your assessment results may have diminished value when applied to the organization at large.

Choose the Participants

At this point you have accomplished four steps: You have decided to move ahead with an assessment; you have engaged a lead assessor; you have a formed the assessment team; and you have selected the projects to assess. There's one more ingredient you need to add to your readiness mix: the assessment participants.

An assessment is not just a look at published processes and the complementary artifacts that arise from the workings on a project. You spend a good deal of time talking with the people who work on the projects (and even with people who work only tangentially on the projects). There are three broad categories of people who you will need to identify as assessment participants:

- Project leaders
- Questionnaire respondents
- Participants in functional area interviews

Let's take a brief look at each category.

Project Leadership

The people who you have managing your projects are key people to include as assessment participants. You need the management view as it is a critical aspect to Level 2 and 3 activities. Plus, management should be able to provide you with an across-the-board look at how the development process is being carried out on the various projects (and in the organization as a whole). Which managers should you select? There's no hard rule, but people in the role of project management, software project management, development management, SQA management, SCM management, and other such roles can provide excellent procedure and practice data for the assessment. Two or three managers from each project might serve as a starting number to consider, but select the managers that best suit your current needs (and who are available and whose participation will not endanger any project commitments). These project managers will be individually interviewed by the assessment team, and they may be called on to coordinate the process of gathering artifacts for review as well to help select the participants for the next two categories.

Questionnaire Respondents

You will send some of the assessment participants the CMM's maturity questionnaire. This is a respondent-completed questionnaire that asks a series of questions that pertain to CMM compliance. It's used as a starting point for investigation. The questionnaires provide a broad look at compliance and help the assessment team members gauge what detailed looks they will need to take in terms of people and projects. There can be a temptation to send the questionnaire out to all participants, and while there is little harm in that it's probably not necessary. The high-level, goal-oriented nature of the questionnaire really makes it best suited to management and so typically from 4 to 10 are sent out at the start of the assessment process. You might identify people who are project leaders, functional area leads, and other key technical positions. Take a look at the KPAs you are assessing and then target your questionnaires to those people who you think can speak to the overall KPA activities on the projects.

Functional Area Representatives

A key part of the assessment process is talking to the people in the organization who work in various areas of software development. When you prepare for an assessment you will need to select a sample of these people to include for interviews. The people you pick should be (to the extent practical) a representative sample of your technical staffs, and it helps if they have had direct experience on the projects on which you are focusing. These people are usually line practitioners, not managers. They are the folks who carry out the processes supported by the organization. They are the ones who have been in the reviews, preparing estimates, and audited for SQA. These people are usually interviewed in small groups of four to eight. You may choose to have four or more of these sessions if you think the circumstances require it, so you'll be able to talk to a lot of people. For this category, choose a range of project roles so you'll have representatives from all areas of the software development life cycle.

Create the Assessment Plan

Steps 1 through 5 prepare you to begin the assessment process. Those steps guide you through the considerations you have to make in order to move ahead with the commitments required. Now that the major planning has been accomplished, it's time to put it all into a plan. By now you have probably noticed that the CMM model is heavy into planning. In fact, quality improvement approaches across industries are generally all pretty high on planning. When a key element of a program is to measure progress you have to know where you started from. If you don't know this you won't know where you've been. The expression "The best map in the world won't help if you don't know where you are" rings true here. A documented plan lets everyone know where the starting point is: what the commitments are, what the scope is, who the players are, what the expected outcome is. During an assessment the plan serves as your management mechanism. It's both your map and your starting point. And it's the best way to measure progress: weighing what happened against what was expected to happen.

Because a CMM assessment is a serious undertaking, involves people across your organization, and requires an investment of time and effort, an assessment plan becomes especially important. The plan will serve three chief purposes. First, it's the document that tells executive management (or whoever is the official sponsor of the assessment) just what is entailed in the assessment. From the plan, executive management should be able to grasp the objective of the assessment, the scope of the effort involved, and the players who must work to bring it off. Second, the plan will serve as a management guide for the assessment team, helping them work within a schedule of time and activity. Third, the plan will communicate to the participants (and the rest of the organization) what will be expected in terms of preparation and cooperation on their parts.

An assessment plan need not be an extensive, complicated document. It's probably best if it is not. In this section we'll look at what I consider to be a minimal table of contents for an assessment plan. You can add more to this if you want to, but you don't have to. Often the company (or the lead assessor) you hire to conduct the assessment will create the plan for you, but it helps to know what might go into a general plan. You will usually have to address seven areas:

- Goals
- CMM scope
- Schedule
- Team members
- Participants
- Reports
- Risks/contingencies

NOTE This template does not include any of the agreement data that might have to be devised to cover any contractual relationship between your company and a third-party assessment company.

Let's take a brief look at each area.

Goals

This can serve as a general introduction to the plan. Here you state the goals of the assessment. This will usually include the reasons for the assessment (elapsed time, sponsor request, reported problems, etc.) and the hoped-for results of the assessment. Hoped-for results might include such accomplishments as CMM Level recognition, problem area identification, and expansion opportunity. The main objective of this section is to clearly state why the assessment is being carried out and what benefits the effort will bring.

CMM Scope

In this section you identify the scope of the assessment. The scope will generally be described in two parts. The first is to identify the CMM KPAs to be considered. This will establish the reach of the assessment. The next is to identify the development projects that will be looked at in the assessment. This will help establish the breadth of the assessment. It is also handy to cite brief reasons for including each KPA as well as the selection logic that governed choosing the specific projects for inclusion.

Events Schedule

The schedule presents two important pieces of information. It breaks down the assessment effort into a series of distinct activities. The following sections (see steps 8 through 20) are the basic steps involved. These should be itemized in the schedule (similar to a work breakdown structure in a software development plan). The schedule will also contain the timeline on which all these activities will occur. It lets everyone know what is going to happen and when.

Team Members

This section identifies the members of the assessment team. By now you ought to have had a chance to appoint members to the team and to get those appointments approved. Here you will also identify the lead assessor and any outside help you have brought in to work on the assessment with the internal team members. With each member name, I would assign a general area of responsibility and a contact number.

Participants

This section officially identifies the participants who will be contributing input for the assessment. Here you should also make sure that you have confirmed participation before you list the folks. This listing will let everyone know who will be required at what points in the assessment activity. With each participant's name I would also include a general assessment role (the participant category), the functional area, and perhaps a contact number.

Reports

This section will identify the documents that will come out of the assessment process. Usually (and minimally) there should be an assessment report that summaries the strengths, weaknesses, and KPA compliance issues uncovered by the assessment. You may have your own list of reports or actions that you wish to have as part of your summary or results activities. They should all be identified here. This section will help executive management understand what data will come out of the process and what information presentation/summaries will be available to them for review.

Risks/Contingencies

Finally in the plan, identify any risks and/or contingencies that might affect the work products, the schedule, or the people involved in the assessment process.

Once the assessment plan has been drafted it's a good idea to review it with your assessment team and then get executive management's approval of it before you consider it officially in motion.

Plan Approval

Here's a good, general law of plan development: If you create a plan thoughtfully, by the time it's written it should be pretty much approved. That is, by the time you've been able to put together a draft of all the information you've been collecting, you should have talked with enough people so that most players included in the plan have already consented to their parts. If you have drafted you plan carefully, and perhaps with the help of steps 1 through 6, the document should be in pretty good shape, and it should be fairly easy to get it approved (naturally, I'm discounting here any change in corporate direction or mission in the environment). You should follow through with the process, however. It's very important to the assessment atmosphere that the plan (as evidence of commitment) is officially approved and adopted by management (or whoever is the formal sponsor of the assessment).

In the spirit of thoroughness and formality, you might want to take the path of moving the plan through the peer review process, the seventh KPA of CMM Level 3. This is a formal process where members of your technical team review a document for clarity, completeness, and potential defects. The process involves reviewer selection, meeting scheduling, meeting facilitation, notes distribution, and so on until an approved draft of the document comes about. I usually recommend that you don't take the assessment plan through a formal peer review process. There are a few reasons for this. First (and obviously), if you are at Level 2 you will have but little, ancillary exposure to the activities described in the Peer Review KPA. Second, your probably don't have a lot of people in your organization who could comment on the plan—few peers. Besides, it's not a hand-off item; it's self-contained; finished once executed. Third, with the real approvers of the plan being the sponsors there's no transition of responsibility that makes a common group review necessary. My usual recommendation is to run the final draft of your assessment plan through a *light* five-step process:

1. Conduct action review.

2. Make executive presentation.

3. Polish.

4. Publish.

5. Distribute.

Let's look at each briefly:

Conduct Action Review

Your assessment plan will contain a series of activities conducted over the course of the assessment. People are going to be associated with these activities. There are your team members, and then there are the assessment participants. The activities will include things like questionnaire response, interviews, document collection, and so on. Before the plan is submitted for formal approval you should confirm with everyone identified in the plan, via a quick plan review, that their parts are recognized and still agreed to. You shouldn't have to commit a lot of time to this review. It's really just confirming a series of scheduled dates and times; however, the step is important because it solidifies the readiness of your plan.

Make Executive Presentation

After the action, review you should know that your plan is clean. At this point you should present it to the sponsor of the assessment for approval and formal adoption. I have seen this done a couple of ways. The first is to present a hard copy of the plan to the sponsors and then let them have a week or so to digest it, ask questions, and so on. From this you will get the feedback you need to finalize the plan and then get the corporate imprimatur on it. This is the path I used to take, and I did it because people always told me that executives don't read plans. Now to me, that makes them sound lazy or disinterested, not to mention homogenous, and so I always tended to respond as if the opposite extreme were true: that all they did was read. Consequently, I probably overreported many of them right up the chain of command, they were excelling just to get away from me.

These days I've backed off that enthusiasm. I'm not saying this is a bad approach; use it by all means if it'll work for you and your team and it's up the sponsor's alley. But here are the quirks I've found with it. First, the sponsor usually knows from a general perspective what an assessment is and what it means strategically to the organization. The detail doesn't really concern them; and it shouldn't; that's what concerns you. So they shouldn't really need to review the minutiae of the schedule and the activities, not unless they just want to do so. A full review might be unneeded effort. Next, executives really don't like to read. And now I better understand why. Brevity is blessed in business. And when the business is information, as in information management, and the pace is fast and the demand escalating, what counts is the point. And when you consider that a CMM assessment is probably a parallel effort in most organizations—that is, an effort that runs beside the day-to-day business mission—you can see how a sponsor might simply prefer the when, where, and how much. It's expedient to present the assessment plan in a brief overview meeting. Hit the chapter highlights, open for questions, and leave copies for later review with a sign-by date clearly noted.

Polish

Most of the time, using the preceding approach, changes will be minor (considering the plan enters in a quality state). Any changes needed can then made, and a version 1.0 can be submitted for signature.

Publish

It may be you who carries out the plan, but the sponsor owns the plan so it's important that the document is published with the sponsor's signature or with official notification. This not only gives weight to the assessment plan, but it also lends weight and credibility to the process of the assessment itself. Once the plan has been approved and adopted it can be distributed.

Distribute

Distribute the plan to whoever you think might like a copy of it. Perhaps post it for common access. Given, there's probably not an abundance of people who might need to see it, but there might be many who are curious to see it. It's not a proprietary document, so share it as you see fit. But you should probably make sure that it gets into the hands of your assessment team members and the participants you have identified in the plan.

With the assessment plan in place, we can now look at the general details of an assessment. Note that these are general details. Every assessment is different; different leads conduct them different ways. But these steps will give for a feel for the minimum that might go on. I have organized these events into steps, but note that the order here is for the sake of convenience. The steps pretty much occur in the sequence I have here, but they don't all have to.

Train the Team in CMM

In step 3 you selected people to serve on your assessment team. Your team probably has between 4 and 10 members, and you were confined to a few areas of qualification in choosing the individuals. The goal here was to end up with a team with at least a base set of aptitudes in the areas of experience and technical exposure. One of these areas falls under CMM training. All members of your team, at one time or another, had to have satisfactorily completed two courses designed by the SEI: *Introduction to the CMM* and *CBA IPI Team Training*. This is required training, and for important reasons.

A CMM assessment is formal process. It's very different in attitude from the CMM itself. The Capability Maturity Model was designed for flexibility and interpretation. Professional judgment and selective application are perhaps two of the dominant traits of CMM implementation. There is no one right way with it. Consequently, no hard paths are set. One group may implement CMM is a much different way from another, yet both may be valid. Not so with assessments. A CMM assessment has to be a much more rigid process. For assessment results to have any common value, and by this I mean comparative value, they have to emerge from common measures. An assessment team will use a standardized maturity questionnaire to foster commonality. Likewise, the team will need a minimal common background in CMM. The assessment training requirements help ensure this. Everyone on your team must have completed two SEI CMM courses.

The first is the 3-day course, *Introduction to the CMM*. This course gives students an overview of the CMM and begins with an assumption of little knowledge about the model. The course sets up the CMM within the realm of software process improvement and then explains its structure, going over the concepts of process maturity and the set of common features (commitments, abilities, activities, measurements, and verification) used to manage process definition and refinement. It moves through a description of each of the five tiers of the model, mainly focusing on the goals of each. Importantly, this course focuses on the flexibility inherent in the model and the need for professional judgment when using the model. Team members can't really expect to contribute much to an assessment if they lack a basic understanding of CMM. This course is one way, discrete and tangible, that that understanding can be shown to exist in depth within the team.

The other course is just as important, and it's a little more specialized, too. It's the *CBA IPI Team Training* class, another 3-day course. This course helps prepare students to participate on an assessment team. Thematically, the course is focused along two areas: working out the process of conducting an internal process improvement assessment and looking at ways to work as a team in this environment. The course serves as a primer for the assessment process. People who take the course should gain a view as to the scope of an assessment, the constraints on the process, and the roles and responsibilities required of a team who is working together on an assessment.

There are several avenues open for taking these courses. For one, the Software Engineering Institute (with Carnegie-Mellon University) offers these courses in the Pittsburgh area on a regular basis. If the school is convenient to you, you can take them there. You might also find that your lead assessor or the assessor's organization offers SEI-endorsed training classes. Many assessment organizations offer these required training courses as part of their overall assessment package. Ask you lead assessor about this. And the SEI publishes a list of companies internationally who offer CMM training. Chances are, there are people close to you who can handle these training needs.

Prepare the Team

Your team has been formed to contain a certain knowledge base. This makes your team certifiable in the better sense. They have the formal abilities needed to make assessment judgments and conclusions that have weight, show value, and are widely recognized in the IT industry. But that's not to say they've done anything so far. At this point they are just a ready team. Some may never have done an assessment before; all have done *this* assessment before. Because each assessment is different, you'll want to bring your team together for a general orientation early in the assessment project. The purpose of the meeting is twofold: to go over the details of the plan and to prep the members in some techniques of deportment. Both serve a single objective: prepare the team to begin on the assessment proper.

With the whole team present you should go over the details of what will occur over the course of the assessment. You should review assignments, go over materials required, and make sure you have everything lined up that needs to be ready for the various parts of the assessment. Treat this as your first status meeting as well as a prekick-off meeting. Make sure everyone is comfortable with what has to happen and when before you move on.

Next, you should go over the tool of data collection. During the assessment, your team members will be collecting data from four sources, and really from only four sources. They need to understand what each source is and how each is derived. The first is *instrument data*. This is data that comes from the maturity questionnaire. Technically, the questionnaire is referred to as a survey instrument. Your people give out a group of these and then collect them and analyze the ratings. That's the instrument data. The next is *interview data*. At scheduled points during the assessment your team will be interviewing members of the project teams and the organization's technical teams. This effort will include individual as well as group interviews. The information that comes out of these interviews are the interview data. *Document data* is next. It's data that comes from the reviews your team members make of the documented practices and procedures used by the projects as well as the artifacts that have emerged from using the practices and procedures during the life cycle of each project. Finally, there is *presentation data*. This is the data, the final comments actually, that come from the presentation-of-findings meeting you have with the assessment participants. During this presentation, the participants will have the chance to clarify issues, add support for others, and in general complete the data set required for reaching a full assessment conclusion. These four data types will provide the basis for creating the final assessment report.

The next areas for review have arisen from field experience, and I include them as items to consider. As structured as the assessment process is, you can see that there is still a large degree of subjectivity and personal interpretation involved. People not used to serving as gatekeepers of information may have a tendency to leave the gates wide open always, giving the flow full freedom but soaking everything else. That's why four deportment techniques might be discussed. They help set the individual up within a role that supports both information facilitation and refinement. These four areas really fall more into the field of business psychology than IT management, so I will not go too far into them here. But I think they are important enough to mention and encourage for development.

The first is some discussion about interview techniques. Your team will be conducting a series of interviews, some in groups, others individually. In both cases, multiple members of your team will be on the questioning end. You want your people to be able to handle each kind of interview in a way that brings out the best information. For this you will want an environment that is isolated from the busyness of the day-to-day environment. A quiet conference room or even an off-site location is a good place to get away from the bustle. You'll want your team to establish the tone of the interview as friendly and relaxed. It's very important here to somehow stress (without being stressful about it) that this effort is fully unconnected with human resource management or job evaluation or personal accomplishment. The interviewees should feel that the interview is solely about process—and in no way about people. There's a natural tendency with everyone to treat any interview as a forum for judgment, with the judge being the guy with all the questions. And this is a difficult suspicion to dispel. But if your team makes a conscious effort to address this up front it will go a long way to relaxing the participants by time of the meeting. And the relaxed tone is important. This will help the interviewee provide unfiltered information, and you want as much pure, unchecked data as possible. This can be promoted by having your questions organized ahead of time. If a team of questioners bombards someone with a jangle of questions you may get back jangled answers. Keep the questions ordered and smooth, and the discussion should take a logical path. Your team should always defer to the interviewees, stick to schedule, and make the process as effortless as possible.

Another issue is confidentiality. The organization will know via the assessment plan just who is involved in every phase of the assessment cycle. That's important because it is public confirmation that the process is well supported, amply defined, and ready to go forward. But once an assessment starts, an important layer of confidentiality enters the picture. Your team members are working to collect data, but it is not necessary (and to do it, in my opinion, is ill advised) to record from whom the data comes. Data gathered during a CMM assessment should be considered anonymous in nature. One bit of data should be equal in validity with any other bit of data; the personal data source—other than the job function position—should not be factored into your evaluations. Some of the data sources will be naturally anonymous. For example, instructions on the maturity questionnaire explicitly state that information identifying individuals will be used strictly for administrative purposes only. But others will be much more open. You will know in the interviews who explains things what ways, but even here you must make sure that your team enforces a code of confidentiality. It's an extreme statement to write this, but it's very true: Your assessment participants should in no way be held individually accountable for anything they say or do during an assessment. If an engineer takes the opportunity to rant and rave against management, to harangue people on staff in the strongest terms, and to come out with what appears to be one outrageous lie after the next about the shop, you have to simply note it and say thank you. If he's wrong, his data scores will disappear in a sea of facts. But it runs counter to the spirit of CMM (and sound management practice in general) to use the revelation as an opportunity for some kind of corporate intervention into that person's work life. Because the job of your team is to assess process and not people, stress to them the importance of confidentiality and help them practice it.

One way to foster confidentiality is to plan your interviews and meeting sessions so that no two people present are linked in the chain of command in the organization. This frees people from perhaps feeling that they have to check what they say during a discussion. If you can keep people on the same job level or separate from their reporting group, they may feel more comfortable expressing their individuals opinions, observations, and concerns.

Finally, and importantly, you will need to orient your team to the rules of corroboration. What is this? It's a way to derive probable fact from a collection of opinions. Newspaper and television reporters are trained in these rules and (though this doesn't really apply here) it's an important defense against libel. How do you know that what one person tells you is true? Well, you get corroborating data. Someone else—an independent someone else—tells you the same thing with very similar details. One person might be fabricating, but the chances that two people came up with the same fabrication are very slim. When your team members go out into the field data collecting for the assessment they will have to be aware of and practice a small set of these rules. There should be two independent sources for each observation. For example, if you want to know that the ABC project conducted a series of requirements reviews, you'll need at least two separate people reporting that they observed the meetings being conducted. To go further, you should also seek to confirm this via other data sources. The comments from an interview are good, but there should also be some evidence of the activity acknowledged elsewhere, such as responses to the questionnaire or in the review of some of the project artifacts. If the data point comes up in at least two independent data gathering sessions you can safely count it as a fact. In general, you are looking for events or artifacts that spread through the project team like a web. It is very rare in the practice of CMM that a key practice or process area is solely confined to one person or to an area so isolated that its work doesn't seep into other areas. The audit trail that your people will be assimilating should touch on a full scope of people, practices, and artifacts. Seek this corroboration across the project. If you so do, holes in the system will become immediately obvious.

This team preparation will give your people the skills they need to go forward. You might handle this in a single meeting or as a series of meetings over time. The important thing, though, is to be very comfortable that your assessment team is ready to implement the effort in a way that will fold harmoniously into the daily activities of the organization.

Hold Kick-Off Meeting

Here's where the active part of the assessment begins. Up until now you've been planning and preparing. In the next five steps you and your team will carry out the investigations that go with an assessment. This usually starts off with some form of kick-off meeting. But I don't really view this one as a regular kick-off meeting. Software project kick-off meetings are usually formal affairs, a bit here-we-go enthusiasm blended with general orientation. You can use the same approach on an assessment kick-off meeting, but in reality it can be much more abbreviated.

An assessment kick-off meeting can include the assessment team members and as many of the participants who are free to attend. The real point of the meeting is to mark the beginning of the assessment. You can also use it for other things, too. You may use the meeting to formally introduce the members of the assessment team. You may also use it to brief the participants again on their roles and responsibilities. And you may want to take the opportunity to go over the schedule and the major milestones in the process. The sponsors may choose to be at the meeting, but it's not absolutely necessary that they are.

Another good use of the kick-off meeting is to request from the participants the first round of documents that you will need as part of assessment analysis. Usually these are the project's documented processes and procedures, the written templates and guides that are used to plan and manage the project. If you can come to the meeting with a list of these ready you can then distribute the requests to specific people and give them a window of time in which to get the documents to your team or else steer your team to them.

Keep the meeting as brief as possible, but you might also consider this final opportunity. If the managers you have chosen to respond to the maturity questionnaire are at the meeting this is a good time to get the questionnaire in their hands. This takes us to the next section . . .

Administer the Maturity Questionnaire

A logical starting point in your investigation is to get a high-level look at where the projects stand in relation to the CMM. A tool to get this view is the CMM maturity questionnaire. This is the basic starting point for any assessment. The questionnaire is a series of questions that help clarify what processes and practices are in place for software project development. For example, one of the questions asks if the people performing requirements analysis for the project have been trained to perform their duties. The respondent can answer the question one of four ways: Yes, No, Don't Know, and Does Not Apply. "Yes" means they have been trained; "No" means they have not; "Don't Know" means the person answering question does not know either way; and "Does Not Apply" means that that issue is irrelevant to the assessment at hand. There are 42 questions that focus on Level 2 of the CMM and 45 questions that focus on Level 3. Most of the questions can be answered "Yes" or "No" pretty easily. Because the questionnaires are usually sent to project managers or technical leaders working on the project, and because the questions themselves are of a high level and general nature, the complete process is not complex nor does it usually require any investigation of the part of the respondent. But the use of the "Does Not Apply" response should be well-understood. It should not be a common answer for most CMM assessments.

"Does Not Apply" is a response reserved for justifiable exceptions to CMM practice. Some of the recommendations and activities described in the model can be ignored on implementation with the shop still being viewed by the SEI as in proper compliance. In other words, you can be assessed as a CMM Level 2 shop without having to implement everything in Level 2, given that those omitted items have no real place in your business. I have not encountered a lot of real examples of this in the development environment. For example, I know of plenty of places that would prefer not to manage their projects using a software development plan, but they lack a justifiable reason. It's not enough to encounter a question that implies an ignored activity and sweep it away with "Does Not Apply." If in reality, and on further investigation, it does apply the issue will indeed affect the assessment results. The most common area I have seen where "Does Not Apply" comes into play is in the area of subcontractor management. Many IT shops, working on Level 2 programs, simply don't farm work out to subcontractors. Everything is done in-house. This business practice justifies ignoring the Subcontractor Management KPA, and in doing so a shop is still able to be considered Level 2 compliant based on the remainder of its practices.

As you give the questionnaires out, it's a good idea to go over them briefly with the respondents, as a group or one at a time. You might want to give them only the questions that pertain to the KPAs you are addressing in your assessment, although there is no harm in letting them complete the whole thing. In relation to the issue of confidentiality I mentioned earlier, the respondent may notice that the start of the questionnaire prompts for a good bit of identifying and descriptive data from the respondent. This is used only for administrative purposes: to track data and follow up on it. It's helpful to stress to the respondents that this data will not be used to link people with responses in any way; that end of the assessment is kept strictly anonymous.

How much time should you give people to get the questionnaires back to you? A knowledgeable project manager could probably tick off all Level 2 and Level 3 questions in half an hour. But let them have as long as they like, and as long as you can allow. A week may be a bit long; a few days may be better. See how you have scheduled this in your plan. You can perform some other tasks while the questionnaires are still out, like document collection and the beginnings of that analysis. But a major thrust of the investigation will occur only after you have had a chance to study the questionnaire results. A good method for managing this process is to split it up into three steps. First, give out the questionnaire with any explanations needed. Then, halfway through the response time contact each respondent to see how things are going and to remind them of the turn-in date. Finally, at the turn-in date, have your team make the rounds for the collection. In this way you can stay on top of this first step in the process, and you can also be visible enough to provide any help or guidance that the respondents may ask for. If you distribute the questionnaires to only a handful of people (4 to 10 is the range recommended by the SEI), and if you choose as respondents those people who have broad managerial and oversight responsibilities on the selected projects, then you should have no problem getting the completed questionnaires back on time with the assurance that the people with the right knowledge had a hand in completing them. You will have both expedient results and sound beginning data.

Examine Questionnaire Results

Your first feel for the degree of CMM compliance comes at this step. Once your team has collected the questionnaires, they can go about the process of analyzing the responses. Don't be concerned with having to score the questionnaires. They are not really designed to be converted into quantitative data. The questionnaire responses are best used when taken as signposts along the assessment road. They'll point the way to areas of strength as well as areas of weakness. When you get the questionnaires back and start to look them over you'll see that each one paints a certain picture of CMM compliance. Taken together, you hope that they paint a consistent picture across all the projects being assessed. They might, and then they might not. Your evaluation of the questionnaires should first consider them as individual responses to be understood and then as a consolidated impression that also needs to be understood.

For each single questionnaire response you should first tackle the issue of clarity. You'll want to make sure that the response is complete and that there are no ambiguities in any of the answers. To help with this, you can make notes in three areas: Begin by going over the response for completeness. If questions have been skipped, you may want to contact the respondent and go over the missing data. Next, check the responses for vague answers. If answers are not clearly marked (double marked, out of the boxes) you may want to contact the respondent also. Finally, as a general recommendation, note wherever the answers "Don't Know" or "Does Not Apply" have been indicated. I find that it's a good practice to confirm these choices with the respondents, especially if they occur frequently on one questionnaire. At this point you have a set of solid questionnaire responses in your hands.

Now you move to the issue of compliance. Each questionnaire can be marked with a broad indication of what KPAs appear to be fully present and which ones appear to have gaps. This is a general mapping to the CMM. You can use this mapping then to begin to identify areas where additional investigation would be helpful. For example, a "Yes" to the question of whether requirements analysts are trained in their jobs may prompt you to make a note to ask to see the training materials or to see a list of the people who have competed the regimen. Go through each response and check each question this way. It will lead you into the next step of the investigation process.

With the individual questionnaires analyzed you can then look at the responses as a whole. What you'll be comparing here is the higher-level CMM mapping from each. And what you are looking for are three things: areas of strong compliance, "Yes" responses that appear in common across responses; obvious gaps, "No's" that most of the respondents agreed on; and conflicts, the recognition of capabilities by some that were not recognized by others. Common areas of compliance agreement usually indicate some degree of valid process and practice activity. The common citing of gaps likewise usually indicates a neglected area. Those questionnaires that conflict with each other tend to point to areas that are in a state of flux or a state of development within the organization. These areas especially may need to be explored further in order to arrive at a good picture of what processes and practices are in place and are being used by different projects.

Based on the group analysis of the questionnaires, your assessment team can produce an overall map of CMM compliance. The map produced here should actually be a fairly accurate representation of what you should begin to find in the next steps of the process.

Examine Process and Practice Documents

The next tasks in the assessment process will be to begin to confirm what the questionnaires have told you. This will involve probing into two areas: Are the development rules governing how the project ought to run CMM compliant? and, Is the project actually run according to those rules? Documented processes and practices should reveal the first answer. A look at project artifacts and discussions with team members should reveal the second.

The first is a somewhat passive activity and occurs off-site. But first you must ask the assessment participants to provide these documents to your team. There are a few ways to go about this. If your participants are CMM savvy or have been through an assessment before, they probably have a pretty good idea of what to provide. You might prompt them with a general list or some other form of reminder. If your participants are new to CMM or are going through their first assessment they may need more help. Because the CMM doesn't tell a shop what kind of process documentation it should maintain there are no lists of this, that, and the other thing that you can hand out in checklist form. You'll have to prepare a cue list that helps the participants understand what *kinds* of documentation would be helpful. It may take a round or two of collecting to make sure you get it all, and you might even have to have some of your team visit on-site to help find and identify the stuff.

Once you have collected the documentation you will want your team to sift through it and map it to the CMM. This can be a simple matter, or it can be an intricate matter. Some shops that have carefully modeled their development activity on the CMM may produce documentation that maps clearly and cleanly. With other shops it may be a different story. In their natural progressions over time some shops may have developed processes and practices that contain subsets and supersets of capabilities, and these must be culled through in order to pull out those relevant to the CMM. You might begin this part of the investigation by first summarizing the documents by KPA and then begin to look further into each KPA area to decipher the detail.

The time and effort involved in this step naturally depends on the amount of documentation you have to review, the size of your team, and their familiarity with CMM. From this effort should emerge two things, a more detailed compliance map, further distilled from the questionnaire level, and a new set of notes on things to ask about and items to look for as the investigation moves ahead. . .

Conduct On-Site Interviews

Until now the assessment activities have mainly been conducted off-site, that is, without the direct involvement of the assessment participants. Your team members have put forth most of the effort. They have administered the questionnaire and studied the responses, and they have reviewed the process and practice documentation used by the various projects to manage development. Both of these activities have given your team a solid foundation to now look into the practical matter of what actually happens during project development.

Every step in the assessment process is important, of course, but I think that the step of on-site interviews is where the true and full CMM picture takes shape. In your assessment plan you will have identified what interviews will be taking place and with whom. Your team now has a suite of knowledge at its disposal: It knows the general direction of CMM compliance from the questionnaires, it knows some of the details of CMM implementation, and it has at the ready its questions and areas for clarification to complete the whole picture. Now the on-site interviews can begin. You can do this in any order or combination you like, but you'll probably end up speaking with three groups of participants: project leadership, midline managers, and functional area representatives. You can handle the interviews in just about any way that you like. You might want to prepare the participants by forwarding to them in advance a list of particulars you would like to address, with requests to have available certain project artifacts. Or you might go in with a more casual manner and then use what's uncovered in the initial meeting to define details of what to look at in a follow-up meeting. Both ways work fine. Just remember to conduct the meetings to promote openness, focus on process, and maintain confidentiality.

Project leaders are typically interviewed individually by members of the assessment team. There's no ideal time for these individual meetings, but they need not be marathon sessions. The length will depend in large part on the issues open at the time, the number and types of KPAs being looked at, and the experience of the players on both sides of the table.

The same holds true for the other interviews. Midline managers are typically interviewed in groups of four to eight or so. So are the functional area representatives. In these groups, interviews avoid including people in the same chain of command or with direct reportings to others in the group.

During these interviews, seek not only to define the areas of weakness (where CMM compliance is not well-supported) but also to get a full picture of where CMM implementation has been strong. This is where corroboration becomes valuable. Seek to gather as many independent sources for the emerging conclusions as possible. Seek the facts across the spectrum of data you have. If you believe the report that a project's requirements analysts have been trained in their analysis duties, look for evidence of this in the process documents (perhaps a rule to train), in the artifacts from the project (perhaps a training memo), and in interviewees' confirmations that such training is offered and did take place.

These rounds of personal interviews will just about complete the investigation picture. From these you can request and then collect any artifacts to support the assessment, and you may even have the need for a few more follow-up sessions to nail down some final points. It's important to conduct the assessment according to schedule, especially the on-site portion, but do not feel pressured to wrap it up early or without the information you need. When you come to the point where you will begin to draft the results of your findings, make sure you have looked into them thoroughly. Be comfortable and confident that what you now understand about the organization and its projects truly reflects the real business nature of thing.

Consolidate the Information

At this step you are pretty much done with the assessment proper. There is still some room for fine-tuning the data and better understanding the results. But at this point—after the questionnaires, the document reviews, the interviews, and the artifact reviews—you should pretty much know how the organization stands in relation to the CMM. That is, your team should know. Now is the time for the team to regroup, compare notes, and consolidate their findings. A good way to move forward with this task is to get the team together and review what you have uncovered for each KPA against which you were assessing. You want to rate the organization as having satisfied or not satisfied the expectations inherent in each KPA. There should be a team consensus here. Several things will help build the consensus. First, the hard data collected during the assessment should tell a strong tale. Second, the softer answers to the interview questions should also have revealed much. It will be easy to identify significantly lacking areas: The data will simply not be there to support them. But it may be harder to reach consensus when it's a close call. When considering this type of situation, remember the flexible spirit of the CMM while keeping in mind what a commitment to process improvement entails. Also bear in mind that an organization can have weaknesses in a KPA, but that weakness needn't prevent it from satisfying the goals of that KPA. You can satisfy the goal and still have room for improvement. Carefully review the goals for each KPA assessed. Ultimately you will have to rate each as Satisfied, Unsatisfied, Not Rated (if you skipped it), or Not Applicable (if it doesn't apply to your shop).

You can't count a KPA as a whole as being satisfied if any of the goals remain unsatisfied.

What your team should finally end up with after this review is an in-depth picture of each KPA as practiced by the organization. For each KPA your team should be able to identify both areas of process and maturity strength, as well as areas of process and maturity weakness. From this you can put together a KPA satisfaction rating, and then from this rating you can surmise where you stand in terms of Level 1, 2, 3, and so on. This last step here—rating a level—is one of the more visible aspects of a CMM assessment, but it's really one of the least important. The focus should be on KPA activity and on the ever-evolving effort at process improvement. This is where the real development benefits emerge.

Prepare Draft Findings

At this point your team should prepare a draft of the assessment findings. These findings may or may not be presented in a version of the final assessment report. But they do need to be complete, well organized, and backed by the right kind of support data. You have thought the findings through in step 15; now you need to organize them. The purpose here is to get the assessment findings in what may end up being close to their final shape. Everyone on the team should have a hand in this. The report produced will, in effect, be authored by all members. Consequently, everyone should agree as to the findings and should be able to address any issues that come about due to the findings. In other words, the team must be ready to present its conclusions to the organization. But even here you are not quite ready to mark the findings as official or conclusive. You need to take the final quality control step of running the findings past the participants for their take on the conclusions. Once this step is competed you will have collected all the input you need to formulate the final report.

Present Draft Findings

The final data gathering session in the assessment is the presentation of the draft findings to the assessment participants. This review is typically handled in multiple sessions to avoid reporting chain links. The objective here is for the assessment team to let the participants know what they have found and what they have interpreted the findings to mean. This is not simply a heads-up style meeting. This is a final chance for the participants to review the collected data, to ask questions about it in relation to CMM, and to provide further data should they feel some areas have not be fully represented. Just as the assessment team should share a close opinion as to the ultimate findings, so should the participants. The assessment might consider going over the course of the assessment: from the collection methodology, to the points looked at in CMM, to the summation and general conclusions.

Areas of disagreement should be noted and addressed, and ample time should be provided for the reconciliation of conflicting views. We hope that these will be few. If you based your findings on what you read and heard from the participants you should both be pretty much in consistent agreement.

One thing to be aware of at this time is the "pass-fail" feelings that may be generated from the presentation of findings. Usually an assessment is begun with a specific goal in mind: "We want to be recognized as a Level 2 (or 3) shop." If achievement of that goal is demonstrated through the assessment, well and good. But if it is not reached, there may be a general feeling of let-down, an anti-climatic, back-to-square-one resignation. I don't know how to avoid this, even though it is antithetical to the whole spirit of CMM. It sounds corny saying this, but any software development shop that is engaged in a conscientious process improvement program, is implementing it in line with CMM recommendations and is going to the time and expense to organize and conduct a valid assessment—well, in my opinion, that's a shop with a lot going for it. The kind of attention to detail evident probably spills over aplenty into the quality of its products. To as great a degree as possible, treat the assessment findings as a snapshot in time, stress a path to improvement, and establish some clear directives that can be immediately implemented to begin moving there.

Publish the Final Assessment Report

You have reached the endline here at step 18. The assessment is now finished. Time has been devoted to collecting data, reviewing data, organizing data, and re-reviewing it all with everyone involved. Now it's time to put your final conclusions on paper. Your final assessment report can take any shape you think best (your lead assessor should have some good practical experience here). But it should probably mimic your assessment plan in some way. The plan is what your sponsor used to approve the start of the process, so it might make sense to follow that structure in reporting the findings from the process. At any rate, what you should probably *always* provide in the report includes the following: a restatement of the purpose of the assessment, recaps of the projects and the KPAs assessed, identified areas of strength, identified areas of weakness, a KPA-satisfaction summary, and (if desired) a final Level rating. You may also wish to include in the report recommendations for action: short-term and long-term activities to address the findings in the report.

Deliver Report

With the final report finished, you can deliver it to the sponsor. The sponsor owns the results of the assessment, and all materials should at this time be relinquished to the sponsor. Remember that, even if this has been a formal CMM assessment, the sponsor need not release the findings of the report. That is the sponsor's choice exclusively. The sponsor can also elect not to send the results to the SEI; however, it is in the spirit of CMM to do so. The SEI will use the data to continue building its international repository of performance data, and this is used in a myriad of beneficial ways: to refine the CMM, to identify industry trends, and to enhance other management programs. The SEI will protect the confidentiality of all data received and will even support this through the use of nondisclosure statements. Deliver the report to the sponsors, but you will have to leave it to them as to what to do with the data, both internally and externally. Your final step (given that report delivery is simply a hand-off) will be to present the findings to the sponsors.

Hold Executive Session

The assessment process closes by opening a door on the future. Usually report delivery is followed with a presentation to the sponsor's executive management in order to present the findings and discuss any implications the findings hold. This can usually be accomplished in an overview meeting. The general objective of the meeting should be to clearly establish where the organization stands with regard to CMM and then to establish where the organization should move from here.

Timeline for an Assessment

How long does an assessment take? The answer depends on many factors: the size of your organization, the number of projects being assessed, the size of the projects being assessed, the level of experience of your team, and so on. I can offer you a general timeline, one that will give you a feel for the amount of time the whole process might take. Just as Steps 1 to 20 are designed not to teach you to become an assessment specialist, so too these timelines are not meant to be read as hard boundaries. Take them as a mechanism to help orient you and perhaps help you plan for future assessments. I split the timeline up into five parts:

Planning. This includes the steps to decide on the assessment, chose a lead assessor, pick an assessment team, train the team, create and approve the assessment plan, and prepare the team to begin the assessment. For these activities you might allow a span of 7 to 9 weeks.

Off-site review. This includes such activities as the kick-off meeting, questionnaire distribution and analysis, and document review. For these activities you might allow a span of 4 to 5 weeks.

On-site interviews. This step includes the interviews with the assessment participants and the collection of project artifacts to support the process and procedure reports. For these activities you might allow a span of 2 to 3 weeks

Prepare draft report. This includes drafting the report narrative, presenting the initial findings, and then refining them as needed with a degree of reinvestigation. For these activities you might allow about 3 weeks.

Prepare final report. This includes creating the final report, delivering it to the sponsor, and presenting an overview of the findings to the sponsor. For these activities you might allow a span of about 2 weeks.

Table 16.1   Typical Assessment Activity Time Requirements

Planning	7–9 weeks
Off-Site Review	4–5 weeks
On-Site Interviews	2–3 weeks
Prepare Draft	3 weeks
Prepare Final report	2 weeks
Total	**18–22 weeks**

Summary

As you have seen from the steps outlined in this chapter, an assessment can be a pretty intensive undertaking, taking time, money, and the use of your people. But the assessment process is essential to the progress of process improvement programs. To organizations serious about SPI and the CMM, I would recommend a full assessment every 18 to 30 months, depending on the maturity of your program. The assessments do not *have* to be formal in the sense of SEI endorsement and use of authorized lead assessors (although that's certainly not a bad idea), but they must occur. It is through regular periodic assessments that the full shape of your program comes into focus. Its practice should be an integral ingredient of any software development quality program. The key to knowing where you are is to assess where you stand. Continue this over time, and you'll know very well where've you've been and where you ought to go.

References

Ahern, Dennis, Richard Turner, Aaron Clouse. (2001). *Cmmi Distilled: A Practical Introduction to Integrated Process Improvement.* Addison Wesley Longman, Inc.

Bomarius, Frank and Markku Oivo. (2000). *Product Focused Software Process Improvement : Second International Conference, Profes 2000, Oulu, Finland, June 20–22, 2000: Proceedings International Conference Profes 2000 Staf.* Springer-Verlag New York, Inc.

Braithwaite, Timothy. (1994). *Information Service Excellence through TQM: Building Partnerships for Business Process Reengineering and Continuous Improvement.* ASQ Quality Press.

Bustard, Dave (Editor), Mark Norris (Editor), Peter Kawalek (Editor), David Bustard. (1995). *Systems Modeling for Business Process Improvement.* Artech House, Inc.

Cassidy, Anita and Keith Guggenberger. (2000). *A Practical Guide to Information Systems Process Improvement.* Saint Lucie Press.

Caputo, Kim. (1998). *CMM Implementation Guide: Choreographing Software Process Improvement.* Addison Wesley Longman, Inc.

Emam, Khaled El, Walcelio Melo (Editor), Jean-Normand Drouin (Editor). (1999). *Spice: The Theory and Practice of Software Process Improvement and Capability Determination.* IEEE Computer Society Press.

Emam, Khaled El (Editor) and Nazim H. Madhavji (Editor). (1999). *Elements of Software Process Assessment & Improvement.* IEEE Computer Society Press.

Florac, William A. and Anita D. Carleton. (1999). *Measuring the Software Process: Statistical Process Control for Software Process Improvement.* Addison Wesley Longman, Inc.

Grady, Robert B. (1997). *Successful Software Process Improvement.* Prentice Hall.

Grady, Robert B. (1992). *Practical Software Metrics for Project Management and Process Improvement.* Prentice Hall.

Kehoe, Raymond and Alka Jarvis. (1995). *ISO 9000-3: A Tool for Software Product and Process Improvement.* Springer-Verlag New York.

Kitchenham, Barbara A. (1996). *Software Metrics: Measurement for Software Process Improvement.* Blackwell Publishers.

Koomen, Tim and Martin Pol. (1999). *Test Process Improvement: Step-by-Step Guide to Structured Testing.* Addison Wesley Longman, Inc.

Lientz, Bennet P. P. and Kathryn P. Rea. (1998). *How to Plan and Implement Business Process Improvement.* Harcourt Brace College Publishers.

Lientz, Bennet P. P. and Kathryn P. Rea. (1999). *How to Plan and Implement Business Process Improvement: 2000.* Harcourt Brace College Publishers.

McGuire, Francis A. (Editor). (1986). *Computer Technology and the Aged: Implications and Applications for Activity Programs.* Haworth Press, Inc.

Putnam, Lawrence H. and Ware Myers. (1996). *Software Management: Planning, Reliability, and Process Improvement.* IEEE Computer Society Press.

Raynus, Joseph. (1998). *Software Process Improvement with CMM.* Artech House, Inc.

Sharp, Alec and Patrick McDermott. (2001). *Workflow Modeling: Tools for Process Improvement and Application Development.* Artech House, Inc.

Stimler, Saul. (1974). *Data Processing Systems: Their Performance, Evaluation, Measurement, and Improvement.* Stimler Associates.

Wilson, David N. (Editor) and Terence P. Rout (Editor). (1998). *Software Engineering Set: Implementing a Quality Management System and Software Process Assessment and Improvement.* Computational Mechanics, Incorporated.

Zahran, Sami. (1998). *Software Process Improvement: Successful Models and Strategies.* Addison Wesley Longman, Inc.

Annotated Level 2 Preassessment Questionnaire

Requirements Management Questions

1. Are system requirements allocated to software controlled to establish a *baseline* for software engineering and management use?

   In other words, does the software team keep the requirements document up to date, so that any changes can be traced across the life of the project, and these changes can be incorporated into new plans/schedules/etc?

2. As requirements change, are software plans, activities, and products changed to *keep consistent* with these requirements' changes? Are requirements maintained and accurately reflected in project plans, activities, and products?

   This is related to Question 1. The idea here is that requirements are so critical to a project that they must be the basis for all project plans and activities. The requirements must be carefully tracked and the project adjusted if and when the requirements change.

3. Is there a written organizational *policy* for managing system requirements allocated to software?

   The project should not begin without a policy (brief and succinct), signed by executive management, that states that the project will follow specific requirement management processes.

4. Has *responsibility* been established for analyzing the system requirements and allocating them to hardware, software, and other system components?

   There should be evidence that someone or some people on the project team was specifically appointed to analyze the requirements (for completeness and quality) before any work was begun to build to them. This prevents "blind acceptance" of potentially poor requirements.

5. Are requirements received and *analyzed* for quality?

   This relates to Question 4. Here the point is that *documented* requirements need to be received by the team and then analyzed by the appointed people. You can show evidence by a Requirements Analysis Report, status meeting minutes, etc.

6. Are allocated requirements documented and *configuration controlled*?

   This relates to Questions 1 and 2. The requirements document, because it is the basis for all work, must be kept consistent (version controlled) as requirements change or are adjusted over the life of a project.

7. Are *resources and funding* provided for managing the allocated requirements?

   Managing the requirements appropriately will take a certain amount of time and expense. You should be able to show on your project that you allocated human resources and capital expenditure in a manner appropriate to the scope of the activities.

8. Are those responsible for managing the system requirements *trained* to perform their activities?

   It's not enough to just appoint people to manage the requirements. You need to show that the people you appointed have been trained in the specific processes and procedures your project will use for requirements management.

9. Do software engineers *review the requirements* before they are incorporated into the software project?

   This relates to Questions 4 and 5. The idea here is that you just can't start working on the project until your team understands the requirements. You need to show that the software team has reviewed the requirements in order to establish a common understanding of their functions and comfort with their scope.

10. Does the software group use the allocated requirements as a *basis for software plans, work products, and activities*?

    You just show that all project planning (and this can be handled in your policy or process) is based first on the documented requirements.

11. Are *changes* to the allocated requirements reviewed and, once approved, incorporated into the software project?

    This relates to Question 6, version control. If the requirements change at any point during the project, you must be able to show that you adjusted the plans, schedule, costs, etc., to account for the changes. The idea here is that when the scope of the project changes, you must conscientiously change the plans of the project.

12. Is *traceability* of the requirements to their source requirements maintained?

    CMM is not super-strict about this, but the practice is a good one. You should keep an audit trail or a history of the changes to each requirement so that you can track the original intent, the modified intent, and the source of the change. This is a management mechanism that will help you measure effectiveness and efficiencies.

13. Are *measurements* made and used to determine the status of activities of managing requirements? (Examples include status of allocated requirements, change activity, cumulative changes, etc.)

    This relates to Question 12. To facilitate process improvement, you need to periodically collect measurements of the requirements management activities for your project. These measurements will be analyzed to discern strong areas and weak areas and ways to improve the RM processes.

14. Are activities for managing requirements *reviewed* with senior management on a periodic basis?

    Questions 14, 15, and 16 are all related. The goal here is to facilitate process improvement by reviewing how the processes for managing requirements went during the course of the project. The Software Project Manager should meet with senior management or the program group manager to discuss the big picture and meet with SQA to discuss any details SQA should also monitor RM activity during the life of the project, and maybe even with an outside consultant to investigate any new trends or developments in the discipline as a whole. Meeting minutes will usually serve as adequate evidence for this activity.

15. Are activities for managing the requirements *reviewed* with the project manager on a periodic and event-driven basis?

    (See Question 14 above.)

16. Is there an independent *quality assurance representative* or group that reviews and/or audits the activities and work products for managing the requirements?

    (See Question 14 above.)

Project Planning Questions

1. Are software *estimates* documented for use in planning and tracking the software project?

   The idea here is that the estimates you use to build a software development plan (cost, effort, schedule, etc.) can't be made up. They have to be documented on paper. Ideally they should be derived using some type of formula, and you should also document any risks or assumptions used when coming up with the estimates.

2. Do affected groups and individuals agree to their *commitments* related to the software project?

   The software development plan should contain (implicit or explicit) the commitments the project team will make to executive management and the customer. But the planner cannot just come up with the commitments without the team as a whole reviewing and approving the commitments. You should be able to show that the team was able to review and comment on the project plan before its official adoption.

3. Is there a written organizational *policy* for planning a software project?

   The project should not begin without a policy (brief and succinct), signed by executive management, that states that the project will follow specific project planning processes.

4. Is there a person designated to be *responsible* for negotiating commitments and developing the project's software development plan?

   There should be evidence that someone has been specifically appointed to plan the project and make the commitments necessary to realize the project goals. A staff assignment form or some other resource designator should suffice for this.

5. Are *plans coordinated* and commitment obtained from individuals and organizations responsible for performing and supporting plan execution?

   This relates to Question 2. Again the idea is that the planner does not plan in a vacuum. The planner must solicit planning data from the team and then run the results by the team prior to approval.

6. Is there a documented and approved *statement of work*?

   Before a planner can begin planning a project, a written SOW should exist. The SOW is a brief written overview of the purpose, scope, and objectives for the project. The SOW aligns the planner in the right direction for planning activities.

7. Are *responsibilities* for developing the software development plan assigned?

   There should be evidence that a project planner was specifically and officially assigned to produce an appropriate plan for the project.

8. Are *resources and funding* provided for planning the software project?

   Realistic software planning will require a capital commitment on the part of project management. You should be able to show that you have allocated adequate human resources and capital funding in a manner appropriate to conduct project planning activities for the project.

9. Are software managers, software engineers, and other individuals involved in the software project planning *trained* in software estimation and planning procedures?

   You should be able to demonstrate that the people who participate in project planning activities are trained to do so. This involves a few areas. The planner should be trained in the process of producing a plan (what steps to take to create it and get it approved), as well as in the contents of the plan (what kinds of information should a plan contain). The other team members should be trained in how to provide estimates from their various areas that will need to be delivered to the planner.

10. Does the software engineering group *participate in the proposal?*

    Many projects are not just software development projects. They might involve hardware, systems engineering, systems integration, etc. The software development effort then is a project within a larger PROJECT. The idea here is that the software engineering project team is not left out of the larger aspects of PROJECT planning. The software project team, or its representative, should have a voice in overall PROJECT planning.

11. Is software project planning *initiated in the early stages* of project planning?

    This relates to Question 10. The planning for the software development should begin early on with overall PROJECT planning. This ensures adequate opportunity for the creation of consistent, coordinated, and realistic plans.

12. Does the software engineering group participate with other affected groups in the *overall project planning* throughout the project's life?

    This relates to Questions 10 and 11. The idea here is that the software project team is not isolated from the other related project teams during the course of the overall PROJECT. There should be a mechanism for overall status consulting and feedback among all participating groups (such as status meetings, review meetings, etc.).

13. Are software project commitments made to individuals and groups external to the organization *reviewed with senior management* according to a documented procedure?

    Before any project commitments are made to anyone outside the organization, they should be first reviewed and approved by senior management. This activity, to be made official, should be conducted according to a written procedure, and the project plans should retain a copy of this procedure.

14. Is a *software life cycle* with predefined stages of manageable size identified or defined?

    Part of the project plan should contain a description of the software development life cycle being used on the project (waterfall, spiral, RAD, etc.). The selected life cycle should be accompanied by the appropriate Work Breakdown Structure affiliated with the methodology.

15. Is the project's software development plan developed according to a *documented procedure*?

    The planner cannot just create a plan that suits his or her fancy. The plan must be created according to a documented procedure. The procedure will usually point to a template for the contents of the plan and outline the steps that must be followed to create the plan and get it officially approved.

16. Is the software project plan *documented*?

    This one is obvious: The plan can't just exist in one's head. It must be documented so that all team members have access to it.

17. Are project *tasks and responsibilities* established?

    The documented software development plan should contain (in addition to other things) a list of tasks and the teams that will be responsible for executing the tasks.

18. Are *software work products* needed to establish and maintain control of the software project identified?

    The documented software development plan should specifically identify the work products that will be produced during the project life cycle. This will usually range from such items as user manuals and source code modules, to SQA audits, configuration management audits, and status meeting reports.

19. Are project attributes like *size or complexity* estimated?

    The plan should contain (somewhere in it, usually in the budget or schedule section) some sort of estimate that quantifies the size or complexity of the project. You can use any sizing method you want: lines of code, function points, etc.

20. Are *estimates for the size* of the software work products (or changes to the size of software work products) derived according to a documented procedure?

    Questions 20, 21, and 22 are all related. The idea here is that the people who need to turn in estimates to the project planner (the analysts, designers, coders, tech writers, testers, etc.) do so in a way that is consistent across groups. To do this you should provide them with some type of estimating formula or procedure they can all use. This ensures both consistency within the project and a tool for measuring effectiveness across projects (for the purpose of process improvement).

21. Are *estimates for the software project's effort and costs* derived according to a documented procedure? Are historical data or models used to determine the project effort and cost?

    (See Question 20 above.)

22. Are *estimates for the project's critical computer resources* derived according to a documented procedure?

    (See Question 20 above.)

23. Are *schedules* established and maintained? Is the project's schedule derived according to a documented procedure? Are subordinate plans established and maintained?

    The schedule for the project should be derived from the estimates turned in from the project team members, and you should use a documented procedure to turn the estimates into a formal timeline.

24. Are *software risks* associated with cost, resources, schedule, and technical aspects identified, assessed, and documented?

    Part of the plan should contain a listing of all the risks and assumptions that were taken into consideration when developing the plan. Identifying these will assist with contingencies should any plan changes arise. They can also be used to help plan future projects similar in size, mission, and scope.

25. Are plans for the project's software engineering *facilities and support tools* prepared?

    If your project is going to require the scheduling and use of shared computer resources, then you must make sure that this planning is reflected in the overall plan. As this may be a critical path item—if you don't have access to it, the project may grind to a halt—you should work its use carefully and appropriately into your plan.

26. Is a plan for *needed knowledge and skills* developed for the project?

    In the planning stages of the project, you will need to think through many items (cost, schedule, methodology, etc.). But you will also have to plan for the right kinds of resources you will need for the project: the experience levels, the technical skill sets and the right business knowledge. This should be accounted for in the project plan.

27. Is software *planning data* recorded (estimates, assumption, etc.)? Is there an activity to reconcile the plan to reflect available and projected resources?

    When you create the project plan, you need to keep the raw numbers that you used to generate the cost, schedule, resource requirements, etc. These can be kept in an appendix to the plan. These raw numbers can be consulted in the future to improve estimating and planning processes. You should also have an opportunity with the first draft of the plan to revise in order to address any fixed resource, cost, or schedule constraints.

28. Are *reviews* of project plans with stakeholders conducted?

    When a draft of the plan is complete, you should allow the various members of the project team to review it prior to approval. Executive management as well as the client should also have an opportunity to review it. The idea here is to gain common consensus on the suitability of the plan prior to its implementation.

29. Are *measurements* made to determine the status of software planning activities (for example, milestone completion against the plan, work completed against the plan, effort expended against the plan, etc.)?

    Throughout the planning process you should keep measurements of the planning process. For example, you should be able to compare how long it took to create the plan against the various size and cost estimates contained in the plan. You are free to come up with your own measures. Their intent should be to provide you with data by which you can analyze the effectiveness of the planning process with a view toward improvement.

30. Are activities for software project planning *reviewed* with senior management on a periodic basis?

    Questions 30, 31, and 32 are all related. The goal here is to facilitate process improvement by reviewing how the processes for project planning went during the course of the effort. The Software Project Manager should meet with senior management or the program group manager to discuss the big picture and meet with SQA to discuss any details. SQA should also monitor planning activity. Meeting minutes will usually serve as adequate evidence for this activity.

31. Are activities for software project planning *reviewed* with the project manager on a periodic and event-driven basis?

    (See Question 30 above.)

32. Is there an independent quality assurance representative or group that *reviews and/or audits* the activities and work products for software project planning?

    (See Question 30 above.)

Project Tracking and Oversight Questions

1. Are actual results and performance *tracked* against the software plans?

    The idea here is to be able to demonstrate that the software project manager not only actively tracked the activity for the project, but did so against the activity that was detailed in the software development plan. This is essential to CMM: to create a plan and then to follow it. The tracking activity should focus on monitoring actuals versus planned for the following general areas: component size and cost, schedule, general progress, technical activity, required resources and facilities, and risks.

    See Questions 16, 17, 18, 19, and 20.

2. Are *corrective actions* taken and managed to closure when actual results and performance deviate significantly from the software plans?

    This relates to Question 1 above. When it appears that project activity is deviating from the plan, the software project manager must be able to show that corrective actions were taken to adjust either the plan or the project activity; in essence and to realign the two so that they are in sync.

    See Questions 16, 17, 18, 19, 20.

3. Are changes to software commitments *agreed* to by the affected groups and individuals?

    You should be able to show that project changes were not just blindly thrown into the mix. It is important to assess the changes and then have them reviewed with all affected parties prior to official adoption. Affected parties can be the project team, executive management, the client, etc.

4. Is a project *software manager designated* to be responsible for the project's software activities and results?

    There should be evidence that someone has been specifically appointed to manage the project and track the activities and commitments necessary to realize the project goals. A staff assignment form or some other resource designator should suffice for this.

5. Does the project follow a written organizational *policy* for managing the software project?

    The project should not begin without a policy (brief and succinct), signed by executive management, that states that the project will follow specific project management processes.

6. Is the software development *plan* for the software project documented and approved?

    This is essential. In order for the project to begin, a documented and approved Software Development Plan must exist.

7. Does the project software manager explicitly assign *responsibility* for software work products and activities?

   At the start of the project, usually at a kick-off meeting (or something similar), the project manager will go over the plan with the team. During this review, the manager should explicitly assign (through a task form or similar type of document) which team members are responsible for which specific work products.

8. Are adequate *resources and funding* provided for tracking the software project?

   Conscientious software project management will require a capital commitment on the part of executive project management. You should be able to show that you have allocated adequate human resources and capital funding to provide a project manager to oversee software development activities for the project.

9. Are software managers *trained* in managing the technical and personnel aspects of the software project?

   You should be able to demonstrate that the people who participate in project tracking activities are trained to do so. This involves a few areas. The PM should be trained in the process of tracking against the plan (what steps to take to manage it). The other team members should be trained in how to work within the tracking arena.

10. Do first-line software managers receive *orientation* in the technical aspects of the software project?

    You should be able to show that prior to beginning work on the project, the team members received orientation to the general technical approach and architecture for the project.

11. Is a *documented software development plan* used for tracking the software activities and communicating status?

    (See Question 6 above.)

12. Is the project's software development plan *revised* according to a documented procedure?

    The project should have available to it a documented procedure that is used to guide how changes to the project's plan are initiated, assessed, reviewed, approved, and distributed.

13. Are software project *commitments and changes to commitments* made to individuals and groups external to the organization reviewed with senior management according to a documented procedure?

    The project should have available to it a documented procedure that is used to guide how changes to project commitments (such as scope, schedule, cost, etc.) are initiated, assessed, reviewed, approved, and distributed.

14. Are approved changes to commitments that affect the software project *communicated to the members of the software engineering group* and other software-related groups?

    (See Question 3 above.)

15. Is the *size* of the software work products (or the size of the changes to the software work products) *tracked* and corrective actions taken when necessary?

    (See Questions 1 and 2.)

16. Are the project's *actual work*, product, and task attributes *tracked* and corrective actions taken when necessary?

    (See Questions 1 and 2.)

17. Are the project's *progress* and performance *tracked* and corrective actions taken when necessary?

    (See Questions 1 and 2.)

18. Are the project's *critical facilities* (like computer resources) *tracked* and corrective actions taken when necessary?

    (See Questions 1 and 2.)

19. Is the project's software *schedule tracked* and corrective actions taken when necessary?

    (See Questions 1 and 2.)

20. Are software engineering technical *activities tracked* and corrective actions taken when necessary?

    (See Questions 1 and 2.)

21. Are software *risks* associated with cost, resource, schedule, and technical aspects of the project *tracked*?

    (See Questions 1 and 2.)

22. Are actual *measurement data* and replanning data for the software project recorded?

    (See Question 25 below.)

23. Does the software engineering group conduct periodic internal *reviews* to track technical progress, plans, performance, and issues against the software development plan?

    Here and in Question 24 below, CMM wants to see evidence of two things. First, that periodic technical status reviews are conducted for the project. These can be software specific status meetings, even internal to the individual teams. Second, evidence that general, overall status meetings were held with all project members (or their representatives) as a way to check on the coordinated progress of the project as a whole.

24. Are *formal reviews* conducted at selected project milestones according to a documented procedure? These reviews address the accomplishments and results of the software project.

    (See Question 24 above.)

25. Are *measurements* made and used to determine the status of the software tracking and oversight activities (for example, the effort expended in performing tracking and oversight activities; change activity for the software development plan; changes to size estimates of the software work products, etc.)?

    Throughout the tracking you should keep measurements of the various activities. You are free to come up with your own measures. Their intent should be to provide you with data by which you can analyze the effectiveness of the tracking process with a view toward improvement.

26. Are activities for software project tracking and oversight *reviewed* with senior management on a periodic basis?

    Questions 26, 27, and 28 are all related. The goal here is to facilitate process improvement by reviewing how the processes for project tracking went during the course of the effort. The Software Project Manager should meet with senior management or the program group manager to discuss the big picture and meet with SQA to discuss any details. (SQA should also monitor the tracking activity.) Meeting minutes will usually serve as adequate evidence for this activity.

27. Are the activities for software project tracking and oversight *reviewed* with the project manager on a periodic and event-driven basis?

    (See Question 26 above.)

28. Is there an independent *quality assurance representative* or group that reviews and/or audits the activities and work products for software project tracking and oversight?

    (See Question 26 above.)

Software Quality Assurance Questions

1. Are quality assurance activities *planned*?

   At the beginning of a project, when project planning starts, the SQA group should develop an SQA plan specific to the project. This plan, while it can serve as a standalone document, should also be (at the end of the process) integrated into the overall software development plan.

2. Does quality assurance provide objective *verification* that software products and activities adhere to applicable standards, procedures, and requirements?

   Using the plan as a map for activity, an SQA analyst should provide SQA services according to the plan for the project. The role of SQA is to keep the project in line with accepted standards, practices, and processes.

3. Are affected groups and individuals *informed* of quality assurance activities and results?

   The SQA is a role integrated with the other activity of the team. When the SQA analyst inspects the practices and processes, he should quickly report the results back to the team so the team knows how it is doing on an on-going basis.

4. Are identified noncompliance issues *escalated* as necessary for resolution?

   If the SQA analyst encounters a noncompliance issue that cannot be resolved by working *with the project manager within the project team*, then SQA should take the issue to executive management for resolution. This should be a rare event, but if it does happen, it means there is a serious process or practice issue at hand. And so it should be addressed at a high level.

5. Does the project follow a written organizational *policy* for implementing quality assurance?

   The project should not begin without a policy (brief and succinct), signed by executive management, that states that the project will follow defined SQA processes.

6. Is there a group *responsible* for coordinating and implementing quality assurance for the project?

   There should be evidence that someone or some group has been specifically appointed to conduct the SQA activity and audits fore the various phases of the project. A staff assignment form or some other resource designator should suffice for this.

7. Are adequate *funds* provided for performing the quality assurance activities?

   To properly oversee process quality, the project must have an SQA resource attached for the life of the project. You should be able to show that you have allocated adequate human resources and capital funding in a manner appropriate to conduct the SQA activities for the project.

8. Is there a maintained *budget* for the quality assurance group?

    Questions 8 and 9 are related. You should be able to show that you have pro-vided adequate resources and funding for the project in order to support the role of the SQA analyst and the conscientious implementation of the SQA plan. You can prove this with such artifacts as an SQA budget item in the plan; SQA staff assignment sheets for the project, a project org chart, and other such related material.

9. Are adequate *resources* provided for performing the quality assurance activities?

    (See Question 8 above.)

10. Are members of the quality assurance group *trained* to perform their activities?

    You should be able to demonstrate that the people who serve in the SQA group are trained to do so. This involves a few areas. The SQA analyst should be trained in the process of SQA planning and auditing. The other team members should receive orientation as to what SQA will expect of them during the project and also an overview of the value and the role of SQA on the project.

11. Do members of the project receive *orientation* on the roles, responsibilities, authority, and value of the quality assurance group at project inception?

    (See Question 10 above.)

12. Does the quality assurance plan adhere to documented *procedures*?

    This relates to Question 1. Every project needs an SQA plan developed specifi-cally for it. To make sure that the SQA plan is comprehensive and adequate, you should provide the SQA planner with a documented procedure for developing the SQA plan. This is usually evidenced by two items: a template outlining the contents of the plan and a short process that details how to create the plan and what steps to take to get it officially approved.

13. Are the quality assurance group's *activities* performed in accordance with the plan?

    This is important. You should be able to show evidence that, during the life of the project, the SQA analyst actually carried out the SQA activities detailed in the plan. This is central to the spirit of CMM: You create a plan, then you follow the plan.

14. Does the quality assurance group *participate in the preparation* and review of the software development plan, standards, and procedures?

    In addition to creating an SQA plan for the project, the SQA group should review initial drafts of the software development plan (created by the software project planner/manager). The purpose of this step is to allow SQA to catch early on any deviances from standards, practices, and processes that might have crept into the plan. This can be evidenced by review meeting minutes or review notes.

15. Does the quality assurance group *review* the software project activities to verify compliance?

    Questions 15 and 16 are related, and tie back to Questions 2 and 13. SQA should perform two general duties on the project. 1) SQA should periodically audit the project activities; that is, the activities of the various teams. This is to ensure practice compliance. 2) SQA should also audit specific work products (identified in the SQA plan) to measure standards compliance.

16. Does the quality assurance group *audit* designated work products to verify compliance?

(See Question 15 above.)

17. Does the quality assurance group *report* the results of its activities to the software project group?

This is related to Questions 15 and 16. Once the SQA analyst has conducted an audit, it is important to report back to the project team the results of the audit. This is usually done via some form of audit report. The idea here is to let the team know how it is doing in terms of compliance as the project is going along. This gives the team the ability to correct any process deviances that might be occurring.

18. Are *deviations identified* in the software activities and work products documented and handled according to a documented procedure?

When an SQA audit encounters a noncompliance issue during an audit or inspection, it should be corrected according to a written procedure. The procedure should state the steps necessary to record the issue, present the issue to the team, resolve the issue, and then verify its resolution.

19. Are *measurements* used to determine the status of the quality assurance activities?

To facilitate process improvement, you need to periodically collect measurements of the SQA activities for your project. These measurements will be analyzed to discern strong areas and weak areas within the SQA process, and help point to ways to improve the SQA role. These measurements can be anything you find helpful, such as the total number of noncompliance issues, the team areas where most issues arose, etc.

20. Are quality assurance activities *reviewed* with senior management on a periodic basis?

Questions 20, 21, and 22 are all related. The goal here is to facilitate process improvement by reviewing how the processes for SQA went during the course of the effort. The SQA analyst and the Software Project Manager should meet with senior management or the program group manager to discuss the big picture and maybe even meet with an outside independent consultant for an objective third-party analysis.

21. Are quality assurance activities *reviewed* with the project manager on both a periodic and event-driven basis?

(See Question 20 above.)

22. Do experts independent of the quality assurance group periodically *review* the activities and work products of the group?

(See Question 20 above.)

23. Are there provisions in place for *user feedback*?

    In addition to SQA reviews with project management and executive management, the members of the project team should be provided some kind of mechanism to provide feedback on the SQA role to management and to the SQA group. A simple questionnaire or project review meeting can account for this.

24. Is the quality assurance plan *integrated* into the overall software project plan?

    (See Question 1 above.)

25. Are the *roles and responsibilities* of the quality assurance group clearly defined?

    Part of the SQA plan, and thus part of the overall software development plan, should be a section that details just what role SQA will play on the project and what activities SQA will carry out. The purpose of this is to let the project team know just what they can expect from the role of SQA regarding their work and activities.

Subcontract Management / Supplier Agreement Management Questions

1. Are suppliers and products *selected* to satisfy project requirements?

   You should be able to show that you selected the product/vendor because it had the ability to address specific product needs. To do you should have a documented procedure in place that outlines how the vendor/product is reviewed and then selected for participation in the project. See Questions 13 and 14 below.

2. Are *agreements* with the suppliers established and maintained?

   You should be able to show that products/vendors were managed through a formal contractual arrangement in which commitments were clearly delineated.

3. Are the supplier's performance and results *monitored* to ensure that the agreement is met?

   A member of your project team has to be appointed to continually monitor vendor performance.

4. Does the project *accept and transfer* products from the supplier?

   You must have a formal mechanism in place for your project to review, accept, and assume (legal) ownership of the contracted-for products.

   Part of this mechanism may include an acceptance test process as well as a procedure for work product transfer (the steps to monitor the transfer.) See Questions 24 and 25.

5. Does the project follow a written organizational *policy* for managing subcontractors or suppliers?

   The project should not begin without a policy (brief and succinct), signed by executive management, that states that the project will follow specific management processes for handling subcontracted work.

6. Is a person designated to be *responsible* for establishing and managing subcontracts or suppliers?

   There should be evidence that someone as chief contact has been specifically appointed to manage the plans and activities of the subcontractor. A staff assignment form or some other resource designator should suffice for this.

7. Are adequate *resources and funding* provided for selecting and managing the subcontractors or suppliers?

   To properly oversee the subcontractor's activities you should be able to show that you have allocated adequate human resources and capital funding for the oversight activities.

8. Are those responsible for establishing and managing subcontractors and suppliers *trained* to perform these activities?

   You should be able to demonstrate that the people who serve in vendor management are trained to do so. You should also be able to show that the vendor managers have been trained in the scope, mission, and purpose of the project so that they can manage from an informed perspective. See Question 9 below.

9. Do those responsible for managing the subcontractors or suppliers receive *orientation* in the technical aspects of the subcontract?

   (See Question 8 above.)

10. Is the work to be subcontracted *defined and planned* according to a documented procedure?

    Your project should have a documented subcontractor management plan in place that details exactly what is expected of the vendor/product. The following items should be featured as part of the plan: the exact needs that the vendor will fulfill (the high level objectives and services) and the system requirements that will addressed by the vendor services/product. This plan should be considered part of the contract between the project and the vendor, and this plan should be by the vendor manager as the chief tracking tool during the course of the project. See Questions 11, 12, 15, 16, and 17.

11. Have the *needs* to be fulfilled by sources outside the project been determined?

    (See Question 10 above.)

12. Have the project *requirements* for the products being acquired been established and maintained?

    (See Question 10 above.)

13. Is the subcontractor or supplier selected based on an *evaluation* of the ability to perform the work, according to a documented procedure?

    (See Question 1 above.)

14. Have *off-the-shelf products* been selected to satisfy the project's requirements?

    (See Question 1 above.)

15. Are the *contractual agreements* between the project and the subcontractor or supplier used as the basis for managing the subcontract?

    (See Question 10 above.)

16. Is the subcontractor's *development plan* reviewed and approved by the project?

    (See Question 10 above.)

17. Is the documented and approved subcontractor's development plan used to *track* the software activities and communicate status? Is the supplier's progress and performance monitored and evaluated against the supplier agreement?

    (See Question 10 above.)

18. Does the project management conduct periodic status/coordination *reviews* with the subcontractor or supplier?

    Questions 19, 20, 21, and 26 are all related. The idea here is for project management and vendor management to regularly track what the external group is doing in relation to the project. You should conduct three kinds of reviews: informal status reviews, technical progress reviews, and general project reviews.

19. Are periodic technical *reviews* and interchanges held with the subcontractor or supplier?

    (See Question 19 above.)

20. Are *formal reviews* conducted at selected milestones according to a documented procedure? These reviews address the subcontractor or supplier's accomplishments and results.

    (See Question 19 above.)

21. Are the subcontractor or supplier's quality assurance activities *monitored*?

    Part of the vendor management activities is to actively monitor the vendor's SQA and CM work. This is to ensure the project team that the external resources are practicing the proper project management disciplines in accordance with internal disciplines.

22. Are the subcontractor or supplier's configuration management activities *monitored*?

    (See Question 22 above.)

23. Is an *acceptance test* conducted as part of the delivery of the subcontractor or supplier's products, according to a documented procedure?

    (See Question 4 above.)

24. Is the transition of the acquired products from the supplier to the project *monitored*?

    (See Question 4 above.)

25. Is the subcontractor or supplier's performance *evaluated* on a periodic basis, and is this evaluation reviewed with the subcontractor or supplier?

    (See Question 19 above.)

26. Are *measurements* made and used to determine the status of the activities for managing the subcontractor or supplier (for example, the cost of the activities for managing the subcontractor compared to the plan, the actual delivery dates for supplier products compared to the plan, etc.)?

    To facilitate process improvement, the vendor manager should periodically collect measurements of the vendor management activities for the project. These measurements will be analyzed to discern strong areas and weak areas within this area. These measurements can be anything you find helpful.

27. Are activities for managing the subcontractor or supplier *reviewed* with senior management on a periodic basis?

    Questions 27, 28, and 29 are all related. The goal here is to facilitate process improvement by reviewing how the processes for subcontractor management went during the course of the effort. The vendor manager and the software project manager should meet with senior management or the program group manager to discuss the big picture and then meet with SQA to discuss any details. Meeting minutes will usually serve as adequate evidence for this activity.

28. Are the activities for managing the subcontractor or supplier *reviewed* with the project manager on a periodic and event-driven basis?

    (See Question 27.)

29. Is there an independent *quality assurance representative* or group that reviews and/or audits the activities associated with managing the subcontractor or supplier?

    (See Question 27.)

Configuration Management Questions

1. Are configuration management activities *planned*?

   At the beginning of a project, when project planning and SQA planning starts, the Configuration Management group (or analyst) should develop a CM plan specific to the project. This plan, while it can serve as a standalone document, should also be (at the end of the process) integrated into the overall software development plan.

2. Are selected *work products* identified, controlled, and available?

   A major part of the documented CM plan is the identification of what work products will be managed. This can be as basic as the software source code and technical documentation, or it can be very extensive, to include project plans, schedules, etc. Once these work products are identified they need to be actively controlled for change over the life of the project. This is usually accomplished by managing them through some form of Library System, which houses the current and past versions for reference.

   This is further addressed in Questions 12 and 13 below.

3. Are *changes* to identified work products controlled?

   The chief role of the CM analyst (and this should be documented in the CM plan) is to track and manage changes across the identified work products.

4. Are affected groups and individuals informed of the *status and content* of software baselines?

   During the course of the project, the CM analyst must periodically issue reports to the project team that update the team as to the status of the configuration management library, including the latest versions of baselined software. A regular configuration management status report can account for this.

5. Does the project follow a written organizational *policy* for implementing configuration management?

   The project should not begin without a policy (brief and succinct), signed by executive management, that states that the project will follow defined configuration management processes.

6. Is there a *board* having the *authority* for managing the project's baselines?

   A Change Control Board or a Configuration Management Board must exist, and the project team must have access to it.

7. Is there a group that is *responsible* for coordinating and implementing configuration management for the project?

   There should be evidence that someone or some group has been specifically appointed to conduct the configuration management activities for the project. A staff assignment form or some other resource designator should suffice for this.

8. Are there adequate *resources and funding* for performing configuration management?

To properly conduct configuration management and version control activities, the project must have a CM resource attached for the life cycle. You should be able to show that you have allocated adequate human resources and capital funding in a manner appropriate to conduct the CM activities for the project.

9. Are members of the software engineering group and other software related groups *trained* to perform configuration management activities?

You should be able to demonstrate that the people who participate in configuration management activities are trained to do so. This involves a few areas. The CM analyst should be trained in the processes relating to CM. The analyst should also be trained in any CM tools being used on the project. The other members of the project team should be trained in how to work within CM guidelines.

10. Has a configuration management plan been prepared for each project according to a *documented procedure*?

This relates to Question 1. Every project needs an CM plan developed specifically for it. To make sure that the CM plan is comprehensive and adequate, you should provide the CM planner with a documented procedure for developing the plan. This is usually evidenced by two items: a template outlining the contents of the plan and a short process that details how to create the plan and what steps to take to get it officially approved.

11. Is a documented and approved *configuration management plan* used as the basis for performing configuration management activities?

As with SQA, this is important. You should be able to show evidence that, during the life of the project, the CM analyst actually carried out the CM activities detailed in the plan. This is central to the spirit of CMM: You create a plan, then you follow the plan.

12. Is there a configuration management *library system* as a repository for the software baselines?

(See Question 2 above.)

13. Are the *work products* to be placed under configuration management identified?

(See Question 2 above.)

14. Are *change requests* and problem reports for all configuration items initiated, recorded, reviewed, approved, and tracked according to a documented procedure?

You should use a documented procedure that guides how your project will deal with change requests. This procedure should detail the steps required to initiate, record, assess, review, and approve change requests.

15. Are changes to baselines controlled according to a *documented procedure*?

You should use a documented procedure that guides how your project will release new software baselines.

16. Is the release of products from the baseline library controlled according to a *documented procedure*?

    You should use a documented procedure that guides how your project will manage checking-in/checking-out products from the library system.

17. Is the status of configuration items recorded according to a *documented procedure*?

    You should use a documented procedure that guides how your project will record the status of configuration items in the library system.

18. Are *standard reports* documenting configuration management activities and the contents of the baselines developed and made available to affected groups and individuals?

    (See Question 4 above.)

19. Are *baseline audits* conducted according to a documented procedure?

    This is related to Question 20 below. You should use a documented procedure that guides how your project will conduct baseline audits. This is the activity where the CM will inspect the contents of the library system to audit the integrity and the work-traceability of all the entries and work products in the system. From this should emerge an audit report. Baseline audits should be conducted at regular intervals during the life of the project. These intervals should be identified in the CM plan.

20. Are *records* established and maintained of configuration items?

    (See Question 19 above.)

21. Are *measurements* made and used to determine the status of configuration management activities (like the number of change requests processed per unit time, work completed, effort expended, etc.)?

    To facilitate process improvement, you need to periodically collect measurements of the CM activities for your project. These measurements will be analyzed to discern strong areas and weak areas within the CM process and library system and help to point to ways to improve the CM role.

22. Are configuration management activities *reviewed* with senior management on a periodic basis?

    Questions 22, 23, and 25 are all related. The goal here is to facilitate process improvement by reviewing how the processes for CM went during the course of the effort. The CM and the software project manager should meet with senior management or the program group manager to discuss the big picture and meet with SQA to discuss any details. Meeting minutes will usually serve as adequate evidence for this activity.

23. Are configuration management activities *reviewed* with the project manager on both a periodic and event-driven basis?

    (See Question 22 above.)

24. Does the configuration management group periodically *audit baselines* to verify that they conform to the documentation that defines them?

    (See Question 19 above.)

25. Does the *quality assurance group* review or audit the activities and work products for configuration management and report the results?

    (See Question 22 above.)

Samples of Level 2 Policies

ACORN Corp.

ACME PROJECT

Policy for Requirements Management

Control: Version 1.1
Effective: 11/30/00
POC:

Overview
The purpose of Requirements Management is to establish a common understanding between the customer, ACORN senior management, and the ACME development team concerning the requirements that will be addressed by the software project. Requirements Management involves establishing and maintaining this understanding over the life of the project. To promote this, the ACME project team will manage the requirements in such a way as to ensure their proper documentation, thorough review, and consistency with all project activity. This approach covers both the technical and non-technical (e.g., delivery dates) requirements related to the ACME project. In support of this, the following activities are hereby endorsed by ACME project management and ACORN senior management as points of policy for Requirements Management conduct.

Policy Points

1. All requirements relevant to ACME will be documented.

2. System requirements allocated to ACME will be controlled to establish a base line for software engineering and management use.

3. Software plans, products, and activities will be kept consistent with the system requirements allocated to software.

4. ACME software project management will establish responsibility for analyzing the system requirements and allocating them to hardware, software, and other system components.

5. ACME software project management will make sure that adequate resources and funding have been provided for managing the allocated requirements.

6. As necessary, members of ACME's software engineering group (and other software-related groups) will be trained to perform their Requirements Management activities.

7. ACME's software engineering group will review the allocated requirements before they are officially incorporated into the software project.

8. ACME software project management will use the allocated requirements as the basis for all software plans, work products, and activities.

9. The ACME project team will review any changes to the allocated requirements before they are incorporated into the software project.

10. ACME software project management will take defined measurements throughout the course of the project to determine the status of the activities for managing the allocated requirements.

11. ACME's software project management will review the activities for managing the allocated requirements with ACORN senior management on a periodic basis.

12. ACME's software project management will review the activities for managing the allocated requirements with the general project manager on both a periodic and event-driven basis.

13. ACME's software project management will facilitate reviews and/or audits by the software quality assurance group on the activities and work products for managing the allocated requirements and will receive compliance reports from the SQA effort.

❖

RESPONSIBILITY: ACME Software Project Managers are responsible for implementing this policy.

APPROVED:

_____

ACME Software Project Management　　　　　　　　　Date

_____

ACME Project Management　　　　　　　　　　　　　　Date

_____

ACORN Senior Management　　　　　　　　　　　　　Date

ACORN Corp.

ACME PROJECT

Policy for Requirements Management

Control: Version 1.1
Effective: 11/30/00
POC:

Overview

The purpose of Requirements Management is to establish a common understanding between the customer, ACORN senior management, and the ACME development team concerning the requirements that will be addressed by the software project. Requirements Management involves establishing and maintaining this understanding over the life of the project. To promote this, the ACME project team will manage the requirements in such a way as to ensure their proper documentation, thorough review, and consistency with all project activity. This approach covers both the technical and non-technical (e.g., delivery dates) requirements related to the ACME project. In support of this, the following activities are hereby endorsed by ACME project management and ACORN senior management as points of policy for Requirements Management conduct.

Policy Points

1. All ACME requirements will be documented.

2. ACME requirements will be approved by the software managers and impacted groups before any project commitments are made.

3. Software plans and activities for ACME will be kept consistent with any changes to the requirements.

❖

RESPONSIBILITY: ACME Software Project Managers are responsible for implementing this policy.

APPROVED:

ACME Software Project Management   Date

ACME Project Management   Date

ACORN Senior Management   Date

ACORN Corp.

ACME PROJECT

Policy for Software Project Planning

Control: Version 1.1
Effective: 11/30/00
POC:

Overview

The purpose of Software Project Planning is to establish reasonable plans for performing the software engineering and managing the software project. Software Project Planning involves first establishing the commitments to be delivered under the work and
then developing estimates for the work to be performed and defining the plan to perform the work. To promote this, the ACME project team will manage software project
planning in such a way as to ensure the use of approved requirements as the basis for all
planning, provide for the review of all commitments and development plans, and facilitate the proper control of the plan over the course of the ACME project. In support of
this, the following activities are hereby endorsed by ACME project management and
ACORN senior management as points of policy for Software Project Planning conduct.

Policy Points

1. Before project planning begins, an approved Statement of Work will exist for the
    project.

2. Software estimates developed for use in planning and tracking the software
    project will be documented.

3. Software project activities and commitments will be documented.

4. Groups and individuals that are impacted by established project commitments
    will agree to their commitments prior to work.

5. ACME project management will appoint a software project manager who will be
    responsible for negotiating commitments and developing the project's software
    development plan.

6. ACME software project management will be sure to allow for adequate
    resources and funding for planning the software project.

7. Software managers, software engineers, and other individuals involved in ACME
    software project planning will be trained in the estimating and planning proce-
    dures applicable to their areas of responsibility.

8. The ACME software engineering group will participate on the project proposal
    team.

9. ACME project management will initiate software project planning in the early stages of, and in parallel with, the overall project planning.

10. ACORN senior management will review software project commitments made to individuals and groups external to the organization prior to commitment approval.

11. The ACME software development plan (SDP) will be created according to a documented procedure.

12. Estimates for the size of the software work products, the cost and effort of the project, needed computer resources, project timeline, and any related risks will all be documented and derived according to a documented procedure.

13. ACME software project management will record and save all software planning data.

14. ACME software project management will take periodic measurements to determine the status of the software planning activities.

15. ACME software project management will review the activities for software project planning with ACORN senior management on a periodic basis.

16. ACME software project management will review the activities for software project planning with the ACME project manager on both a periodic and event-driven basis.

17. ACME software project management will allow reviews or audits by the software quality assurance group on the activities and work products for software project planning and will receive reports on the results.

❖

RESPONSIBILITY: ACME Software Project Managers are responsible for implementing this policy.

APPROVED:

_____

ACME Software Project Management   Date

_____

ACME Project Management   Date

_____

ACORN Senior Management   Date

ACORN Corp.

ACME PROJECT

Policy for Software Project Planning

Control: Version 1.1
Effective: 11/30/00
POC:

Overview

The purpose of Software Project Planning is to establish reasonable plans for performing the software engineering and managing the software project. Software Project Planning involves first establishing the commitments to be delivered under the work and then developing estimates for the work to be performed and defining the plan to perform the work. To promote this, the ACME project team will manage software project planning in such a way as to ensure the use of approved requirements as the basis for all planning, provide for the review of all commitments and development plans, and facilitate the proper control of the plan over the course of the ACME project. In support of this, the following activities are hereby endorsed by ACME project management and ACORN senior management as points of policy for Software Project Planning conduct.

Policy Points

1. Only approved requirements will be used as the basis for ACME project planning.

2. The project's commitments on ACME will be negotiated between project management, the software managers, and other impacted managers.

3. Affected groups will review the software size estimates, effort and cost estimates, schedules, and other commitments prior to approval.

4. Senior management will review all commitments made to external organizations regarding ACME.

5. The ACME Software Development Plan will be managed and version controlled.

❖

RESPONSIBILITY: ACME Software Project Managers are responsible for implementing this policy.

APPROVED:

ACME Software Project Management   Date

ACME Project Management   Date

ACORN Senior Management   Date

ACORN Corp.

ACME PROJECT

Policy for Software Project Tracking and Oversight

Control: Version 1.1
Effective: 11/30/00
POC:

Overview

The purpose of Software Project Tracking and Oversight is to provide adequate visibility into the actual activities and progress on ACME so that management can take effective actions when performance deviates significantly from the software plans. Software Project Tracking and Oversight involves tracking and reviewing the software accomplishments and results against documented estimates, commitments, and plans, and adjusting these plans based on the actual accomplishments and results. This is accomplished through continuous interteam communications and reviews. In support of this, the following activities are hereby endorsed by ACME project management and ACORN senior management as points of policy for Software Project Planning conduct.

Policy Points

1. ACME software project management will track the actual the results and performances against the software plans. This tracking will include the size of the software work products, the project's effort and costs, the critical computer resources, the schedule, and the project risks. ACME software project management will take corrective actions as necessary based on the tracking data.

2. Software project management will take corrective actions and manage to closure when actual results and performance deviate significantly from the software plans.

3. Software project management will obtain agreement to changes to ACME software commitments from the affected groups and individuals.

4. Software project management will use the approved ACME software development plan as the basis for managing the ACME project.

5. The software project manager will explicitly assign responsibility for software work products and activities to be delivered by the ACME team.

6. Software project management will be sure to provide adequate resources and funding for tracking the software project.

7. Software managers, as needed, will be trained in managing the technical and personnel aspects of the ACME software project, and first-line software man-

agers will receive, as needed, orientation in the technical aspects of the software project.

8. Software project management will revise the ACME software development plan according to a documented procedure.

9. Software project management will review software project commitments and changes to commitments made to individuals and groups external to the organization with senior management according to a documented procedure.

10. Software project management will communicate approved changes to commitments that affect the software project to the members of the software engineering group and other software-related groups.

11. Software project management will record actual measurement data and planning data for the software project.

12. Software project management will conduct periodic internal reviews and scheduled formal reviews to address the accomplishments and results of the software project at selected project milestones according to a documented procedure.

13. ACME software project management will review the activities for software project tracking with ACORN senior management on a periodic basis.

14. ACME software project management will review the activities for software project tracking with the ACME project manager on both a periodic and event-driven basis.

15. ACME software project management will allow reviews or audits by the software quality assurance group on the activities and work products for software project tracking and will receive reports on the results.

❖

RESPONSIBILITY: ACME Software Project Managers are responsible for implementing this policy.

APPROVED:

_____   Date
ACME Software Project Management

_____   Date
ACME Project Management

_____   Date
ACORN Senior Management

ACORN Corp.

ACME PROJECT

Policy for Software Project Tracking and Oversight

Control: Version 1.1
Effective: 11/30/00
POC:

Overview

The purpose of Software Project Tracking and Oversight is to provide adequate visibility into the actual activities and progress on ACME so that management can take effective actions when performance deviates significantly from the software plans. Software Project Tracking and Oversight involves tracking and reviewing the software accomplishments and results against documented estimates, commitments, and plans, and adjusting these plans based on the actual accomplishments and results. This is accomplished through continuous interteam communications and reviews. In support of this, the following activities are hereby endorsed by ACME project management and ACORN senior management as points of policy for Software Project Planning conduct.

Policy Points

1. A software development Plan (SDP) is maintained as the central tool for tracking the project.

2. The project manager (PM) is kept informed (by all subgroup and team managers) of the project's status and issues.

3. Adjustments to the SDP or to the project team are made when the SDP is not being achieved.

4. Changes to the SDP are reviewed by all impacted groups before the changes are implemented.

5. Senior management review all changes to the SDP that impact commitments to external groups.

❖

RESPONSIBILITY: ACME Software Project Managers are responsible for implementing this policy.

APPROVED:

ACME Software Project Management   Date

ACME Project Management   Date

ACORN Senior Management   Date

ACORN Corp.

ACME PROJECT

Policy for Software Configuration Management

Control: Version 1.1
Effective: 11/30/00
POC:

Overview

The purpose of Software Configuration Management is to establish and maintain the integrity of the work products for ACME throughout the project's software life cycle. Software Configuration Management involves identifying the configuration of the software (i.e., selected software work products and their descriptions) at given points in time, systematically controlling changes to the configuration, and maintaining traceability of the configuration throughout the life cycle. The work products placed under Software Configuration Management include the software products that are delivered to the customer (e.g., the software requirements document and the code) and the items that are identified with or required to create these software products (e.g., the compiler). In support of this, the following activities are hereby endorsed by ACME project management and ACORN senior management as points of policy for Software Project Planning conduct.

Policy Points

1. All SCM activities for ACME will be documented; this ACME SCM plan will be created according to a documented procedure, and the plan will be used as the basis for performing all SCM activities.

2. ACME SCM will control changes to identified software work product and inform affected groups and individuals of the status and content of evolving work products and software baselines.

3. ACME project management will establish a board having the authority for managing the project's software baselines (i.e., a software configuration control board-SCCB), and will appoint a group to be responsible for coordinating and implementing SCM for the project (i.e., the SCM group).

4. ACME project management will establish a Configuration Management library system as a repository for the software baselines.

5. ACME project management will provide adequate resources and funding for performing SCM activities.

6. Members of the SCM group, as necessary, will be trained in the objectives, procedures, and methods for performing their SCM activities, as will members of the software engineering group and other software-related groups.

7. ACME SCM will control changes to baselines according to a documented procedure.

8. ACME SCM will create products from the software baseline library and control their releases according to a documented procedure.

9. All ACME software baseline audits will be conducted according to a documented procedure.

10. The ACME configuration manager will take periodic measurements to determine the status of the SCM activities.

11. The ACME SCM group will periodically audit software baselines to verify that they conform to the documentation that defines them.

12. The ACME SCM group will allow software project management to review the activities for SCM (with ACORN senior management) on a periodic basis.

13. The ACME SCM group will review SCM activities for software project tracking with ACME project management on both a periodic and event-driven basis.

14. The ACME SCM group will allow reviews or audits by the software quality assurance group on the activities and work products for Software Project Tracking and will receive reports on the results.

❖

RESPONSIBILITY: ACME Software Project Managers are responsible for implementing this policy.

APPROVED:

_____

ACME Software Project Management   Date

_____

ACME Project Management   Date

_____

ACORN Senior Management   Date

ACORN Corp.

ACME PROJECT

Policy for Software Configuration Management

Control: Version 1.1
Effective: 11/30/00
POC:

Overview

The purpose of Software Configuration Management is to establish and maintain the integrity of the work products for ACME throughout the project's software life cycle. Software Configuration Management involves identifying the configuration of the software (i.e., selected software work products and their descriptions) at given points in time, systematically controlling changes to the configuration, and maintaining traceability of the configuration throughout the life cycle. The work products placed under Software Configuration Management include the software products that are delivered to the customer (e.g., the software requirements document and the code) and the items that are identified with or required to create these software products (e.g., the compiler). In support of this, the following activities are hereby endorsed by ACME project management and ACORN senior management as points of policy for Software Project Planning conduct.

Policy Points

1. Responsibility for SCM is specifically assigned for the project.

2. SCM processes are implemented throughout the project life cycle.

3. SCM is implemented for all projects within the organization.

4. The projects are each given adequate access and resources within the SCM environment.

5. Software baselines and general SCM activities are audited by management on a regular basis.

❖

RESPONSIBILITY: ACME Software Project Managers are responsible for implementing this policy.

APPROVED:

_____   _____
ACME Software Project Management   Date

_____   _____
ACME Project Management   Date

_____   _____
ACORN Senior Management   Date

ACORN Corp.

ACME PROJECT

Policy for Software Quality Assurance

Control: Version 1.1
Effective: 11/30/00
POC:

Overview

The purpose of Software Quality Assurance is to provide management with appropriate visibility into the processes being used by the ACME project to ensure quality output. Software Quality Assurance is responsible for reviewing and auditing the software products and activities from the project to verify that they comply with the applicable procedures and standards. SQA is also charged with providing software project management and other appropriate management with the results of these reviews and audits. In support of this, the following activities are hereby endorsed by ACME project management and ACORN senior management as points of policy for Software Project Planning conduct.

Policy Points

1. Appoint a group to be responsible for coordinating and implementing SQA for the project (i.e., the SQA group).

2. Provide adequate resources and funding for performing the SQA activities.

3. Train members of the SQA group to perform their SQA activities.

4. Orient the members of the software project on the role, responsibilities, authority, and value of the SQA group.

5. Plan software quality assurance activities. Prepare an SQA plan for the software project according to a documented procedure. Perform the SQA group's activities in accordance with the SQA plan.

6. Objectively verify adherence of software products and activities to the applicable standards, procedures, and requirements.

7. Inform affected groups and individuals of Software Quality Assurance activities and results.

8. Ensure that noncompliance issues that cannot be resolved within the software project are addressed by senior management.

9. Have the SQA group participate in the preparation and review of the project's software development plan, standards, and procedures.

10. Have the SQA group review the software engineering activities to verify compliance.

11. Have the SQA group audit designated software work products to verify compliance.

12. Have the SQA group periodically report the results of its activities to the software engineering group.

13. Document deviations identified in the software activities and software work products and handle according to a documented procedure.

14. Have the SQA group conduct periodic reviews of its activities and findings with the customer's SQA personnel, as appropriate.

15. Make and use measurements to determine the cost and schedule status of the SQA activities.

16. Have experts independent of the SQA group periodically review the activities and software work products of the project's SQA group.

❖

RESPONSIBILITY: ACME Software Project Managers are responsible for implementing this policy.

APPROVED:

_____

ACME Software Project Management   Date

_____

ACME Project Management   Date

_____

ACORN Senior Management   Date

ACORN Corp.

ACME PROJECT

Policy for Software Quality Assurance

Control: Version 1.1
Effective: 11/30/00
POC:

Overview

The purpose of Software Quality Assurance is to provide management with appropriate visibility into the processes being used by the ACME project to ensure quality output. Software Quality Assurance is responsible for reviewing and auditing the software products and activities from the project to verify that they comply with the applicable procedures and standards. SQA is also charged with providing software project management and other appropriate management with the results of these reviews and audits. In support of this, the following activities are hereby endorsed by ACME project management and ACORN senior management as points of policy for Software Project Planning conduct.

Policy Points

1. Software quality assurance practices are in place on all projects.
2. The SQA team retains an independent channel for reporting to executive management.
3. Senior management periodically reviews SQA activities and results.

❖

RESPONSIBILITY: ACME Software Project Managers are responsible for implementing this policy.

APPROVED:

_____

ACME Software Project Management   Date

_____

ACME Project Management   Date

_____

ACORN Senior Management   Date

Notes

Introduction

[1] Mark Paulk, et al. (1994). *The Capability Maturity Model: Guidelines for Improving the Software Process.* Addison Wesley Longman, Inc.

Chapter 1

[1] See the SEI's Web site at www.sei.cmu.edu. My italics.
[2] Paulk, et al., p. 123.
[3] I worked with one Level 1 shop, a major telecom company, with 6,000 IT employees.
[4] Data sources available at the SEI Web site.

Chapter 2

[1] Paulk, et al. (1994), §7.1.
[2] Ibid., §7.2.
[3] Ibid., §7.3.
[4] Ibid., §7.5.

[5] Ibid., §7.6.
[6] Ibid., §7.4.
[7] Ibid., §7.1.
[8] Ibid.
[9] Ibid.
[10] Ibid.
[11] Ibid.
[12] Ibid., §7.2.
[13] Ibid.
[14] Ibid.
[15] Ibid.
[16] Ibid.
[17] Ibid., §7.3.
[18] Ibid.
[19] Ibid.
[20] Ibid.
[21] Ibid.
[22] Ibid., §7.5.
[23] Ibid.
[24] Ibid.
[25] Ibid.
[26] Ibid.
[27] Ibid., §7.6.
[28] Ibid.
[29] Ibid.
[30] Ibid.
[31] Ibid.
[32] Ibid., §7.4.
[33] Ibid.
[34] Ibid.
[35] Ibid.
[36] Ibid.

Chapter 3

[1] Paulk, et al. (1994: Addison Wesley), p. 173. Emphasis is mine.

Chapter 4

[1] Subcontractor management is covered in Chapter 7.
[2] Cited from *Process Maturity Profile of the Software Community 2000 Update— SEMA.3.00.*

Chapter 5

[1] Paulk, et al. (1994: Addison Wesley) p. 49.
[2] Ibid., p. 129.
[3] Ibid., p. 138.
[4] Ibid., p. 150.
[5] Ibid.
[6] Ibid., p. 184.
[7] Ibid.
[8] Ibid., p. 174.
[9] Ibid., p. 175.
[10] Ibid., p. 49.

Chapter 6

[1]That's why we don't have a policy for what to do when a tree falls in the forest and there's no one around to hear.

Chapter 8

[1] Paulk, et al. (1994), §8.1.
[2] Ibid., §8.2.
[3] Ibid., §8.3.
[4] Ibid., §8.4.
[5] Ibid., §8.5.
[6] Ibid., §8.6.
[7] Ibid., §8.7.
[8] Ibid., §8.1.
[9] Ibid.
[10] Ibid.
[11] Ibid.
[12] Ibid.
[13] Ibid., §8.2.
[14] Ibid.
[15] Ibid.
[16] Ibid.
[17] Ibid.
[18] Ibid., §8.3.
[19] Ibid.
[20] Ibid.
[21] Ibid.
[22] Ibid.
[23] Ibid., §8.4.
[24] Ibid.

[25] Ibid.
[26] Ibid.
[27] Ibid.
[28] Ibid., §8.5.
[29] Ibid.
[30] Ibid.
[31] Ibid.
[32] Ibid.
[33] Ibid., §8.6.
[34] Ibid.
[35] Ibid.
[36] Ibid.
[37] Ibid.
[38] Ibid., §8.7.
[39] Ibid.
[40] Ibid.
[41] Ibid.
[42] Ibid.

Chapter 9

[1] Paulk, et al. (1994), §8.1.
[2] Ibid.
[3] Ibid.
[4] Ibid.
[5] Ibid.
[6] Ibid.

Chapter 10

[1] Paulk, et al. (1994), §8.2.
[2] Ibid.
[3] Ibid.
[4] Ibid.
[5] Ibid.
[6] Ibid.
[7] Ibid.

Chapter 11

[1] Paulk, et al. (1994), §8.3.
[2] Ibid., §8.4.
[3] Ibid., §8.5.

[4] Ibid., §8.6.
[5] Ibid., §8.7.

Chapter 12

[1] Paulk, et al. (1994), §8.5.
[2] Ibid., §8.4.

What's on the Companion Web Site

This book's companion Web site, www.wiley.com/compbooks/persse, includes other CMM-related materials, divided into three general categories of information. First, we provide a series of tips and practical explanations to help you implement specific areas of the CMM. Second, we make available a series of sample processes (in part, taken from the book). If you find that they fit your basic needs, you can use these as they are, or you can use them as a foundation to begin shaping your own customized processes. Third, we present a series of sample forms and artifact listings that you may find helpful in creating the kind of audit trail that helps you both evaluate how your processes are working and sets up the kind of supporting documentation you will find helpful during an assessment.

Download the material, use it as is, or re-shape it. We hope it helps you begin your CMM program in an effective and efficient manner.

Index